CHASING TRAINS

TRAINS

THE LIFETIME STORY OF THE FOUNDER OF THE COLORADO RAILROAD MUSEUM

ROBERT W. RICHARDSON

UNKNOWN TO MOST AKRONITES was this big bridge, located close to Main Street, where Train 95—the morning mixed train of the Akron, Canton & Youngstown—has just pulled away from the little Main Street station. Mikado No. 401 is shown in this view, with coach No. 15 and mail car No. 11 on the rear. I always preferred the opposite train because the coach would then be on the end of the consist. This scene was shot during June of 1937, and the mixed train was short due to the continuing recession in the tire industry prior to World War II.

CHASING TRAINS

THE LIFETIME STORY OF THE FOUNDER OF THE
COLORADO RAILROAD MUSEUM
ROBERT W. RICHARDSON

Heimburger House Publishing Company
Forest Park, Illinois

Front Cover

Engine No. 473 of the Denver & Rio Grande Western was being used as the switcher at Durango, Colorado when this winter scene was recorded during the week of December, 1950. John Dieckman was working his last day of a long career as an engineman on the D&RGW. His final time was spent as an engineer of one of the railroad's K-28 outside-frame 2-8-2's.

Back Cover

The dramatic scene was taken behind the last car of the Silverton train in 1982. Robert W. Richardson, left, and Gordon S. Chappell were about to depart for Durango, Colorado, a distance of about 49 miles. The beautiful snow-covered mountain in the background is Mount Kendall, just east of the Rio de las Animas, while the Animas Canyon is to the right (south).

Library of Congress Control Number 2004110409
ISBN: 0-911581-56-1
Second Edition
Printed in the United States of America

Editor: Russ Collman; production manager: Dell A. McCoy; editorial consultants: Augie Mastrogiuseppe and Robert A. LeMassena

Heimburger House Publishing Company
7236 West Madison Street
Forest Park, Illinois 60130
www.heimburgerhouse.com

PREFACE

ROBERT W. RICHARDSON is indeed a railfan's railfan—a living legend—and a treasure among those who "chase trains" professionally, or as an avocation. Possessing a fascination with trains and railroading as far back as 1931, this interest quickly developed, along with his keen sense of history, into a lifelong career of chasing, riding and photographing trains.

This book has long been awaited. Bob was encouraged over the years to write down his reminiscences. His unique journeys throughout the United States and northward into Canada, as well as south of the border into Mexico and Central America, and into overseas countries—following the rails over many thousands of miles—led to adventures that few railfans have experienced. Bob, with his journalistic penchant, is a great storyteller, and those of us who have been privileged to travel with him, on automobile trips around Colorado's renowned "narrow-gauge circle," will never forget the factual and interesting accounts of the way it used to be on the narrow-gauge railroads.

Details, such as what was located at Porter, Colorado, on the legendary Rio Grande Southern, or how the Denver & Rio Grande Western operated heavy-tonnage trains east over Marshall Pass, or the difficulty of railroading through snowstorms, would hold the listener spellbound. At times, the conversation would shift to the time he was establishing the museum at "South Alamosa" and publishing his **Narrow Gauge News,** to chasing the East Broad Top line in Pennsylvania, to riding short lines in Texas, or military railroad stories from Iran. Interspersed through the stories would be the descriptions of people, from a cantankerous railroad official, a dedicated engineer, a lackadaisical trainman, hard-working sectionmen, a blasé local businessman, a tourist customer at his motel, or a novice railfan. Bob's ability to "size-up" people, weaving this human element into his railroad stories, created an engrossing historical tapestry.

Bob has pulled together many of the best of these fine oral accounts of history for this book. These well-written stories will make the reader feel as if Bob is sitting next to you, conversing. Now in print for the first time, in a splendid illustrated volume produced by **Sundance Publications,** railfans the world over can enjoy these episodes.

Not only being a sharp observer, mentally recording his travels, Bob's talents with photography resulted in an important collection of photographic images—many complementing these trips. Like all railfans, Bob chased, rode and photographed the Class One mainline trains and locomotives. However, what really interests and excites him to this day are the small, unusual, out-of-the-way "backwoods railroads." So, he studied the **Official Guide** and ventured to the likes of a Tionesta Valley Railway in Pennsylvania, to the Smoky Mountain Railroad in Tennessee, to the Live Oak, Perry & Gulf Railroad, a woodburning-locomotive operation in Florida, and to the Yucatán Railways in Mexico. And, who but Bob Richardson recorded in memory and on film, during the 1940's, the

Wichita Falls & Southern Railroad in Texas?

The documenting of these lines and countless others certainly was not on the minds of the local folk who resided in the railroads' backyards. Many of the railroads that Bob was visiting were literally disappearing before his eyes.

Bob understood the need to preserve some of the better examples of the "age of steam," and he became a leader in the historic railway-preservation efforts in the United States. After seeing preservation attempts fall short on steam and electric lines back East, as well as the lost opportunities by individuals and a state agency, when Colorado's historic Midland Terminal Railway ceased operations, Bob launched the idea of a railroad museum. From a small start in Alamosa, this museum developed over the years into the noted Colorado Railroad Museum in Golden, just west of Denver. His Herculean efforts in preserving equipment and documents of the Rio Grande Southern and the Denver & Rio Grande Western railroads—almost single-handedly—became the basis of a major collection that is constantly studied, photographed and admired.

Upon returning to his native Pennsylvania in 1991, Bob deposited his vast collection of railroad-photograph negatives of steam and electric line at the Denver Public Library's Western History Department. Sorting of the negatives has occurred with the assistance of library volunteer, Jim Hurt, to the level that access is now possible by railroad-company name. As the library proceeds with the digitization of our Western History photographic collections, sections of the Robert W. Richardson Collection will be some of the first images scanned by computer. This step will improve access-and-reproduction services, as well as ensuring the preservation of the original negatives. Almost 300 of these Richardson views were selected to accompany the text in this volume.

Bob's intent in photographing railroads was to document what was disappearing. He admirably succeeded in this objective. However, in this pursuit, he often created works of art—images that will endure as classics in railroad history. As you page through this book, pause on the page with that image of the Sheffield & Tionesta Railway's mixed train, approaching out of the foggy morning. Bob's favorite photograph, and rightly so, you can feel the atmosphere of that day long ago. Look at the view of the Denver & Rio Grande Western's locomotive piled high with snow, on that bitter-cold January day in 1949, high on Cumbres Pass. Contemplate the lonely miles of the San Luis Valley, as one of the last freight trains heads north beside the majestic Sangre de Cristo Mountains. Our hats are off to this adventurous railfan from Pennsylvania. Bob, may you always have a green order board and a clear track ahead.

— Augie Mastrogiuseppe
Curator of Photographs
Western History/
Genealogy Department
Denver Public Library
June, 1995

BACK DURING THE 1930's, most railfans wore hats and neckties, and we often wore business suits as well. For this trip on October 17, 1937, I was given a specially printed cap badge. Here, I was leaning out of the cab of Kelley Island Lime & Transport Company's locomotive No. 67, a double-truck Shay engine. This interesting operation was located at Marblehead, Ohio.

INTRODUCTION

WHY "CHASE" TRAINS? Why put so much effort and time into photographing locomotives, interurbans and trains? The simplest answer would be from the obvious fact that most of us acquire a lifelong interest in some avocation that to others is a puzzle. Why we select a particular interest as a hobby is something that is indeed an enigma and baffling to explain.

With me I suppose it all began on Memorial Day of 1931, when I rode the final train on Ohio's last narrow-gauge railroad. Up to that date, I had always expressed a fascination with railroads, and I had spent many an hour (or day) just watching them. However, that day was different for I had taken the family Kodak camera along and used up an entire roll of film. Some of the resulting pictures were poor, but it really made little difference as the good ones were lost when I loaned the negatives to a man who never returned them.

The pictures in *Railroad Magazine* were fascinating, and I learned that many persons were taking photographs of engines and trains. For years, I had been keeping a scrapbook of pictures printed in newspapers. The engines and cars of the little Ohio River & Western narrow-gauge line went to scrap with few photographs snapped of this railroad's last days. To me, it seemed a great loss that those vignettes were forever lost, unrecorded.

So, armed with a folding Kodak 3A camera, I started taking pictures of railroad scenes. The infamous Great Depression was on, and there were few dollars available for film. My subjects were picked with care, and my travels were limited by that Depression. Even so, many a tank of gasoline—at 19 cents a gallon!—was wasted in the pursuit of elusive steam locomotives and electric interurbans!

Long trips during that decade were few. Visits to relatives in Pennsylvania provided some opportunities farther afield. But by the mid-1930's, a rare trip to Washington, D.C., another to the East Broad Top narrow-gauge line in 1936, and one that fall to Tennessee to see the East Tennessee & Western North Carolina (also narrow gauge) were outstanding events, increasing my growing collection of "railfan" photographs.

Four years spent working in Columbus, Ohio, at the end of the decade widened my field of subjects with the big motive power

of that area. It was also the era of the fan trip coming into popularity. Regional fan trips consumed many rolls of film during long weekend outings. Ohio had few short lines. The large railroads seldom could be bothered with handling small groups in special movements. So, our trips were mostly on the rapidly vanishing interurban lines, and this included whatever steam power was in their vicinity.

With a low military draft number, I quit the editor's post at *Linn's Weekly Stamp News* early in 1941. With a similarly situated friend, we went on a last grand fling of railroading by going during the early summer on a trip to see the Colorado narrow-gauge railroads. However, the military changed their needs, and a change in age limits postponed the draft for a while.

Then came my really big chance to see railroads over a large part of the United States, an unexpected "perk" (in my view) of a temporary job with the Seiberling Rubber Company. With their sign truck I was to check with dealer outlets to locate and place indoor and outdoor advertising, making local arrangements, etc. Eventually, it took me over a good half of the U.S., and to my delight, this provided frequent opportunities to use my cameras while seeing some interesting and unusual lines. Up to that time, the company had difficulty keeping anyone on such a job, as it involved layovers at out-of-the-way places. There was nothing to interest the average young fellow, and the stays were so short as to preclude making local acquaintances.

My bosses puzzled at receiving none of the usual complaints from me and checked up by means of the salesmen and branch managers "...to see what he's up to." (Incidentally, I wish I had some of those reports to include here!) My boss called me in to his office to order that I put the cost of train trips and film on expense reports. He hated traveling and commented, "It's our fault you have to go to such out-of-the-way places and put up with those awful accommodations."

So, I included the trip costs on the reports, but not the cost for film for fear some auditor might want them. During the conversation, my boss asked where it was that I had breakfast on a streetcar. That puzzled me, until I found that the office girls, in nosily checking my reports, had somehow confused the electric Illinois Terminal Railroad with a streetcar line. And while I was riding an ITR train I had breakfast one snowy morning in their parlor-café trailer while en route to St. Louis.

To tease these snoopers, on several occasions on mixed-train trips I would have the conductor cut me a cash fare for a few cents for passage from one obscure siding to another. The girls in vain tried to solve those expense entries, even with the aid of a boy friend in the shipping department who had a copy of the *Official Guide.* One conductor entered into the idea when I explained, with great enthusiasm, selecting from some old forms some places from which track had vanished.

As for an avid interest in railroads, my mother had uncles who worked on the Pennsylvania Railroad as a baggageman, trainman and yardmaster. My father grew up in Corning, New York, and as a kid he watched the goings and comings of Erie, Lackawanna and New York Central trains. His Sunday walks with me as a small child in Akron, Ohio, could always be counted upon to include the Union Station, occasionally a roundhouse or interurban terminal—just as today's parents take their kids to the airport by car (no walking). And a pigeon-racing club found out that I was just the one to escort a crate of birds to some station 50 or more miles distant, there to release the birds from the crate. The club paid my train or interurban fares and gave me a dollar or two extra. During later years, some relatives of mine would wonder, "How did he get so interested in trains?"

My intended railroad career was short, as was my bout with higher education. After graduating from high school at 16 to go to work in the Akron, Canton & Youngstown's roundhouse, my parents signature was needed, but was refused. So, I was pushed to register at Akron University. However, I never attended a class, and I went to work for a wholesale hardware company instead.

Mainline hotshot trains were not as great an attraction to me as the short lines, particularly the ones that were small and obscure. The outfits with minimal listing in the *Official Guide* were often very interesting, well worth the effort to find and explore. Their people, too, were more friendly and tolerant of picture-taking than were the employees of the big roads. The little lines and weedy branches were often barely escaping the scrap heap. It was sad to realize that their days were numbered. Their com-

ings and goings were seldom, if ever, recorded on film. I used to think of all their impressive action lost forever, their notch in time having vanished with the smoke. Small motive power and cars with fading, peeling lettering were things I delighted to find and photograph. When I sold my golf set one rainy, discouraging summer, I kept one iron just for swishing weeds obscuring forgotten rolling stock!

An incentive with all this was to exchange photographs with other railfans. Often these developed into longtime correspondence, exchanging information from distant points I would never get to. We generally did not take our photographs with any thought of their ever being published, particularly in a book. There were not any railroad books being published then, so the sole rare picture to be published might be one used in *Railroad* or *Trains* magazines.

Sometimes, with a borrowed Keystone camera, I took 16-mm movies, but not extensively. A roll of film cost $5.00 for just a few minutes. Not much of that could be afforded during the Depression. (With awe, I have watched the video cameras being used for pan shots that far exceed what one 100-foot roll of 16-mm film could do, and all for the cost of a few cents.)

Color slides were added to my outings around 1950, after I selected a 120-size camera and chose Agfa, Ansco and Kodachrome color films to get large 2¹/₄ x 2¹/₄-inch slides. The slides were beautiful and could be projected on a full movie screen. On some days I shot only color slides—no black-and-white at all—something I eventually bitterly regretted. For a few years later, disaster struck, when it was discovered that all those color slides were turning into awful reds and browns. It sadly turned out that Agfa, Ansco and Kodachrome color slides were not permanent films.

During 1962 I switched to a 35-mm camera, a Leica, and routinely asked various Leica fans what that camera's idiosyncrasies were, only to be informed that there were none. Shortly thereafter, I went on a trip to Mexico to shoot railroad pictures. I had permits to photograph the engine terminals that were soon to be dieselized and shot over 30 rolls of film. When this film was developed, some 32 rolls looked like dirty window panes—over 1,000 slides ruined! It turned out that the Leica did have a peculiarity, for it occasionally got a small piece of film stuck in the shutter! The Leica almost got thrown into Clear Creek, averted only by a cash offer from an employee, who got a bargain on the promise to keep the camera out of my sight. Since then, I have enjoyed years of reliable use from two Pentax cameras.

At first, the tendency was to take shots at a three-quarter angle, but it was soon realized that made for a monotonous collection. As a result, this was expanded to scenes of trains, general views of the lines, stations, depots and types of cars, especially cabooses. Considerable effort was made to shoot bridge-and-trestle scenes. And snow scenes I particularly tried hard to get. Only after the legendary Rio Grande Southern narrow-gauge line was abandoned did I realize that virtually no one ventured to visit such remote lines during the winter. And I have regretted very much that I did not make a better effort to cover this line and others like it during the winter months. Of course, one big deterrent was the lack of good all-weather highways in those days, and one venture out along the RGS west of Durango ended with my vehicle in the borrow pit. Fortunately, a couple of ranchers soon retrieved the pickup truck from its embarrassing position.

While in Texas, I tried using at least some action scenes with both a 16-mm movie camera and the "616" for still shots. I did not see the movie results until I was back in Akron, and never again tried such dual shooting. The movies were exasperating to watch, for just as the train became really interesting, the scene "cut"! Another "booboo" was taking the advice of a camera-store clerk to use a red filter to bring out the clouds. It certainly did that, but the trains were just black silhouettes!

In 60 years of photographic activity, it should be clear that I have taken as many duds as anyone else, and have had disasters to equal others. Like the time the developer ruined most of my film taken on the ET&WNC back in 1936, for example. I am just grateful that most of the time the camera just "grabbed" what was hoped for. It is humbling to think of the several thousand ruined color slides and all the wasted trips, as well as days of efforts that came to nothing. However, there were far more days that turned out to be all right. Above all, I kept in mind that it was only a hobby, not a matter of life and death, so I seldom found myself being grimly serious in the pursuit. And I could even laugh at my own mistakes and what were sometimes wretched results. Things like racing in the car, then puffing up a hillside to snap an oncoming Baltimore & Ohio articulated engine, with a tall column of smoke rising high in the sky —a great shot, but no film in the camera! Or after a long wait, finding an oncoming Louisiana & Arkansas 4-6-0 smokily chuffing along with its wooden train, and then, as the shutter clicked, the shutter fell apart!

Still… nearly all of it was fun, and some latter-day satisfaction comes from seeing the photographic successes giving pleasure to others by appearing in railroad books.

— Robert W. Richardson
Bellefonte, Pennsylvania, 1995

WHEN YOU HAVE a delayed timer on your camera, it obviously means you can take pictures of yourself. However, the relatively short 10-second scramble to get into the picture sometimes results in odd posing. The subject of this photograph (apart from myself) was one of the three coaches of the Akron, Canton & Youngstown Railroad. Dating from the 1890's, and obtained from predecessor companies, these open-platform wooden coaches were used on the Akron–Delphos mixed trains. This run provided a scenic, leisurely ride across northern Ohio.

TABLE OF CONTENTS

Continued next page......

Table of Contents Continued...

ROBERT W. RICHARDSON was serving his country as a member of the U.S. Army when this view was photographed in Iran.

AUTOBIOGRAPHICAL SKETCH OF ROBERT W. RICHARDSON

ROCHESTER, PENNSYLVANIA, is my birthplace, which was on May 21, 1910. Perhaps my lifelong interest in railroads got started in this town along the mainline of the Pennsylvania Railroad. Rochester was the sort of place where the residents would walk down to the town's depot area to watch the trains roar past on that busy four-track line.

Events on the PRR were common topics of conversation. Conway Yard, a few miles up the Ohio River toward Pittsburgh, was the largest railroad yard in the world, and quite a number of Beaver County residents were employed there.

My family moved to Akron, Ohio, in 1915, where my father had a job as a steamfitter in the booming tire industry. After this move, I suppose my interest in railroads was heightened by the fact that we lived within a block of the Akron Union Station and the mainline of the local electric interurban system for years. After graduating from high school in 1926, I registered at the Akron University, but I never showed up for classes. Instead, I went to work for a wholesale hardware company.

While in high school, I took a class in printing, and after being laid off from my hardware company job during the beginning of the Great Depression, I gradually worked the printing equipment I had gathered as a hobby into a small print shop. But in 1937, I sold the little shop and went to work as editor for **Linn's Weekly Stamp News** at Columbus, Ohio, the largest philatelic-circulation publication in the United States—which it still is today (in 1994). I had started stamp collecting as a kid, and have never completely dropped it, keeping up my interest over the years, and I still have several specialized collections and attend the larger exhibitions.

During 1941, I quit my editorial post, as I was about to be drafted into the army; however, the age brackets for draftees were temporarily changed, so I went to work for the advertising department of the Seiberling Rubber Company at a temporary job. This position required me to check out Seiberling dealers' advertising in the Eastern and Southern U.S. The travel entailed in this job enabled me to see and photograph many trains in out-of-the-way places.

My boss at Seiberling had difficulty keeping earlier people on the job, and he was very pleased that I did not complain. In fact, he encouraged me to take off days to see railroads, since that seemed to keep me satisfied about traveling to some of the areas I was sent to.

After being inducted into military service in 1942 and going through "boot camp," I was sent with a U.S. Signal Corps detachment to the Persian Gulf Command at the end of that year. For two and a half years I served in Iran, which was a "back-door route" to supply the Russians during World War II. On a furlough in Iran, I got to ride the Iraq State Railways meter-gauge line [slightly wider than three-foot gauge in the U.S.], as well as the railroads in Palestine, which is now Israel. On the way home, I completed an around-the-world trip by way of Egypt.

Back in Akron, Ohio, after the war, I resumed working for Seiberling Rubber Company and continued to photograph trains in

out-of-the-way places. Then, in 1948, I went into a business partnership to build and operate a motel "out West" in Colorado—Alamosa being the location selected, down in the middle of the vast San Luis Valley, near the heart of "narrow-gauge country," as railfans call it. The mountain regions of western Colorado were very short of tourist accommodations at that time, and postwar tourism was growing rapidly. So, we decided that Alamosa would be the best business location from among the various cities considered along what was referred to as the "Narrow-Gauge Circle."

Not known at this time was a management decision at the Denver & Rio Grande Western Railroad to eliminate all of the narrow-gauge lines... *even if they could make a profit as a result of postwar tourism.*

Alamosa had an annual D&RGW payroll of over $1 million at that time. Fortunately, a timely discovery of crude oil and natural gas in northwestern New Mexico saved the narrow-gauge freight line between Alamosa and Durango for many more years.

However, in 1958, I ended my business interest in what was called the "Narrow Gauge Motel" of Alamosa, Colorado, and in the settlement, I found myself owning several historic narrow-gauge locomotives and half-a-dozen cars, along with tons of other railroad items—and no place to take them. Eventually, I formed a partnership with Cornelius W. Hauck of Cincinnati, Ohio, and we established the Colorado Railroad Museum in 1959, at a site just east of Golden, Colorado. We also built a small motel and operated if for a few years, until it was sold to others a few years later. Operating both businesses was just too much for me; it involved too many 16-hour work days.

With the gradual abandonment of narrow-gauge lines by the Denver & Rio Grande Western, as well as the total demise of the

ROBERT W. RICHARDSON and Mrs. Frances Plummer are shown here at the main entrance to the Colorado Railroad Museum in Golden. Mrs. Plummer's son, Rob, worked for the museum, and the family lived next door, to the east, and the Plummers were good neighbors. They operated Golden's jewelry store, a center for information about the area. Naturally, the goings-on at the railroad museum provided much for Golden to discuss. Their son, Rob, was our first employee and one of the best. Rob got the job as a result of fleeing from his home on occasions of dinners and lodge doings, and he was over at the museum so much that I hired him! His mother was a well-known cook and host. Invitations to dinner there were never declined. In a stupid bit of surveying, through error, our property line went right through their kitchen, and this was the subject of much joking. We pretended sorrow at losing not only that kitchen, but also its products! After Wendell Plummer passed away, I escorted Frances to some of her lodge events, and some of her relatives expressed concern when four of us went on a trip to Hawaii. I think she liked to tease them. Now, she is Frances Plummer Strawn, and she lives in the much warmer climate of San Diego, California. Notice that the name of the museum was whimsically called "Delay Junction."

Rio Grande Southern in the scenic San Juan Region, I had purchased a number of pieces of rolling stock. Sometimes the money was borrowed, but I preferred to stay out of debt. The D&RGW did not really want to sell much of anything, preferring to take much more profitable write-offs by scrapping the engines themselves. This attitude likely saved me from going into serious debt! But the legendary RGS was a veritable museum itself, and upon its abandonment, I bought whatever I could. For example, at Dolores, Colorado, there was a three-way stub switch, which had been constructed in 40-pound rail, originally laid in 1890, when the RGS was constructed at that location. All kinds of long-out-of-date track fittings were collected, including about 40 harp switchstands from the 1880's, which the RGS had purchased from the Denver & Rio Grande Railroad.

At what was the joint D&RGW-RGS depot at Ridgway, the office was jammed with tons of old files, a result of never cleaning house in this historic old building, and these files I bought. They filled several freight cars, a Galloping Goose railbus and numerous pickup-truck loads. These railroad papers detailed the operating history of this mountain narrow-gauge railroad in remote southwestern Colorado. Thus, they were unique, as other comparable records of similar narrow-gauge railroads had been destroyed many years ago.

For the next 33 years, I worked as the

MY ONLY GLIMPSE of Hawaii before 1975 had been from the deck of the steamship "Mauritania," during a couple of days halt at Pearl Harbor in 1943. On the way, I had no idea at the time we were en route to Iran. During those two days, amid the wreckage caused by the Japanese on December 7, 1941, I could see many trains on the very busy three-foot-gauge Oahu Railroad from a distance. There were many long passenger trains and many double-headers. Most of us on the ship promised ourselves to return to Hawaii; however, my return was postponed until 1975, when I joined Frances Plummer, her brother and his wife on a tour. The Oahu Railroad was long gone by then, although I had seen some of its former engines and freight cars on the Ferrocarril de El Salvador during the 1960's. However, as we checked-in at the hotel on Maui, I heard a locomotive whistle. Inquiry at the hotel desk brought only the assurance that there was no railroad around there. Nevertheless, on the following day, I thought I heard it again, and just on the other side of the golf course, I found a little engine steaming along the Lahaina, Kaanapali & Pacific Railroad, trundling along with open cars—loaded with tourists!

A JOURNEY on the Rio Grande's "California Zephyr" was always an enjoyable outing. On this particular day, things were tinged with a bit of sadness, as the shortened route—just to Grand Junction—was having its last run. Yet, to the very end, the service was impeccable, the diner was first class, and the great train went out as it came in, in the best of a long tradition of superb passenger trains.

manager, or executive director, at the railroad museum at Golden—hardly a desk job, as for the first few years, we were always building track, or we were repairing and repainting various-and-sundry items. In any case, by the late 1980's, I decided (despite good health) it was time to leave the museum post, and I finally retired during the summer of 1991.

In the meantime, we had established the Colorado Railroad Historical Foundation, and after I retired, the operation of the museum was now their problem, overseen by a group of carefully chosen trustees, who would have the best interest of the museum as their primary goal.

Today, I live in retirement in a pleasant small town in central Pennsylvania, many miles east of the city where I was born. Bellefonte is on what was formerly a Pennsylvania Railroad line. And this little town has been the place where I have labored to put together the material for this book of railroad memories, photographs and maps from an enjoyable lifetime of "chasing trains."

— *Robert W. Richardson, 1995*

THE MODELERS AT BOULDER, Colorado, who maintained Engine 74 in the city park there, loaned us the so-called "bear-trap" cinder catcher they had built from Colorado & Southern patterns for that 2-8-0. So, in April of 1987, on the occasion of the final-runs anniversary on the South Park line, we operated No. 346 with our single ex-C&S stock car and the little four-wheel C&S way-car (caboose). It made an unusual and authentic 50th anniversary train, for in 1937, Engine 346 had been on loan to the C&S, and she handled the last livestock train on the South Park—into Jefferson. The engine has a steel cab instead of the original wooden one, a result of a wreck on the C&S at Kenosha Pass in 1936. After the last stock train in 1937, there was a mix-up, and the crew put No. 346 into the Como roundhouse and dumped the fire. Then, the crew got an automobile ride back to Denver. The men were supposed to have run the 2-8-0 back to Denver, so the engine could be loaded onto a flatcar and sent back to the D&RGW. As a result, a crew had to be taken back to Como, where No. 346 was fired up, and the men ran the engine light to Denver.

D&RGW ENGINE 346 saw little use by 1946,

except for sometimes serving as a helper during livestock season, or on the Silverton mixed train, or at other times, operating as the yard engine at Durango. The rest of the time, the engine sat in the terminal at Durango, with stack capped. C-19 No. 346 had extra piping on the steam dome for use with a fire hose when needed, and there was a tool box atop the cab, for when the 2-8-0 worked the yard as a switcher. During May of 1947, the Montezuma Lumber Company discovered that their ex-D&RGW C-16, Engine 271, was ruined, because the crown sheet was scorched. The D&RGW was down to their last two C-16 engines and could spare neither of them; however, they offered No. 346 for the $3,000 they had put into the engine's last overhaul. In any case, the career of the C-19 was short on the lumber company's line. The McPhee lumber mill burned down during the next January, and early in 1948, No. 346's last use was to provide the motive power for the scrap train that removed the Montezuma Lumber Company's last five miles of track—southwest of Dolores. After that, the 2-8-0 first sat at Durango and later at Dolores, waiting for a buyer. As it turned out, I was the buyer, when I came along and bought the engine in 1951.

FAVORITE ENGINES OF MINE

ALMOST EVERY RAILFAN has some favorite locomotives or rolling stock. The number-one favorite of mine, I suppose, is the one engine I bought with considerable misgivings at the time, former 1881 Denver & Rio Grande Western narrow-gauge 2-8-0 No. 346. She looked so forlorn sitting on the remnant of the lumber-company spur at Dolores that I yielded to the offer of the scrap dealer, who was reluctant to cut up the little Consolidation because there would not be much profit in it for him. He was glad to find someone to take the problem off his hands for a mere $800.00. No doubt, my bond with No. 346 is the result of the ensuing trials and travails as I tried to get her moved to Alamosa, Colorado, and then to rescue the 2-8-0 once again years later, when in dissolving a partnership, I nearly lost all my investment. And then, the happy surprise in 1962 was when the D&RGW engine successfully steamed and operated at the Colorado Railroad Museum in Golden, Colorado, for the first time. Since that delightful occasion, the D&RGW's No. 346 has continued to perform to the delight of thousands of fans over more than 30 years.

No doubt, I could name some other engines that have had particular appeal for me. There was the bantam Baldwin 4-4-0 used by the decaying lumber railroad along Tionesta Creek in Pennsylvania on the Sheffield & Tionesta Railway. A friend and I one summer day battled a million mosquitoes to re-letter her tender, so we would have better photographs on the next day's run. My preferences seemed to be for the smaller motive power, like the Wheeling & Lake Erie's Atlantics, and the heavier passenger power of roads like the Southern, New York Central and Baltimore & Ohio.

There are interurbans, too, that are among my favorites. In Ohio, the wooden No. 21 of the Ohio Public Service Company, the handsome *Lima Limited* No. 166 of the Lake Shore Electric and similar-era cars of the Cincinnati & Lake Erie.

BY THE YEAR 1941, the interurban era in Ohio was almost completely over. Ohio Public Service Company combine No. 21 was one of two of the early original wooden cars surviving. The other car, No. 6, was a straight passenger car. We had several fan trips riding these cars, paying the extra $100.00 of the estimated costs to have them used in place of the lightweight steel cars on the last Sunday runs, during July of 1939. "Save the

21!" was frequently heard. So, as president of our railfan club, I went to the offices of the power company in Cleveland and bought No. 21 for $300.00. This was my first involvement with the preservation of railway items. Eventually, in 1947, we gave the interurban car to the newly formed Ohio Railway Museum at Columbus, where she remains—sometimes operating on their line at Worthington, Ohio.

Then, there is RGS Engine 20...

I suppose my favorite Rio Grande Southern engine was No. 20, the last of a trio of Ten-wheelers the RGS had acquired from the defunct Florence & Cripple Creek Railroad. Many railfans believed that Engine 20 was the most impressive of the limited locomotive roster of the RGS. It was in August of 1951 when No. 20 moved my dead engine, No. 346, in a freight train out of Dolores for Durango. It was the first freight train that had operated over the line in months, due to a bridge being out. It was a rather rainy day, and No. 20 was about out of sand. The track was not only rusty, but weeds also

were plentiful, and the 20 had to work hard.

Heading upgrade from Mancos for the summit of Cima hill, No. 20 stalled on some of the sharper curves. The conductor set the brakes on the caboose, then the engine backed gently to bunch the slack. After that, she started off, as the conductor leaned out with his club ready on the brake wheel to kick off the caboose brakes just as the slack stretched out to that car. In this fashion, the sharper curves were negotiated. Even so, at each of two sidings, a car was set out. The 346 had a dome almost full of dry sand, but in the steady downpour there was no way to transfer it to No. 20 and keep it dry during the handling.

AFTER BEING DISCHARGED from the U.S. Army in September of 1945, I took a Western trip. After arriving in Durango, Colorado, I rode in the mail truck over to Dolores, planning to ride out of there on the next morning's "Galloping Goose." All afternoon I waited to snap pictures of a double-headed freight train; however, it arrived after dark. Unfortunately, I was unaware that at the same time, Rio Grande Southern No. 20 was loading livestock that afternoon in Lost Cañon, just a mile from town. Anyway, late in the afternoon, I was surprised to see No. 20 rolling into town, with a string of stock cars. And on the following morning, the three locomotives would try to get that livestock to Durango without delay. *So...* this picture of No. 20 represents my first experience with southwestern Colorado's legendary Rio Grande Southern Railroad!

At the time, I thought the stalling of the engine on the sharp curves was due to the weather, weeds, rust and lack of sand. However, it was not until moving her dead at the museum that I learned the real reason the engine seemed so weak on curves. The worn laterals of the center pair of blind drivers let those wheels slide off the rails, so that on the RGS, they would have been spinning in air, effectively changing the engine from a 4-6-0 to a 4-4-0 on those sharp curves! No wonder No. 20 could not get the tonnage around the curves without getting a good run for them!

The whistle of RGS No. 20 can still be heard, though, as the 1951 movie, *Ticket to Tomahawk* (filmed on the Silverton Branch of the D&RGW), can be seen when "oldies" are repeated on television. Few viewers of the movie realize that a complete wooden copy of the engine was built for use in some of the movie sequences that supposedly showed No. 20 being dragged across the mountains ahead of tracklaying.

THE VANISHING AMERICAN

WELL NAMED, the "American" type—the onetime ubiquitous 4-4-0—had been the most common type of locomotive for decades, from the 1850's onward, when U.S. railroads were growing by many thousands of miles. However, by the time I arrived on the scene with cameras, very few engines of this wheel arrangement were to be found. From the 1890's onward, heavier locomotives had been replacing them, such as 4-6-0 "Ten-wheelers" and 4-4-2 "Atlantics," especially during the early part of this century, when steel cars began to replace wooden ones. By the 1920's, the American type was to be found only on light-duty branches, short passenger trains and on shortlines, either unable to re-lay tracks or to buy larger engines. The Great Depression quickly sent most of the remaining engines to the dead-lines and scrap.

A GROUP OF RAILFANS from Buffalo, New York, arranged for a fan trip on June 15, 1941, on the Pennsylvania shortline known as the Coudersport & Port Allegany Railroad. So, a carload of us fans from Akron, Ohio, joined the occasion. The track between the named points on the railroad is flat, and the line was rather straight. After turning the engine, the crew gave us a fast trip from Port Allegany to Coudersport, 18 miles away. The line beyond to Newfield Junction involved a steep grade, past the headwaters of the Allegheny River. Moreover, there was a brief, hard rain shower as we rolled along the line. The Coudersport High School Band, in "nifty" braided-and-plumed uniforms, rode in the gondola behind the engine, as hot sparks and heavy rain combined to change those attractive uniforms into awful messes.

So, it was a continual search to find these elusive 4-4-0 engines. Here and there, they still powered a two-car passenger train or a short mixed train. The 10-mile Cadiz Railroad in Kentucky had for its total motive power two of these engines, which handled the 26-minute run very nicely as late as 1945. The seven-mile Ferdinand Railroad in southern Indiana had for its motive power only its little No. 3, with two trips per day, fitting-in with school schedules of the county high school, whose students were its regular passengers.

In Pennsylvania, the Coudersport & Port Allegany Railroad had a fast-stepping specimen used on the portion of the line between its two principal points; however, for the stiff climb beyond Coudersport, past the headwaters of the Allegheny River, the road had to rely on heavier power. The Maryland & Pennsylvania had one last 4-4-0 on hand to spell its often-balky gas-electric car. A similar situation prevailed on the Huntingdon & Broadtop Mountain. The Sheffield & Tionesta had seen business for its two-car passenger train vanish with the lumbering activities, but its bantam Baldwin American still worked a short mixed train once or twice a week. The mighty Pennsylvania held on to at least one 4-4-0, and the railroad saved it in storage for years in the locked-up Northumberland roundhouse.

VERY FEW RAILROADS used 4-4-0 American-type locomotives as late as 1942—once the most common wheel configuration in the United States. The Cadiz Railroad in western Kentucky used two of them as its motive power for its 10-mile line that ran a daily train to make the connection with the Illinois Central at Gracey, Kentucky. Here, on January 24, 1942, the Cadiz Railroad's locomotive No. 8 was waiting for the Illinois Central connection, with a freshly refurbished "Jim Crow" combination car on the tail end. This mixed train provided an interesting little ride, and the road's president, W. C. White, seemed to be the conductor on that day.

Nevertheless, Texas was surely the last stronghold for 4-4-0 locomotives. The Southern Pacific's Texas & New Orleans Railroad lines had obtained about 25 of the engines during the early 1920's, the last big order for such engines ever to be handled by the Baldwin Locomotive Works. Officials had wavered between steam and gas-electrics to handle the large number of lightly patronized lines in Texas, and they had settled for both types, but favored steam. As it turned out, when the gas-electrics wore out, the small steam engines took over those runs, too, but their number of trains was steadily shrinking. Throughout the war years, T&NO managed to get by, using everything in its stables, dating back to the 1880's, but with the end of the war, any small engine needing $500 or more in repairs was to be set aside for scrapping. As a result, the lines of dead engines grew long at San Antonio and Houston.

So, in driving around T&NO territory, it paid to keep an eye on any approaching smoke, especially if it was near the scheduled time for a gas-electric train. And sure enough, occasionally a 4-4-0 would come along at a good rate of speed—over 40 mph—hauling a couple of heavyweight passenger cars. Unfortunately, I usually did not have the time to turn around and try to get ahead for a photograph. The evening trains from Fort Worth and Austin were handled by larger and older 4-4-0 types, which could be heard at night working for all their worth down through the "sags," and then they would slowly clear the top of the next rise along their rolling terrain—usually handling tonnage, with a heavyweight Pullman car on the rear end.

The Katy owned a fleet of Americans, dating from around 1915, and some oil boom along its northwestern lines. These 4-4-0's handled a two-car train at up to 50 mph from

21

Wichita Falls to Woodward, Oklahoma, and from Waco, via Cisco, out to Stamford, in cattle-ranching country. The train out of Waco left just after 6:00 a.m., but during mid-summer it could be photographed in bright sunshine as it headed out of town. The fast-stepping well-maintained engines made the 452-mile round trip in just under 16 hours, with numerous stops along the way, as it handled the mail and express for many post offices and little stations.

The vast Missouri Pacific system was able to get down to just three American types, for light rail and roadbed on the oldest part of the system, from Bloomington, Texas, to Austwell and Seadrift on the Gulf, some 50 miles distance in all. One at a time, the remaining 4-4-0's would handle a mixed train, with a caboose for crew and passengers, daily except Sunday. Small diesel-electric engines on order at the time were expected in 1946, which would end the use of the three engines. Then, the Kingsville shop could cut them up for scrap. The station agent did not take kindly at all to an inquisitive Yankee poking around his domain, asking questions, and he avoided telling me that on one Sunday a change-off would occur, and the replacement engine was even then steaming light toward Bloomington. The august Lucius Beebe was to have no better fortune at this place, after I had told him he might find a 4-4-0 in use.

RAILFAN EXCURSIONS DURING PRE-PEARL-HARBOR TIMES

RAILROAD MAGAZINE, during the decade of the 1930's (the Great Depression years), became oriented toward "railfan interests." During this time, the magazine changed from one that served a readership that was primarily made up of railroaders to one that catered to railfans, which gradually became the majority of its readers.

Our small handful of railfans in the Akron, Ohio, area, read about a new activity in the issues of *Railroad Magazine,* the "fan trip." So, we began to look around, with the hope that we could have some fan trips in our part of the country. The idea was very attractive... to spend a day on a special excursion train, consisting of selected motive

power and cars, which would feature "photo run-bys" at prearranged places.

Unfortunately, northern Ohio did not have much in the way of steam-powered trips that would be practicable. The Pennsylvania Railroad wanted a minimum of 125 regular passenger fares to run a special, an impossible number for us. Besides that, people expected "excursion trains" to cost less than regular scheduled runs! The local Akron, Canton & Youngstown Railway had only three coaches, two of which were used on the daily-except-Sunday mixed trains. And the AC&Y was not interested at all in running a special consisting of the two passenger cars, plus cabooses. The various captive lines, owned by the steel companies, were paranoid regarding passengers or cameras. The only shortline nearby was the Pittsburgh, Lisbon & Western Railroad, whose sole passenger equipment was a Brill gasoline-powered railbus. The general manager was willing to charter the railbus to us for a round trip from Lisbon to New Galilee, Pennsylvania, for something like $30.00, the same amount they charged local high-school groups during the football and basketball seasons. However, he decreed that no photography would be permitted. While he did not give any reason, we learned that his little road had been taken over by Pittsburgh Consolidated Coal Company, and coal companies generally were like the Russians, paranoid regarding cameras. This was too bad for us, as the route was scenic and included a 997-foot-long steel trestle on a curve. The fact that the main road ran between the round-house and the turntable at New Galilee was also an interesting "plus" for railfans.

Anyway, we organized the Eastern Ohio Chapter of the new National Railway Historical Society, a name that helped considerably when we negotiated for fan trips. Fortunately, none of the people we dealt with ever asked us about size of the NRHS at that time. The NRHS had been formed at Lancaster, Pennsylvania, in 1935, and at the time we were chartering fan trips had fewer than 300 members, almost all of whom were trolley fans in the large Northeastern cities.

Of necessity, we turned to the rapidly vanishing interurban lines to have fan trips. They had a number of advantages, including the fact that their charter rates were low, often less than $50.00 for a car or train for a whole day. And they were flexible and toler-

THE LAST SURVIVING narrow-gauge engine of the Pennsylvania system was this 1916 Mogul. During a fan trip on the nearby Stark Electric Railroad, the PRR foreman of the East Canton backshops surprised us by using a crane to lift the small 2-6-0 from a storage corner in the boiler shop, then move it by cable outside, using planks for a third rail. This little engine is now at Waynesburg, Pennsylvania, at the county historical society's museum.

ant. All of them were facing extinction in the not-very-distant future, and our dollars were most welcome.

Our first fan trip was on the Stark Electric Railroad, a 40-mile line between Canton and Salem, Ohio. It came about as a result of my being "drafted" to give a program on the Railway Post Office for the annual banquet of the Alliance Philatelic Society. Downtown Alliance was on a short spur that connected with the Stark Electric's mainline. It was a warm spring evening, and the windows of the second-floor banquet room were open behind me as I was introduced to present my address. I had barely begun speaking when down the hill came a Stark Electric car, with screeching flanges and other noises. So, I paused and announced, "I yield to the Stark Electric." When the car finally stopped behind me and the thumping of the airpumps subsided, the motorman proceeded to change the ends of the trolley poles as I resumed my talk. However, I first stated that I would be glad to yield to the Stark Electric anytime, and I expressed the hope that we would be able to hear those sounds for many years to come. I went on to tell the audience that just as philatelists like to collect postage stamps, we railfans treasure photographs of all kinds of interurban cars. And I mentioned that out in the back area of the Lake Park carbarns outside town were some old and now-unique interurban cars, which we would surely like to catch out in the daylight.

Afterward, a man came up and thanked me for the kind words for "his little line," and he introduced himself as the receiver, O. K. Ayers. He went on to promise that if we would come down some Saturday, he would be glad to bring out those old cars for us to photograph. That led to our excursion trip, which was about eight hours long, using a variety of equipment. From the back of the carbarn they brought out two four-wheel Birney cars, formerly used in city service, and they took us to downtown Alliance in those little trolleys. As other old cars rolled out of the barn, a mild breeze whipped up clouds of years of dust! For the portion of the trip to Salem, the crew had cleared tools and gear out of their line car and placed some folding seats inside for us. No. 20 had been an original car of the line, dating from the early 1900's. And the crew showed us how fast the old car could run, with the pleasant brass chime whistle sounding almost continuously as we sped through the rolling countryside.

On another fan trip, we arranged with the foreman of the PRR's huge East Canton roundhouse and repair shop to tour that facility. Our original request was just to see the Pennsy's last narrow-gauge engine, stored in the boiler shop. However, the foreman included the entire operation during our visit. As for the little 2-6-0, off the suspended Waynesburg & Washington line, the foreman surprised us by having the Mogul moved outside on the transfer table. He had lifted the engine and tender from her corner spot with a crane, then he laid a "third rail" of planks and pulled the 2-6-0 out on the table. She had been all cleaned up, and green flags were flapping in the breeze.

The largest remaining interurban line in northern Ohio during the late 1930's was the Lake Shore Electric Railway, with a 120-mile mainline from Cleveland to Toledo, plus several short branch lines. Its main shops were at Sandusky, and like most interurban lines, as the operation gradually declined, it featured a collection of all kinds of out-of-service cars. This included passenger, freight and work equipment. Some of the passenger cars dated back to 1902, and they were still in good operating condition. Economic conditions had let the track get weedy and rather rough, but the cars were well maintained. We were able to have only a couple of special fan trips on the LSE before this line bowed to the inevitable in 1938.

At the height of interurbans, which was around 1910–1920, the Lake Shore Electric ran "Lima Limiteds" in connection with other lines, and even through cars to Fort Wayne, Indiana. They still had the last of the big wooden cars built for this service, a beautiful specimen of the car builder's skill at the Niles Company. This interurban we chartered for one trip, even taking the car on her only trip (perhaps) on the short branch to Lorain, Ohio. There, residents turned to stare as this big orange-and-cream car lumbered through the city streets.

The LSE's newest cars were heavy steel cars, equipped with railroad couplers for operating in trains. The scheduled time for the express runs for the 56 miles from Sandusky to Toledo was just five minutes short of two hours. The LSE manager, crews and dispatcher decided to give us a fast limited run, and all other cars were ordered to take siding for our special. We probably got the fastest interurban ride ever for all of us! The big car bounced and rolled on the often rough joints, as we clipped quite a few minutes off the normal time. This part of the line was rather flat, and most of the track was tangent, with slight curves.

We did not journey to Sandusky to watch the scrapping. Most of us took little interest in such sad things. Often, toward the end, a crew member or official would give us lanterns, old tickets, whistles, etc. They seemed to be glad that someone liked to have such mementos. On impulse, the crew of the last run from Cleveland to Beach Park told us, "You fellows might as well take that headlight. We haven't any more use for it!"

Things finally got down to only two lines left, the 15-mile Inter-City Rapid Transit Company, between Canton and Massillon, and the Youngstown & Suburban Railway. The Inter-City's charter rates were low and provided several Sunday-afternoon specials. It looked as if it would be the last of all of Ohio's interurban lines. However, in 1941, disaster struck when the city council demanded (backed by Ohio laws) that the Inter-City repave the tracks through the city, which was about half of their trackage. It was not the trolleys that had worn things down so that the streets were rough. Massillon's main streets had become through highways, with much truck traffic. For this small company to relay and repave miles of double track was financially impossible. As a result, the company abandoned trolleys and went to buses. Ohio law required paving between the rails and 18 inches outside the track, and in Massillon that was most of the street!

So, the Y&S became the last line to abandon interurban service, operating city service in Youngstown to a suburb, and a couple of trips per day over the 22 miles to Signal, or to Leetonia on a short side spur. It was the freight traffic that kept the line in existence. The Pittsburgh Consolidated Coal Company had built a coal-unloading facility on the Ohio River at Smiths Ferry. They also had constructed a private line to connect with the Pittsburgh, Lisbon & Western at Negley, Ohio, which used the Y&S to deliver coal to the Youngstown steel mills in competition with the Pennsylvania Railroad, which fought all this every way they could. So, freight trains traveled this route, sometimes using steam locomotives of the PL&W, and at other times—north of Signal—the Y&S used their steeple-cab motors (electric locomotives).

When approached about a special excursion run, Lloyd Lyon, the manager, was rather somber, and he asked many questions.

24

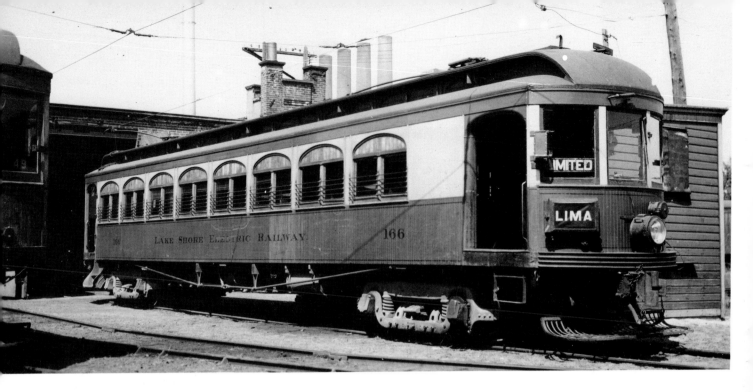

THE VERY ARCHETYPE of the interurban car in Ohio was this grand specimen, which remained operable up to the end of the Lake Shore Electric Railway in 1938. We fans from Akron, Ohio, chartered trips on interurban No. 166 on a couple of times. No. 166 was the first item of rolling stock that we gave serious thought to "saving" from the scrappers. No one even talked of a museum at that time. The problem then was twofold—where (or how) could we raise the money, and where could we put the car in a safe place after we bought it? Unfortunately, we could not solve either problem. At this time, the Great Depression was on, and most of the fans were young fellows, and we just did not have the kinds of jobs that permitted us to contribute much. And where could we keep the car in safety—a big 65-foot car like this? So, when abandonment came, the magnificent car body was sold off to sit in a field somewhere and rot away.

He obviously had never heard of a "railfan excursion." I learned later that he was thinking of the kind of excursions they had operated for rowdy steel workers, carrying them to and from football games, which had required a strong police presence. After some thought, he quoted a price for a special run. (It seems to me that it was just under $50.00.) He also soberly agreed that we could stop at the carbarns to take pictures. Their passenger fleet was down to five lightweight steel cars, but they had some non-revenue items that had been converted from passenger cars, as well as a couple of electric locomotives.

Advance ticket sales were good, so we chartered two cars. When we boarded the cars on Sunday morning, Mr. Lyons and several people from his office were present, including the company's special agent. When we stopped at the shops, the fans just did the usual things, examined the equipment, took pictures and asked many questions. Finally, just before we were to board the cars and resume the trip, Mr. Lyons came to me and commented something to the effect that he did not see any need for his people to go on the trip, other than the motorman, of course. He then explained that they did not know what to expect, since he remembered the problems the football specials caused. So, he had the chief engineer and others present to try to keep things from becoming such a riot. He complimented us on our behavior, and remarked that it was a relief that we were not like the football celebrants. He obviously had been very worried about us.

So, on a wintry day in 1947, we made our final trip on the Youngstown & Suburban, now giving up its passenger business. Eventually, in the down-sizing of the steel industry, the coal barges no longer unloaded at Smiths Ferry. And now, the lightly used rails into Youngstown are part of a new shortline, the PL&W Scenic Railway, which operates weekend trips for a few miles on the former PL&W out of Negley, Ohio. They rebuilt a Porter 0-4-0T into a 2-4-0, added a tender and removed the engine's saddle tanks, and it rolls along a very scenic and out-of-the-way line, trundling a couple of steel coaches and

THIS SCENE WAS SHOT during our fan trip to Marblehead, Ohio, on July 3, 1938. The Kelley Island Lime & Transport Company had about a dozen Shays here, with some 60 of these geared engines in all of its operations. Happy and proud Superintendent Sauvey was standing in this view, second from the right.

a caboose. In 1994, the crew was wondering if someday they might venture all the way to Youngstown. As it comes along the line, the engine looks like a reincarnation of the Denver & Rio Grande's famed "Montezuma" in standard-gauge form.

What about our fan club in Akron? We mostly just acted as a sort of committee arranging trips. We never had much in our treasury, as it seemed if we made some bucks on one trip, we were sure to lose it on the next one. I never was able to get out of the job of president. In the print shop I would print the postcard notices of trips, the tickets, and if there was enough time, a special timetable or folder for the trip was run off. These latter printed materials I saved as mementos and now treasure them as prized collector's items. While living in Columbus, I would go to the shop on evenings, spend hours making a timetable setup, for the printer to run off the next day. All those small figures, between brass rules for the lines, represented a great deal of work to set, something that today is a forgotten skill: hand typesetting, us-

ing metal type. Old-time printers are open-mouthed at the speed with which ruled forms are turned out today without touching type or brass rules.

At that time, we were the farthest west chapter of the National Railway Historical Society. Several of the members had their own ideas of what we should do, and they formed a new chapter, based in Canton. This was known as the Midwest Chapter. So, we decided just to be our own local club, and turned in the Eastern Ohio charter and became the Akron Railroad Club. And thus, I finally got rid of being president and having to referee factions. The club flourishes today and still holds monthly meetings at Akron, and when they do have a special run—as they did last October on the Ohio Central Railroad—they have a turnout of 200 or more. This doubleheader was sold out.

We had two special excursions on the narrow-gauge East Broad Top Railroad in Pennsylvania, which came about by learning that we could have an engine and three coaches for $65.00, for not more than eight hours. We splurged, adding $10.00 for each run for two additional coaches! These excursion runs were in 1946 and 1948. We and others would have had more trips on the line, but the company gave up on running specials after a man in Pennsylvania ran a trip that caused many problems for the EBT.

Railfan trips sometimes had some side effects that were surprising. One trip was on the Monongahela West Penn's line from Marietta, Ohio, to Parkersburg, West Virginia. This run used an old car that seldom saw daylight anymore. At the carbarns, there was a kid who obviously had a great interest in electric traction. Several of us talked it over and invited him to come along on the outing. He had a great time, and I had forgotten this until reminded at a recent Hoosier Traction Meet at Indianapolis. This meeting is an annual get-together of traction fans, masterminded by Dr. Howard Blackburn, the erstwhile "kid" of long ago, who grew up with a lasting interest in electric traction.

George Silcott's mother called me when I was living in Columbus to ask if I would take George—then 14 years old—on an upcoming fan trip in northern Ohio. She guaranteed that he would be no bother and would behave. She said he was afraid if he asked me, the answer would be "no." George became quite a traction enthusiast, and as a young adult, showed some skill at helping the new Ohio Railway Museum at Columbus get underway. Learning that the Erie Railroad had a fleet of six gas-electric cars for sale, he bought them (with his own money, as the club had none), sold five of the generators and motors individually, and the bodies separately. He kept the best car for the museum, and its generators solved the museum's need for 600 volts for trolley operation. The gas-electric car in effect became a small power plant for the museum. He made over $10,000 in all of this, and turned that over to the new museum, starting them off in the black. All this educated him to the world of diesel-electrics, too. Gradually, George became a dealer in and rebuilder of small diesel locomotives, and he has conducted this business successfully all over the country.

⚑ RAILFAN EXTRA ⚑

THE MIXED TRAIN

ONCE COMMON on American railroads, the "mixed train," could be seen all over the country. As the name infers, this type of train was a mixture of freight and passenger equipment. Common on short lines and on branch lines of the larger railroads, such trains often handled all the traffic on some lines—their schedules fluctuating with the amount of business at hand. Often, neither their departures nor their arrivals were anywhere near the times listed in the timetables. Surprisingly, a few actually stayed close to their scheduled times. Many would spend hours doing way-switching at stations en route. Some of them handled Railway Post Office equipment, and these trains, because of constant nudging by the U.S. Post Office people, attempted to meet their schedules, as lineside post offices and various other mail routes expected on-time connections.

Improved roads and the automobile had siphoned off most of the passenger business of mixed trains by the 1930's. During the Great Depression years, many mixed trains had very few passengers, so few on some of them that they were rare. Because of this, the equipment gradually changed from a coach or two, to a combination baggage-coach, with only a few seats for passengers. This combine often was an old secondhand wooden affair, showing its age by a sagging body and end platforms. When age overtook some of these old cars, they would be retired and replaced by a caboose—sometimes a "side-door caboose" with space for express and small L-C-L freight shipments, and perhaps four plush seats from the old coach would be installed in this hybrid caboose.

On the six-mile Flemingsburg & Northern Railroad in Kentucky, after the connecting Louisville & Nashville took off their passenger train, the F&N's passenger business plummeted to zero. When I showed up to ride the F&N, the crew offered me a ride in the engine, piled with express packages on the pilot beam. And shortly after I climbed aboard the locomotive, the train took off for the junction, leaving the caboose behind. When I went to pay my fare, the superintendent (who was one of the crew members) told me that since I had not had passenger accommodations, he hardly felt a fare should

ALL OF US HAVE our favorite trains and favorite engines, and mine is easily this little train, that once ran irregularly in the beautiful Tionesta Creek Valley of northwestern Pennsylvania. No. 11, a 4-4-0, was a bantam Baldwin American type locomotive, bought by the Sheffield & Tionesta Railway in 1915. It was used to handle their two-car passenger train then serving a valley filled with lumbering activity. Now, during August of 1941, Newtown Mills is just a ghost-town site, nothing more than a field. The train at this time was depending on coal shipments from a truck mine, and it might run one or two times a week, or not at all.

be collected—even if they had to stop once to recover my hat, which blew off when I leaned out to observe some point of interest they wanted me to see.

On one September day, I had a pleasant ride aboard the old coach of the Sheffield & Tionesta Railway, along scenic Tionesta Creek. Their combination car had become unsafe to use, with rotten sills, and the last caboose had been spurred out in even more decrepit condition. I wondered just how solid the coach might be! Next June, when traveling by that way with a day to spare, I went for a ride again and learned I was the first passenger since riding it myself the previous fall. Perhaps they felt the photographs I had given them were better than collecting fare, for none was collected.

Sometimes to show up as a passenger on such poorly patronized trains was an annoyance to the conductor, who would have to report the fare or ticket on a special report form and place it in an envelope to go to the company office. Showing up like this on the AC&Y's mixed train brought a grumbling protest from the conductor that he would now have to fill out a report. His attitude was that he wished I had not come aboard.

With an agreeable crew—and most of the men were quite friendly—a trip on a mixed train was a pleasant adventure. The leisurely stops for way freight and switching were made at small places for which the arrival of the train broke up the quiet monotony of things in these small towns and decaying villages. Often the local kids would be waiting to climb aboard and enjoy brief rides in the combine or caboose as the switching progressed. On one such trip, the crew actually took them for a ride for a couple of miles, then stopped so they could get off and happily hike back home along the track... their day made. They had ridden on a train!

Generally, taking pictures of mixed trains was easy; there was little rush to get up ahead at a station stop, as there was for a regular passenger train, whose stop often was brief. And if some trestle or other point of interest was a good scene to photograph, the mixed train could be posed briefly for such a shot.

There were some exceptions, of course. Like the Atlanta, Birmingham & Coast Railroad from Brunswick, Georgia, a nearly 80-mile branch to the little crossroads of Sessoms, deep in the pine forest, where the branch met the mainline. Delayed by a derailment in the yard, the short train—tailed by a wooden baggage car and an attractive wooden coach of long ago—took off at as fast a rate of speed as the old Ten-wheeler on the point of the train could manage. Fortunately, the track was mainly flat (if you could call it that) and almost tangent, but it was not well-ballasted, and the coach bounced drunkenly, and the old oil lamps constantly flickered. A passenger daring to attempt to walk down the aisle to the water cooler, had to grasp the back of each coach seat firmly to stay upright. Sessoms was reached on time, and the headlight of the Atlanta train was not yet showing. I am sure that was the fastest mixed train I ever rode; it seemed to me that we were doing at least 50 mph most of the way.

The slowest mixed train? Perhaps the Bellefonte Central Railroad's mixed, which made passably good time on its outward journey of 18 miles to State College, Pennsylvania, and the return trip did seem we might make the 3:30 p.m. scheduled arrival back at Bellefonte. However, the sun was getting low in the west, and we were still a couple of miles short of Bellefonte, and having missed lunch, I was looking forward to whatever culinary specials lie ahead. But upon inquiry, the conductor estimated it would take another two hours for switching before we would reach the station. This equated to starvation, so off I trudged down the track. It was long after I was in the restaurant that I heard the engine whistling for the station.

The shortest mixed train? Definitely, none could be shorter than the Flemingsburg & Northern's engine-only consist.

The longest? Not infrequently, a mixed train might consist of 30 to 40 cars; however, on occasion—as at grain-harvest time or at seasonal livestock-loading periods—the train could become 60 to 70 cars in length. Some of the trains on the Santa Fe's secondary lines got very long, and the mixed train through Amarillo, Texas, looked as though it was a mile long on the one-and-only time I saw it.

As mentioned previously, some railroads looked on passengers as a nuisance. The Prescott & Northwestern in Arkansas only accepted passengers on its Friday train, although the train hauled the combination car on all the other days. In the South during the "Jim Crow" era, taking pictures from the rear platform was a "no-no" if that happened to be the end of the car that was restricted to "colored" passengers. On a couple of occasions, I was firmly told that I could not stand on that platform to take pictures. However, instead, I could only do so from the "white"

end of the car, which would be when the train was going in the other direction, of course. The "Jim Crow" requirements led to the construction of what was known as the "Southern combination car," in that the baggage-express doors and compartment were in the center of the car, separating the two passenger compartments. On combination cars of the usual arrangement, which had only one passenger compartment, there was sometimes a dividing wall between the two sections. And in some cases, there was a movable partition to accommodate fluctuations in the numbers of "white" and "colored" passengers.

Some companies equipped the combination car with a cupola, so the trainmen could keep an eye on the freight cars ahead, this being a particularly desirable feature on those lines with less-than-good track. The Denver & Rio Grande Western equipped the little narrow-gauge combine of the Pagosa Springs Branch with a cupola, after many derailments—and in some instances, the derailed car was dragged for a considerable distance because no one from the rear of the train could see what was happening ahead. On the narrow-gauge *Chili Line* route of the D&RGW to Santa Fe, New Mexico, the coaches used on those trains had bay windows installed to serve the same purpose.

After going around the world via the U.S. Army during a three-year stint, in July of 1945 I found myself turned loose at Indiantown Gap, Pennsylvania, for a 30-day furlough. Looking through the *Official Guide* at the army-camp travel office, I was intrigued to learn that the Gap was located on a branch served by a mixed train. Moreover, one that headed into the mountains to the north. And on its journey to Lykens, some 40 miles away, the train traversed a switchback! That did it, and the plan to immediately head home for Akron, Ohio, was put on hold at the idea of exploring a new railroad, and in the U.S.A.

The day turned dark and gloomy, spitting rain occasionally, as the Reading's camelback 2-8-0 trailed about a dozen freight cars with the typical wooden combination car. Once past the mountain, the track wound through endless worked-over and largely idle anthracite mining areas, with endless huge piles of culm (anthracite-slack dumps), presenting a very dreary aspect. Even on a bright, sunny day, that area would hardly look attractive.

WITH THE TENDER piled high with sawmill scrap, Engine 100 was handling the mixed train of the Live Oak, Perry & Gulf, near Live Oak, Florida. Notice the engineer has added brass flag holders to the engine. This was Train 3, and the date was February 20, 1942. The handsome 4-6-0 was hauling a train consisting entirely of boxcars (except for the combine), several of which were typical composite wood-and-steel freight cars of this period.

There was not any opportunity to snap a picture or two at the switchback, and by early afternoon, Lykens was reached. However, I did manage to shoot a picture or two of the engine and train while the 2-8-0 was being turned on the armstrong table. In addition, there was time for a Hershey candy bar and soft drink at a store in the rather neglected-looking town. Arrival at the origination point of the mixed took place late in the afternoon at Lebanon, where a mainline connection was made to Harrisburg, Pennsylvania. After the disappointing trip on the Reading, I looked forward to something hopefully better, and a PRR train landed me in Mount Union, to ride on the morrow the East Broad Top's mixed train.

The weather failed to improve noticeably, but the scenic Aughwick Valley and the familiar route of the East Broad Top were a great change from the previous day's trip. The husky narrow-gauge 2-8-2 ahead had a string of empty coal cars (steel hoppers) from Mount Union, and a dozen or so passengers had boarded the combine. The crew members were friendly, although they expressed surprise that a G.I.—after being away for years—would detour on his trip home to ride their little road. However, by mid-afternoon I was back on the Pennsy and headed for Akron aboard a passenger train, with no more railroad detours.

CHASING THE PAST

BESIDES "CHASING TRAINS," it was fun to seek out the grades of abandoned lines in Colorado, as well as the grades of lines never completed or used. It is likely that at no point will we ever be able to claim that all of these grades have been found and identified. When Mac Poor compiled his monumental book, **Denver, South Park & Pacific**, in the 1940's, he did not know about the tons of old records forgotten in Denver. Not until the end of the Colorado & Southern Railway in the 1960's, and when C&S structures were being torn down, did these sooty records turn up. Even then, much of this material was destroyed before tons of the remaining records were given to the Colorado Rail-

road Museum by the authority of Burlington Route official, John M. Budd. At this time, much of it was already loaded to be cut up at a nearby scrap-paper plant. With that highest okay, C&S President John Terrill was most helpful, even though the auditor strongly demurred that this was contrary to all his lifelong training, which was to give nothing away.

Scattered through this vast amount of sooty material were all kinds of data, information long wondered about, etc. At the time Mac Poor's *DSP&P* was published by the Rocky Mountain Railroad Club in 1949, it was the finest railroad book yet produced. A number of other people had read it, revised it, added to it, proofread it and so on, notably Ed Haley and Richard Kindig. However, one odd thing ensued. While at Alamosa one time on a visit, Mac sadly admitted that he found few buyers had ever read the entire book. Nearly everyone had read the Alpine Tunnel chapter, enjoyed the photographs, etc., but they had read little of the balance of the book. From his comments, it seemed to me that barely five percent had read the entire book—a shame.

There already was a considerable interest in the remote Alpine Tunnel among railfans. Photographs of the massive rotting doors and snowsheds, the rusty track at the western portal, the little "depot" (the telegraph office) and the tilting boarding house, along with the ruins of the stone enginehouse, had intrigued many. During the summer, when taking a day off, and some visitor from a distant point was willing to go along, they often wanted to go to Alpine Tunnel if asked. So... during the next 30 years I certainly visited this site many times. Nevertheless, I have to admit that each time I saw something interesting I had not noticed before.

Perhaps the remoteness of this site and that it had to be approached on foot truly impressed visitors, making it almost a "holy place" in their minds. To approach from the west, an automobile could be driven only a short distance beyond Pitkin. From there, the tunnel site could be reached only on foot, on a hike along the old South Park's long-abandoned grade for about seven miles. From the eastern side of the tunnel, what passed for a road ended at the site of the ghost town of Hancock, after a long, rough drive up a back-country road that followed Chalk Creek. Then, one had to hike for over three miles, stepping over rotten ties, rocks, brush and weeds to reach the curve past the sagging doors at the eastern portal. At that point, one could see the cave-in that had closed the tunnel during the 1930's.

After living in Alamosa, at an elevation of 7,500-feet plus, I got used to high elevations, and was able to keep going on high-country hikes. However, I would have to stop many times for the lowland hikers to catch their breath, before they could continue a few hundred feet farther up the trail or grade. A trail led over the top of the tunnel, across Alpine Pass, and down to the other side. It was always a "must" to take along a heavy jacket or raincoat for this hike, even in the middle of summer. Even though the hike might start with a cloudless blue sky at 8:00 a.m., by noon, thunderheads probably would be boiling up, and it was not unusual for them to be followed shortly thereafter by booming thunder and rain. There might even be sleet or snow, which could briefly whiten the ground within a few minutes. And the air would rapidly become quite cold, helped by strong gusts of wind.

At one time the two of us on a hike over the pass sort of crawled into the shelter of some low "buck brush," to be shielded from stinging sleet, feeling as though someone was pelting us with a battalion of "BB" guns. On another hike, lightning lit up the cloud-filled sky, and at 11,000 feet above sea level, one certainly feels close to that lightning—much too close. We hurriedly shed our pockets of the souvenir spikes we had picked up from the grade! And the air had that odd odor of "when you are too close to lightning," *much too close!*

There was still an opening of perhaps two or three feet below the arch of the western portal of the tunnel. And equipped with strong flashlights, one could peer into the timber-lined bore. Beyond the foot or more of water backed-up against the debris at the entrance, one could see the track reaching toward the apex, and the stately rows of California redwood timbers still firmly supported the sides and roof. "Spooky" was the way some viewers termed it. Each visiting group would pull

away some of the dirt and rock rubble, which continually came down on the portal. However, they lost ground over the years, and at the last report I heard (in 1994), the opening under the arch requires one to drop down several feet through huge boulders. This is definitely a hard-hat place now!

Of course, the visitors would go home with memories of Alpine Tunnel never to be forgotten. And they would tell others, leading to thousands of visitors making the trip to the old DSP&P tunnel site each summer. A uranium miner bulldozed the grade from Quartz (a short distance above Pitkin) all the way to Woodstock Curve, a distance of six miles. Later, a county road grader managed to shove the ties off the grade along the Palisades and beyond, finally reaching the last mile or so of track still in place at what was Alpine station. The Gunnison County crew felt it was worth their effort, for they were able to obtain a good supply of rail for cattle guards all over the county. However, while still in place, the DSP&P track showed the peculiar strength of the type of track fittings the old South Park line used.

Rail joiners were a common failure on railroad tracks after the Civil War, as rails became larger. The commonly used splice bar would crack and break, and the early angle bar, which extended down to cover the foot of the rails, was a great improvement. Nevertheless, inventors were kept busy "improving on the improvement." A Mr. Fisher invented what was widely advertised in the 1880's as "The Fisher Rail Joint," which was a flat plate about 28 inches long. It was spiked to two ties and the rail joint was made midway on the plate, with each rail bolted down to large "U" bolts. This never looked to me as though it was a good, reliable joint, but its strength was demonstrated on the long-abandoned track. A large boulder (weighing several tons), fell down and hit the inner rail, pushing it inward on the track by more than a foot. However, the joint still held the two rails firmly together. The miner who bulldozed the grade above Quartz shoved hundreds of these relics down off the grade. For years afterward, happy railfans might find one and cart it home. The Fisher rail joiner was used on many railroads, and with rail much heavier

CHASING THE PAST: After the Colorado & Southern turned over the Baldwin Branch to the Denver & Rio Grande in 1911, the old South Park depot at Gunnison served as a section-foreman's home. Unfortunately, after the abandonment of all the D&RGW trackage in Gunnison during 1955, the old stone building sat squarely in the path of the newly rebuilt portion of U.S. Highway 50, and the depot was demolished. A contractor had offered to move the building; however, there was no agreement locally on a new site. This depot was typical of the high quality of construction on the legendary narrow-gauge Denver, South Park & Pacific. Stone was also used for culverts, and some of them still function where roads have been built on the DSP&P grade.

than the South Park's 40- and 45-pound steel. Of course, as rails got much larger, better rail joiners were devised, and the Fisher went into the scrap heaps. However, the slang term "fishplate" is used to this day to refer to a rail joiner.

Colorado has many abandoned railroad grades, and some railfan tourists have annually spent vacations just exploring and photographing these old grades—matching various photographic sites published in railroad books with the places visited. These grades range from mainlines, like the Colorado Midland, to almost invisible lumber-company grades, devoid of ballast and usually located just where a spring freshet would wipe them out. Untreated ties would last for 40 or 50 years in Colorado, depending on drainage and location, of course. Some of these grades once were obvious for their rotting debris.

The steel mill at Pueblo was a ready market for railroad scrap, but when many items were abandoned, economic conditions made it worthwhile for only the rails to be hauled out—leaving behind the spikes. Often, the spikes were from the 1880's, and they were of cast iron, not steel. They were worthless to later track crews,

as the iron would deteriorate. Subsequently, we learned at the museum, just driving one of them into a tie might cause the head of the spike to fly off. And if it hit someone's shin, that person would be limping for several days! Occasionally, a switchstand posed a problem to load aboard flatcars with rails, and it would be left behind, particularly if it was an old "harp" style cast-iron version—as would often happen on the railroads of Otto Mears. However, very few visiting railfans were able to haul off more than an old spike or two, or perhaps a slice of old rail. Believe it or not, one narrow-gauge fan hauled an old South Park tie all the way to Connecticut, probably a unique happening!

It often seemed to me that we were trying to catch up with those long-vanished trains of yesteryear, as we hiked along the grades and studied the books and historic photographs. Every inch of the abandoned Rio Grande Southern has been hiked and examined, and the volumes produced by Sundance Publications undoubtedly will greatly increase that activity. A considerable amount of imagination is needed to visualize those grades, as they once were long ago, when the rails were shiny and the trains were rolling. Decades later, curious railfans hiked the grades and scanned books and old pictures to tell them what they could never catch up with or see.

While photographs are the equivalent of the thousands of words required to tell you what is in each picture, the complete facts have to be gleaned by reading the old paper records of the railroad operations during that time and at that place in the scene viewed by the photographer. Most railroads would "clean house" now and then; however, it was often the case that records just piled up and were forgotten until the space was needed or a building was torn down.

As happened with the famed South Park line, most of it was abandoned in 1937; however, visiting fans gave brief attention to the old records left behind at abandoned stations. These records would have added much to our knowledge of that unusual railroad, but most of the paper work was scattered around or burned at trash dumps. So, I used to put much time and energy into saving all the old records I could locate. For many years, I read through tons of this material, gleaning many interesting bits of trivia, finding the answers to some puzzling things that old photographs did not explain.

Buried under inches of soot in an old Colorado & Southern building in Denver were hundreds of linen drawings and prints of unfinished extensions of the various routes that formed the C&S in 1898. The Union Pacific of the 1880's had grand plans to construct standard-gauge lines into South Park and beyond, even into the San Juan region. This explains why some early locomotives had names of places in the San Juan Mountains of southwestern Colorado. Likewise, the Burlington Route had sent out surveying-and-location parties to plan for a line that was to reach into the Crystal River Valley's coal seams. The CB&Q even had located sites for their enginehouses on this never-built line. The Moffat Road left behind maps of various lines to Utah, descriptive of the rugged regions beyond Craig (in northwestern Colorado). This is mute witness to the many hard-working surveying crews and field engineers of what was the Denver & Salt Lake Railroad (now part of the Southern Pacific's D&RGW lines).

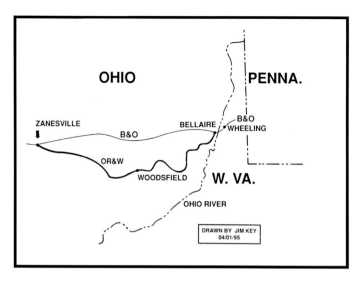

FOR A DIFFERENT WAY of getting home to Akron from Columbus, Ohio, I had ridden a Toledo-bound New York Central passenger train to a station where it crossed the Akron, Canton & Youngstown. From this point I boarded the mixed train on a warm summer day on August 20, 1939. The two scheduled mixed trains of the Akron, Canton & Youngstown met at the rural community of New London. It was like riding on an observation car and having it all to yourself!

OHIO'S LAST MIXED TRAIN

MIXED TRAINS had almost completely vanished from Ohio by the end of the 1930's. Competition from electric interurban lines had by that time killed most of the short line and local passenger trains, as well. However, one lingered until 1951, the Akron–Delphos mainline run of the oddly named Akron, Canton & Youngstown, which never got anywhere near either Canton or Youngstown, but was merely a 7.5-mile switching road until it absorbed the Northern Ohio Railway in 1920. This was accomplished by obtaining a long-term lease for this streak of rust from the parent New York Central system. Thereby, the belt line acquired the "Akron & Delphos Railway Post Office," and it was the discontinuance of this mail service by the Post Office Department that enabled the AC&Y to end its mixed trains. By 1951, virtually no one rode the trains, which often

handled some 35 cars of mostly through freight between the two terminals. Even so, the train did a little switching along the way, as the road crossed most of the railroads in the northern part of Ohio.

A ride on the train was a pleasant way to enjoy the rolling countryside of rural Ohio— for the AC&Y route missed large cities, and most of the listed flag stops were merely sidings or very small places. The road had in-

herited three open-platform coaches from the Northern Ohio, and it was like a private observation trip to ride aboard one of these cars. Several times, if I was in no hurry to return to Akron, I chose to make the AC&Y trip the final portion of my journey. Once, when coming from Toledo, the first portion of my trip was via a typical New York Central local, hauled by a handsome Pacific locomotive and consisting of two head-end cars, tailed by two coaches. At Arlington, 40 miles east of Delphos, I swung aboard the AC&Y coach, to find myself to be the only fare-paying passenger, although there were several company employees aboard the train. Thereupon ensued a pleasant springtime six-and-one-half-hour trip to Akron. At the time the road averaged around $27.00 in fares per month, most of it from shorter trips than mine.

Another time, while coming from Chicago, I found the mighty Pennsylvania Railroad declined to stop most of its trains at Delphos, but the PRR did have one that left Chicago—coaches only—about midnight, which arrived at Delphos shortly after 6:30 a.m. This allowed two hours for breakfast, as well as for any Pennsy delays, before boarding the AC&Y for its 8:30 a.m. departure. Sleep in the PRR coach was disturbed twice by conductors checking tickets, and I counted on them to wake me for the Delphos stop. I awoke shortly after dawn to see a large building gliding by me lettered "Lima" something! And I immediately realized with a shock that I had overshot the station of Delphos by some 20 miles!

Determined to catch the mixed train if possible—as no other rail connections lay ahead via the Pennsy—I consulted a taxi driver at the depot, who agreed (for a modest sum) to take me north to Vaughnsville. Apparently, he had never heard of the place, and when we got there, he wondered if I was certain this was where I wanted to go. There was a farmhouse near the grade crossing, upon whose front porch a curious housewife appeared, evidently attracted by the first taxi cab ever to visit Vaughnsville—which, apart from her farm home, consisted of only the AC&Y's siding and station sign. The taxi driver, solicitous of my future, offered to come and get me if I found myself stranded, and he gave me a telephone number to call.

Perhaps an hour later, I heard a crossing blast from a whistle, still miles to the west.

Eventually, an AC&Y Mikado came into sight, with her long train, as I stood by the siding and waved a white handkerchief until the startled engineer acknowledged with a long blast of the melodious steam whistle. Some 30 freight cars rumbled past me, slowing as the brakeman—now on the top of the cars—waved the engineer to a smooth stop that spotted the coach steps practically in front of me. The unsmiling conductor reached down to help me with my luggage to board the car as he highballed ahead again. Again, I found myself to be the sole passenger for the all-day ride. There was no diner or buffet, of course, but at New London, where we arrived an hour or so after noon, sustenance was obtained while switching progressed at this station.

My last trip over the AC&Y was a variation of the above. Discharged from the Army of the United States at Camp Benjamin Harrison during September of 1945, I scorned the bus routing the army discharge clerk was insisting upon, who stated, "You can't get to Akron by train!" I quickly informed him to the contrary, so he thereupon paid out the minimum in cash as I headed via the camp bus to the Indianapolis Union Station. There, I boarded a crowded "Big Four" train headed for Cleveland, but rode the train for only the 54 miles to Muncie, Indiana. Soon, a captivating little local train of the Nickel Plate Road came along on its run from Frankfort, Indiana, to Lima, Ohio. A white-striped 4-6-0 headed a three-car train that already was a museum piece of wooden cars of 1905 configuration, with classic windows and a general design soon to vanish from American railroads forever. What a change in passengers, too, with no crowd of G.I.'s, but instead, there was a somewhat hushed handful of civilian passengers. The Big Four had so many G.I.'s aboard that it almost seemed to be a troop train. The Muncie station also was rather quiet and calm, a pleasant change.

From Lima, Ohio, I caught a late afternoon westbound Pennsy local after lunch, and I stayed overnight at Delphos. I had plenty of time the next morning to board the AC&Y's 8:30 mixed train. Just for old time's sake, after four year's hiatus, I went up ahead to the RPO car and mailed several postcards to get the distinct postmark for "Train 90." I never did learn why the AC&Y increased the Northern Ohio Railway's num-

THE AKRON, CANTON & YOUNGSTOWN was misnamed, for it never went near either Canton or the steel town, Youngstown. In fact, the road went in the opposite direction! The switching road that took over the streak of rust during 1920, had been known as the Northern Ohio Railway before becoming the AC&Y. It ran from Akron to Delphos, Ohio, a distance of 161 miles. For many years, the AC&Y used light 4-6-0 and 2-8-0 steam engines. However, the company finally built up the former Northern Ohio so that the it could buy a number of husky 2-8-2 Mikados in 1926. The locomotive in this view, No. 400, was the first one in the series. This 2-8-2 was in the AC&Y engine terminal at Brittain yard in Akron, Ohio, and the date was January 25, 1939. Notice the bell positioned out in front of the feedwater heater. Yours truly was standing on one of the pilot steps.

bers of Trains 1 and 2 to such high numbers. Was this a joke by someone in the railroad's office? One superintendent was noted for things like this.

After four years of military service, it was indeed a pleasant day not to see any G.I.'s, and to sit quietly there and watch the rolling green countryside of Ohio from my rear-end plush seat. It was 5:00 p.m. when the train pounded across North Main Street to spot the postal car and coach at the box-shaped little Akron depot. Six times a week the mixed brought the home-going rush-hour traffic of automobiles and trolleys to a halt, until the two rear-end cars were uncoupled and the forward portion of the train cleared the busy street.

As I headed to cross the street, the brakeman told me that he would wait for me to get across before he pulled the pin on the coupler and signalled the engineer—a very considerate act on his part. Then, hoisting my barracks bag over my shoulder, I headed up the hill the six blocks to home. However, at Summit Street, at the top of the steep curving grade from Main Street, I stopped to wait for a scene that years before, we grade-school kids used to enjoy. Shortly after the U.S. mail and Railway Express shipments were unloaded, the train came back across Main Street again to couple up. Then, the entire train backed down until the engine was a block past the depot at the edge of a big trestle. With her steam up, whistle blowing and bell ringing, the locomotive pounded across Main Street again, and she came working hard up the grade—a tall column of smoke rising in the sky. After a friendly wave from the engineer and the rear brakeman, Train 90 was gone, heading for the AC&Y's Brittain Yard, four miles away. It was a nice way to complete an around-the-world trip that had taken four years.

37

A BELT RAILROAD

BELT RAILROADS usually did not merit the attention of railfans like the other railroads did, and the Akron & Barberton Belt Railroad was one that went its way ignored by most of the railroad camera fans. The A&BB line started out in the 1890's as a scheme of the "match king," Ohio C. Barber, and he made feints of building it all the way to Cleveland, as well as to other points.

Eventually, the property became worth much more during the 1900's, due to the rise of the rubber industry. As a result, the three railroads serving Akron bought the line; however, the Baltimore & Ohio and the Erie let the Pennsylvania do the operating. As a grade-school kid, I was intrigued by the obviously secondhand PRR engines and their passenger whistles. Apparently, at one time, the Pennsy even had one of their Atlantics trying to handle the hilly belt line in East Akron.

THE AKRON & BARBERTON BELT railroad lived up to its name. It wound around and through Akron, with steep grades, curves and numerous street crossings. However, the tire-and-rubber industry's boom times were over by the 1980's, and this once-busy switching road in East Akron has been abandoned, and the tracks were being torn up in 1995. Engine No. 16 was a Baldwin 0-6-0, one of four ordered just before the severe financial crash of 1929. Two of the 0-6-0's sat in storage, unused from the date of their delivery in 1930, until needed during World War II.

UNTIL DIESELS TOOK OVER in 1948, the Akron & Barberton Belt Railroad used Baldwin 0-6-0's, which dated from 1930. It was difficult to

find the A&BB's trains out in open spaces, as the switching road wound through industrial areas for almost its entire route. This photograph of engine

No. 15 was taken at the south side of Barberton, Ohio, on October 22, 1942. Notice the two crew members on top of the tender.

This railroad had a connection with the Northern Ohio Railway via a line through the Copley swamps, and this became a problem during the 1930's, as an underground fire was undermining that track. So, the Pennsy unloaded its answer to the danger. Obviously, as the road obtained four new Baldwin 0-6-0 switchers just as the Great Depression began, it was not desired to risk them on that track, as no wrecking crane would dare to venture out there. As a result, the Pennsy sent over a Class A-3a 0-4-0T, No. 5076, which had been equipped with a tender. The switcher had been sitting idle somewhere for so long that she still had the big steel box headlights, and right away, two new electric headlights were applied to the engine—front and rear. And apparently, the little No. 5076 never had any trouble in the swamps.

In 1913, the A&BB had purchased some Baldwin Moguls, and three of them survived into the 1930's, Nos. 1, 6 and 7. However, business was down in 1930, when the new 0-6-0's arrived, Nos. 15, 16, 17 and 18, so only two were used in service, while the other two sat in storage in the Pennsy's South Akron yard for years.

The Akron & Barberton Belt line tapped the Goodyear and General tire plants, as well as numerous allied industries. The worst grade was westbound—toward Barberton—when it left the Goodyear plant and embarked on several miles of grade involving many street crossings. This resulted in a great amount of whistling, as the engineers tried to get the most out of their engines. This took place as the locomotives tackled the line from Beaver Street to cross busy Exchange Street and climb on up the grade.

ON NOVEMBER 16, 1941, the Akron Railroad Club had its last pre-war excursion. We chartered a two-car outing on the Akron Transportation Company's single trolley line, which extended through its namesake city from the western suburb of Kenmore to Ellet on the east side. This was the last remaining portion of the once-vast Northern Ohio Traction & Light Company empire. These electric cars were new when I was a kid of about 10 years old. And one day, my parents let me ride alone on a similar two-car train all the way to Ravenna, Ohio. This was a town about 25 miles away, some of it a high-speed run. At the town of Kent, I watched trains of the Erie Railroad for hours, mainly because this road had large facilities at this location. Although my picture looks as if we had a three-car train, the regular city car followed the special run. The motorman had pulled his trolley up close behind our cars, giving that appearance.

THE TOWN OF KENMORE was a post-World War I suburb of Akron, Ohio, and Kenmore Boulevard had been laid-out with a double-track trolley line in the center strip. This electric line went on to Barberton and Wadsworth. A streetcar that dated from those "big-boom times" for the tire-and-rubber industry, still plied the line in March of 1947. Unfortunately, this well-designed route was soon to be abandoned.

Although the new engines came with "doghouse" shelters on the tenders, the union demanded cabooses, so the PRR supplied two. Incidentally, the belt line had only one other piece of rolling stock, a flatcar.

The A&BB, unlike so many of the small railroads I "explored," has survived, enlarged and prospered. With the decline of the tire industry, the local Erie and the Pennsyl-vania lines vanished into abandonments or became part of successor companies who did not want them. As a result, some of this mileage in the general Akron and suburban area became part of the A&BB. Then, in 1994, the new Wheeling & Lake Erie Railroad became the owner and .has changed the belt line's name to the unique "Akron & Barberton Cluster Railway."

DURING THE SUMMER of 1941, Line Car 1022 of the Akron Transportation Company was out on a rare trip on the East Akron portion of this trolley line. On a February night in 1928 I had ridden the last of the big red interurban cars on the final run of this line to Canton and beyond. At that time, the line was part of the vast Ohio Traction system. My parents did not approve of my outing, or my arrival back home at around 1:00 a.m.!

LOWER LEFT: The Youngstown area had a heavy concentration of railroad operations. Yet, on our few forays with cameras, our results fell far short of what we expected. The Baltimore & Ohio moved much traffic to and through the area. And for the freight trains operating to the west, the B&O employed their recently acquired fleet of ex-Boston & Maine 4-8-2's. These Mountain types were notable for their extremely loud whistles, which had to be toned down because they were too loud in the flat country of western Ohio, and on to Chicago. Here, on June 13, 1948, these engines apparently had just set out their train of coal cars. Then, the two locomotives headed for the engine terminal, with one of the small B&O cabooses in tow. No. 4260, a 2-8-2 Mikado type, and No. 5585, a 4-8-2 Mountain type, were photographed on June 13, 1948.

LOWER RIGHT: The Moraine backshop of the Cincinnati & Lake Erie is in the background in 1939, as this electric interurban car was awaiting scrapping. When the Cincinnati & Lake Erie took over the Cincinnati, Hamilton & Dayton in 1930, it put on new lightweight high-speed cars. However, it kept this heavier series of CH&D cars for use on the line to the south, toward Cincinnati. This car, No. 106, was never relettered for the C&LE. Railfans living in the Dayton area chartered this car and two others for the line's last three-car train.

EVERY AFTERNOON, while I lived in Columbus, Ohio, during 1937–1941, the Chesapeake & Ohio's Train 35 departed for Toledo at 3:15 p.m. with this attractive consist. C&O motive power was noted for its smooth-running machinery. So, when the local officials viewed an engine of the "Standard Railroad of the World" (the Pennsylvania Railroad) with clanking siderods, they asserted they would tie-up the locomotive for backshopping if it belonged to the C&O! This interesting view of C&O 4-6-2 No. 467 was photographed on May 2, 1941.

THE DETROIT, TOLEDO & IRONTON

BY THE LATE 1930's the Detroit, Toledo & Ironton Railroad, once the property of Henry Ford, had only a mixed train in service. This train carried a Railway Post Office between Springfield, Ohio, and Jackson, Ohio (in the southwestern part of the state). This 109-mile

CONSOLIDATION No. 201 was being "blown down" outside the roundhouse in Jackson, Ohio, during May of 1939. This 2-8-0 was typical of the motive power used on the southern end of the Detroit, Toledo & Ironton Railroad.

trip was covered in four and one-half hours.

One Saturday in 1938, I went for a jaunt on this mixed train. It had only a short consist, just the locomotive, a former Pennsylvania Railroad 2-8-0 and the steel combination car. The train operated on the excellent DT&I track at up to 50 mph, with the result that we had rather long halts at stations along the line, to let the timetable catch up with us.

Detroit, Toledo & Ironton crews had no good words for Henry Ford, who (among other faults) in their view had a stubborn insistence that crew members all do something useful during delays—not just loaf around. Trainmen were expected to pick up litter while flagging and—yes—even to pluck weeds growing in the track. Henry wanted a neat-appearing railroad! Nevertheless, despite their reminiscence of the times of Henry Ford, I noticed that the brakeman was plucking weeds around the vicinity of the depot platform!

The Consolidation-type engine looked as if someone had wiped down the entire tender and boiler jacket, while the aluminum numbers and the DT&I herald were clean and bright. In addition, the steel combine was neatly painted and clean, both inside and out.

However, when the Pennsylvania Railroad took over the DT&I line, the words about the PRR management from later DT&I President Towle were: "The Pennsylvania people ruined a good railroad."

STANDARD PRR 2-8-0 ENGINES replaced older, lighter motive power on the Detroit, Toledo & Ironton after the Pennsylvania Railroad obtained control of the DT&I. Ex-PRR 2-8-0 No. 412, which was switching at Springfield, Ohio, on March 15, 1941, is an example. However, DT&I practices instituted by the great Henry Ford when he owned the road, could still be seen. Mr. Ford equipped each engine with a complete tool box for the engine crew's use. Besides that, the attractive DT&I monogram herald was in shiny metal on the tenders, and unlike the PRR, the engines were kept wiped down and clean.

UNTIL THE HARD TIMES of the Great Depression ended the practice during the 1930's, once a year this former PRR Atlantic would be steamed-up. And Detroit, Toledo & Ironton officials would tour the line in the road's business car. By 1939, the shop crews at Jackson, Ohio, had even pilfered the headlight glasses for other engines. This 4-4-2 had been built at the Pennsy's Juniata shops in Altoona, Pennsylvania, in 1901. The Henry Ford era's raised DT&I monogram and numerals were typical of this road.

A GAS-ELECTRIC TRAIN SET had been purchased by the Detroit, Toledo & Ironton during the 1920's; however, when the motors wore out in the early 1930's, the daily passenger train became a mixed. In any case, on January 2, 1939, there were no freight cars to handle, and this short train sped along at up to 50 mph. Then, the train would have to kill time at each scheduled stop, waiting for the departure time to arrive. Never much of a passenger line, the DT&I only had this round-trip from Jackson to Springfield, Ohio. No. 400 was the first of a number of PRR engines the road obtained.

TRYING TO SHOOT A PICTURE of this Firestone Tire & Rubber Company locomotive required patience. The 0-6-0 had to cross a city street between the fenced-and-guarded plants in South Akron, Ohio—the only place available to snap a view of No. 1. In any case, the engineer of the switcher solved the problem for me. As he laughed about the lurking special agents (security guards), he unlocked a gate in the chain-link fence and invited me to shoot away. Handily, the Pennsy roundhouse was next to the Firestone plant, so help for the 0-6-0 was near when needed.

FIRESTONE TIRE & RUBBER 0-6-0

OF THE GIANT RUBBER FIRMS in Akron, Ohio, only the Firestone Tire & Rubber Company had its own switch engine. It worked the vast expanse of the southern Akron factory district, also serving the subsidiary Firestone Steel Products plant. In all its work, however, it stayed behind fences, except that to get to the steel products operation, she had to cross a city street. The only other "resident" of the street was the Pennsylvania Railroad, which had at its end—a distance equivalent to several city blocks—its freight yard and roundhouse.

Determined to obtain a picture of Firestone No. 1, I parked my car one day on the street to wait for the engine to cross it. I brought along a book to read, and I was peacefully engaged in reading when alongside pulled a car containing two gentlemen who just "sort of" had that air of being company police (called "security guards" today), although no badges were in sight. They demanded to know what I was doing there, so I plainly told them the truth, that I was waiting for the engine to cross the street and planned to snap a picture of it. To this, they strongly demurred, alleging that photographs of the 0-6-0 were not permitted. To which I replied that they could ban it on Firestone property, but this was a city street, and as a taxpayer and citizen, I had as much right as anyone to be there, and they had no authority over me. They asked for and were given my name, etc., and they drove off, leaving me guessing if they would return with reinforcements, or more likely would not allow the engine to venture out in public. Neither happened, and about 20 minutes later, the engine, running light, crossed the road. This switcher was an undistinguished Lima-built 0-6-0, equipped with a slope-back tender, and the attractive gold Firestone logo was emblazoned on the tender sides of the switcher and under the windows of the cab.

On another occasion, I thought I might try again for another picture, and the engine and crew were resting just inside the Firestone fence. The engineer walked over and remarked that he had seen me take the previous picture, and when I mentioned the company police, he just laughed and invited me in to take a picture if I desired, an invitation I accepted.

The Firestone company's "coal-and-iron police" had a tough reputation, and eventually, Harry Bennett, their feared chief, was hired by the Ford Motor Company. And he masterminded the riotous confrontations as unionization erupted during the 1930's. Indeed, he became so irresponsibly powerful that he tried to oust Henry Ford Jr. from control of the company his father founded.

ON OCTOBER 17, 1937, our railfan club in Akron, Ohio, sponsored a fan trip on the Ohio Public Service Company's interurban line from Oak Harbor to Marblehead, Ohio. There, Superintendent Sauvey showed us his unusual mixture of Lakeside & Marblehead Railroad and three-foot-gauge Kelley Island Lime & Transport Company engines. He then took us for a ride out to the quarry roundhouse, using four Shay geared engines and his boxcar "coach."

A BIG DAY AT MARBLEHEAD

THE KELLEY ISLAND Lime & Transport Company, which headquartered at Cleveland, Ohio, had over 60 Shay geared engines on their roster, mostly narrow-gauge. They operated these Shays on their quarry lines in five states. During 1937, I wrote to Superintendent Sauvey at Marblehead, Ohio, and asked him if we could look over his Shays and the four 0-6-0 standard-gauge engines of the Lakeside & Marblehead Railroad—which shared the ancient stone enginehouse and yard (all dual-gauge)—when we had a special run on the interurban line to Marblehead. When he replied that we certainly would be welcome, we had no indication of the kind of welcome.

When the old wooden Niles combine came to the end-of-track opposite the L&M terminal, we were greeted by the whistles tied down on Shays and the 0-6-0's! The racket had islanders out in the lake thinking that a big fire was in progress! Then, Mr. Sauvey took us three miles out to the quarries and the narrow-gauge enginehouse, with the first quadruple-headed fan trip ever! He explained his only "coach" was a boxcar with benches, and he thought most of the male passengers "...wouldn't mind riding the engines." The crew consisted of one man who would drop off an engine to check the fire and water on another engine, then drop off that engine to check on another one, and so on, for the entire trip. It was quite a day, but one 100-percent traction fan did not like the Shays at all. He demanded that he be allowed to skip all this steam nonsense and ride back on his ticket to Toledo in the regular interurban, which had arrived. When we refused, he later filed a complaint with the Ohio Public Utilities Commission!

ON AN EXCURSION to Marblehead, Ohio, on July 3, 1938, Superintendent Sauvey took us for a ride again, using his boxcar "coach" and as many engines as needed to carry the overflow from that single car. "Robby" Robinson—in a white shirt—was an engineer on the Baltimore & Ohio's "Capitol Limited," and he admitted that it was a mistake to wear his diesel outfit around coal-burners!

THE SHAY GEARED ENGINES in this scene were at the Kelley Island Lime & Transport Company's quarry roundhouse, near Marblehead, Ohio, on July 3, 1938. Some of these small Shays dated from among the first constructed at the Lima Locomotive Works. Engine numbers beginning at the left are: Nos. 71, 69, 67 and an unidentifiable fourth Shay.

ON NEW YEARS DAY of 1939, we Ohio fans used the holiday to see what could be photographed. In the Columbus Union Station, No. 112 of the Norfolk & Western was going to handle the morning passenger train to Portsmouth, the connection with the mainline. Railfans in those days, like me, wore hats and neckties!

LARGE MALLETS of both the Pennsylvania Railroad and the Norfolk & Western often were seen working on the same tracks at Columbus, Ohio. Here, on March 21, 1941, is the Pennsy's No. 7332 0-8-8-0, at the left, and the N&W's No. 1455 2-6-6-2. Mallets were necessary for the long-and-heavy transfer drags that moved through town.

NORFOLK & WESTERN Mallet No. 1422 was doing switching chores at Columbus, Ohio, on November 5, 1940. The N&W's only other switch engines were their 4-8-0 types, a strange wheel arrangement. Notice the long, heavy N&W coal cars, equipped with six-wheel trucks. The N&W moved long coal drags to Eastern cities.

THE LAST NARROW-GAUGE LINE in Ohio, the Ohio River & Western, was making its final run from Bellaire to Woodsfield on May 30, 1931. Engine 9671, which was a 4-6-0, a car of gravel, 2-8-0 No. 9669, a boxcar, a mail-express car and two coaches (packed with last-trip riders) made up this train. A subsidiary of the Pennsylvania Railroad, the engines were numbered for their system. However, freight cars were lettered for the OR&W, while passenger cars and locomotives received PRR lettering!

OHIO RIVER & WESTERN RAILWAY
"CROOKEDEST RAILROAD IN THE WORLD"

IT IS TRUE that the people of the local area of this little narrow-gauge railroad called the line: "The Crookedest Railroad in the World." And when I first came across this term, I just dismissed it as a local brag. But it turned out they were not very far off, for in

LOCAL PEOPLE called the Ohio River & Western the "crookedest railroad in the world," and it
did have some claim for this appellation. Its 45
miles of track seemed to be continually curving,
featuring 64 bridges and trestles, as well as two
tunnels. The largest trestle was this 500-foot span
near Key, Ohio, nine miles and 600 feet higher

than Bellaire, on the Ohio River. The last train was
posed on the final run, May 30, 1931. Me? I rode
the train, and from the steps of the rear coach I
watched the photographer. It was a trip never to
be forgotten. The cars between the two engines,
except for the load of gravel, were "deadheads,"
to be set out at an old mine spur for scrapping.

my travels and readings of railroads all over
the world, there were few that seemed to
employ more curvature per mile than this 45-
mile line. The paved and gravel roads of today emphasize what a contorted terrain it
wound through. There were 64 trestles and
bridges, of which the most impressive was a
500-foot "S"-curved one along a hillside. The
Ohio River & Western Railway used the
routes in part of two small streams, and
when it had to cross watersheds, it employed
two tunnels to do so.

Until 1928, this narrow-gauge line had
existed in its original length, extending 67
miles beyond Woodsfield, the Monroe Coun-

ty (Ohio) county seat, and to Zanesville to
the west. This other mileage was more sedate
for most of its length, as far as sharp curves
were concerned, and the line even enjoyed
some tangent trackage. Gobbled up in the
early part of this century, when the several
large railroad companies seemingly were
contesting for ownership of the OR&W, the
Pennsylvania Railroad operated it as a separate company. Engines and coaches were lettered just like their standard-gauge counterparts: "PENNSYLVANIA," but other rolling stock was designated "OR&W."

It was the final run of this line, on May
30, 1931, that started me to take train pic-

tures, and I must add that my initial efforts were hardly good enough to spur me further. Moreover, the only good negatives were loaned to a railfan who just never would return them.

At Bellaire, Ohio, across the Ohio River from Wheeling, the OR&W shared a Pennsylvania Railroad yard, station and roundhouse. Immediately after passing through the suburb of Shadyside, the line started its twisting, constant steep-gradient route. The train required nearly four hours—if it was on time—to negotiate the run, in typical mixed-train style, daily except on Sunday. The last run was on Memorial Day, and many locals went for short rides. In fact, an extra coach had to be added from storage in the Shadyside yard. The railroad served various little post offices and rural routes, and for this purpose, the passenger train carried the "Bellaire & Woodsfield" R.P.O. in the head-end car. As the last trip included some deadhead equipment to be set out at spurs, two engines were needed, Engine 9669, a 2-8-0, and No. 9671, a 4-6-0. The PRR had set aside in its general numbering system the 9660–9670 series for narrow-gauge use, hence the ridiculously high numbers. Conversely, the coaches had the lowest numbers on the whole system: "3" and "11."

This was the last narrow-gauge line in Ohio, a state that during the 1870's and 1880's had seen numerous lines flourish and usually quickly withered or changed to standard gauge. The OR&W's ancestors had been involved in great plans, too, none of which matured (obviously). During the interurban era, it was even planned to extend the line and electrify it.

PENNSYLVANIA RAILROAD management people never liked Mallets. So, the system used them only for heavy switching at Columbus, Ohio. Heavy transfer drags, consisting of coal loads, moved through the city's rail yards, and only a Mallet or a combination of other engines could handle these trains. The Mallet was No. 7649, photographed during July of 1940.

BOTH THE PRR AND THE N&W used large Mallets as heavy-duty switch engines at Columbus, Ohio. The 10 Pennsylvania Railroad engines were built for the place and the usage; however, the Norfolk & Western engines were older types of motive power, replaced by faster articulateds on the mainlines. Both used the same tracks at Columbus. The engines were PRR No. 7332 and N&W No. 1455, which were photographed on March 12, 1941.

GAS-ELECTRIC TRAINS of the PRR met daily-except-Sunday at Akron Union Station for many years. Doodlebug No. 4656, with a postal-car trailer, was at the left, running as Train 605 for Columbus. No. 4652 was the Akron–Hudson "accommodation" train, which made several trips to connect Akron, Ohio, with the main Cleveland–Pittsburgh line. It was a car like this that was destroyed in a head-on collision at Cuyahoga Falls, with a double-headed freight train, and over 40 passengers were killed in the fire. Rapidly, the PRR changed the gasoline-electric cars to use diesel fuel. The date for this scene is May 9, 1948. The stretch of track at the right was the final section of the Erie Railroad to be double-tracked, in the 1920's.

DURING THE DEPRESSION of the 1930's, Pennsylvania Railroad engines and passenger cars might get new paint and lettering once in five years, so a freshly turned-out Mallet, like No. 7335, was rare indeed at Columbus, Ohio, in 1937.

AN IMPORTANT SUBSIDIARY of the New York Central system was the Pittsburgh & Lake Erie Railroad. The P&LE handled many passenger trains between Pittsburgh and Youngstown, Ohio, for itself and the Baltimore & Ohio. This is Train 85 as it left Warren, Ohio, in June of 1947. It was on its way to Cleveland via the Erie's trackage. The train was headed by Pacific No. 9551.

PASSENGER TRAINS of the Wheeling & Lake Erie Railroad were last equipped with new cars during the days early in the 20th century, when George Gould was coming close to establishing a coast-to-coast railway network. By 1936, the Atlantic type engine and wooden cars was a one-and-only passenger train of this old-time style for Ohio. Daily, the W&LE train made the round trip of 304 miles from Cleveland to Wheeling, West Virginia. Mogadore provided a good photo opportunities during the Depression years of the 1930's.

THE WABASH RAILROAD'S 2-8-2 No. 2428 was doing switching at Okolona, Ohio, on November 16, 1940. This was a way stop for this Toledo-to-Fort Wayne, Indiana, freight train, which used the old caboose at the left. The schedule called for five hours to cover the 93-mile route. However, with occasional stops like this, it usually took much longer to make the run.

WABASH LOCAL FREIGHT TRAINS CARRIED PASSENGERS

THE WABASH RAILROAD had an unusual arrangement for the benefit of the few passengers for out-of-the-way "flag-stop" places. Such individuals could ride in the caboose of the scheduled local freight train, but they must have purchased a ticket in advance, as the conductor was not permitted to take cash. So, on one November day in 1940, Bill Schriber and I met early in the morning—before dawn—at Toledo's Union Station and bought tickets to Fort Wayne, Indiana. First, we had to convince the night clerk that there was such a train and service, then we had to hire a taxi to take us out to the Wabash freight yard, where we had to find the correct caboose. This arrangement required that passengers had to board and depart from the train wherever it might be, and small type warned in the timetable not to expect to step off at a depot platform.

The route was flat, marked by long stretches of tangent track, not-infrequent stops to do local switching, and there was a rear-end brakeman who ate continuously throughout the trip. He even scrounged edibles from adjacent fields, which he would cook on the caboose stove. Lunch for us and the rest of the crew was at Napoleon, Ohio, although we were not quite 40 miles along the way from Toledo. Long before that, we had pulled onto a siding to await the passage of the night train from St. Louis, powered by a high-wheeled 4-4-2 Atlantic, which made fast work of the flat terrain.

Our arrival at Fort Wayne was after dark, and we got back to Ohio by boarding the Nickel Plate's double-headed eastbound train en route to Cleveland. After a few hours "layover" in Cleveland, we boarded the Baltimore & Ohio's two-car Wheeling train, which was powered by a slippery 4-4-4. This train let me off at Akron, while Bill went on to his home at Massillon, Ohio.

THE GENERIC MALLET

POPULAR with railfan photographers were the so-called "Mallet," a generic term used by railroaders and fans alike for all locomotives with two sets of drivers and four cylinders, i.e., two engines joined together to operate as one locomotive, with only one boiler (usually). While the older engines of this type were indeed "Mallets" (named for the Frenchman who invented them), with one set of cylinders much larger than the second set, which used the boiler's steam for a second time, before exhausting with the odd double-stack noise so typical of these large locomotives. The newer mallets were actually *not* "mallets," but rather were simply "articulated" engines, wherein all four cylinders used steam directly from the boiler. Most railroads used mallets for helper service, something suited to their slow speeds.

Columbus, Ohio, had an unusual terminal area. Heavy coal trains operated through the city, right past the Union Station, en route to Lake Erie points. To get these long trains through without tieing-up things, the Pennsylvania Railroad employed powerful mallets, 10 huge 0-8-8-0's. The Norfolk & Western employed their older mallets as switchers, augmenting some 4-8-0 types. Both the Norfolk & Western and the Chesapeake & Ohio brought articulated locomotives into town at the head of coal drags, which loped along from the Ohio River Valley at about a steady 30 mph. One could find a PRR 0-6-0 or a mallet switching at the freight-depot tracks, and the N&W similarly used whatever locomotive was first out. If a crosstown freight train stalled, the PRR would couple perhaps as many as three locomotives on the head end, making odd mixtures of wheel arrangements and classes.

By just roaming through a vacant field between the Union Station and the Norfolk & Western freight yard, a couple of miles to the north, there were many photographic possibilities. However, during the Great Depression years, the Pennsylvania Railroad only cleaned and repainted things about every five years. As a result, the gold-leaf lettering and numbering were grime-coated, and although the human eye could read them, the photographic film of that period rejected it, and often, negatives were not readable. Of course, an engine just out of the paint shop looked fine—except this happened so infrequently, it was unlikely one would see PRR motive power in this pristine condition.

THE VAST NEW YORK CENTRAL system operated Mallet locomotives on its eastern Ohio coal branch, from Phalanx to Dillonvale. In addition to extra freights, a daily mixed train handled a steel combine, which included a Railway Post Office compartment. NYC articulated-engine No. 1948 was making up the train at Phalanx, Ohio, on June 18, 1941.

STEEL COMPANY RAILROADS

THE STEEL COMPANIES had their captive railroads, sometimes distinguished from rather limited in-plant railroad operations. Most of these lines attracted railfans as they generally had neatly lettered locomotives and cabooses, although it has to be admitted that their freight cars were often battered, bent and sagged, and they had the general appearance of being at the end of their lives.

Cleveland had the Newburgh & South Shore Railway, The River Terminal Railway and the Cuyahoga Valley Railway. Taking photographs depended on catching their engines at some place where they could be seen and photographed from public property — like a street — even though the companies were hostile to that as well. The N&SS did get out in public a little more often than the other two lines, although the writer never spent much effort trying to snap pictures of their 0-6-0 types. The Cuyahoga Valley seemed to switch only the Otis Steel Company, and I never found it even close to a fence. So, my

sole picture was of a dirty 0-6-0 at quite a distance — broadside—taken by poking my camera through a chain-link fence.

The River Terminal line had some unusual 0-6-2 engines, which later teased fans when they were sent to the Birmingham, Alabama, steel plants. The RT switched the Republic Steel and Corrigan-McKinney Steel Company works. And no doubt there were other corporations included in the maze of steel plants. Through this wended a paved Cleveland street, so on one Saturday morning, Bruce Triplett and I parked our car, and with cameras ready, we waited until one of the rare 0-6-2 switchers crossed the street. Results were indifferent, what with other street traffic and smoke. However, out of the yard office came a steel-company security cop, with a shiny badge of the Corrigan outfit. He demanded to know what we were up to, to which we replied fully, and then, he demanded the films. To that, we dissented, pointing out that we were on public property, and there was nothing illegal in taking pictures in such a place. But he insisted that we come down to his office, and we finally

60

WHEN MY FRIEND, Bruce Triplett, and I tried to snap pictures of these unusual River Terminal Railroad engines from a nearby street, we had a steel-company cop come over demanding both cameras and film. The steel firm's switching in-house railroad was this busy line, but what particularly caught our attention were the engines with a wheel arrangement of 0-6-2. Obviously, we did not give the steel company's "hawkshaw" our film of this rare switch engine!

agreed, although we stipulated that since we would be there at his invitation. And that did not give him property rights over either the cameras or films, and I mentioned that if he tried to take any of them, he would be charged with criminal assault and various other things.

We really were not concerned, but we felt we had better find out how far such an outfit might go. We also had the policy that one could plainly explain to those few persons who were suspicious of our photography just how harmless it was. Anyway, he called someone in the steel company office, who evidently did not take it very seriously, who just told the cop to get our names, addresses and phone numbers, as well as what our occupations were. But we never spent the effort to get a better picture of an 0-6-2.

After World War II, steam locomotives were being scrapped at a great rate, and one day at Akron, one of the Pennsy's 0-8-8-0 mallets we used to see at Columbus as a favorite subject, rolled through town, en route to Cleveland—dead—heading for the scrap yard. I found out that the mallet was going to Republic Steel, so the next Saturday I drove up to their office after talking to a stamp collector who worked in the office. He had evidently paved the route well to the en-

gine builder's plates, as the only man in theoffice was obviously waiting only for noon to go home, and he obligingly called down to the River Terminal office to tell them to help me locate and obtain the builder's plates.

At the same little office where the cop had quizzed us a few years earlier lounged some shop men who escorted me into a yard that was not noticeable from the street. Here was a collection of locomotives waiting for scrapping that if in existence today would be considered the most priceless collection on Earth. Eventually, we found the PRR mallet, and after chiseling off the plates, I expressed my appreciation and gave the men a couple of dollars for their efforts. To this, their reaction was to ask if there were any other plates I would like. So, I ended up with one from a Lima AC&Y Mikado, and I could have had a whole PRR Keystone emblem from the front of a K-4 Pacific. However, the man with me that morning was bored by that time, and he wanted to go see something else. So, the Pennsy Keystone went to scrap. But that yard, with a number of parallel tracks, had a collection probably only to be seen in some similar scrap dealer's work yard. Although it was a bright, sunny day, something about all those doomed engines gave a somber feeling to the scene that I have never forgotten.

THE ALIQUIPPA & SOUTHERN was a "captive" line of the Jones & Laughlin Steel Corporation. This meant that railfans had to be somewhat sneaky to photograph their trains—so paranoid was the steel company's management people. However, when I was a child, my first steam-engine ride was in the cab of a steel-mill "dinky" (a small switcher). One of my uncles worked for the steel industry, and he offhandedly gave me a ride aboard the little engine. During later years, such an event would have had the law department of the company fainting from apoplexy. The year was 1935 when this picture was taken, and the Ohio River is in the background.

THE ALIQUIPPA & SOUTHERN

STEEL AND COAL RAILROADS were notorious for their shyness toward cameras. Perversely, they also kept their engines neatly painted and lettered, and they were very attractive to photograph. The Aliquippa & Southern Railroad was one of these company-owned lines, operating entirely within

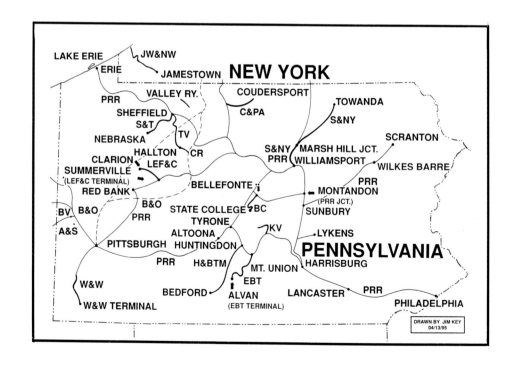

THE ALIQUIPPA & SOUTHERN was situated entirely on the grounds of the Jones & Laughlin Steel works, and photographs were strictly forbidden. To attempt to shoot pictures like this one incurred the risk of being arrested by security guards. Almost as if to tease the guards, we camera fans tried to photograph the neatly lettered and well-maintained A&S engines. In this case,

another A&S engine had derailed just out of sight, to the right. After joining the crowd at the gate, I just could not resist hurriedly snapping a picture of this nearby 0-6-0, built by Porter in 1910. The trolley wires back of No. 108 were for the company's "Woodlawn & Southern" electric traction line, which operated from the steel mill to a suburb above Aliquippa, Pennsylvania.

the confines of the Jones & Laughlin Steel Corporation's plant at Aliquippa, Pennsylvania, the company town. The enginehouse was located near the main gate, and the railroad shared space in this structure with the company-owned electric streetcar system, known as the Woodlawn & Southern, with Woodlawn being the suburban heights above Aliquippa, with a better residential area.

As luck would have it, one day during the 1930's, "yours truly" and a couple of my cousins were driving to Pittsburgh one day to see railroads, and upon seeing a crowd at the main gate, we walked over, and I took my Kodak "616" camera in my hip pocket. It seemed that one of the 0-6-0 engines had derailed right inside the gate, and a crowd of steel workers had gathered around, and the guard at the gate was diverted with all the commotion going on, so we joined the

crowd. From our vantage point I was able to shoot a picture of the carbarn, yard trackage and one of the 0-6-0's, resplendent in fresh paint... before the guard noticed us and hustled us out.

This was not my first visit to this steel plant, however. At the age of 8 or 10, I was taken by one of my uncles, a foreman at the plant, for a ride in the cab of one of the narrow-gauge engines the company used then. I cannot say that I recall any particular details; however, the Eastern steel plants usually started out small, and they had narrow-gauge tracks where mule- or horse-drawn cars were used. As the plants grew, they eventually obtained steam locomotives for them. These little narrow-gauge switchers were certainly among the most elusive engines insofar as railfan photographers were concerned.

THE BEAVER VALLEY RAILROAD was a three-mile switching road, chiefly in Beaver, Pennsylvania. It connected with the Pennsy at one end of the line, and at the other end, it connected with the Pittsburgh & Lake Erie. The Beaver Valley's No. 2 was side-tank 0-4-0T, rather derelict by 1932, and their No. 3 was a saddle-tank 0-4-0T. About half a mile of track was in the center of a street in Beaver, on a grade. There were a few small industries around Beaver, providing a livelihood for nearly daily service on the railroad. Not only did the small four-wheel engines have a tough time

working up the grade with a consist of loaded boxcars, but when going in the opposite direction, the loads pushed against the engine. So, one day, when a careless driver of a power-company truck was hauling some long poles on a dolly, tried to beat the train across a street crossing (forgetting about his extra-long load), No. 3 just could not stop quickly enough. Several freight cars pushed the engine into the poles, scattering them in all directions. When No. 3 required overhauling in the late 1930's, the company management bought a small diesel-electric switcher.

THE BEAVER VALLEY RAILROAD

AN ODD THREE-MILE LINE in Beaver County, Pennsylvania, had part of its trackage in a residential street of the little town of Beaver. There was also a two-stall enginehouse at the end of town, and several small industries were served by this little short line. The Beaver Valley Railroad connected with the Pennsylvania Railroad at Vanport and with the Pittsburgh & Lake Erie at the other end of the line. Two secondhand 0-4-0T tank engines provided the motive power, and they had some difficulty controlling

trains of several cars on the street portion, as the loaded cars would push the engine on the downgrade. Eventually, the management purchased a small diesel engine during the 1940's.

WHEN I RODE the Bellefonte Central Railroad on September 16, 1939, they had so much switching at the lime plants a mile or more from Bellefonte, Pennsylvania, that I walked back the last mile into town. I had skipped lunch at State College earlier in the day so I could photograph the BC train. Lime products are still big business in Centre County, and this industry provides considerable traffic for the Nittany & Bald Eagle, the successor to what was a Pennsylvania Railroad line through Bellefonte.

WHILE RETURNING from the New York World's Fair in September of 1939, I took a few days to search for and go for rides on some shortlines. At Bellefonte, Pennsylvania, I found this 2-8-0 switching, and upon asking the conductor what the train's destination was, he replied, "The college." So, I paid my fare and rode on the mixed train the 18 miles to the town of State College. At that time, this rural Pennsylvania community was just another small town, with a small college. The Bellefonte Central train had a couple of cars of coal for the school's boiler room. On the return trip we halted a mile from Bellefonte's station, and when I learned that they might be switching cars for an hour or two, I hungrily walked back to Bellefonte. When I visited Bellefonte, I certainly never expected to become a resident of the area some 50 years later. All that remains of the BC line is a turntable outside Bellefonte, and the "little" State College has grown so much that what was a right-of-way through the rural countryside is now hidden by business buildings and houses.

OUR AKRON RAILROAD CLUB decided to go for a trip on the Bessemer & Lake Erie Railroad during 1947. So, we wrote their office in Pittsburgh to see if we might visit their Greenville shops and roundhouse. They were agreeable to that, and they gave us a fine tour of about the neatest of such facilities I have ever seen. However, no cameras were allowed (after all, the B&LE road was owned by steel companies). When we also went for a trip to Erie, Pennsylvania, the northern terminus of their daily passenger train, the conductor suggested a solution for us upon hearing that management had banned picture-taking. He simply stopped the train next to a large open field and held it there while we used up our film. The B&LE had distinctive Pacific engines, and the passenger equipment seemed to be New York Central rolling stock. Many years later a book

on the Bessemer line was published, and the railroad's master mechanic mentioned how few pictures of the steam era he had located—as if he did not know why!

THE LOGGING RAILROADS in western Pennsylvania are all gone now. However, in 1947 the paper mill at Johnsonburg used this leftover Shay to switch incoming pulpwood in its yard. A small mountain of this pulpwood is visible at the left. The dual gauge track was for use of the mill's three-foot gauge trio of saddletank 0-4-0T engines, which hauled small cars of pulpwood into the mill. These little switchers really hustled along, with the result that the track was scattered with pulpwood, and one did not want to stand close when such a train was coming near, for fear of being hit by a piece of wood.

JOHNSONBURG PAPER COMPANY

THE PAPER MILL at Johnsonburg, Pennsylvania, employed a slightly different method of feeding the processing mill with pulpwood. With the local forests cut-over, the mill was getting its pulpwood from as far away as Canada during the late 1940's. The Johnsonburg Paper Company's three-truck Shay, No. 12, worked only the Johnsonburg yard. The track, however, was dual gauge for the use of the three-foot-gauge fleet of 0-4-0T engines and four-wheel cars used to feed the mill from the huge yard of pulpwood. The enginehouse was off limits, but the trains could be seen bouncing along at a good rate of speed, with pulpwood occasionally sliding off the little cars.

THE CLARION RIVER RAILWAY

A SAD SIGHT in November of 1945 was the gracefully designed Baldwin Ten-wheeler, sitting in a light snow at Hallton, Pennsylvania. This engine needed some firebox work, and a welder inexperienced in locomotive work had attempted the repairs, resulting in—as has happened elsewhere—the engine needing a new firebox and being inoperable. And, of course, under the circumstances of the little 11-mile Clarion River Railway, this was an impossible matter.

The No. 119 had been idle at Williamsport, Pennsylvania, after the Susquehanna & New York Railroad was abandoned. Williamsport was the headquarters of the Susquehanna Chemical Corporation, which owned the

IN PENNSYLVANIA during 1947, some children went to school by train. Here, on October 27, the Clarion River Railway had stopped its train at the ghost-mill site of Portland Mills, so children from isolated Hallton could continue their trip to Ridgway High School a few miles away. Three times a week, the Heisler geared engine, No. 17, handled the train, with the home-made combination car on the rear. The other two days a week, a gasoline-powered locomotive handled the car. The road between Hallton and Portland Mills was so poor—especially during the winter months—that school buses ventured no closer than the site of this ghost town.

BEING READIED in October of 1947, this ill-fated locomotive would soon be scrapped. No. 119 had started out as a new passenger engine in 1921, for the Huntingdon & Broad Top Mountain Railroad. Then, when a gas-electric "doodle-bug" took over the duties of this 4-6-0, the engine went to another shortline in Pennsylvania, the Susquehanna & New York Railroad. By the end of World War II, No. 119 was again idle, and without checking things very well, she was purchased by the 11-mile Clarion River Railway to replace their worn Heisler geared engine. Four days after this picture was taken, No. 119 made her first trip on the Clarion River Railway—very carefully—as the trim Ten-wheeler was somewhat heavy for the CR track. Then, when the firebox needed repairs, some faulty welding ruined the 4-6-0. The third rail in the track at Hallton was for the use of the former Tionesta Valley Railway, used by its train to bring in loads of chemical wood from a loading point, several miles to the north. The mill is out of sight, behind Engine 119.

Clarion River Railway, as well as the chemical wood plant at Hallton. No. 17, the CR's Heisler, was about worn out. As a result, the executive of the SC Company—without checking too much—bought No. 119, not realizing she was much too heavy for the CR's rails. Moreover, there was neither a turntable nor a wye on the line, so the engine would have to back in one direction on the railroad. These problems were ended with the firebox disaster. Engineer Bert Lyle and Fireman Jack Rimer had nursed No. 17 to the limit of their abilities, but the Hallton enginehouse lacked much in the way of major repair facilities. Its

two tracks provided out-of-the-weather space for one narrow-gauge Tionesta Valley Railway engine and one standard-gauge Clarion River engine. No. 119 just sat out in the open air.

The chemical plant was also in its final years of operation. Producing charcoal and acetic acid by "cooking" what looked like pulpwood, its aging machinery was obsolescent, as was happening with the other remaining plants in that part of Pennsylvania. As was true for everything else connected with the dwindling forest industries, its remaining time was short. As late as 1941,

AT CARMAN, PENNSYLVANIA, the Clarion River Railway train met the Baltimore & Ohio's passenger trains five times a week. The southbound B&O train sometimes did not even stop. It just threw off a mail sack; however, on some days it unloaded a supply of bread for Hallton's company store. No. 17, a 50-ton Heisler, had been built in 1919 for the Tionesta Valley Railway. Much later, the engine was sold to the CR and was changed to standard gauge. If major repairs were needed, it would be sent to the TV's Sheffield shop by simply putting it on narrow-gauge trucks. Three times a week, the Heisler made the 11-mile trip to this junction as late as 1948.

Tionesta Valley Railway trains had operated five or six times a week. It moved consists of a dozen or so loads of wood to Sheffield Junction, leaving the cars there in exchange for empties brought up from the Hallton mill by the crew working out of Hallton. However, the Tionesta Valley died during World War II. For several years, wood was trucked to a spot alongside Highway 66, where it was loaded onto cars for the mill. There was no suitable year-around road into Hallton for trucks; in fact, even other vehicles had a difficult time getting in and out, as we railfans found when the road was muddy.

The Clarion River ran trains five times a week, and it had a contract to haul the high-school students between Hallton and Portland Mills, where the schoolbus met the train. This arrangement was made with the railroad because the schoolbus could not negotiate what passed for a "road" between those points for a large part of the year. Three days a week the Heisler engine made the round trip, meeting the Baltimore & Ohio at Carman, exchanging mail and L-C-L shipments with the southbound passenger train there. The other days, the Brookville gas locomotive would operate the train to the junction. And this meant that some days, either engine would be switching cars at the mill, which had dual-gauge trackage.

One time, while watching the crew switching near the enginehouse, I was suddenly alarmed to realize that a string of pulpwood rack cars was starting to move. Hastily dropping my camera, I rushed around picking up anything I could find in the form of chunks of wood. And I firmly laid several pieces on the rail, trying to get a wheel to "bite" into it and thus stop the cars. However, it took about three chocks before the cars stopped. If the cars had run away, they would have dropped down to the low bridge over the creek and raced up into the mill yard. The railroad crew saw what happened, but said little. However, at a later date, they gave me the builder's plate off No. 17, presumably because of that episode.

Operations were unusual in that the Clarion River line brought in cars of wood from the Baltimore & Ohio and shipped out company products in that direction. The

THE STEAM-ENGINE CREW of the Clarion River Railway operated the narrow-gauge train to the wood-loading site several miles to the north of Hallton, Pennsylvania, two days each week. On these two days a week, a two-man crew handled the contract calling for the railroad to transport the school children, using this small four-wheel Brookville-built gasoline-powered engine and the road's homemade combination car. It was during the spring of 1941 when this picture was taken, and the site of the view was yet another one of the ghost towns during this lumbering era.

chemical company also owned some 17 miles of the former Tionesta Valley Railway's line, reaching from Hallton northward toward Sheffield Junction. At Hallton, there was a mixture of dual-gauge trackage. The nondescript U.S. Post Office at Hallton served as the railroad depot as well. One crew operated both narrow- and standard-gauge trains.

The Brookville-built gas locomotive had a small annex on the rear of the enginehouse. In the nearby weeds sat a motorcar that looked somewhat like a schoolbus, which had been used before the Brookville engine was obtained. The Brookville unit could handle one or two freight cars if it was necessary to do so.

On the alternate days—usually on Tuesday, Thursday or Saturday—the steam crew would take the narrow-gauge engine and caboose and a string of empty wood flatcars up to the loading spot at Highway 66, just a couple of miles short of Sheffield Junction. Until the Tionesta Valley Railway was abandoned in 1942, this line had gone as far as the

junction, as most of the wood came from Sheffield loadings. On the return run to Hallton, the train would have perhaps a dozen or more loads of wood. At this time, the only "roads" into the Hallton area were dirt, or mere dirt trails, both impassable during wet weather. An attempt was made to drive on one of them after a rainstorm one day, and this found us sliding around and hitting bottom, unable to find a place to attempt to turn around safely. One of the so-called "roads" we used to follow the train has been abandoned during more recent years, deemed simply as not needed.

During the summer of 1948, the crew was busy tearing up the narrow-gauge trackage, and not long afterward, the Clarion River line also was scrapped.

THE EAST BROAD TOP RAILROAD

ON ONE JULY FOURTH WEEKEND, Bruce Triplett and I decided to look up the narrow-gauge East Broad Top Railroad in south-cen-

AFTER BEING FREE of the U.S. Army for the first time in three years—on a 30-day furlough—August 1, 1945, was a day to do something different. So, what better way was there to enjoy the U.S.A. again than to take a side trip on my way home on the narrow-gauge East Broad Top Railroad? This was the Mount Union station, and there was a large amount of mail and express from the Pennsy. Out in the yard, a number of empty coal cars were waiting to be coupled into the train. The 9:15 a.m. departure time would put me at the end of the EBT—or nearly so—at noon. And I would have time to find some nourishment at the Robertsdale store before the return trip began. The crew expressed surprise at a G.I. riding with them, but the men were obviously pleased that I thought of their little line as a goal en route to my home. The lush scenery of Broad Top Mountain seemed like a jungle after 2½ years in the barren desert and dusty Empire of Iran.

tral Pennsylvania. His father wanted to visit a friend in Bedford, not far southwest of the EBT, and this provided an excuse for the trip. What with one delay or another, we did not get an early start on Monday morning. However, the distance was not great—maybe 30 miles—over winding roads that seemed to go every direction except where we were headed.

The East Broad Top timetable in the *Official Guide* showed that the train departed from the south end of the line just after noon on holidays. We arrived at "Alvan" to see only an empty track, a good hour after the scheduled departure time. Despairing of catching up with the train along unknown roads in that area, we drove a couple of miles along the track to Robertsdale. There, we went in the local store for a soft drink.

Standing there, taking our time, we suddenly were startled to hear a locomotive bell —and nearby, too! In a chorus, we asked the storekeeper what that was, and his calm reply was, "The train." And so it was, but it was not steam-powered, as we had hoped for, but it was the Gas-Electric "M-1," built by the EBT. It was then that we learned to examine a timetable beyond the initial point, for it showed the train ran south to the end-of-track at Alvan, then immediately backed to the wye at Robertsdale, to layover for nearly an hour and a half before heading north. The EBT was a line where one could miss the train by an hour at the end of the line, and then have ample time to catch it only two miles away.

Not knowing what reception to expect, we climbed aboard and paid our cash fares to Mt. Union, 33 miles away. After all, the EBT was a coal-company railroad, and we had learned that "coal-and-iron police" were to be taken seriously, as those companies were as paranoid as the Russians when it came to picture-taking. The East Broad Top

turned out to be the pleasant exception. The crew seemed delighted to have a couple of real fare-paying passengers, and the car was obligingly stopped for us at the tunnels for photographs. And the crew let us ride up in the noisy engine room if we wished.

At the Orbisonia shop yard, we picked up a flatcar for Mt. Union, apparently the only thing moved on the holiday, besides the doodlebug. On the return there, the crew put the car away and walked home. We could not resist peering in the windows of the locked-up shop and roundhouse. And we were walking away when a man in a business suit came our way from the depot. Immediately, we thought, "Oh, oh! Here's

trouble!" Another surprise... The gentleman asked how we liked the trip, then, after looking at his watch, he mentioned that he had some time before dinner and, "Would you like to see the shop and roundhouse?"

So... we saw that fantastic machine shop, with all the belts and various projects underway. In the roundhouse sat half a dozen handsome narrow-gauge Mikados, and there was even a saddle-tanker in one corner! And under canvas was the historic private car, the "Orbisonia." After the tour was over, our guide gave us his card, and only then, did we learn that he was the vice-president and general manager of the road, a Mr. C. O. Jones. Incidentally, Bruce had spied a marker

THE TAIL OF THE WYE at Robertsdale, Pennsylvania, was where the East Broad Top's daily train laid-over for an hour before heading back north with whatever coal cars were ready. On our first holiday visit to the EBT in 1935, we knew the northbound train left the southern end of the line at Woodvale at about noon. After arriving there about an hour late, we thought we had hopelessly missed the train. Not very happy about the situation, we drove for about a mile, until we found the Robertsdale store. While glumly eating Hershey candy bars, we were startled to hear an engine bell, and we discovered that the train was sitting on the wye! If we had studied the timetable, we would have seen that after leaving Woodvale, the train (on time at noon), did not leave Robertsdale—two miles to the north—for another hour! In this view, Engine 17 and one of the old wooden combines, No. 15, were photographed on August 1, 1945.

WHILE I WAS ON A FURLOUGH during 1945, I stopped at Mount Union, Pennsylvania, to take a side trip on the narrow-gauge East Broad Top Railroad. Taking one last picture of No. 18, a 2-8-2, and No. 15, a combination coach, I headed for the nearby Pennsy to catch a train for Akron, Ohio. This Mikado and combine still survive, as scrapping was held off after abandonment of the EBT. During recent years, the EBT has operated tourist trips on a few miles of the line, and prospects look bright for 1995. I rode this combine again in 1994, during trips of the road's "Fall Festival," with four of the engines steamed up for a good display of narrow-gauge motive power.

ON LABOR DAY, 1947, the narrow-gauge East Broad Top's little gas-electric car, the M-1, was substituting for the daily steam-powered train. Tomorrow's mixed train sits at the right, ready to leave with a combine at the rear. The train will head out about 8:00 a.m. Although the wooden coaches were old, they were equipped with roller-bearing trucks!

lamp on the scrap pile, and he asked if he might have it—and it was his!

The two of us, together or separately, visited the line on other occasions. And during one visit, the shop was working "full blast," belts "flip-flip-flapping" busily, as the shop-men were overhauling one of the two standard-gauge switchers. The engine sat on special narrow-gauge trucks, having been moved from Mt. Union in that manner. The regular trains were all mixed or freights, featuring the road's steel hopper cars, trailed by a combination baggage-coach. We never got up early enough to ride or see the 5:30 a.m. "Miners' Train" from Orbisonia, which carried several ancient, but roller-bearing equipped coaches for miners en route to work at the south end of the line.

Upon learning that a special train, consisting of an engine and three coaches, might be chartered for only $65.00 for an eight-hour day, our Akron Railroad Club chartered a Sunday outing on two occasions during the

1940's. Learning that we could add more coaches at $10.00 each, we splurged and had four-car trains! With "photo run-bys" at bridges and tunnels, a great time was had by all, including the crews!

THE AKRON (OHIO) RAILROAD CLUB chartered this special train on the narrow-gauge East Broad Top Railroad, after we learned about the line's very low rates for excursions. This special, consisting of Engine 15, a sleek 2-8-2, and four passenger cars, was operated on July 4, 1948. Our enjoyable excursion trip featured numerous photo stops and photo run-bys. Years later, operations were suspended on the EBT because the coal business was not very profitable. However, during very recent years, the owners of the line—not wanting to scrap it—have operated tourist trains on several miles of track, from Orbisonia, Pennsylvania. As these lines are being set in type, it appears that the EBT will operate again in 1995. A dedicated group of railfans, under the name of the "Friends of the East Broad Top," has worked hard to publicize the line and get tickets sold.

Unfortunately, the coal business fell on hard times, and despite a seemingly endless supply of good Broad Top Mountain coal in reserve, the road closed down in the 1950's, and it was sold to a scrap dealer. However, Mr. Kovalchik held off and eventually, his son began running weekend tourist trains on five miles of the line. The balance of the track was in the status of "service suspended." These tourist runs have continued through 1994, but what will become of the little road beyond then is not known. One can only hope that this narrow-gauge line is saved.

Four of the locomotives put on a great "Fall Spectacular" on October 8 and 9, 1994, running a variety of passenger, freight and mixed consists. Even the "M-1" doodlebug made trips over the line. The unusual shop, with its belt-powered machinery, however, has been silent for many years, but it has been kept intact just as when the men left work one day years ago.

ON MY WAY HOME on furlough, after 2½ years in Iran, I photographed the Huntingdon & Broad Top Mountain's 4-4-0 while I was between trains at Huntingdon, Pennsylvania. The H&BTM train was departing for Bedford with its daily train when I snapped this view. Old No. 30 had been stored in the roundhouse until called back to duty after the road's gas-electric car was severely damaged in a train wreck.

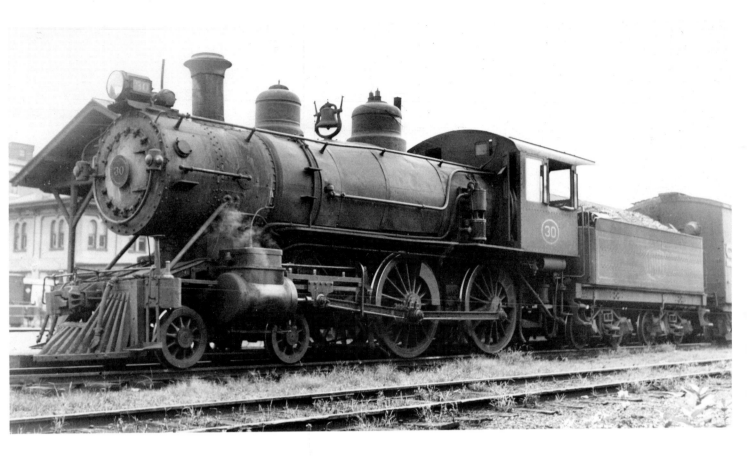

DURING THE LATE 1930's, the Huntingdon & Broad Top Mountain Railroad brought this engine out of storage after a head-on collision wrecked its gas-electric passenger car. This old 4-4-0 that hauled the H&BTM's daily train formerly was a Pennsylvania Railroad engine, partially obvious by the tell-tail cap stack. Originally, No. 30 was operated with a big "standard" steel-box headlight of the PRR, presenting to passengers from the big road a sort of "spooky" reminder of an earlier era. No. 30 was at the station in Huntingdon, Pennsylvania, during 1938.

AFTER THEIR 4-4-0 passenger engine was worn out, the Huntingdon & Broad Top Mountain Railroad used one of their low-drivered 2-8-0's—in this case, No. 37. For a coach, the road rebuilt a gas-electric car wrecked in a collision during the 1930's. Fifty-foot milk cars, such as the Supplee Milk reefer in this view, often were hauled by the line—as this of November 7, 1947, portrays. After the road was abandoned, Dr. Stanley Groman of Sand Point, New York, bought this locomotive and some cars. And the 2-8-0 was operated under steam part of the way to his new "Rail City."

THE DAILY PASSENGER TRAIN of the Huntingdon & Broad Top Mountain is shown here as it was arriving at Huntingdon, Pennsylvania, in November of 1947. Actually, the bridge across the Juniata River was Pennsy trackage, and it still stands as part of a spur of the Conrail system.

THE SHOP AREA and yard of the Jamestown, Westfield & Northwestern Railway, at Jamestown, New York, was a crowded place. At the right are the two electric-traction locomotives that handled a daily train of interchange freight cars. Interurban cars, Nos. 301 and 303, are at the left. On August 23, 1945, the electric line was fairly busy hauling passengers to points along Chautauqua Lake, which the interurban line followed for many miles. In this service, the traction road frequently used its last observation car, No. 312—especially during the summer tourist season.

JAMESTOWN, WESTFIELD & NORTHWESTERN RAILWAY

EVER HEAR of the "Yewish Northwestern," which ran out of "Yamestown," New York? The Salzberg family purchased various small railroads during the 1940's, as part of their scrap-dealer business, and then proceeded to operate them, at least for a few years. One of these was the last interurban line in New York state, the Jamestown, Westfield & Northwestern Railroad, which operated a scenic route along the eastern shore of Chautauqua Lake, and went over the hump to drop down to Westfield, on the shore of Lake

THE LAST OBSERVATION CAR of the electric Jamestown, Westfield & Northwestern, No. 312, was wyeing at Jamestown, New York, on July 20, 1947. The car had just made a trip from Westfield, New York, much of it along the shore of Chautauqua Lake. The 32-mile line had a short life remaining for it, as a scrap firm had bought it, and it would soon be dieselized. There was a good market for all that copper wire in the overhead! The JW&NW was a very popular line with the fans, as it was one of the last interurban railroads in the East.

IT WAS MARCH 4, 1947, and it will soon be time for the 10:00 a.m. run of the Jamestown, Westfield & Northwestern's big red interurban car, which will depart from Westfield, New York, for Jamestown. Unfortunately, time had run out for the electric line, and soon, passenger service would be discontinued, and the line would be converted to diesel-electric freight service (briefly, as it turned out). A New York Central train was roaring past the station in the background.

Erie. This 32-mile route had enjoyed a large passenger business during the summers, and the line also provided a year-around connection with the New York Central at Westfield. A considerable amount of carload freight was handled by steeple-cab freight motors. However, the automobile and changing trends had taken away most of the passenger business.

IT WAS MARCH of 1947, and I was en route home from Boston, Massachusetts, intending to take the JW&NW interurban to Jamestown. At that point, I was going to catch the Erie's "Pacific Express" and be home by late afternoon. However, the trolley line was snowed-in along miles of its winding line over the ridge from Lake Erie. Fortunately, an electric locomotive was plowing trackage north, and soon had the line open. And I made my connection at Jamestown in time. It seemed as though a New York Central train went roaring through Westfield every few minutes.

To the very end—in 1947—the bright red Jewett-built electric cars plied the route, and the pride of the fleet was No. 312, a big observation car. The railroad's Jamestown terminal was jammed into a small space that was also used by the Erie Railroad. Many of the residents of Jamestown were of Scandinavian descent, and the pronunciation of "J" came out as "Y," and the traffic manager, Mr. Pickard, used to smilingly acknowledge he was a man on the "Yewish Northwestern." His Jewish sense of humor enjoyed the road's final nickname.

Coming back to Akron from Boston during March of 1947, I took a train for Buffalo, New York, buying space in a Pullman berth, intending to get the morning local from there to Westfield. Thence, I would go by JW&NW to Jamestown and catch the Erie's *Pacific Express*, and be home in Akron, Ohio, by late afternoon. Waking up the next morning, I raised the window shade to be surprised to see a light doubleheader pass, plowing snow as a blizzard raged. Very late in the morning I disembarked in a snowbound Buffalo, with

nothing moving on the city streets, including trolley cars abandoned in drifts, so I trudged several blocks along a narrow path to a hotel. On the following morning, I arrived at Westfield, where the agent informed me that a plow had left Jamestown early that morning to try to open the line.

I spent some time watching the parade of snow-plastered NYC trains, then walked down to the interurban wye. Around the curve came an electric steeple-cab locomotive, its plow pilot throwing snow off the track. Within a few minutes, the crew had the interurban's trolley pole up, and as the heaters warmed the car, we took off. At places, the snowdrifts were so high, as we climbed the winding grade out of Westfield, that one could not see out the window. But the big steel car was geared for the climb, and once over the ridge, the snow gradually diminished until long before reaching Jamestown, it was only a few inches deep. Chautauqua Lake was a wintry scene, quite unlike summer recollections. And so the proud *Pacific Express*—on time—deposited me in Akron 24 hours after I had planned.

ELECTRIC LOCOMOTIVE No. 301, equipped with a pilot plow, had plowed-out the winding line above Westfield, New York, and had cleared the wye at Westfield. Soon, the snow-plastered red interurban car will be off for Jamestown, New York. I was en route from Boston to Akron, Ohio, during March of 1947, having chosen this means of getting to Jamestown to catch the Erie's "Pacific Express" at that point to travel to Akron. The New York Central's four-track mainline at the left was very busy, moving traffic delayed by the blizzard that hit hard across New York state.

THE KISHACOQUILLAS VALLEY RAILROAD

ON THE WAY BACK from the 1939 World's Fair in New York, I routed myself to see the railroad with the above mouth-filling name. The schedule in the Official Guide showed the Kishacoquillas Valley Railroad operated passenger service over 16 miles, from Lewistown, Pennsylvania, to Belleville. My arrival was timed just right, for down the center of a street came a Ten-wheeler, with two vestibuled wooden coaches trailing behind. It seemed to be making stops, streetcar style, at every block. As the train tied-up, the crew headed for their favorite eating place, and I followed. It was a little cafe, located behind the street in a basement, and the menu was a sheet of paper on which the day's specialties were written in pencil—in Pennsylvania Dutch!

Unable to translate the listings, I selected my choice by pointing to what someone at a nearby table was having. It turned out that the train on Saturdays more or less imitated a streetcar line, or an interurban. After leaving the Lewistown terminal, the train stopped at three street intersections, then eased through a couple of small suburbs to arrive at Reedsville, at a gap in the low mountain range. At this location, the train

AT THIS WYE just outside Lewistown, Pennsylvania, the Kishacoquillas Valley Railroad's steam-powered train exchanged passengers with this "train" going over into the valley of its name. President J. P. Getter supplied his Packard automobile, and passengers rode in it, while mail and packages were hauled on the push-car trailer to Belleville. The Amish kids happily hopped on the trailer, as they and their parents ducked out of sight from the camera. This scene of September, 1939, was not to last long. On my next visit, in 1945, I found that the little KV line was gone.

ON MY WAY BACK from the New York World's Fair during September of 1939, I looked up the intriguingly named Kishacoquillas Valley Railroad. I found a two-car train coming down Main Street in Lewistown, Pennsylvania. However, this line was actually on a spur of the Pennsylvania Railroad, and the track is occasionally used yet today (in 1995). As of this date of this Saturday, the KV line was running frequent trains from the valley of its name into Lewistown, a sort of weekend market-day service.

left the Pennsylvania Railroad branch we had been riding on for six and one-half miles, and we terminated the run at a wye in a grove of trees.

Although there was not any indication in the timetable, at this point, passengers and the mail found waiting for their conveyance an unusual vehicle for the rest of the trip to Belleville, not quite another 10 miles. Here was the railroad president's Packard automobile, sitting on the rails, equipped with flanged wheels and trailed by a push car, fitted with sideboards to handle the mail sacks. The only other passengers consisted of a family of Amish people, the elders seating themselves in the Packard, while their kids happily climbed onto the mail sacks. And away the Packard rolled!

Later, I learned that this little railroad was another one of those local promotions, on the basis of high hopes instead of practicalities, and of course, it had proved to be a red-ink affair from the beginning. Dr. Getter, the railroad's president, underwrote the road's losses, and with his passing, the little line was finally abandoned in the 1950's.

THE RED BANK & DRIFTWOOD Branch of
the Pennsylvania Railroad had several trains a
day from Pittsburgh that stopped at the old board-
and-batten depot at Summerville, Pennsylvania.
At the same time, twice a day, the 15-mile Lake
Erie, Franklin & Clarion Railroad's gasoline-powered railbus also came into Summerville, as
shown in this scene photographed on August 12,
1941. This depot scene was typical of so many
railroad views of this type one could see all over
the U.S. before and during World War II. The
LEF&C was a coal-hauling road; however, the coal
business fell on hard times, and a few years ago,
operations were abandoned. And the track was
torn up in 1994.

LEHIGH VALLEY RAILROAD'S No. 2101, a
rebuilt 4-6-2 Pacific in streamlined garb, was hustling northbound express milk reefers past the
depot at Towanda, Pennsylvania. It was September in 1939, and the word was given to me that
this newly streamlined engine was being run to
the backshop at Sayre, Pennsylvania, for a minor
overhaul. The new passenger train No. 2101
hauled began operating during June of 1939.

LAKE ERIE, FRANKLIN & CLARION RAILROAD

BY THE 1930's, the Lake Erie, Franklin &
Clarion Railroad was a 15-mile remnant of
much larger mileage which started during
the lumbering era in that part of Pennsylvania. However, unlike most of the other roads
that started with a livelihood dependent on
forest products, the LEF&C developed coal
traffic, which it fed into the Pennsylvania
Railroad at Summerville.

For passenger service and closed pouch
mail, etc., this little railroad used a gasoline-
powered motor car, a Brill railbus that cost
$17,500 new during the mid-1920's.

85

ON THE READING, No. 1560, a 2-8-0 Camel-back, was switching cars at Williamstown, Pennsylvania, a small town in the northeastern part of the state. This was in the anthracite-coal regions, and this view was shot on November 1, 1947.

THE READING LINE dominated in the anthracite coal fields of Pennsylvania, but as that mining declined, so did the railroad. This is the Pottstown–Lykens mixed train, shot northeast of Harrisburg, with a typical Camelback locomotive, which was equipped to burn anthracite (hard) coal. At Lykens, the terminal was reached by a switchback, while at places, the line went through large hills of waste dumps. Train 393 had Engine 1560 on the point, photographed near Bunker Hill on November 1, 1947. Notice the whistle board, to the right of the mainline.

SUSQUEHANNA & NEW YORK

A PLEASANT DAY during September of 1939 was spent in a round trip on the mixed train of the Susquehanna & New York Railroad, whose Williamsport, Pennsylvania, terminal was a museum of ancient equipment. For the first 20 miles, the tracks of the Pennsy's Elmira line were used. Then, the S&NY line started at Marsh Hill Junction, a twisting, climbing route to Towanda, Pennsylvania, on the Lehigh Valley rail line. The S&NY was a relic of logging times, and for many years, it had been a busy railroad. No. 119, the husky Ten-wheeler acquired from the Huntingdon & Broad Top Mountain during the late 1920's, handled a train that at times had 11 cars, tailed by a typical wooden combine.

At Towanda, many local folk gathered at the depot to see the new Lehigh Valley streamliner come through town, the *Asa Packer*. On the return trip, the engineer invited me up for a ride in the cab. He was just explaining how he would rather have a few freight cars for braking, when rounding a curve at a flag stop, there was a passenger! Despite his best efforts, the combine did not get stopped until it was several hundred feet beyond the passenger, but we backed up. Upon rolling onto the PRR line, with its heavy rails and high-speed conditions, he opened up Engine 119 and gave me a 50 mph trip toward Williamsport, showing how smoothly the 119 operated at speed. Whether or not the combine back at the rear rode as well, no one said.

After the S&NY was abandoned in 1945, No. 119 was sold to the Clarion River Railway, far too large an engine for that road. Following a faulty welding job, which ruined the locomotive's firebox, No. 119 went to scrap, after having made but one or two trips on the CR... *with great care.*

CIVILIAN CONSERVATION CORPS (CCC) boys working in the north-central hills of Pennsylvania received their supplies in 1939 from this train on the Susquehanna & New York Railroad. This scene was at the little place called Cabin Run. This was a cut-over logging area, and the S&NY and its connections were very busy lines for many years. Notice the truck with the "covered-wagon" back of the cab.

HEADED BY 4-6-0 No. 119, this Susquehanna & New York train was at Towanda, Pennsylvania. I enjoyed a ride in the cab of this Ten-wheeler, and the line used the Pennsy track for the last miles into Williamsport—its terminal. On this stretch of track, the engineer showed me what the engine would do, a good 50 mph. No. 119 originally had been a passenger engine on the Huntingdon & Broad Top Mountain Railroad.

ALL OF US HAVE our favorite photographs, although our judgment is prejudiced by factors others probably would not appreciate. On this foggy morning in August, 1941, the train coming through the site of Newtown Mills, in the Tionesta Creek Valley, seemed to be on a stage. And the fog provided the curtains and drapes. Engineer Bob Smith of the Sheffield & Tionesta would blow a long station blast for each of the long-vanished places, using practiced skill on the engine's melodious chime whistle.

SHEFFIELD & TIONESTA RAILWAY

LUMBERING was the reason for most of the small railroads that had been built in northwestern Pennsylvania. Then, as this source of traffic declined, the shortlines mirrored the conditions by gradually reducing their operations, living off smaller amounts of traffic from other sources. Sometimes, they staved off abandonment for many years. The Sheffield & Tionesta Railway was one of these roads. Like so many other shortlines, it had a brief listing in the *Official Guide*, claiming a daily-except-Sunday round trip into the Great Depression years. This run operated over its 35-mile route from Nebraska, Pennsylvania, to connections at Sheffield with both the Pennsy and the narrow-gauge

Tionesta Valley Railway. By the end of the 1930's, the S&T was down to tri-weekly runs. Although in fact, the train might run only once a week, whenever there was revenue to move.

Most shortlines that survived into the Great Depression years featured discarded rolling stock, in various stages of rust and decay. Old wooden passenger cars had been set aside when there were no longer any passengers to ride them. Home-road (on-line) freight cars in similar fashion sat sagging, paint peeling, waiting for loads that never came. Surplus locomotives, or ones in need of repairs the railroad simply could not afford, were rusting away, being stripped gradually of parts for engines still operating. The S&T outdid any other shortline I ever looked over. It looked as though nothing had

DURING SEPTEMBER of 1939, the planing mill at Nebraska, Pennsylvania, was this declining lumbering point's last industry—soon to close. And a few years later, a dam on Tionesta Creek would put this area under 40 feet of water. Engine 11, the S&T's 4-4-0, had just spotted a couple of empty freight cars at the mill.

been scrapped since before World War I. It was all there, deep in brush and weeds. Once, we counted over 20 locomotives in three gauges. The total number of cars was not known, as some were completely hidden, sitting on tracks also hidden from view.

The terminal at Nebraska had a wye, a leaky water tank; and sitting on the tail of the wye was a large collapsed wooden mill building and shop, out of which protruded a faded PRR open-platform combine and a small Porter Mogul. The present "shop" was a ramshackle shed, in which were kept a mass of tools, parts of all kinds—and sitting up on a shelf in the rafters, peering through the gloom, was a fascinating collection of headlights of various types and sizes. It seemed as though when an engine was set aside, or an oil light was replaced with an electric one, the old headlight joined the collection in the rafters.

Outside—in all directions—was an accumulation of parts of all kinds, most of it hardly visible in the weeds and brush. Behind the ruins of the mill, track continued up the valley, and there sat two homemade passenger cars, a combine and a coach, weathered to bare gray wood. To keep them company was an early Climax geared engine,

shrouded in what looked like a stock-car housing. The passenger cars we were told had been set aside in 1915, during "good times," when a passenger train made two round trips a day, and the S&T had purchased two passenger cars from the Pennsy and ordered a bantam 4-4-0 from the Baldwin Locomotive Works.

On a yard track near the wye sat a 4-6-0, and all lettering, except its number "12," had vanished long ago. The Ten-wheeler had been sitting there for so long that the weight of its drivers had pushed the rails out of sight. Near this engine was a relic of the New York elevated-transit system, an equally rusty 0-4-4T. When the elevated lines were converted to electric power, many of these small engines were sold to shortlines, for they were so light that they were of no use to a road with heavy hauls.

Oldest of the rusting engines was a three-foot-gauge Shay, only the upper half of its boiler visible, sitting behind some derelict log cars, crumbling into punk. This train was the first one in the vicinity, being floated on a raft down Tionesta Creek to do logging work along the tributary Salmon Creek. The S&T listed "four locomotives" on its roster, which meant that besides the two still in use, a

90

AN AIR OF GRADUAL DECAY described the terminal of the Sheffield & Tionesta Railway at Nebraska, Pennsylvania, in 1939. Behind the enginehouse tracks, a ruined lumber mill lay hidden in the overgrowth—its roof fallen in, with a rusting Porter Mogul, No. 5, and a sagging combination car. Everywhere in the weeds lay parts, wheels, rails and discarded scrap. The shed at the right was a storehouse of sorts, and up on the rafters sat a ghostly array of headlights of various types and ages—all taken from old engines, as they were set aside, worn out. These old headlights eventually went to the Henry Ford Museum at Dearborn, Michigan (after I had told one of the museum's agents about this old collection). However, the museum hired—in what was a major error—an "art authority" as director, who scrapped all of the headlights, along with many other things he did not appreciate (because he obviously was not an historian).

couple of the rusting specimens were counted.

Sitting on a two-foot-gauge track were two little Koppel 0-4-0T engines, as well as a couple of tiny gasoline-powered engines. This equipment and other machinery that was rusting away had been used by a contractor to build the seven miles of concrete highway to Tionesta over along the Allegheny River. Unable to pay his bills, the S&T became the owner, in lieu of unpaid freight bills. Included were piles of track segments and rails, a cement mixer on flanged wheels, a fleet of four-wheeled contractors' cars and numerous other things from the times when roads were built in this fashion, employing a small-gauge railroad to move the construction materials. The use of motor trucks for this purpose was rather new during the 1920's. By this acquisition, the S&T became a three-gauge railroad in a technical sense.

Nebraska, Pennsylvania, was a tiny crossroads community, with only a handful of houses visible. There were no longer any

WITH STEEL MILLS in the area, old locomotives and other derelicts ordinarily did not sit around long. The market for scrap metal usually was too good for that. However, the Sheffield & Tionesta Railway was different, and besides two operable locomotives, we counted about a dozen of definitely inoperable ones. This was the oldest derelict, a three-foot-gauge Shay, the first engine in the Tionesta Creek Valley, floated in on a raft. Left to rust away for many years, the old Shay was still coupled to a train.

FOR ITS FINAL DECADES, the little Sheffield & Tionesta Railway had only two operable engines. Sometimes, the repair period for one of the road's locomotives might stretch into nearly a year. Engine 6, a 1903 Porter Mogul was not often seen toward the last. With a typical train, The 2-6-0 was leaving Sheffield, Pennsylvania, with some bulkhead flatcars loaded with so-called "chemical wood" (pulpwood) for the plant at Mayburg, the last industry along the line. This pulpwood was to be "cooked" for charcoal and acetic acid.

mercantile establishments; those had vanished with the lumbermen when the mill closed. There was a ramp alongside the track where coal hoppers were spotted, to be loaded from dump trucks that brought the coal from a mine not too far to the south of the terminal. A small sawmill converted logs to finished lumber, and this provided an occasional revenue carload. The railroad crossed Tionesta Creek to reach the north side at this point, and there at the end of track was their very unusual collection of road-building machinery, dating from the 1920's.

The last two Sheffield & Tionesta engines in use were No. 6, a 1903 Porter Mogul, whose companion, No. 5, sat in rusty disrepair in the collapsed Nebraska mill shop. No. 11, the 1915 Baldwin 4-4-0, was the other engine in use by the road, both alternating while the other was given needed maintenance by the train crew on the days they did

not run. Such repairs were leisurely done, sometimes extending for months. During September of 1939, No. 6 needed about $5.00 in some kind of parts, and it was still waiting for them the following May. No. 11 was used in tearing up the line in 1945, and the engine suffered the misfortune of getting a scorched crown sheet due to the carelessness of the dismantling people. If it had not been for that, this engine might have gone to the nearby Clarion River Railway, which needed a lightweight locomotive.

The S&T railroad followed the south bank of the creek up a beautiful valley its entire distance. The stream dropped gradually, so the grades were not steep. At various points, there were long-disused sidings, usually just spiked shut at the switch points. The switchstands were missing from most of them. No signs indicated the names of these places, although there were 14 of them between the terminal points. At three points,

THE TAIL OF THE WYE at Nebraska, Pennsylvania, was also the engine terminal of the 35-mile Sheffield & Tionesta Railway. This shortline was a relic of the lumbering boom times. The log loader at the right of the engine will never work again; there were no more logs to load. In this visit of September 1, 1940, No. 11, a 4-4-0, was cold, even though that day was its scheduled weekly run. Operations now were tailored for whenever enough freight made a trip practicable.

civilization still was evident. The railroad's office had been at Kellettville, located in a rather nondescript building, but it was no longer used by the S&T. Here, too, was a wye, beyond the tail of which lay the collapsed ruins of a huge sawmill, its machinery visible under the wreckage. There was also another engine at this location, a Heisler whose fate had been to arrive only a year before the mill closed. And the practically new engine had been left to deteriorate—of course stripped by scrap-minded vandals of all brass, copper and small parts. One leg of the wye was so overgrown that we did not suspect that any rolling stock was still on it, until a thrown stone brought a metallic sound, and after prying aside bushes, we found an abandoned log car.

Mayburg was the only busy place on the line, just a few miles beyond Kellettville. A chemical plant at this location was converting what looked like pulpwood to charcoal and acetic acid. A bridge across the creek was used for both rail and road purposes, the track belonging to the Hickory Valley Railroad, which wound through the hills from Endeavor on the Allegheny River to bring carloads of "chemical wood" to Mayburg. The small community of perhaps a dozen houses sufficed for the mill workers. The mill had a Climax engine to do its switching, and sitting in the yard was a Shay in derelict condition. At one time, the HV line had been a busy line of the Central Pennsylvania Lumber Company, a large operator in the forests, dominating the region.

Taking pictures of the S&T was not easy. For most of the 35 miles, the highway was on the northern side of the creek. Although the train ran close to the stream, such a large

LOCOMOTIVES 6 AND 11 were simmering to themselves on an off day at the Nebraska, Pennsylvania, terminal of the Sheffield & Tionesta Valley Railway. This was an outdated scene in 1941; however, earlier in this century, it was a common one in many places in the lumbering regions—small railroads, small engines, a cluttered enginehouse and yard—always appearing that they were in their last days. Notice the strange roof on the old wooden water tank.

amount of brush and trees had grown up since the early days, that even a three-car train was out in an open spot only a few times in the entire distance. One of the best locations was the ghost-town site of Newtown Mills, which by the 1930's was just a large field, with no trace of the mill. Fortunately, there was a bridge near there, which crossed to the south bank of the creek.

At Barnes, just several miles out of Sheffield, the S&T crossed the Tionesta Valley Railway at grade. There were not any gates or signals. When we asked which railroad had the right-of-way, both crews said they had it. And we noticed that trains of both lines approached the crossing rather confidently, although they did look both ways. Later, we learned that a TV train had hit an S&T engine there, knocking it over!

The Sheffield yard was a mixed affair, with both railroads' trackage. The S&T, in order to wye their engines, had to use the Pennsy's main track as one leg, and as that

line was often very busy, the S&T crew would just have to wait for an opportunity to use the track. There was not much interchange with the TV. However, because the narrow-gauge line had a well-equipped shop here, on several occasions, the S&T engines received major overhauling. The Great Depression shut down the huge mill in Sheffield, only to reopen again briefly. Its vast wooden structures seemed to fill two city blocks. The TV line had brought in the last loads of logs during the early 1930's, and after that, logging was finished for this operation.

Passenger revenue must have been as close to zero as it could be, although the trains—when they ran—were "mixed," with the old Pennsy coach, equipped with sooty plush seats, serving as the caboose. During September of 1939, President Klinestiver was loading a car of lumber, and he asked me if I was going to ride the train. On my affirmative answer, he declared, "You don't have a

THE MIXED TRAIN of the Sheffield & Tionesta Railway was arriving at Sheffield, Pennsylvania, in November of 1941. A couple of tankcars of acetic acid from the Mayburg plant, a carload of chemical wood for the Barnes (Sheffield) plant and a boxcar of lumber made up the consist of this rather uncertain mixed—except for the old wooden coach on the rear end of the train. The coach had seen no paying passengers in nearly two years! The narrow-gauge third rail was for the use of the Tionesta Valley Railway, whose terminal was at Sheffield.

ticket." When I asked where I would get one, he said, "from me," and he collected 90 cents, but he neither gave me a ticket nor a receipt. The crew, upon hearing of this, was indignant, and I then learned the crew did not expect anyone to pay! Probably that was the last fare paid to ride the S&T. During the next May, I learned that in the meantime there had not been any passengers.

Trackwork was minimal, and when I rode the pilot beam for a few miles one hot day, I was not very reassured when often I noticed that the rails ahead of the engine visibly trembled as the pilot wheels came near to them. I got off at the first opportunity!

The Sheffield & Tionesta was supposed to make a run twice a week, on Tuesday and Friday. So, Bill Schriber and I had left Massillon, Ohio, late one Thursday evening after he got off work. After a slow drive of 190 miles, we reached the foggy town of Nebraska, just after dawn. Soon, the engine crew showed up and gave us the bad news that because a car of coal was not yet fully loaded, the run would be made the following day, Saturday. It was too late for us to reach any other nearby trains that might be operating, such as the two segments of the Tionesta Valley line. So, what were we to do with the full day on our hands?

As we looked at Engine 11, the 4-4-0, which would be the motive power tomorrow, we talked about cleaning up the lettering on the tender, as it was rather dingy from its original application back in 1915. However, the grime of 25 years did not clean off very well. The crew was agreeable to us re-lettering it, but the nearest can of aluminum paint would be at Sheffield, 35 miles away! So, we made the 70-mile round trip, and be-

THE NARROW-GAUGE Tionesta Valley Railway had its terminal in Sheffield, Pennsylvania. The engine-house is at the right in this 1939 view, virtually a museum of considerable variety, ranging from the original engines of 1882, down to fairly new Heisler geared locomotives. The TV's derrick was sitting on the track leading to the general office building and depot. Notice the dual-gauge trackage in part of this yard.

fore noon, in the midst of a million hungry mosquitoes, we started the job. We seemed to spend more time and effort swatting insects than in applying paint, and their attacks did not help steady our hands with the paint brushes. We hoped that the results would show in the next day's photographs.

Saturday was very foggy, and No. 11 was wreathed in clouds of steam, as the air-pumps wheezed noisily. We had stayed overnight in Sheffield, and had brought along lunches for a long day. We watched No. 11 couple three loads of coal ahead of the ancient, faded Tuscan-red coach. Then, we drove off to wait hopefully at Newtown Mills ghost-town site, praying that the fog

would lift for a picture. The open field at this location was the best open place on the entire 35 miles of S&T track.

Engineer Bob Smith was faithful to all the vanished places in the timetable of long ago. And he sounded the pleasantly modulated Baldwin passenger whistle in a long station blast, as he approached the spiked switches. The whistle echoed nicely in the valley... at first far off, and then, as it came closer... until the short train emerged from a cloud of morning mist, as if the creek beyond was a backdrop of a stage... and the engine slowly steamed by us and then vanished into the fog.

Was all our effort worthwhile? We both

thought so. Perhaps as much for the associations as for the result, this view is one of my favorites. The train and the open field itself are long gone, for the waters backed by the Tionesta Dam now cover the site of Nebraska and Newtown Mills.

TIONESTA VALLEY RAILWAY

BY THE END of the 1930's, the Great Depression had brought about the demise of nearly all of the narrow-gauge lines east of the Rocky Mountains. Only the East Broad Top and the Tionesta Valley continued to operate in Pennsylvania, a state that up until

very recent years had more such railroads than any other state east of the Mississippi River. The Tionesta Valley line originated during the logging boom of the 1880's, and it still continued to make a meagre existence in the years before World War II. This narrow-gauge line hauled many carloads of so-called "chemical wood."

The last train of logs was hauled into Sheffield during the mid-1930's, and after that, the huge lumber mill at Sheffield was permanently idle. Only one log car was left in the yard, with a section of the last big hemlock tree that was cut for rail shipment. By the late 1930's, the Tionesta Valley operated five or six days a week, making a round trip on the 13 miles of track from Sheffield to

THE TIONESTA VALLEY RAILWAY and its connecting Clarion River Railway were two lines that we Ohio railfans visited whenever the opportunity came along. Sometimes, it was just a short detour from some other trip, as happened on April 27, 1941. My costume on that spring day was hardly suited to a lumber railroad! The little caboose was the last of some home-built four-wheel bobbers, formerly used on the numerous logging branches of this narrow-gauge shortline.

IN THE TRANSFER YARD at Sheffield, Pennsylvania, cars of both gauges were positioned on either side of a long platform. The Tionesta Valley Railway's boxcars had old-fashioned outside ladders, long banned from modern freight cars.

THE RAILROAD CREW from Hallton, Pennsylvania, with their old Mogul No. 10 of the Tionesta Valley Railway, was at the closed depot at Sheffield Junction in August of 1941. Not too many years in the past, this was an important junction point with the Baltimore & Ohio branch northeast of Pittsburgh. Prior to 1912, it also was narrow gauge, and the interchange of both passengers and freight made this little place important for many years. At the left was the engineer, Robert Lyle, while the fireman was Jack Rimer. The two men at the right are unidentified.

Sheffield Junction, where the line met the Baltimore & Ohio. The track ran on beyond to Hallton, a distance of 19 miles, but a crew from the plant at that point used TV engines to take the wood loads to their mill.

In 1936, the Sheffield enginehouse, in effect, contained a collection of engines that was a museum. There were the first two engines of 1882, No. 1, a 4-4-0 named the *Wild Pigeon*, No. 2, a 2-6-0 named the *Black Bear*, and a couple of small ALCO Moguls. One medium-size Heisler, four Climaxes and four large Heislers were the newest and heaviest engines the road had. Strangely, across each of their fire doors—except for two of the Heislers—the insurance company the TV used had hung a chain with a warning that the engine must not be steamed-up.

The last crew preferred the Heislers, so the men alternated between using No. 16 and No. 19. On the 4.0-percent grade from Brookston to Sheffield Junction, one of these Heislers could haul a dozen loads of wood. And in the process, they sounded as if they were coming along at a good 35 mph, although they actually were moving at a mere five or six mph. Outside the enginehouse, there was a convenient crane, which was used for the sole purpose of changing the smokestacks, as the seasons changed. For summer and fall, when things in the wooded hills often were very dry (compounded by thick growths of giant ferns, which burned as if they were paper), the engines used a balloon stack. After winter snows came, the stacks were switched back to the straight design. Side-door cabooses trailed behind the trains, and there were even a couple of four-

ENGINE NO. 10, a Mogul of the Tionesta Valley Railway, was making one of her final runs during August of 1941. Soon, No. 10 would be exchanged for a Heisler geared engine, No. 19, and go to Sheffield for scrapping. Belvidere trestle was one of the few open places on this brushy route.

wheeled "woods bobbers," as they were called by the crewmen.

Many miles of track still remained, such as along the East Branch; however, by 1936, only one wood-loading track remained active, at the tail of a spur reputed to have an extremely steep 7.0-percent grade. The train bound for the junction would make the short side trip up the East Branch, bring out a couple of loads, and then go roaring up the grade to spot a couple of empties, the exhaust making a steady roar of sound. The East Branch was the scene of the last logging on the line. Gradually, trains brought in long strings of log cars to Sheffield for scrapping.

The Tionesta Valley line was very hospi-

table to us Ohio railfans. The crew invited us to ride with them and extended it to "anytime." The little caboose had an odor of burning pine, and the crew delighted in pointing out to us the places along the route that were once of importance—vanished towns and mills and branch lines. Superintendent Gibson even invited us up to his second-floor office in the brick structure serving as a combined freight depot and office building. Supplying us with copies of the final timetable, he, too, invited us back, remarking that our visits did a world of good for the crews, explaining that they got very bored, doing the same thing on every run, "...and they've worked with each other for so many

UNTIL THE LOGS were exhausted, the Tionesta Valley Railway used Moguls like No. 10, an ALCO product of 1904. The little 2-6-0's were used to handle the mainline trains. In the winter, these engines would have a straight stack, while in the summer and fall, they would have a balloon stack, as fires were easily started when things were dry. Just north of Hallton, the southern end of the line, the crew had spotted No. 10 on a wooden trestle for our cameras. The date was August 19, 1941.

years they've run out of stories." Our presence served to break the boredom and lift the spirits of the crew. He explained that his little narrow-gauge road obviously was in its final years of operation, and he said this knowledge also was depressing to the men.

Of course, each of us got to run the Heisler a little, while the crew was doing the Sheffield Junction switching. I found the throttle tricky, and one had to give steam to a light engine carefully, and just as carefully apply the air, or else the little geared engine would slide an incredible distance (or so it seemed), really shaking up this amateur! The engine crew was familiar with both Shays and Climaxes, and declared that the Heisler was the best all around. The "V" drive required less maintenance than either of the two other types of geared engines.

For track inspection and other purposes, the Tionesta Valley had a four-wheeled velocipede with wire-spoke wheels, bicycle seat and pedals, and this device also was tried. It could clip along at a rapid rate, but it was so light that if one hit a bad rail-joint, with perhaps a quarter inch or more of "lip," the cyclist and his machine were likely to be bounced completely off the rails. The railroad still had a hand-pumped car, but track crews had a variety of homemade gasoline-motor section cars.

Passenger service had ended about 1932, a mixed-train schedule, and the last two passenger cars sat rotting away at Sheffield, destined to become hunter's cabins. The B&O had a connecting mixed-train service as well, although it was standard gauge, having been converted in gauge in 1912. The Sheffield Junction depot had been boarded-up for years.

The TV had much dual-gauge trackage at Sheffield, of course, as well as for the two miles to where the Barnes mill spur took off. Standard-gauge boxcars and tankcars moved over this segment easily, as the TV engines were equipped with three-position couplers. The mill at the end had a small Class "A" Climax, still lettered for its previous owner,

the Lewis Run Manufacturing Company. The yard crew consisted of only one man, who ran the engine, fired it, got down to throw the switches, made the couplings, etc., all of which kept him busy. When a couple of us railfans showed up just to watch, we found ourselves more-or-less "drafted" to become helpers in his switching duties, and as a reward, he let us run the little engine. This was a reward that really made us regret to leave, as we were as happy as kids who had received a new toy!

However, all good things must end, and in 1941 the Tionesta Valley applied to abandon, and by the following year, it was scrapped. Several years later, at the end of World War II, the three Climax engines sat in the weeds awaiting buyers, but all else was gone.

The Clawson Chemical Company of Hallton bought the line south of the junction, along with Heisler No. 19, a couple of ca-

booses and numerous wood-rack cars. Wood was loaded from highway trucks at the highway crossing, as no passable roads existed to Hallton, so this line stayed in use until the Hallton mill closed. Three days a week, the crew would operate the Clarion River Railway, and the other two days, the men would make a trip with No. 19.

When the connection was broken with the abandonment north of Sheffield Junction, the Hallton line was using Tionesta Valley Mogul No. 10, a small-drivered 2-6-0 product of ALCO manufactured in 1904. No. 10 was in need of shopping, but it turned out to be cheaper to buy TV Heisler No. 19 as a replacement. Engine No. 10, we were sad to learn, was then scrapped.

Without a turntable or wye at Hallton, 2-6-0 No. 10 would back to Sheffield Junction, and one of their favorite stories was about one trip when a black bear just sat in the track and would not move, despite whis-

HEISLER GEARED ENGINE No. 19 of the Tionesta Valley Railway had brought a dozen loads of "chemical wood" to Sheffield Junction on this day in June of 1941. A crew from the southern end of the line, at Hallton, Pennsylvania, would come up a couple of times a week to exchange empties for loads. The plant at Hallton produced charcoal and acetic acid from the pulpwood. The flatcars were rather crude versions of bulkhead flats.

BY EARLY IN 1942, the Tionesta Valley Railway was abandoned, and during that year the line was torn up from Sheffield to Sheffield Junction. Before this occurred, the line south of the junction was sold to the chemical plant at Hallton, Pennsylvania. This company continued to receive their wood supplies by railroad cars loaded at a highway spot, near the junction. Engines were also exchanged. No. 10, the Mogul, was turned back to the Tionesta Valley, and No. 19, a Heisler, was received in exchange. The new owners, the Susquehanna Chemical Corporation, repainted and relettered for the Heisler.

A TYPICAL CABOOSE on the Tionesta Valley Railway is shown here. Built at Sheffield, Pennsylvania, by Scandinavian carmen without blueprints, showing how skilled these carpenters were. After all were abandoned in 1948, the bodies became hunter's cabins, etc. One was retrieved and taken to Connecticut to a machinery museum. This is the way Caboose 111 of the TV line looked on October 26, 1947. Notice that the side door was on only one side of this hack.

PICKING UP LOADS of wood at the State Highway 66 end of the line, the Heisler would haul the loads to the mill at Hallton, Pennsylvania. As there was neither a turntable nor a wye, the engines backed the empty flatcars to the yard. The narrow-gauge railroad of the Susquehanna Chemical Corporation was photographed on May 22, 1948.

A TIONESTA VALLEY TRAIN was drifting along near the ghost-mill site and town of Pigeon Run, Pennsylvania. It was photographed on July 12, 1947, during the last full year on the last portion of this little narrow-gauge road.

AS THE WATER TANK at Pebble Dell was accidently burned, the beaver pond at that point became the engine supply. A syphon arrangement was being used by Fireman Jack Rimer on May 22, 1948.

LITTLE CLASS "A" CLIMAX geared engine No. 2 was used as the mill engine by the Clawson Chemical Company plant at Barnes. This place was located on the Tionesta Valley Railway, just outside Sheffield, Pennsylvania. The Climax was still lettered for its earlier owner, "Lewis Run Mfg. Co." The engineer was a one-man crew, and he was delighted when we showed up, because he could get us to throw switches and couple-up cars, rewarding us by letting us run the little No. 2 now and then. These happy occasions ended in 1941, when the mill shut down, and the engine went to scrap. The specially toned Climax whistle, with its distinctive tip, can be seen here. It had a distinctive low tone, sounding something like a "squnk!"

tling of the engine. Several extra people were riding on the tender, so one threw a lump of coal, which hit the bear on the nose. Instead of taking off, the bear came charging down the track, apparently intending to climb up on the engine's low-slung tender. The fireman ended the event by employing his squirt hose, spraying hot water on the animal, causing the black bear to scamper away.

When the chemical plant at Hallton closed in mid-1948, the remaining narrowgauge track was torn up, and Heisler No. 19 was cut up, too. The standard-gauge Clarion River Railway also was abandoned, as there was no further traffic for it to haul out to the B&O connection.

THE VALLEY RAILROAD
"THE SHORTEST IN THE U.S."

THE VALLEY RAILROAD of Westline, Pennsylvania, made it into Ripley's *Believe It or Not* lists by its claim to being the shortest railroad in the United States: one mile. This was true, except that to be exact, the railroad actually operated an additional 15 miles on Pennsylvania Railroad-owned track, which connected at Kinzua, Pennsylvania, on the big road's Oil City–Buffalo line. Years before, when I showed up to look it over on a

FOR MANY YEARS, the Tionesta Valley Railway controlled and operated the Clarion River Railway. They built this rather crude little railbus at the Sheffield shops to carry the school children from Hallton to Portland Mills, as close as the poor roads permitted the school bus to come. A similar railbus was built for the narrow-gauge line north out of Hallton. Finally worn out, the management bought a small Brookville gasoline-powered vehicle to replace it. Woebegone wooden "T V Ry M 55" was photographed on April 26 of 1941.

hot September day in 1939, the Valley Railroad was an 11-mile operation, featuring twice-a-week mixed-train service from Westline up the creek valley to connect at Kushequa with still another of the many little railroads that were a feature of northwestern Pennsylvania's forest industries, going under the famous-and-tremendous steel trestle of the Erie Railroad, which spanned the wide valley at this point. The Mount Jewett, Kushequa & Riterville Railroad was the connecting road, and by virtue of its "Kushequa Route" connection, the Valley line could handle freight and passengers to several larger railroads, including the Erie, the Baltimore & Ohio, the Buffalo, Rochester & Pittsburgh and the Pittsburg, Shawmut & Northern. However, the Great Depression ended all of that with the abandonment of the Kushequa Route, and the Valley line also abandoned its trackage back to Westline. Today's riders on the Knox, Kane & Kinzua tourist line can look down from the great bridge and see the grade of the Valley Railroad far below.

Westline had a "chemical plant," which converted what looked like wood pulp into acetic acid and charcoal, trundled out by Shay No. 2 to the PRR connection. It also obtained revenue freight from another mill at Morrison, 15 miles from Kinzua, which handled its own switching by using a Heisler converted to a gasoline locomotive by removing the condemned boiler and installing the mechanism of a Mack truck!

The 15 miles was in fearful condition, with rotten ties and overgrown brush, and riding in the caboose, I learned on the way back from Kinzua why the caboose was coupled directly behind the engine, with the freight cars behind the crummy. There was a sudden crash from the Shay ahead, and the train stopped! Rails had turned over, and all three trucks were in a mess of rotten ties and poison ivy. The crew matter-of-factly walked several feet ahead, found a few fairly solid ties, spiked down rerailers, and then—after uncoupling from its train—the Shay demonstrated one of its best features as it ground through the mess, rolled up on the rerailers,

107

THE NO. 2 SHAY was switching cars near Kinzua, Pennsylvania, during September of 1939, on the Valley Railroad. The weedy track in the foreground is the mainline. Shortly after this picture was taken, the rails spread and the entire engine was on the ties. However, within 30 or 40 minutes, the crew had No. 2 back on the rails, demonstrating the power of a Shay geared locomotive.

AT MORRISON, PENNSYLVANIA, on the Valley Railroad's line, the chemical mill's Heisler geared locomotive had worn out. So, mill mechanics used a Mack truck to produce this hybrid engine to do the mill's switching! Photographed in September of 1939.

THE VALLEY RAILROAD made Ripley's "Believe It or Not" syndicated cartoon series by its claim to being the shortest railroad in the U.S., one mile. As its two-inch listing in the *Official Guide* said, "Operates one mile of track, providing connection with the Pennsylvania Railroad at Westline, Pa." Actually, since 1919, the Valley Railroad also operated the 15 miles of PRR from Westline to Kinzua, Pennsylvania. The big road declined to come any closer over the neglected track! No. 2 Shay was the only engine remaining, and its sole car was this converted PRR boxcar (Type NX23), rented from the big road. Here, at Westline, cars were being weighed at the track scale on July 15, 1947.

and in 20 minutes, the engine was back on the rails. Then, the cable on the tender was attached to the caboose, which was dragged through the chewed-up ties, and in 40 minutes, we were on our way; however, the boxcars were left to await the section crew, which would have to go down and install a few new ties.

It had been a hot and very humid day, even though the trees arched over the train for most of the way, it seemed no cooler in the shade. The day ended in a relaxing swim in a natural pool in Kinzua Creek, a spot which the brakeman had announced was his goal as soon as we tied-up.

Today, the mill is gone, Shay No. 2 and the Heisler motorized engine have long since been scrapped, leaving only memories of all the train activity that once was a feature of that beautiful area in Pennsylvania.

WEST PENN RAILWAYS, in the "coke region" of western Pennsylvania, had a bargain on Sundays. It was a low-priced Sunday pass, good for two adults and as many as six children. When riding on this roller-coaster route from Greensburg to Brownsville, kids looking for a free ride would attach themselves to passengers who had passes, and the motormen just smiled and offered no objection. The line had many trestles, some of them curved, in order to cross the various steam-road lines. The West Penn cars had no air-brakes, just magnetic brakes to stop, with hand brakes to hold the cars in place. Here, No. 735 was crossing one of the trestles on September 6, 1948.

A THREE-WAY MEET on the West Penn Railways was taking place at Hecla Junction, Pennsylvania, in the "coke region" of the state. Changes in steel operations and coke manufacturing caused a great decline in traffic on this broad-gauge interurban line, which led to its abandonment during the late 1940's.

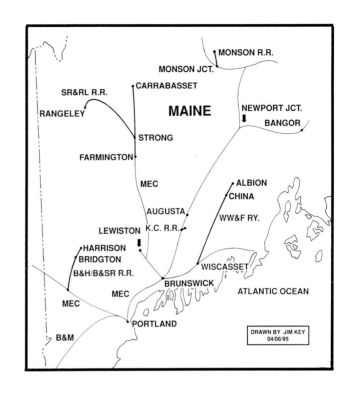

MAINE

MONSON R.R.
MONSON JCT.
CARRABASSET
SR&RL R.R.
RANGELEY
NEWPORT JCT.
BANGOR
STRONG
FARMINGTON
MEC
ALBION
CHINA
AUGUSTA
WW&F RY.
LEWISTON
K.C. R.R.
HARRISON
BRIDGTON
B&H/B&SR R.R.
WISCASSET
MEC
MEC
BRUNSWICK
ATLANTIC OCEAN
MEC
PORTLAND
B&M

DRAWN BY JIM KEY
04/06/95

NEW ENGLAND RAILROADING

NEW ENGLAND in 1947 had an amazing number of passenger trains, specially for me, as I had just spent over a year in Texas, Louisiana and Mississippi. The number of trains operating on very short runs was amazing, reflecting the density of population to sustain them.

Upon returning to Boston from Haverhill, a little over 30 miles away, I was lucky to pick the southbound Canadian Pacific Railway's *Alouette*. For a little extra fare, I was able to enjoy a short trip in this handsome parlor-buffet-observation car. This was truly a beautiful wooden car, with a varnished-wood interior, and a number of creaks could be heard to emphasize the wooden construction. These cars made daily round trips between Montreal and Boston, using Boston & Maine trackage for the Boston entry.

The Boston & Maine's North Station was a very busy place, with a large number of commuter trains. Only recently had their last 4-4-0 engines been retired from these operations; however, there was much of interest on the head ends of these trains, including a number of Moguls (2-6-0's). The passenger cars were mostly wooden, many of them open-platform coaches, and there were some combination cars, as well. One early evening, while watching all of this, I decided to go for a trip. So, I selected one of these trains made up of open-platform equipment, with a 2-6-0 up ahead. I do not recall the end of the line now, but perhaps I should. After making a number of stops, we pulled into a small sub-

urban station. When I inquired what time the return trip would be from a crew member, I received the startling reply that it would be the next morning around 6:30 a.m.! However, the crew was sympathetic when I explained I had just gone for the ride and I was from "way out west in Ohio." After some discussion, the crew pointed out a bus stop nearby, directing me to take it to where it met the end of a trolley line. At that point, a ride on a trolley would eventually take me back downtown in "Beantown." It was a long trip, but about two hours later, I sighted the Statler Hotel, my haven.

Boston had a great amount of commuter traffic, much of it utilizing trolley lines. If one

MY FIRST SKI-TRAIN RIDE was aboard this special train of February 22, 1947, operating on the Boston & Albany Railroad of the New York Central system. I was stuck for the weekend at some town along the line, and observing a ski-train poster, I got up early on Sunday morning and joined the crowd. I was told that the B&A train included coaches from as far away as New York City. The station at North Adams, Massachusetts—our destination—was at the end of an upgrade line. Although the engine was working very hard, she finally bogged down in the snow-covered yard, simply unable to haul us any farther. So, we all hiked up along the track to the station, where the passengers vanished into buses bound for the ski slopes. Not being a skier, I had hours to kill examining North Adams. Late in the day, the mob of passengers came back to the station, and a few of them were limping. Since the return trip was downgrade, it was faster and smoother.

studied the maps, almost any point could be reached easily by electric traction. However, some lines already were being discontinued, as one day we drove for miles along a double-track route being dismantled.

The Boston & Albany subsidiary of the New York Central Lines also operated many suburban trains. They seemed to go by as frequently as one would expect on a streetcar line during the rush hours. One station was within walking distance of the Statler Hotel, and several times I went over there just to watch the railroad action. The B&A employed several wheel arrangements of husky tank engines on these trains, types of engines I had never seen anywhere else—2-6-6T and 4-6-6T types.

NEW ENGLAND STATES... 4

While stuck at Springfield, Massachusetts, one weekend, I saw posters advertising a ski train to North Adams, up in the far northwestern part of the state. Although I was not a skier, for something different, I

bought a ticket, and at dawn I climbed aboard a long string of coaches, some of which I understood had started at New York City. Up ahead a husky Mikado made reasonably good time on the winding route. The train followed streams, and the snow (which had been only three or four inches deep at Springfield) kept getting deeper, as the miles passed.

The North Adams station was at the end of a long grade, the snow was over the rails, and the Mikado was working very hard as we neared the town. However, the train kept going slower and slower, and soon there were jars and jerks, as the engine lost her footing. Finally, we came to a stop out in the

yard, quite a distance from the station. The engineer tried hard, but he could not get the heavy train going on that slippery track. So, the passengers unloaded in the yard and trudged through the snow to the ski buses waiting at the station. Me? I was wearing galoshes, so I made my way along by using the path beaten by the skiers. I got a couple of shots of the train, finally getting up to the station to await the return run. Then, I spent the rest of the day exploring snowy North Adams. The return run, mostly downgrade, was easier on the engine crew, and late at night, we detrained at Springfield.

While in New England and studying maps and timetables, I realized that in dis-

FARMINGTON, MAINE, looked like this during 1921. Engine No. 10 was a 2-4-4T of the Sandy River & Rangeley Lakes Railroad, while the Maine Central's No. 284 was a 4-6-0. The old-fashioned ball signal controlled the crossing of the two railroads, the SR&RL being two-foot gauge, while the Maine Central was a standard-gauge line. The mail-express car of the SR&RL can be seen in this view. Postmarks reading "Farmington & Rangeley R.P.O." are highly prized by collectors.

tance, the Newfoundland Railway was within reach—a reach of over 1,000 miles from Boston. When I tried asking questions at the ticket office, I got the impression that no one went to Newfoundland during the winter. This was despite the train schedules that listed Pullman cars, including a through Pullman from Boston to Halifax, Nova Scotia. This trip involved the Boston & Maine, the Maine Central and the Canadian Pacific. From Halifax it was nearly 300 miles to Sydney via the Canadian National. At that point, one took an overnight steam ship to Port-aux-Basques, Newfoundland. The 3-foot 6-inch-gauge "Newfie," as they called the railroad, spent 25 hours (at least) for the

547-mile trip to St. Johns, the eastern end of the line. However, the Newfoundland Railway trains had diners and sleepers, and I had read a little about this trip.

All of this became increasingly attractive,

THIS WAS THE JUNCTION of the two-foot-gauge Sandy River & Rangeley Lakes Railroad with the Maine Central at Farmington, Maine. The ball crossing signal at the time this picture was shot—circa 1932—commonly used in New England, a holdover from early times of railroading. The slang term "high ball" came from the using this kind of signal, meaning "clear track ahead."

despite the fact it was midwinter, with its shorter days. I had neither been in that part of Canada before, nor had I traveled on any of those railroads. I had some vacation time due me, and wintertime was not the best time to be dragging tire dealers outdoors to measure their buildings and negotiate for signs. So, my boss was agreeable, but he voiced some skepticism that he never expected to see me alive again, as Newfoundland always seemed to most Americans to be as remote as Europe. And it was a far less desirable destination, particularly during the winter months.

So, I made my reservations for Pullman space, double-checked times and schedules, stocked-up on film and made other preparations, almost as if embarking on a trip to the Arctic regions. And that is what actually happened. Mother Nature evidently viewed my venture as an unfriendly act, and the whole venture went down the drain. The railroad agent advised me that a severe storm had disrupted everything, and most notably the steamer connection to Newfoundland. Everything was snowed-in, iced-in and at a standstill, and no one was sure just when things would get close to normal again. As a result, I never got to see and ride the Newfie, and it is sad to note that it has gone the way of abandonments, as indeed

have all the trains I had planned to use on that grand excursion. However, even in good summer weather, New England railfans rarely ventured up that way. I had heard many descriptions of Newfoundland from former neighbors in Akron, who—when I was a kid collecting stamps—would save the stamps of that remote "British colonial outpost" for me.

THE BOSTON & MAINE'S smallest locomotive was this little Plymouth four-wheel gasoline-powered engine, in use as a shop switcher. Many railroads bought these small engines during the 1920's to replace old steam power. They were used at repair shops and roundhouses for switching. Their short length enabled them to handily spot much larger steam power on turntables.

A NARROW-GAUGE TRAIN on the two-foot gauge Edaville Railroad was photographed in December of 1946, while still being built. The track wound through the cranberry bogs of Ellis D. Atwood. In its early years, this little road moved many tons of materials used in the production of the "Ocean Spray" brand of cranberries. It was a typical wintry day on Cape Cod, foggy and chillingly cold. Engine 7 and the cars all came from former two-foot-gauge railroads in Maine.

VISITING THE TWO-FOOT-GAUGE EDAVILLE RAILROAD

FOR NEARLY 50 YEARS the Edaville Railroad was well known to railfans as the place to see two-foot-gauge equipment from the former Maine narrow-gauge lines. And the fans could not only see this equipment, but they could ride trains pulled by the little engines. However, when it first was started by Ellis Atwood laying tracks through his cranberry bogs, it was a secret in New England. This was true even though the Edaville was less than 50 miles from Boston, just off well-traveled highways to Cape Cod. I learned how much of a secret it was during a winter Sunday, when I found myself laying-over in Boston, with nothing planned for the day.

The company I was working for had sent me to help the Boston branch office with the advertising needs of the New England tire-dealer outlets. On Saturday, I learned that there was a daily New Haven train going down toward Cape Cod. So, on Sunday, I presented myself at the information stand in South Station, shortly before the scheduled departure of the train at 8:00 a.m. I told the person at the stand I wanted to know which station to go to nearest to South Carver. It turned out that he had never heard of South Carver. When I described why I was inquiring—that the widely advertised "Ocean Spray" brand of cranberries came from that place, etc.—it just did not help one bit. Of course, they had never heard of the Edaville Railroad either. I had run head-on against the New England attitude that something 50 miles away might as well be in another country. With the train about to pull out, I asked the conductor, who also was not any help except to suggest that the fireman might know, as he came from down that way. The fireman managed to come up with a suggested place, and I swung aboard the train just as the "highball" was sounded.

Wareham was very quiet that Sunday morning, but there was one taxi cab, whose driver was totally uninformed as to Edaville, Ocean Spray's manufactures, etc. He finally "thought" it might be a place about two miles away, but he remarked, "Ahm not shuah, you know." So, we took off, and as we neared the place, there in plain sight of anyone was a steam train operating and a cluster of cars—only two miles from his "hack stand"! Up to that day I had always looked upon hotel desk clerks and taxi drivers as fountains of information, with answers to all questions. But this was not so in New England!

Engine 4 of the Edaville line, an 0-4-4T, with a couple of coaches, was standing ready to depart, at a time when there was probably not three miles of track. All sorts of material around the place indicated things were still being constructed. The trip ended out amid the bogs, where a small gasoline locomotive waited to assist in reversing the train, as no wye or loop was available yet.

A tall, friendly gentleman seemed to be in charge of things, and he turned out to be Ellis Atwood. He had noticed my arrival by taxi, and we were soon in conversation. He was amused by my tale of how no one

117

seemed to know about his place. He smilingly explained that 50 miles was a great trip for most New Englanders, and that most Bostonians would consider the journey one to be taken only after considerable thought. I was learning that in my jaunts with the company salesman, who spent two days making short trips of 50 or 75 miles. This was all the more interesting, as I had just come from a long stay in Texas, where it might be suggested during the middle of the afternoon to drive to Houston. And this was a trip of some 265 miles from Dallas!

Mr. Atwood explained his plans, outlining planned track expansion, acquisition of further car bodies and rebuilding them into operating cars. He also said he intended to add other railroad items, as well. He offered a ride in the engine cab, and although I was wearing a new tan topcoat, I risked it in the little cab. Despite the narrow track, the engine rolled along rather smoothly, indicating that someone had made the track very seaworthy—Ocean-Spray seaworthy! I also got to look inside the beautiful little parlor car Rangeley, about which I had read in magazines. This car was the gem of all the equipment on the Edaville line. It had operated on the Sandy River & Rangeley Lakes Railroad in Maine, to the Rangeley Lakes region on

that fairly large—indeed the largest of Maine's half-a-dozen two-foot-gauge railroads. Unfortunately, none of these lines are operating any longer.

It was a cold, gloomy day, but my topcoat survived the cab ride with hardly any noticeable soot or cinder effects! The taxi man soon arrived on call, and he exhibited bored disdain as I told him what was there and what was going on. He showed disbelief when I ventured an opinion that his business would profit from the project. I also found that the conductor and brakeman of the New Haven train back to Boston had no interest in my information. In fact, I got the feeling that the next person who might inquire like I had, would surely get little from them. One would think that railroaders would be a little intrigued by coal-burning steam locomotives operating on but two-foot gauge? But not them. I also informed the "information" persons at South Station, who barely listened. I was to learn down through the years that the Edaville Railroad never reached the number of visitors hoped for, and I was not surprised. I felt Mr. Atwood understood his region well, and he never expected his little railroad would see many visitors. It was sort of a private project, where visitors were made welcome—if they could find the place!

THE VANISHING INTERURBAN

IN THE QUARTER CENTURY or so beginning during the 1890's, the electric-interurban railway lines grew to include thousands of miles in the Midwest and East, as well as in other parts of the U.S. Almost as rapidly, these lines vanished during the following 20 years, so that by 1945, Ohio had only one small interurban line still operating. During 1925, Ohio had 2,500 miles of electric-interurban railways. While I was growing up in Akron, the big red electric cars were frequent sights on city streets, and sometimes there were even three-car "Limited" trains, which shooed the growing automobile traffic out of the way. Actually, it was the growing automobile traffic that was shooing the interurbans out of existence. Commonly, the electric interurban's mainlines had been built at the side of intercity roads, preventing the widening of those roads. At night, the blinding glare of interurban car's arc headlights was a feature very unpleasant for motorists, as I learned on the Akron–Canton road, which I drove on fairly frequently.

Our little railfan club in Akron learned that we could have fan trips on the remaining lines for modest sums, and several times a year, we would arrange these outings. These trips featured the use of some unusual car, with visits to carbarns and the posing of older interurbans for photographs. So-called "photo run-bys" were a feature of these fan trips. The transit companies and their personnel were tolerant and obliging, perhaps because in the back of their minds was the realization that soon all would be gone. They seemed to appreciate our attention.

Costs were low, so we could plan our first trip on the Stark Electric Railroad for a fare of only $1.45, and requiring only 35 passengers to break even. But even so, a few fans thought the price was too high in 1936! For part of the trip, from Alliance to Canton and Salem—about 40 miles in all—the company used their line car, which had been

PORT WASHINGTON, Wisconsin, about 29 miles from Milwaukee, had one of those typical sharply curved reversing loops that interurban lines featured. One of the articulated cars of the Milwaukee Electric—actually considered two cars by the MER&T—had no difficulty with this loop. The three-truck unit was numbered "1188-1189."

built from one of their early wooden cars, stored in the carbarn for many years. And the foreman of the Pennsy's East Canton shops gave us a tour and dragged out of storage and polished-up the PRR's last narrow-gauge locomotive for us.

The Lake Shore Electric Railway, tottering on the brink of abandonment, gave us a speed run on their mainline from Cleveland to Toledo, a re-enactment of what their heavy steel cars used to do every day in limited service. On another trip, we spent much of the day at the Sandusky shops, as numerous relics of earlier times were moved around for photographs. The LSE fleet included operable cars in good condition from their beginnings in 1902. The company had always taken pride in their equipment, and they continued to maintain their interurban rolling stock in good condition until the end in 1938. While some companies operated shabby, worn-out cars—not so with the Lake Shore Electric line.

Too often, there was a carelessness in operations that could cause disaster, as most interurban lines did not have block signals, and they relied only on telephoned train orders and clearances. Typical was the Fairmont–Clarksburg line in West Virginia, which wound through the "hollows" of the coal-mining country. One day I was pacing the interurban company's southbound wooden relic of the early 1900's, and while I drove a few miles ahead searching for a good photo site, I was startled to find a freight motor coming in the opposite direction, pushing a tankcar. I became truly alarmed when that short consist passed the only siding, and I raced frantically for some lane or road crossing to intercept the oncoming passenger car—without finding any crossings. And then, along that winding route, both cars fortunately came toward each other on a rare section of tangent track. The freight motor backed to the siding it had

THE LARGER DIVISION of the Monongahela West Penn interurban system centered on a main-line from Fairmont to Clarksburg and beyond, to Weston, in deepest hilly West Virginia. Business was good in 1947, and even the oldest (and original) cars of the line were kept busy. However, in 1944, the two separate divisions of MWP were sold to the City Lines of West Virginia (*not* an affiliate of the villainous National City Lines). Nonetheless, CLWV intended to convert the system to buses after the end of World War II, and this was accomplished in 1947. A small number of Ohio railfans chipped-in to buy one of these classic original cars, and we gave it to the Connecticut trolley museum. In this view, an old MWP interurban, No. 228, was at the small town of Shinnston, West Virginia.

LIGHTWEIGHT INTERURBAN No. 110 had handled the last run out of Columbus, Ohio, during October of 1938, as a Cincinnati & Lake Erie car. Along with five other high-speed lightweight cars, No. 110 was sold to the Cedar Rapids & Iowa City Railway. There, she served until that Midwest interurban line dieselized and became a freight-only carrier. A crowd of passengers was waiting to board No. 110 in downtown Cedar Rapids in October of 1945.

BY OCTOBER OF 1945, the Des Moines & Central Iowa Railroad was one of the last electric interurban lines. The road's mainstay was freight traffic, but passenger service was maintained on the 35-mile mainline up the Beaver Valley to Perry. When the Lake Shore Electric Railway was abandoned in 1938, three of its heavy steel cars were bought from the Ohio line. Re-equipped with a baggage compartment, snowplow pilots, locomotive bells and dual-end controls, the old cars could handle carload freight when necessary. After 10 years of operation, these cars were retired and scrapped. Luckily, I was able to have a pleasant round trip aboard one of these cars (which I had ridden earlier on the LSE in Ohio) by stopping off at Perry from a Milwaukee Road train.

passed, but I never did learn what the tank-car contained, probably gasoline... or it may have been empty. (See Page 153 for pictures.)

Most frightening of all my experiences took place in January of 1941, when the Indiana Railroad was abandoning practically all of its remaining interurban system. I wanted to write up a story for *Linn's Weekly Stamp News* about the final run of a very unusual Railway Post Office, the "Ft. Wayne & Newcastle R.P.O.," which made a daily round trip in a compartment behind the motorman in a heavy-steel electric car. Collectors prized the postmarks of things like this, and the clerk often carefully postmarked covers for them. To comply with regulations, the postal compartment had no connecting door to the motorman's compartment. Armed with a cab permit, I chose to ride with the motorman north of Newcastle, as it was soon dark, and a good view of the track ahead was interesting to watch.

A few-hundred feet to our left was a parallel track of the Nickel Plate Road, and the motorman assured me we would see nothing on that line, as they only had a daily local train, which was long gone. He was concerned about the location where we would meet the line car, as he did not have a special order covering it—only knowing that it had gone out in the morning, preparing substations, etc., for the end of operations, and he had no idea of where it would be up ahead. This IRR line north to Fort Wayne had been the scene of one of the most terrible interurban wrecks, when long ago, two passenger cars had hit each other hard, and the ensuing fire killed most of those passengers who survived the crash, an event never forgotten by those who worked on the interurban line.

On a long curve through the trees, the motorman excitedly spied a headlight! Immediately, he started braking the car, but the cold temperatures—close to zero—and a light snowfall had the big car just sliding for hundreds of feet. And as the headlight came nearer, he ordered me to open the car door and "Jump!" We were passing poles, trees and a jumble of fences along the sloping grade, and any jumping into that looked to me as no better a choice than being ground up by the line car. It seemed much longer, but perhaps only half a minute passed, when the motorman shouted "Wait!" And I must admit this was one of the most welcome words I ever heard. It turned out that there was a Nickel Plate work train on the parallel track, heading south on the seldom-used line.

At the next stop, I got off and went back

INTERURBAN LINES were few and far-between during October of 1945, when I stopped off to take a ride on the Fort Dodge, Des Moines & Southern Railroad. A typical FtDDM&S car was at the terminal in Des Moines, being loaded with express shipments for the 86-mile trip. As this had been a steam railroad that had been electrified, the motormen had cap badges lettered "Engineer." This road was unlike other Iowa interurban lines, having always relied on freight service.

to the passenger compartment, figuring that it was a much safer place to be!

IOWA—THE LAST STAND OF THE INTERURBAN

BY THE 1940's, most of the electric interurban lines of the American Midwest had gone to the scrap heap. Virtually nothing survived beyond World War II. Iowa was the single exception, having five such operations, each very different from each other in operations and equipment. Consequently, railfans going to and from Colorado would spend some of their available time in the "Hawkeye State," enjoying these relics, soon to vanish, also. I was no exception, and during October of 1945, while traveling by train, I made a num-

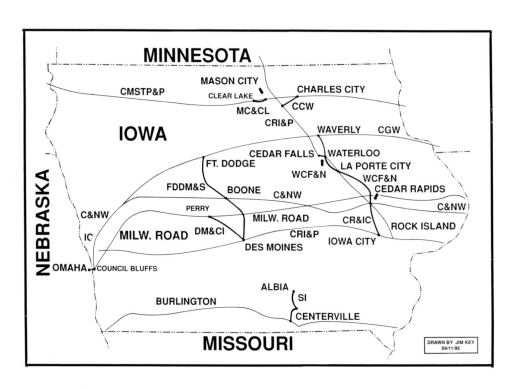

INTERURBAN CAR No. 82 was a typical car on the FtDDM&S, shown here as it waited at Boone, Iowa, during October of 1945. The electric line had a good carload-freight business, and some points of special interest, including two large, high steel bridges. About 15 miles of line survives today out of Boone, including one of the bridges—156 feet in height. The road hauls tourists behind a 2-8-2 steam locomotive purchased in China. The company also has a short electric operation in Boone.

ber of side trips to the interurban lines, both en route to and from the narrow-gauge lines of Colorado.

The five lines ranged in size from the 13-mile Charles City Western Railway to the 85-mile Fort Dodge, Des Moines & Southern Railway. All of these lines handled freight to and from steam-railroad connections. Three of these lines had freight-only mileage besides their main routes. Passenger business was rapidly declining from the World War II boom, and four of the companies had only two to four passenger runs per day. One, the Cedar Rapids & Iowa City line, had nearly hourly service. The well-known CR&IC had the most modern interurban cars, previously operated on the famous Cincinnati & Lake Erie in Ohio.

Iowa had plenty of steam-railroad passenger service, so it was easy to reach these electric-traction lines. First on my list was the Cedar Rapids & Iowa City Railway. As I walked over from the Cedar Rapids depot, I found a car I had last seen in Ohio seven years earlier, apparently destined for scrap. This handsome lightweight interurban car was in the process of turning around on a wye in the street. The C&LE had purchased a fleet of these sleek, steel lightweight cars in the 1930's, and now I was to ride on one again—this most modern of interurban cars. Despite numerous stops, the trip took just under an hour to reach Iowa City, source of most of the road's passenger traffic, from the state university. En route, we met a couple of steeple-cab locomotives (or "motors," as they were commonly called), with a dozen or more freight cars for interchange. It was this business that was destined to keep this line in existence to this very day (as of 1995). However, the CR&IC was dieselized many years ago.

North of Cedar Rapids ran the 59-mile mainline of the Waterloo, Cedar Falls & Northern Railway. This electric line operated through slightly rolling farmland. In fact, the land was so flat in some places that on a later trip, the car I was aboard seemed to be in the middle of a vast lake for many miles during flood stage of the Cedar River. This line still employed its original steel interurban cars, one of which had an observation platform. It was handsomely fitted inside as a parlor car. However, that type of business had van-

TWICE A DAY this interurban made a round trip to Waverly from Waterloo, Iowa. Most of the traffic had gone to the highways, and the end of the Waterloo, Cedar Falls & Northern Railroad was only a few years away. Happily, I rode on this heavyweight car to Waverly in 1945.

ished, and the WCF&N no longer advertised these deluxe cars. This line also had a good freight business, and it advertised that it had the belt traffic of the Cedar Falls area. A total of 140 miles of line served the many industries along the route. It also operated the local streetcar service from Waterloo to Cedar Falls.

The WCF&N operated with two runs each day on a 22-mile branch north of Waterloo, terminating in a town called Waverly. The company employed an old heavyweight wooden combination baggage-passenger car. At one time, when I had a day to "kill" (when the tire company had me covering Iowa), I went for a little day's outing. This trip started with this old car on one of her runs to Waverly. The Chicago Great Western had a passenger train coming west from Oelwein. Upon studying my *Official Guide*, I saw that if I took that train just 6.5 miles west to Shell Rock, I could catch a northbound Rock Island passenger train there to Marble Rock. There, in turn, I could ride on the smallest of the Iowa interurban lines, the Charles City Western, which connected with the Rock Island.

I was totally unprepared for what the

Chicago Great Western had coming. In fact, I was expecting a steam-powered train. So, I was not prepared with my camera when an old McKeen self-powered "doodlebug" car glided smoothly to a stop—with her sharp prow front end and distinctive round "porthole" windows. Trailing behind the doodlebug was a car that would be a gem in any railroad museum, one of McKeen's little round-end combination Railway Post Office and Railway Express cars. It looked as if it was an oversize tinplate toy train! I never got a picture of this train, although I tried to find the opportunity. The original noisy gasoline engine had been replaced with a gas-electric power unit, which accounted for the McKeen car sneaking up on me. If this car had been equipped with the original "rackety" engine, the McKeen unit could not have surprised anyone, including me!

Shell Rock was not much of a place, but within an hour, a Rock Island 4-6-2 Pacific came in view, hustling a short passenger train, consisting of heavyweight cars. This was a typical Rock Island local, filling-in between their streamliners, the famed Rockets. About 40 minutes later, I was deposited at Marble Rock, and there was the connecting

FOR FAST RUNS on the 60-mile electric line from Cedar Rapids, Iowa, to Waterloo, Iowa, the Waterloo, Cedar Falls & Northern had two of these heavyweight observation cars. Originally, these handsome cars provided cafe service as well, intended to be a deluxe operation. This was one of the five surviving interurban lines of Iowa that lasted into the 1940's.

Charles City Western interurban car. It was an old wooden affair, one of two the line had, and after boarding the car, I found that I was the sole passenger. Apparently, the motorman was used to having no passengers at all, just handling mail and express items. Once we were moving, he abandoned the controller and sat down facing me, not in the direction we were travelling! Somewhat nervously, I must admit, I kept eyeing the Iowa countryside through the front windows, but he knew what he was doing. There were no road crossings of importance, and anyway, I had a suspicion that he was just doing this performance to tease me. He succeeded!

Charles City was the site of a large farm-machinery plant, the owner of the little interurban line. No doubt, such ownership obtained better freight rates and service from the three connecting steam-powered roads. The electric car was equipped with MCB couplers, so she could handle carload traffic if necessary. However, most shipments went direct from Charles City on connecting lines. Any traffic man could see those couplers were a good investment—"leverage" it might be called—for better freight rates!

On the way back to Marble Rock, the motorman even let me run the car for a couple of miles. And no doubt, lonely for genuine passengers, he invited me to be sure to return when I could. At 4:00 p.m., the returning Rock Island Pacific could be heard whistling, and in less than an hour and a half, I was back at my starting point, Waterloo. I had been gone for nine hours, traveled 124 miles and probably had not spent more than $3.00 in fares. Today, such a jaunt is impossible, but back then, there were passenger trains everywhere. A study of the *Official Guide* would reward anyone with many a day's adventure that included variety.

The Des Moines & Central Iowa Railroad had 72 miles of line, but most of it was freight only, and it operated in connection with the electric terminal line at Des Moines. The 35-mile mainline passenger service to Perry, northwest of Des Moines, did not have much patronage. In 1938, the company bought three of the Lake Shore Electric Railway's newest cars, upon that road's abandonment. The newer LSE cars replaced the DM&CI's old wooden ones. However, the LSE interurbans were heavy steel cars, which the DM&CI modified. They installed baggage doors and plow pilots for Iowa's winter snowdrifts. These LSE cars I had also ridden and photographed when our club had several fan trips on the line during the 1930's. With their MCB couplers, they could move carload freight, although their steeple-cab locomotives were better able to perform this service.

At 85 miles, the Fort Dodge, Des Moines & Southern was the longest of the Iowa passenger-carrying lines. The FDDM&S interurbans were their original wooden cars, rebuilt considerably with new round roofs and fitted with steel underframes. They featured locomotive bells on the roof, above the motorman's cab. This interurban line still had a fair amount of passenger business, and four trips were operated every day, including the city of Boone, location of the company's shops and offices. The turnaround track at the northern terminal in Fort Dodge featured an incredibly sharp-and-constricted loop of track. To watch one of those big cars move quickly into and around that loop was something hard to believe.

Motorman Ottoway invited me to ride up in the cab with him. We crossed two very large and long trestles, one of which was asserted to be the largest in Iowa. Interestingly, his cap badge read "Engineer," and then I learned that the line had originally been constructed as a steam-powered railroad. And Mr. Ottoway had been a locomotive engineer before the line was electrified. Somehow, he had gotten into building little live-steam 4-4-0 engines to supply the local market for such equipment at amusement parks and carnivals. From this, he had branched out into supplying engines, cars and track sections that could be moved from one to another of the numerous farm festivals and harvest-time county fairs that were held in the Midwest. And he had a proposition for me when he learned that I had not yet gone back to work for the tire company.

Mr. Ottoway had contracts to supply his trains for a number of these agricultural affairs, and he wanted me to handle one of these movable trains for him. It was an attractive deal financially, provided Mother Nature did not create a rainy summer and fall. I had some experience with such a small live-steam locomotive when several of us

railfans bought a former amusement-park 4-4-0, which ran on 15-inch-gauge track. We had rebuilt the little engine, and we laid trackage at Massillon on some suburban property of one of the fellow's parents. However, despite the attraction of spending a long summer running a live-steam "railroad," I thought it over for a while, but I decided to return to the tire company. Long afterward, in Colorado, a couple of the little Ottoway trains turned up, being used at parks or offered for sale.

Iowa had two other electric lines. One was the 25-mile Southern Iowa Railway, south of Des Moines, which was headquartered at Centerville. This line was primarily a coal hauler for electric utility companies. However, it was a friendly outfit, and on several occasions, it operated excursion trips for railfan groups, using its last passenger car of very homemade appearance. The other electric line was the 12-mile Mason City & Clear Lake, which still had passenger service in 1945. However, the MC&CL was very hostile to fans and cameras—the management being somewhat paranoid. Many years later, I visited the place. It was being operated by people who were themselves enthusiasts. And they were preparing to operate an electric-traction tourist line, along with operating their very good freight service.

Fifteen miles of the Fort Dodge line, including the 156-foot-high steel trestle, now operates as a tourist carrier. Engineer Ottoway would like it, I am sure, for they bought a new 2-8-2 from China to haul their trains.

All the rest of the Iowa interurban lines are gone now, except as noted regarding the Cedar Rapids & Iowa City Railway. The freight-only "Crandic" (as the Cedar Rapids & Iowa City was affectionately called), is still busy hauling trains at Cedar Rapids.

THE LAKE ERIE & NORTHERN Railway and the Grand River Railway were electric-powered subsidiaries of the Canadian Pacific Railway. From Port Dover, Ontario, on Lake Erie, the combined lines added over 60 miles to the parent company. Heavy all-steel passenger cars were operated in trains as needed, while freight traffic was handled by large electric locomotives. Occasionally, we railfans from Ohio would make the trip around the eastern end of Lake Erie to spend a day on these lines. During later years, groups would charter a ship for more direct connections!

ACROSS CANADA AND THE PACIFIC NORTHWEST

MY JOURNEYS by train had mostly been in the United States, with only short trips into Canada, chiefly in the Toronto area. However, as dieselization took over in the mid-1950's, passenger trains everywhere began to vanish in the prelude to Amtrak and Via in the late 1960's. So, I decided I should see the Canadian mainlines while they still had their much-advertised transcontinental passenger trains. It was not practicable for me to get away from the museum for a couple of weeks during the summer or fall, so winter it would have to be—particularly as at that time of the year, I could leave the museum in the capable hands of several students on winter break.

The first trip was to feature the Canadian Pacific from Winnipeg west to Vancouver, British Columbia, a 1,400-mile portion of the road's 2,500-mile mainline across Canada.

So, from Denver the finely equipped Burlington streamliner took me to Chicago. Then, another Burlington hop was made to St. Paul, Minnesota. From there, it was by Great Northern to Fargo, North Dakota, 262 miles out in the snow-covered prairies, where the wind had piled drifts on the rural roads we passed. No longer did the GN have a through train from St. Paul to Winnipeg, with sleepers and a buffet-lounge car, which served breakfast. Now, a single RDC car (a Budd "railroad diesel car") bounced along at a good clip through the frozen countryside.

THIS SCENE WAS RECORDED at Kitchener, Ontario, on May 31, 1947. The cars of the Lake Erie & Northern–Grand River interurban train were substantially built, as was the line itself and the brick depot at Kitchener. Notice that this Canadian electric line used trolley poles instead of pantographs on its big steel cars. This was unusual for a line of this type.

Winnipeg was cold and snowy, but this was typical winter weather in Manitoba. Not only did many of the citizens wear their winter headgear of fur hats, but the police did so, also.

The Canadian Pacific's famed *Canadian* streamliner was still a great train, an all-reserved train, with its sleek vista-dome cars and justly renown dining cars. The dining car ensured that I was going to gain weight on this trip! For hundreds of miles, the scenery was mostly rather flat prairie land, buried in a foot or more of snow. Then, beyond Calgary, Alberta, we entered the Rocky Mountains, and their scenic wonders were unlike anything that could be seen from a train in Colorado. The familiar scenes used in CPR advertising folders and posters were even more impressive when seen from the train. The snow got deeper, and finally — beyond Banff — the adjacent wires were seem-

ingly resting on snowdrifts, crusted with inches of ice and snow. There was ample evidence that snowplows had been out keeping the tracks clear, because we gradually fell behind the timetable. Even after dark, the scenery often was impressive, as the headlight swung around curves far ahead.

I had been counting on seeing the Banff and Lake Louise area of the route in daylight. However, the train was running late, and darkness had fallen by the time we reached those places of great scenic repute. However, from the dome car the silhouettes of the great snowy peaks were very impressive.

Evidently, the railroad was having serious trouble with the storm that was just ending. During the night, we became nearly eight hours behind schedule, which meant that it was my good fortune to see the canyons of the western slopes of the Canadian

THIS INTERURBAN TRAIN of the Niagara, St. Catherines & Toronto had to cross the Welland Canal on this drawbridge. The NStC&T had been a very busy interurban line in the Niagara Falls area. However, traffic demands were forcing the company to give up the most lucrative parts of their system. Heavyweight cars like Nos. 135 and 132 frequently operated in trains out of Niagara Falls, New York. Not long after this 1947 view was shot, the St. Catherines–Niagara Falls interurban service was abandoned. However, lightweight cars continued to operate on the short Thorold–Port Colborne line in Ontario until March of 1959. In any case, carload freight service remained as a viable operation on the Niagara, St. Catherines & Toronto Railway.

Rockies in broad daylight—on a bright sunny day. Thompson Canyon and particularly the Fraser Canyon made the lateness of the train worthwhile. After all, I had no connections to catch at Vancouver, so the time was unimportant. At times, I could also see the Canadian National line, which shares the same canyons. It certainly impressed this traveler with the difficulty of building Canada's transcontinentals.

On the next day, at Vancouver, I had an idea to go for a ride on the Pacific Great Eastern (now the British Columbia Railway). The PGE was famous for its remote-and-scenic route, its passenger trains consisting of sleek RDC cars. Certainly, this was the longest route I had ever heard of for these self-propelled diesel cars, which had been made famous by the Budd Company. However, things were all quiet on the PGE, as it was closed by a strike. Nevertheless, by riding a bus across the Lions Gate Bridge to North Vancouver, the PGE terminal, I spied a column of smoke down by the nearby waterfront. And the bus driver let me off at the closest point, providing me with a couple of blocks walk... and a surprise! There was a three-truck Shay geared engine working

A SURPRISING TREAT for railfans in Vancouver, British Columbia, into the 1960's, was this solitary steam locomotive switching along the waterfront in North Vancouver. A relic of the logging era of steam-geared engines, this three-truck Shay's owner, MacMillan Bloedel Company, kept this one for local needs on the waterfront. The date for this view was December 27, 1968.

busily at switching. Lettered for the "Mac-Millan–Bloedel Co.," a large Canadian forest-industry conglomerate, this steam engine was a rare sight to behold. I was told this Shay was the sole steam locomotive operating in western Canada.

Later, I was disappointed to learn that I could not go to Vancouver Island and see what Victoria might be like in winter. However, I discovered that the British Columbia capital was cut off by the results of the same storm, and there was damage to the docks and the ferry-boat service had been shut down. I had read about the Esquimault & Nanaimo line on the island (a CPR subsidiary), which also used Budd RDC cars. And I had idly thought that a winter trip aboard

an E&N train might also be worth trying.

So... I was up early the next day to take the Great Northern's Seattle-bound train, which spent the morning winding along Washington's inland coast, another very scenic trip. And for the return trip to Golden, Colorado, I was aboard the sleek ***North Coast Limited*** of the Northern Pacific, another famous streamliner, as it pulled out of Seattle that afternoon. This train provided a deluxe connection back to Chicago, and then it was via the Burlington Route to Denver on a silver *Zephyr* streamliner.

It had been a long trip for me, involving some of North America's greatest trains, and I had traversed highly impressive routes to and from the scenic Pacific Northwest.

EL DORADO & WESSON RAILWAY

THE OILFIELDS of extreme southern Arkansas provided the livelihood for the little 10-mile El Dorado & Wesson. This railroad delivered many tankcars to the Rock Island and the Missouri Pacific at El Dorado, Arkansas. Besides that, it provided passenger service seven days a week, unusual for a shortline railroad. The coach was a worn-out General Electric gas-electric car, which was handily moved by one of the road's light 2-8-0 steam engines.

THE 10-MILE SHORTLINE called the El Dorado & Wesson Railway, which was located in extreme southern Arkansas, was kept busy moving freight shipments to and from the nearby oil-field discoveries. The ED&W ran a daily mixed train, using any of its freight engines that were available, with a worn-out gasoline-powered motor coach for baggage, express and passengers. Engine 15, a 2-8-0, was recorded on film at El Dorado, Arkansas, on June 2, 1946.

THE BACKSHOP and engine terminal of the 10-mile El Dorado & Wesson Railway was located at Wesson, Arkansas, and it looked like this on June 2, 1946. Engines 11, 17 and 14 are in this scene, with a spare tender in front of No. 11. A fourth engine, No. 16, was in the shop. This view was typical of steam-powered shortlines shortly after World War II.

FEW "NO. 1" LOCOMOTIVES showed up on the larger railroads this late in the 20th century, particularly one as old as the Missouri Pacific. Train 891, between McGehee—Warren (Arkansas), was unusual because its power was a husky 2-8-0 of the MP, numbered "1." The train was passing through Monticello, Arkansas, during the month of June, 1946.

THIS GENERAL ELECTRIC motor car served as a combine on the El Dorado & Wesson's mixed train during June of 1946. Its GE power plant had worn out, and it was removed some time before this date. Many railroads had bought gas-electric cars to replace steam-powered trains during the 1920's and 1930's. However, as their motors eventually wore out (at the time when passenger traffic declined), the cars continued to be used as coaches.

THE FRISCO LINE was hostile toward people with cameras; however, I could not pass up a chance to record this scene from a city street. No. 182, a heavy 4-4-0, and her two-car train was at the brick depot in Fort Scott, Kansas, on April 24, 1949. This short train served to handle all the local passenger traffic on the Frisco's route between Kansas City and Oklahoma.

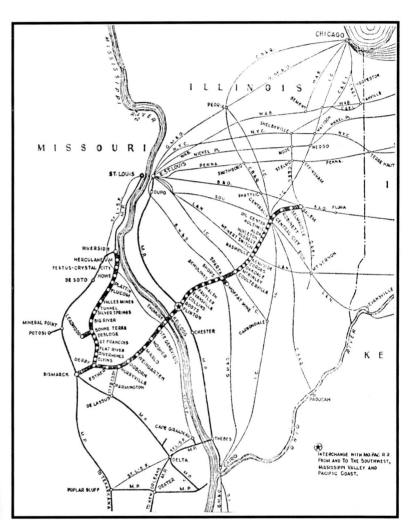

ALTHOUGH FLAG-STOP TIMES continued to be shown in the timetable for this scheduled train of the Missouri-Illinois Railroad, it was in fact listed as a local freight. By December 19, 1941, passenger business had vanished on the Missouri lines of the company that served the lead-mining district of eastern Missouri—a subsidiary of the Missouri Pacific system. A ferry boat over the Mississippi River provided a connection with the Illinois portion of this road. Engine 25 was a typical Missouri Pacific 2-8-0, which was pictured at Flat River, Missouri.

TEN-WHEELER No. 2644 must have been the Missouri Pacific's smallest 4-6-0. Here, No. 2644 was hauling Train 697 between Sedalia and Warsaw, Missouri. This mixed train was operating on a bitterly cold, "zeroish" morning, January 6, 1942. Way car No. 1157, on the rear, was a specially built steel car for such mixed trains.

THIS COMBINATION COACH of the Prescott & Northwestern Railroad was typical of what was used on many shortlines. The P&NW's 31-mile Arkansas line only ran a scheduled steam-powered train on Fridays. On other days, in order to handle a mail contract, they ran a motor car, which also handled express and L-C-L freight. So, if you had to get to someplace on the Prescott & Northwestern line in 1945, you had the choice of Friday only!

WHEN THE INDIANA RAILROAD interurban line was scrapped in 1939, the five-mile Ferdinand Railroad set out its old wooden combine for use as a depot, after buying a steel trailer. No. 305 was obtained from the IRR at a bargain price to replace the old car. The little Ferdinand made two round trips a day to Huntingburg, in southern Indiana, mainly because it had a contract to take the school children to that county-seat town and fetch them back when school ended for the day. Engine 3, a small 4-4-0, was the sole engine on this shortline. The general manager was part of the crew, and he also maintained the engine, car and track.

THE FERDINAND RAILROAD

IN HILLY SOUTHERN INDIANA, a short distance north of the Ohio River, the town of Ferdinand found its only railroad connection to be its own six-mile line, which connected with the Southern Railway, just a mile outside the county seat of Huntingburg. A handful of high-school students was important for the little railroad, which contracted to carry them to and from Huntingburg, where they attended classes. This accounted for the little line making two round trips on each school day. One train operated during the early morning, and the other trip was in the mid-afternoon, to carry the kids back home.

The Ferdinand's sole motive power was a light 4-4-0, devoid of a builder's plate. The line's sole passenger car was a steel car, a former passenger trailer of the electric interurban Indiana Railroad, which the Ferdinand made into a combine by installing a baggage door on each side of the coach.

At about 7:35 a.m. each weekday, the students would hurry into the car, immediately take big sheets of cardboard stashed behind the seats, and using these as playing surfaces across their laps, would play checkers or other games until arriving in Huntingburg. No doubt they resumed playing games on the return trip in the afternoon. The four-man crew included the road's president, and when not running the train, the men did everything else needed on the line, including track work! A one-stall enginehouse and adjoining machine-shop space was the total "shops" of the company. Aside from myself, an occasional townsman would make the trip to the county seat, but it was obvious that other than lumber from the local sawmill and the students, traffic did not exist.

Other than her number, the road's engine carried no name, but she had a pilot on the end of the tender (as well as one on the front end of the 4-4-0), as there were neither turntables nor wyes on the line.

DURING THE MID-1930's, I had ridden aboard a two-car train of the Indiana Railroad interurban line, from Indianapolis to Louisville, Kentucky. This car, No. 305, was the trailer on that train, only it did not have baggage doors in its sides at that time. After the Indiana Railroad was abandoned in 1939, the Ferdinand Railroad obtained No. 305 to replace its decrepit wooden car. Daily during the school season, the Ferdinand line carried students to the Huntingburg school from Ferdinand, Indiana. Notice the large rear-end windows of this combine, typical of the IR's passenger cars.

THE FERDINAND RAILROAD'S train was waiting for a Southern Railway work train to pass, so it could get the children to their school in Huntingburg, Indiana, a mile away. This was the little five-mile line's total rolling stock, No. 3, a small 4-4-0, and combination car No. 305. The headlight was on as it was a gloomy winter morning in southern Indiana's hill country on December 16, 1941.

ON THE MORNING of December 16, 1941, the kids were a little late for school in Huntingburg, Indiana. The Ferdinand Railroad's train had to wait at the junction, a mile from town, until a Southern Railway work train got out of the way. The local school district found it much cheaper to contract with the railroad that run a schoolbus.

BALDWIN LOCOMOTIVE WORKS turned out this 4-4-0 in 1913 for the five-mile Ferdinand Railroad in southern Indiana. This engine was typical of the light power once produced in large numbers for small railroads unable to handle heavy engines. Often, such lines operated trains that were at the most two- or three-car affairs.

THE BUFFALO CREEK & GAULEY'S "passenger train" was somewhere deep in the hills of West Virginia when this picture was taken. Supposedly, the automatic coupler on this little railbus was for towing it when it broke down! A builder's plate on the railbus claimed it was a product of the "Four Wheel Auto Drive Company" of Clintonville, Wisconsin. The date for this view was July 5, 1947, during a coal-mine war, when the non-union mine on this line was under siege.

BUFFALO CREEK & GAULEY

THE BUFFALO CREEK & GAULEY was an 18-mile coal hauler feeding into the Baltimore & Ohio at Dundon, West Virginia—deep in the "hollers," as the local people say in that state. A lumber firm had a branch off the BC&G, which used a Shay geared engine to bring logs, crossing a little stream by simply laying tracks in it (i.e., a ford), highly unusual for a railroad. The BC&G operated mixed trains and filled-out the twice-daily round trips with railbuses, a Brill "doodlebug" and a much smaller vehicle, which had only four wheels and whose body bore the name of the "Four Wheel Auto Drive Company" of Clintonville, Wisconsin. The smaller railbus had a standard coupler in front, which I guessed was most likely used for hauling the car if it failed, rather than for pushing anything.

Dressed in a business suit and customary white shirt, I selected a sunny day to ride the BC&G, and especially the quaint little "B." We carried some closed mail pouches, some packages and occasionally a passenger or two, who seemed to be railroad employees. At one point, we pulled off on a passing siding to meet the mixed train, upon whose pilot beam were perched two crew members armed with a shotgun and a rifle. Maybe they were rabbit hunting I thought to myself.

Widen, the coal-mine settlement on the line, was a typical place, with a small company store, which supplied me with a bottle

THE DAILY PASSENGER TRAIN of the Buffalo Creek & Gauley had paused at a little place called "Cressmont," about midway on the 18-mile line deep in the West Virginia hills. The small railroad also operated a mixed train, which hauled coal from a non-union mine at the end of the line, at a settlement named "Widen." Eventually, this line was abandoned; however, as of 1995, it was reported that the line was about to be resurrected. Does that mean Railbus "B" will run again, too? This unusual gasoline-powered unit was photographed on July 5, 1947.

of Coke and a Hershey candy bar in the way of lunch. To kill time while waiting for the return trip, I walked down a quarter of a mile and snapped pictures of former Baltimore & Ohio engines roaring upgrade to dump cars of culm (worthless waste rock from the coal mine). No one seemed to be around; however, the mine tipple was some distance beyond the store, so I did not venture in that direction.

The trip back down the line was smooth, and nothing of note took place, unless a recently repaired short trestle was seen, which obviously had been the scene of a derailment. It was some time later that I learned that despite the peaceful appearance of the Buffalo Creek & Gauley, I had ventured into a so-called "mine war"—the mine being non-union, and the only road to Widen was under siege by the United Mine Workers. The armed men on the pilot beam of the mixed train's engine were not rabbit hunting. They were keeping an eye out for anything like the damaged trestle, which was not (as I thought) the scene of a derailment, but rather had been blown up with dynamite! On reflection, the reason neither side bothered me was my mode of dress consisting of a white shirt and dark suit must have had them thinking that I was some sort of investigator. A friend of mine and his teenage son, who rode the line about a month after I did, were virtually held on the platform of the company store at Widen by two burly mine guards. They certainly tolerated no photographs, and the guards did not even permit them to venture into the store to have a cooling drink.

DEEP IN WEST VIRGINIA the Buffalo Creek
& Gauley Railroad provided a pleasant day's trip
aboard their odd little four-wheel railbus. At the
mine terminal of Widen, a former Baltimore & Ohio
engine stormed up a spur with loads of culm
(waste coal) to dump. I took all the photographs
I wanted during the day, unaware that a mine war
was in progress, with the mine literally under siege
by the United Mine Workers' union. Perhaps my
white shirt, tie and dark business suit and hat gave
the impression that I was some kind of "federal
agent" nosing around? In any case, July 5, 1947,
was just another nice summer day as far as I was
concerned.

THE FLEMINGSBURG & NORTHERN

AMONG KENTUCKY'S SHORT LINES
was the Flemingsburg & Northern Railroad,
which had all of six miles of track to Flemingsburg Junction, where it connected with
the Louisville & Nashville. Unfortunately for
the F&N, the L&N had discontinued its passenger service on the Maysville–Paris
Branch, so the depot at the junction was now
closed. When I arrived at the Flemingsburg
yard, four men were working on the track,

IT IS NOT CLEAR just who was the most stubborn in this "name dispute." The railroad depot at the left was called "Flemingsburg Junction," in Kentucky. The building at the right was the U.S. Post Office at what the Post Office Department called "Johnson Junction," Kentucky. Eventually, the Post Office people won when the little depot was torn down. This scene was on the Louisville & Nashville and Flemingsburg & Northern railroads on December 5, 1941. Notice the train-order semaphore signal in front of the depot's bay window and a wooden railroad-crossing sign beside

this attractive little rural depot, typical of many small station buildings during the steam age.

MANY SMALL RAILROADS made their own self-propelled cars to reduce the losses of running steam-powered trains. The seven-mile Flemingsburg & Northern Railroad built this gasoline-motored car from an old streetcar. Long out-of-service at the time this photograph was shot in December of 1941, presumably the gasoline engine generated the 600 volts needed to power the electric-traction trucks.

replacing some ties, and since there was no one at the depot building, I inquired when and if the train would run, explaining that I thought I would like to make the round trip. They informed me that it would be about an hour yet, so I wandered around, and eventually, they got the locomotive out of the two-stall enginehouse, reached by way of a three-way stub switch.

Outside the enginehouse was a curious-looking motorcar in faded green, obviously a former streetcar. There was a waycar (ca-boose) in the yard, and an odd flatcar, with coach steps, which presumably was what was left of a wooden coach. One of the men came up to me after placing some packages on the engine's pilot beam, and he an-nounced "If you are ready, we are ready to go." I asked if they wanted me aboard the waycar, and he explained that since I was the sole passenger and obviously interested in trains, they were just going to the junction with the engine, and they "...thought I wouldn't mind riding in the engine." So, off we went on the shortest "mixed" train I ever rode.

En route, a breeze blew my hat off, and the engineer stopped to allow the fireman to run down the track to retrieve it. But they just laughed at my embarrassment. At the junction I noticed that the Post Office people apparently did not like the Flemingsburg

THE SEVEN-MILE SHORTLINE known as the Flemingburg & Northern was hurt badly when the Louisville & Nashville discontinued its scheduled trains on the branch between Lexington and Maysville, Kentucky. By December of 1941, the F&N's last engine had gone to scrap, and the line had to lease a small L&N engine. And although the line showed a mixed-train schedule, there was little to haul. The trip to the junction I made consisted of only the engine, and I was the only passenger—who rode aboard the engine, of course. When I tried to pay the fare, the crew declined, saying that they could not in fairness charge me for riding in an engine! So... I eventually paid them by sending the crew some photographs.

Junction name, and although the small post-office building was next to the depot, facing the tracks, its name was Johnson Junction!

Upon our arrival back at Flemingsburg, with two cars of coal, I asked the conductor (who turned out to be the manager) how much fare I owed, but he smiled and said that since I did not take the caboose, which also served as a coach, and had to ride in the engine, it did not seem they should charge fare for that kind of a ride. So, with thanks to all and a promise to send pictures, I departed with a good feeling about the little Flemingsburg & Northern Railroad.

THE FLEMINGSBURG & NORTHERN line in Kentucky needed a work car. So, the railroad did the obvious. Since its sole remaining passenger car was no longer needed, the company converted it into a flatcar—with coach steps.

ON A COLD JANUARY DAY in 1947, I could not resist shooting this picture of a Chicago & Eastern Illinois train. The C&EI did not cross my path very often, but this view of No. 1915, a 2-8-2, provided a smoky scene for my camera. The attractive Mikado was at Altamont, Illinois, hauling a long freight train.

BELOW RIGHT: Before the Japanese bombed Pearl Harbor and scattered our railfan-club members all over the globe, we managed to have several fan trips in 1941. One trip was on the Monongahela West Penn Public Service Company's Parkersburg line. This was the smaller (separate) division of the system, operating from Parkersburg, West Virginia, to Marietta, Ohio. The larger Clarksburg–Fairmont line (which operated in a mountainous area of West Virginia) was completely different from the Parkersburg line. The smaller line originally operated 14 miles between Parkersburg, West Virginia, and Marietta, Ohio. Later, a 23-mile extension served Beverly, Ohio; however, this extension was abandoned in 1929. Although this was not a big interurban system, it had an interesting variety of newest and old cars. At the carbarn, even the company's line car was out for pictures!

OUR RAILFAN CLUB had chartered an older electric car of the Monongahela West Penn interurban line at Parkersburg, West Virginia. We were about to cross the Ohio River bridge to enter Marietta, Ohio, when Baltimore & Ohio Train 33 came along, so the steam-engine fans had the trolley wait while we took pictures of B&O Pacific No. 5069. This handsome 4-6-2 was hauling a train made up entirely of "standard" steel passenger cars. It was a warm summer day when this daily connection from Wheeling made its regular station stop at Williamstown, West Virginia. The B&O train was heading down the Ohio Valley to Kenova, West Virginia, on August 18, 1940.

THE ILLINOIS TERMINAL system was a heavy-duty electric-freight carrier that operated between Peoria, Springfield, Decatur and Danville, in Illinois, and St. Louis, Missouri. In 1948, the Illinois Terminal still operated fine electric-passenger service; however, patronage was rapidly declining. A large variety of electric-traction locomotives were in use by the road, some not very large, as this small steeple-cab unit portrays, as it was switching at Danville, Illinois. The largest electric locomotives on the ITR had four traction trucks.

FOR MANY YEARS, this spot at the Milwaukee Union Station was a very popular one for railfan photographers. On August 16, 1945, a Milwaukee Road 4-6-0, No. 1112, was heading out of the station with one of the numerous two-car locals. Milwaukee, Wisconsin, was a favorite railfan location, with both electric interurbans and streetcars operating, as well as many steam-powered trains. As you can see, electric-trolley tracks are in the foreground of this scene.

THIS PASSENGER TRAIN was typical of the Illinois Terminal Railroad's scheduled trains—shown here on the Decatur line in May of 1948. Heavy-steel interurban No. 271 was hauling one of the oldest of the line's non-powered trailers. With heavy rail and well-maintained track, these trains operated at a high speed for an interurban line at this late date. On the ITR's St. Louis run, three-car "limiteds" were operated, featuring parlor-cafe service in the rear car. It was a pleasure to ride aboard such a train on a wintry, snowy morning, and it was all charged to my tire-company expense account, too!

WHILE ON A FURLOUGH, after arriving back in
the United States from Iran, a fellow traction fan
and I headed for Milwaukee to shoot electric lines.
During this visit, a Chicago & Northwestern Railway Mikado came along at this point to provide
a change of pace from traction subjects. This was
at West Junction, Wisconsin, on August 16, 1945,
and the C&NW engine was No. 2415.

THE FINE TRACK of the Milwaukee Electric
Railway & Transport Company plainly shows in
this view taken on August 16, 1945, at West Junction on the Waukesha line. This route operated 36
trains each week day. Among the rolling stock
were some articulated cars, one of which is approaching.

150

OVERLEAF: On the short branch to Hales Corners, the Milwaukee Electric Railway & Transport line used its older wooden cars, such as No. 1103. This picture was taken on August 15, 1945, the day after the acceptance of Japan's surrender in World War II. On the day of victory in the Japanese theater of war, the MER&T interurban system had every operable car out on its electric lines, hauling tens of thousands of people into downtown Milwaukee to celebrate. My railfan friend from Akron, Ohio, and I had just seen the busiest interurban line ever! Despite the warm summer weather, the U.S. Army insisted that "neckties shall be worn" and frowned on rolled-up sleeves. However, MP's did not venture out to West Junction, Wisconsin! By the way, this car had not derailed! No. 1103 was going through a very sharp turnout on Route 33. And my friend shot this closeup of the Milwaukee Electric car's front end, while I stood in front of this classic arch-window interurban.

INTERURBAN CAR No. 280 of the City Lines of West Virginia was in the foreground of this view, as a freight motor was pushing a loaded tankcar into the siding—in front of the interurban combine—at Lost Creek, West Virginia. Fortunately, the motormen saw each other in time on a piece of tangent track, and the freight motor (an electric express car) was able to back to this siding, so the passenger car could pass, avoiding a collision. Car No. 280 was typical of the former Monongahela West Penn Public Service Company's eastern route between Fairmont, Clarksburg and Weston, West Virginia.

BEHIND A TANKCAR at Lost Creek, West Virginia, was an electric freight motor of the City Lines of West Virginia—apparently pushing a carload of gasoline. The crew of the freight motor forgot that the regular interurban car was coming against them, as they departed from Weston. And the motor went rolling past the last siding, to my alarm! I had been leisurely pacing the passenger car, watching for some spot to take a picture, and I was shocked to see this freight train go by the last siding! On this winding interurban line—in the hills of West Virginia—overlooking a train order for a meet could lead to disaster!

THE LOUISVILLE & NASHVILLE operated this mixed train, shown here arriving at the mainline connection of Park City, from a trip to Glasgow, Kentucky. Park City was famous for nearby Mammoth Cave National Park. Only a handful of passengers rode aboard the combine anymore. However, at this time, on December 10, 1941, two round trips a day were made on this 10-mile branch. The engine was a 2-8-0, and the Glasgow Railway combine was No. 109.

BEFORE THE POPULARITY of automobiles swept across North America, thousands of people traveled to Mammoth Cave, Kentucky, via the Louisville & Nashville Railway and its 10-mile branch to Glasgow. However, by 1941, this short branch had only a mixed-train connection, with this Southern style "Jim Crow" combine. This car was the only rolling stock of the L&N's subsidiary Glasgow Railway.

MARCH 28, 1942, found me in Shelby, North Carolina, heading back to Akron, Ohio. My notice to be inducted into the U.S. Army during the following month had arrived, so I was en route to home. A couple of miles out of Shelby I found this little three-foot-gauge engine at the transfer point with the Seaboard Air Line railroad. The crew invited me to ride along to Lawndale, 11 miles out in the Piedmont hill country. No. 4's headlight had suffered some misfortune. So, two automobile lamps had been rigged as a replacement, giving the diminutive 2-8-0 sort of a "bug" appearance.

BOTH ENGINES of the Lawndale Railway had been built by Vulcan in 1909. No. 5 had suffered some damage, and as it turned out, she would not be used again. The little line was abandoned during the following year, after its protector, the old mill operator, J. F. Schenck, passed away. So, on March 28, 1942, I was seeing the line for my first and last time. Lawndale was the source of the road's traffic, a huge cotton mill.

THE LAWNDALE RAILWAY & INDUSTRIAL COMPANY

THIS COMPANY used only the minimum space for its listing in the *Official Guide.* And after giving its mileage of 11 miles (enumerating by miles the points on its route), there was the simple statement "Freight Service Only By Motor Truck" in its 1947 listing. Despite the name, there was not any railroad at all. However, there **had** been a railroad, a very interesting little narrow-gauge line, and I was lucky enough to see it and ride it during its last full year of operation.

My military notice had been telephoned to me, and here I was due to be inducted at Columbus, Ohio, exactly one month later. My boss wanted me to do as much advertising work as possible, delaying return to Akron until virtually the last day possible. I had the company's half-ton pickup truck and a load of materials, and he wanted this for storage at Akron during the war. Seiberling for many years had used an Old English "S" as a logo. However, my new boss had redesigned things and got rid of that "old-fashioned" emblem and replaced it with a sansserif angular "S" of blue on an orange background. The swastika—once an innocent emblem employed during the summer time on hundreds of canoes, etc.—was now a

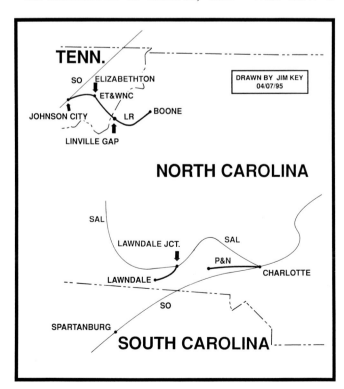

DRAWN BY JIM KEY
04/07/95

THE SOUTHERN STATES... 8

hated-and-feared emblem. The new Seiberling logo had a faint resemblance, which the choice of colors emphasized. In Buffalo, at the tire store in that heavily Polish town, a dealer had in alarm stopped the placing of the new emblem for fear he would get a brick through a window. And this pickup truck I was driving had the new logo emblazoned on its side, on a big sign running the length of the bed! However, I had no problems in the South.

So, during this Saturday in March, I detoured from downtown Shelby to find the Lawndale Railway for a look. I found a junction point with the Seaboard line, and there was a track going up a steep grade, passing a suburban group of houses and a typical cotton mill. Beyond this interchange point, the road more-or-less closely followed the little track. Not really expecting to see a train on the line, I was nearly to Lawndale, when here came the smallest 2-8-0 I had ever seen. This little Consolidation had a green tender, and trailing behind was a wooden boxcar and the smallest combination baggage-coach I had ever seen. The engine lacked a normal headlight; instead, it had a bug-like appearance from a pair of automobile headlights in the usual location.

Without hesitation, I turned around and paced the Lawndale train back to the junction, where a friendly crew smiled at my enthusiasm, posed for photographs and invited me to ride back up the line with them. The fireman said he would be coming into Shelby, and he would get me back to the pickup truck. Meanwhile, a couple of Seaboard freight trains hustled by, which emphasized the diminutive appearance of the little engine and its cars.

The little Lawndale engine made good time as it moved the short train over a rolling terrain, typical of North Carolina's western Piedmont country. Finally, we crossed a

THE LAWNDALE RAILWAY had only one trestle of any importance. It was located at the edge of Lawndale, North Carolina.

THE SOLE PASSENGER CAR of the Lawndale Railway was diminutive No. 101, which had to be the smallest narrow-gauge combine in the U.S. Being a Saturday, when there was no school, the neighborhood kids enjoyed a ride up the hill from the junction, a regular treat by the crew.

WHILE WAITING for the transferring of freight to be completed at Lawndale Junction, a Seaboard Air Line local freight came rumbling by. The contrast between the two gauges is strange.

RAILROADERS also like to watch trains! Everyone joined to look as a Seaboard double-headed through freight went thundering by at Lawndale Junction, in rural North Carolina. Notice the small water tank next to this little narrow-gauge line.

rather large trestle, and we ended our trip at a two-stall enginehouse nestled in the midst of the Cleveland cotton mill, owner of the railroad. There sat the companion engine, No. 5, somewhat out of service, and evidently it was not to run again. I was told that in being repaired a while back, someone dropped an open-end wrench somewhere inside the engine and forgot it. Later, the engine was tooling along to the junction, when suddenly, it stopped, its wheels locked and sliding. The baffled crew—after considerable work—opened up the cylinders and found the missing wrench in one of them. It had slid lengthwise by some jolt of the track and stopped the engine as effectively as a granite wall!

After picking up my truck at the junction,

OUT ON THE LINE, Lawndale No. 4 hustled along at about 25 miles per hour. This was a good speed considering the small diameter of the 2-8-0 locomotive's drivers.

I followed the fireman into town and invited him to have lunch with me as my guest, a small return for a pleasant morning. When we exited the cafe, there was a crowd of the usual Saturday courthouse-square loafers around my truck, as well as a deputy sheriff, standing beside his motorcycle. I had a sinking feeling of real trouble, although I could not think of anything unlawful I had done. The deputy sheriff asked if I had been by the Shelby Junction cotton mill, and the fireman volunteered that I had ridden the narrow-gauge line to Lawndale with them. The officer started to smile, and then said that two women who lived near the mill had come into the sheriff's office very distraught, to the point of hysteria, and they told a tale of a "Nazi spy," with a "big swastika," who was out there. The officer had a sense of humor and pointed to the logo and told me that when he saw that logo, he began to suspect that was the answer to the office's riddle. He said it had gone out on the radio to watch out for someone driving around with a big swastika, and that if anyone stopped me they should call the sheriff's office. And the crowd of gawkers drifted away, in obvious disappointment, as apparently there was no Nazi spy with an Ohio truck license! The rest of the way back to Akron I did not take many pictures, and when I did see something interesting of a railroad subject, I just looked, and I did not drag out my camera.

The two little Lawndale Railway's Vulcan engines of 1908–1909 vintage, with 12 x 16-inch cylinders and 33-inch drivers, weighing about 25 tons, went to the wartime scrap drive. Some of the car bodies sat around for many years, and at one siding, there was a couple of freshly painted boxcars. However, when I got within a couple hundred feet of them, I was almost overcome by the heavy odor of dead fish. Some misguided laborer had transferred a shipment of fish heads into these cars, and like refuse, they had been destined for fertilizer by farmers. The narrow-gauge line also hauled coal in for the mill, but of course, outbound freight consisted of all kinds of cotton products. Some of the cars were built by the railroad, including the little combine, No. 101. The crew told me they never had any other passenger cars, except some excursion cars made from flatcars or gondolas. For many years, the line reached into the town of Shelby, the final two miles by having a third rail at first on the Southern Railway, and then later, via the Seaboard in the same fashion. Around 1941, the third rail was removed, and transfers were made at Shelby Junction.

THE LANCASTER & CHESTER Railway in South Carolina was a line owned by a cotton mill, only 29 miles long, which operates between the towns in its name. The L&C's daily-except-Sunday mixed trains employed these odd cars in this view, in place of passenger cars. The X-702 formerly was a boxcar, which served as a baggage-express car, while the X-701 was a combination caboose-coach, with a few coach seats inside. The passenger portion of the caboose is in the near end, which was fitted with regulation coach steps and leaf-spring coach trucks.

AFTER A WEEKEND TRIP to Charlotte, South Carolina, I returned to Lancaster via the Lancaster & Chester's mixed train. The coach-caboose cupola made a good vantage point to watch the former Detroit, Toledo & Ironton 2-8-0 up ahead. The Lancaster & Chester's engine No. 41 was steaming across the rolling countryside en route to Lancaster.

LANCASTER & CHESTER RAILWAY

ON ONE FRIDAY I found myself in the little cotton-mill town of Lancaster, South Carolina, faced with the prospect of spending a long weekend until Monday or Tuesday, when my company's dealer was expected back in town. Until then, I had little opportunity to explore South Carolina railroads, so I got busy studying the *Official Guide's* timetables and maps. The mill, the producer of the much-advertised "Spring-maid" brand, owned the Lancaster & Chester Railway, which made two round trips daily to Chester, 29 miles away.

Lancaster was also on the Southern Railway's branch line that connected with the mainline at Rock Hill, about 23 miles to the north. I wanted to see and ride the electrified Piedmont & Northern's mainline between Spartanburg and Greenwood. So, after some study, I came up with one of the most complicated of several Southern weekends. The trip started with the Southern Railway's mixed train to Rock Hill, then went via the mainline to Charlotte, North Carolina. After that, it was back to the Southern again to Spartanburg.

The next morning the trip began with the 89-mile journey on the electric Piedmont & Northern, then went by the Seaboard line to Chester, where on Monday morning I boarded the Lancaster & Chester mixed. Despite the variety of lines and trains, only a few photographs were taken. The Southern was very hostile to cameras.

The L&C train, instead of the usual "to-be-expected" old wooden combine, used two side-door cabooses. One of them served as sort of a baggage-express car, and the other one was for the crew and passengers, if any. A half-dozen coach seats indicated that passengers were few. But I could sit in the cupola and enjoy the passing scene of rolling countryside. Along the way, we crossed a branch line of the Seaboard; however, there was no sign of the daily mixed train it professed. It was obvious that the L&C was a good adjunct of the cotton mill, as at Chester, the railroad exchanged traffic with the Carolina & Northwestern, which, however, was a subsidiary of the Southern. All of these connections undoubtedly obtained good freight rates for the mill.

Elliott W. Springs, head of the cotton mill and its railroad, was a flamboyant personage who garnered much fame from some rather daring advertising for Springmaid sheets. After World War II, the L&C took an entire page of the *Official Guide*, two-thirds of it a map. There was a fancy herald for the road, and the slogan "The Springmaid Line." Over 30 persons were listed as vice-presidents, most of them famous at the time in business. Four surgeons were listed, including one in Denver, Colorado, a good 1,800 miles away from any employee who might need him! A relative was "Chief Stewardess," while another man had what must have been the only such listing in the *Official Guide*, as "News Butcher." There was also a "Marine Superintendent," someone at Sapelo Island, Georgia. An Atlanta man was the "Superintendent of Motive Power." But despite all this, the line is now operated for freight and express shipments only—no more mixed trains.

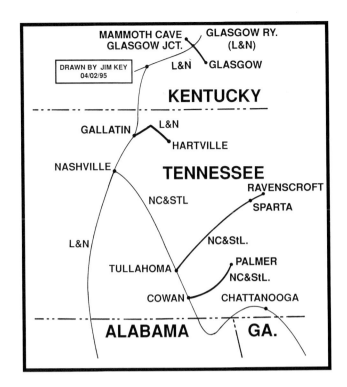

EAST TENNESSEE & WESTERN NORTH CAROLINA RAILROAD

AFTER RIDING the last train of the narrow-gauge Ohio River & Western in 1931, I wondered what other narrow-gauge railroads still existed, and upon checking the *Official Guide*, I found that over 15 still survived. Unfortunately, most of them had a dubious and probably very short futures. My interest in collecting postmarked covers of Railway Post Offices was to see which ones had such service. Other than four such routes in Colorado, there was one each in Maine, Tennessee–North Carolina, Oregon and California. And the one in Maine, the "Albion & Wiscasset R.P.O.," which was on the two-foot-gauge Wiscasset, Waterville & Farmington Railway, ended abruptly with the wreck of its passenger train in 1933.

Eventually, in September of 1936—despite the limitations of the Great Depression—I made the nearly 500-mile trip to Johnson City, Tennessee. I arrived on a Saturday, in time to watch the daily mixed train depart on its 66-mile trip through the Great Smoky Mountains to Boone, North Carolina. Noting a poster for a round-trip excursion for the next day—Sunday—I decided to take that train and then the mixed. **"Ho! For a Day of Mountain Pleasuring!"** is what the poster proclaimed. Fares of about a dollar were quoted to several mountain picnicking places, and fares were not much more to go all the way to Boone and back.

On Sunday morning, I found a neat Ten-wheeler, with three open-platform coaches and a screened-in flatcar, equipped with benches. About a hundred people boarded the train, which, after a fairly level 10 miles past Elizabethton, began its climb, featuring

BY NOVEMBER OF 1942, the East Tennessee & Western North Carolina Railroad was one of the last narrow-gauge railroads in the eastern U.S. Here, at Elk Park, North Carolina, a commuter train was meeting an eastbound freight. The freight train would go on to the end of the line at Cranberry, only two miles beyond Elk Park. To meet a need for workers at the wartime plants near Johnson City, Tennessee, many mountaineers and hill folk were hired, who lived along the ET&WNC. Without good roads or automobiles, train travel became necessary. So, with three old coaches, the narrow-gauge line ran daily trips.

ET&WNC TRAIN 2 of this narrow-gauge line was being made up in the Johnson City, Tennessee, yard. Behind the "Tweetsie" engine is a combination car, No. 15, all that remained of a former all-vestibuled passenger train. This combine was unique among narrow-gauge railroads in the U.S. The car had a Railway Post Office compartment, a baggage-express section and a tiny passenger portion, with plush seats accommodating 10 people. Behind No. 15 was one of the ET&WNC's unique trailers, on a special car. At Boone, North Carolina, the end of the line, a highway tractor will couple up and deliver the trailer to one of the places served by the railroad's motor-truck subsidiary. This scene, photographed on September 21, 1936, was common on the road until the summer of 1941, when a bad storm—a severe cloudburst—wrecked the railroad's eastern segment.

THE ET&WNC ENGINEHOUSE at Johnson City, Tennessee, looked like this in 1936. The stalls at the left and right were for narrow-gauge engines, while the center track was for standard-gauge motive power. To make sure that the wrong gauge engine could not go into the wrong space, the narrow-gauge tracks (in the two stalls at the left and right) did not have a third rail for standard gauge.

TRANSFERING FREIGHT at Johnson City, Tennessee, was a simple matter. The two cars at the right had brought azalea plants down from Pineola, North Carolina, to go out on the standard-gauge connection. For other kinds of loose, bulk freight, such as coal and ore, a small trestle and loading bunker was used. This scene was photographed on September 21, 1936.

the scenic Doe River Canyon. Gradually, we climbed up out of the canyon and ventured through several small communities. Much of the way, any roads were simply little-used dirt, and there would be glimpses of mountaineer's log cabins, and once there was a view of a great fireplace, with kettles swinging over a fire.

In less than two hours, we reached Cranberry, where the principal revenue freight of the line had originated, iron ore. Beyond this station, the tracks climbed through Linville Gap, the highest narrow-gauge railroad point east of the Mississippi River, 4,194 feet above sea level. This part of the ET&WNC was the subsidiary Linville River Railway, and a number of freight cars, and at least one coach, were lettered with this name.

At one little place, beyond a wye in the forest, was a glimpse of a logging railroad. At another place, near Grandfather Mountain, was a switchback, which wound way down into a deep mountain valley.

We dropped down steep grades, on the mountain slopes to reach Boone, a small town in extreme northwestern North Carolina. There was a stop in Boone for a couple of hours for lunch, to turn the train on the wye, and then, back we headed up the steep winding grade for the Gap. At Newland, a small settlement, we took siding to await the westbound mixed train.

Here, at Newland, I decided to catch the mixed train, stay overnight at Boone and come back the next day to Johnson City. The mixed came along headed by another cap-stacked 4-6-0, trailed by its sole passenger

car, then a couple of truck trailers on special low-slung cars, designed for that traffic, followed by some gondolas and boxcars.

The passenger accommodations were very limited. Combine No. 15, when built several decades earlier, had been the head-end car of a train of vestibuled coaches, with the parlor car "Azalea" on the tail end. After a fire destroyed a popular mountain resort, the cars were sold for use in Latin America, except for No. 15. It had a small Railway Post Office compartment, a baggage-express section, and a 10-person-capacity smoking compartment, with red-plush seats. If more than that number of passengers showed up, the overflow passengers sat on whatever they could find in the baggage compartment.

For postal purposes, this was the "Boone & Johnson City R.P.O.," and the clerk ex-

AN INFREQUENT FREIGHT on the East Tennessee & Western North Carolina Railroad—with No. 12 on the point—was approaching Elk Park, North Carolina, on November 18, 1942. The coal loads will be set out at the town, while the empties will go on to the end of the line at Cranberry. At that point they will be loaded with mine props, cut in the Smoky Mountains. I would not see Engine 12 again for over 50 years. It was a delight to see this cap-stacked Ten-wheeler once more, stepping along with a trainload of people on the "Tweetsie Railroad," at a theme park between Boone and Blowing Rock, North Carolina.

THIS WAS A RARITY in 1942, a narrow-gauge commuter train. Engine No. 11, with three wooden coaches, was waiting at Elk Park, North Carolina, to make its late-afternoon round trip to Johnson City, Tennessee. The train would pick up "hill-country" employees of a defense plant at Johnson City and drop them off at various points along the line. Then, the train would layover for the night at Elk Park, and it would take the commuters to work on the following morning. At this time—on November 18, 1942—No. 11 was one of the last three engines of the ET&WNC, Nos. 9, 11 and 12. At the end of World War II, Nos. 9 and 11 would be scrapped, and No. 12 would be sold to some promoters of a railroad in Virginia. Later, the 4-6-0 went to a theme park near Boone, North Carolina, where she still is operating on the "Tweetsie Railroad."

changed mail sacks with numerous small post-office routes scattered through the mountains. The sacks did not seem to be very full, but it was an important service to those isolated mountain people. I rode with the clerk for awhile, who obligingly carefully postmarked some covers I had brought along.

The truck trailers represented an important part of the East Tennessee & Western North Carolina Railroad's operations, its subsidiary "ET&WNC Motor Transportation Company," which not only sent in this fashion freight for points in North Carolina, but also operated some strictly motortruck routes to other points in both Tennessee and North Carolina.

On the way back from Boone on the next day, the train stopped at the junction with the Pineola Branch, which was several miles long. The postal clerk locked up his RPO, and he and I joined the crew on the engine as it backed down the branch to bring out a couple of boxcars that had been loaded with azalea plants. The next day, I saw these cars spotted alongside a standard-gauge boxcar of the Clinchfield Railroad in the Johnson City yard.

The road had dual-gauge track in its yard at Johnson City, and for about 10 miles out, as it moved quite a number of loads of standard-gauge freight for industries. The line's last standard-gauge engine had just been scrapped, and the road was using a husky little narrow-gauge 1907-built 0-8-0 for this switching work. No idler car seemed to be used, and the offset strain of coupling directly to loaded standard-gauge cars was hard on the engine's frame and machinery, and not long afterward, this engine was

CAP-STACKED TEN-WHEELER No. 12 of the ET&WNC Railroad had just set out a car of coal at Elk Park, North Carolina, and she was rolling along on the mainline. In a short time, No. 12 would take the rest of the freight train the remaining two miles to Cranberry, North Carolina. Another "Tweetsie" Ten-wheeler, No. 11, was waiting on the siding for its late-afternoon commuter run to Johnson City, Tennessee, to pick up a trainload of mountaineers, who worked at a defense plant during World War II. The date is November 18, 1942.

A THIRSTY LOCOMOTIVE, 4-6-0 No. 12, of the ET&WNC Railroad, was taking on water at Cranberry, North Carolina, the end of the line in 1942. After the Ten-wheeler's tender tank was replenished, the engine would do her switching chores at Cranberry. The two-track carshed was a busy place at one time. Incidentally, the "Tweetsie's" cap-stacked No. 12 was the prototype for a well-known half-inch narrow-gauge scale model for so-called "garden railroads" (large outdoor model railroads). Although this "G-gauge" Ten-wheeler does not go by its full-size railroad's "Tweetsie" nickname, it is a very accurate scale model of the distinctive cap-stacked engine.

scrapped, when it required an expensive overhaul. It was cheaper to buy another secondhand standard-gauge engine. The 0-8-0 was claimed to have been the heaviest narrow-gauge switcher ever built.

The combined enginehouse and machine shop had three tracks, with doors on the two outer tracks for narrow-gauge engines, while the center track had a much larger door to accommodate standard gauge. With railroader's propensity to eventually do something they should not, I wondered (but did not ask) what would happen if a standard-gauge engine got shunted to one of those narrow-gauge entrances.

To transfer bulk freight, the railroad had a small trestle on which tracks were dual gauge, as were those underneath, so that coal and other such materials could be easily dumped from one gauge cars to the other. The ET&WNC had some wooden hopper cars that looked like illustrations from a long-ago *Car Builders' Cyclopedia*.

In 1940, a terrific storm destroyed miles of this little line, with severe washouts beyond Cranberry, and the mixed runs and the RPO service came to an end. Freight service continued as far as Cranberry.

Then, during the World War II boom, caused by a rayon plant at Elizabethton, as well as a shortage of workers, the railroad agreed to run what amounted to commuter trains for workers both morning and evening, recruited in the mountains. So, for the duration of the war, twice a day a Tenwheeler and three coaches made the round trip. On my way home during November of 1942, on a furlough from Camp Forrest, Tennessee,I stopped off and spent a long day riding these trains. It was dark on the evening run, and the trainmen had a number of special signals to stop and let someone off at their mountain path. The passengers, often without a flashlight, would vanish down a path that only they seemed to know existed.

The crew recalled my earlier trip, and as only the engine went to Cranberry to turn around and obtain water, the railroaders took me along on a freight train headed that way. When at the war's end this narrow-gauge line was scrapped, I never again expected to see No. 12, the little 4-6-0, but 51 years later, in 1993, I was to see the trim Tenwheeler stepping along at the "Tweetsie Railroad," a three-mile line at a family park not far from Boone.

A MIXED TRAIN ON THE LOUISVILLE & NASHVILLE

WHEN TRAFFIC was normal, the Louisville & Nashville's Gallatin-to-Hartsville and Scottsville Branch saw light traffic over the lightweight rails on Mondays and Thursdays. This run was handled by a small Baldwin Consolidation, No. 666, and a waycar (caboose) was used for both crew and passengers, if indeed there were any of the latter. However, during late summer of 1942, Engine 666 had plenty of loads to handle. Hartsville was the unloading place for all manner of supplies for the U.S. Army troops from Camp Forrest, Tennessee, who were on maneuvers nearby.

Our signal outfit had a Saturday to kill, and we were sprawled along the hillside overlooking the busy railroad yard. I had a pass to go to Gallatin, but was not in any hurry to board a busy bus to join hundreds of other G.I.'s in that small county seat. But after talking to an L&N conductor, I learned that his run was a "mixed," and it soon would be ready to return to Gallatin. So, from the harried station agent at Hartsville, I bought a one-way ticket. And as the train departed from the yard, I was on the rear platform of the caboose, waving goodbye to my startled pals. Long before I got to Gallatin, they had spread the word that I had gone AWOL on a freight train. In any case, I am not sure they were pleased when I showed up back at camp that evening via bus.

AN ELDERLY L&N ENGINE was on the turntable at Hartsville, Tennessee, a point then served twice a week—with a caboose for passengers, if any. Having a pass from maneuvers to Gallatin, the county seat, I took this Louisville & Nashville train instead of the bus, and my fellow soldiers thought I was going AWOL. Everyone else rode on the bus, of course. However, the pass did not specify *how* I was to get to Gallatin!

ON TUESDAYS AND FRIDAYS in 1942, this 1903 Baldwin 2-8-0 handled the mixed train of the Louisville & Nashville from Gallatin, Tennessee. This was a light-railed branch to Scottsville and Hartsville, Tennessee. No. 666 was being turned on the Hartsville turntable, powered by hand. On this day, October 30, 1942, the little L&N locomotive had a lot of work to do, as the U.S. Army was holding maneuvers nearby, and Hartsville was the destination of many carloads of foodstuffs and other supplies. In another week, things will be back to the normal one or two freight cars.

NASHVILLE, CHATTANOOGA & ST. LOUIS RAILWAY

WHILE ASSIGNED to Camp Forrest, Tennessee, from April until November of 1942, *The Dixie Line* afforded some pleasant interludes away from that basic-training institution. I am sure the little town and the poor farming countryside enjoyed our presence no more than they did 80 years earlier, when General Nathan Bedford Forrest and his fellow Southerners were making things unpleasant for Yankees in that part of middle Tennessee. World War II had made the old Western & Atlantic of Civil War fame a very important and busy line again. En route in the troop train just south of Nashville, I had a taste of this when we had a "sawby" meet with another southbound train and a long northbound freight train.

The Nashville, Chattanooga & St. Louis Railway had too few locomotives and only a few of what it had were of fairly modern and heavy types. All the NC&STL engines had cap stacks, a hallmark of the company. Four daily passenger trains traveled between Nashville and Chattanooga. So, there always seemed to be something going on—coming through little Tullahoma (the station serving Camp Forrest).

Whenever I could obtain a daytime pass to town on a nice day, it was a short hike beyond the town limits to pick a shady spot along the rolling mainline and just watch trains, and even try for pictures. Sometimes, it seemed the first hint of an approaching train was the pant of the airpumps, whose exhaust was placed up alongside the engine's smokestack. The passenger trains apparently were tonnage affairs, including every coach the line could muster, plus plenty of head-end cars. Every third day, the famous *Dixie Flagler* passenger train passed through. This was an all-coach streamliner between Chicago and Miami, which started out on the Chicago & Eastern Illinois, then went by the L&N, NC&STL, AB&C, ACL and the Florida East Coast.

A couple of times, a pass with farther limits permitted me to ride a train the less-than-30-minute ride south to Cowan, at the foot of the steep grade to the old tunnel. Most trains needed a helper engine attached at Cowan, and a mixture of 2-8-0's, 2-8-2's and even a 2-10-0 were put on the head-end of passenger trains at this station. Three old Mallets were kept busy helping the freight trains. Cowan was a great place to watch the action.

One day, I was accosted by a local dentist, wearing a white jacket, who proceeded to tell me (seeing I was in uniform), "Soldier, there's a war on. You shouldn't be taking those pictures." He went on to identify himself as chairman of some local patriotic organization. At the time I was standing on the station platform, and a number of other people turned out to be locals—railroaders—also just killing time by watching trains. A couple of these men turned on the dentist and virtually ran him back to his drills with various sarcastic comments ringing in his ears. I was assured that I could take all the "blankety-blank" pictures I wanted. Back at the barracks, when a couple of the fellows heard of my little trip, they decided to go to Cowan. (After all, just about anywhere except Camp Forrest and Tullahoma was deemed to be an improvement!) When they went down to the town, a not-too-sober off-duty foreman invited them to ride in a Mallet with him, and before they really had looked the engine over, they were running it! They and the foreman had a great time running it up and down the yard!

A short branch line from Cowan went up to some coal mines, and it was served by a mixed train; however, I never found an opportunity to ride it. Out of Tullahoma was another mixed run to Sparta, 60 miles to the east, using an old wooden RPO-express car and an attractive wooden vestibuled coach. The local railroaders suggested that if I liked unusual railroads, I should be sure to ride the Centreville Branch sometime. This branch line left the mainline west of Nashville to wind incredibly through a very hilly region. Originally, this branch had been built as a narrow-gauge line, and it still exists today (as of 1994) as an independent short line.

One of the passenger trains was named *The Lookout*, and it carried a coach-observation car with an open platform on the rear, as well as an observation-coach-café car. For a weekend pass to Chattanooga, this was a very fine trip, through a very scenic region, with names of places vaguely familiar from Civil War history—following the Tennessee River the final 30 miles, once so vital as a

FOR BRANCH LINES, local freight trains and even as helpers, the NC&StL railroad relied on a fleet of these Ten-wheelers. Engine 281 was typical of the road's motive power—equipped with a cap stack and an exhaust pipe for the airpumps, which often was the first noise heard from an approaching train.

CUMBERLAND MOUNTAIN posed an operating problem between Nashville and Chattanooga, Tennessee, with miles of grades up to 2.4 percent, as the line climbed to a tunnel. Three 1915 Baldwin 2-8-8-2 Mallets were built for use as helpers at this point, operating from the small town of Cowan, Tennessee.

military objective. In the Chattanooga Union Station sat The General, the famous 4-4-0 from the "Great Locomotive Chase" of 1862. When the Confederates had control of the Western & Atlantic at the time, a group of Yankees had stolen the engine from its passenger train in Georgia, and they planned to wreck the railroad as they progressed northward to Chattanooga. They failed in their attempt, and in the National Cemetery atop Lookout Mountain we saw the marble monument to them, with *The General* carved on top of it.

SMOKY MOUNTAIN RAILROAD

SOME RAILROAD NAMES are intriguing, and I remembered that the Smoky Mountain Railroad was listed as running from Knoxville, Tennessee. Since I would be routing myself that way during a November, 1942, furlough to Ohio, I wrote the manager and was assured that the daily mixed train indeed did depart at 5:30 a.m.

The Southern Railway passenger train I took was running late. And it was not too many minutes before 5:30 in the morning when I went to the Knoxville ticket agent on duty to inquire where I would find the Smoky Mountain train. To my dismay, he very shortly told me that there was not any "...such railroad in Knoxville, soldier. You are in the wrong city." When I told him I had just recently had a letter from the road's manager, he somewhat snarlingly repeated his reply, adding that he had been an agent for many years and certainly knew what he was talking about. So, I asked him if I might look at his *Official Guide*, as by now I was half convinced I was in the wrong place. However, the *Guide* sustained me, and I said to him to listen, and when I read what it said in the *Guide*, his reply was a wave of his hand, and he turned his back toward me!

It was now just about 5:30 a.m., so I hurried outside and over to a bus station, where I got a taxi whose driver also had never heard of the Smoky Mountain line. Never-

theless, by asking some questions, we found the SM freight yard, a few tracks alongside a house, which must have been the railroad's office. *Too late!* Hanging above the bridge over the river was the smoke of the just-departed train! It turned out that by a switchback arrangement, the SM got up on the Southern Railway grade, and it then used its bridge to reach its own line, which branched off beyond the Southern span.

So, I rushed back to the local bus station,

THE SOUTHERN RAILWAY had some rather old and lightweight boxcars in November of 1942. (Notice the truss rods under the wooden cars.) They were being switched by two Smoky Mountain Railroad engines at their junction with the Southern at Knoxville, Tennessee.

176

where—within an hour—a bus was departing for Sevierville, and about half way to this town, we passed the mixed train, smokily working along behind the smallest 4-6-2 Pacific I had ever seen. At least by going by bus, I arrived at Sevierville in ample time to select a spot to snap a picture of the oncoming train—in fact, three trains. A Tennessee Valley Authority (TVA) dam was being built, and the other two trains were working on the construction branch. So, the Sevierville yard was a busy place, with plenty of railroad action for my camera.

The return to Knoxville was a pleasant trip aboard the mixed train, and as I told the crew about the Southern Railway station agent, they decided they were going to have a talk with that man—a talk I would have enjoyed hearing. They were scornful of his having worked in Knoxville for over 20 years and still did not know which railroads operated in town.

THE TURNTABLE AT SEVIERVILLE, Tennessee, was the best spot to photograph Mogul No. 206 of the Smoky Mountain Railroad, in what was an otherwise crowded and busy yard. A Tennessee Valley Authority (TVA) dam was under construction nearby, and many of the materials came via the SM line and a special spur. The contractor's engines operated in and out of Sevierville. No. 206 had two builder's plates, the original of 1910, and a second for an extra-order boiler in 1920.

THE COLUMBUS & GREENVILLE

"THE DELTA ROUTE"—as the Columbus & Greenville Railway was called—was a 168-mile line crossing the upper part of Mississippi from Columbus, Mississippi (near the Alabama border), to its western terminal at Greenville, on the Mississippi River (across the river from Arkansas). The railroad had been part of the Southern Railway, but became an independent line due to some financial matters affecting the big rail line. In the *Official Guide*, the C&G employed a full-page map and stressed "dependable freight

THE COLUMBUS & GREENVILLE'S No. 404, a 4-6-0 Ten-wheeler, was heading the daily mixed train as it rolled westward out of Indianola, Mississippi, during May of 1946. Cut-in the consist was a hopper car about half full of coal, to enable the train to return from Greenville, on the eastern trip on the following day. A coal strike was taking place at this time, and the C&G "Delta Route" had obtained just one car of coal in days. This enabled the road to make a round trip with this mixed train. The old cars at the right are in the C&G's Bridge & Building outfit service.

THE ABANDONED Fort Smith & Western line in Arkansas supplied this series of light Mikados for the Columbus & Greenville Railroad. I had tried my luck at this Sunflower water tank several times, but this was my last try. It was during May of 1946, and the white supremacists were very active at this time. Our dealer at nearby Indianola had cautioned me to "remembah you ah the only Yankee in Sunflower County," and then, the conductor of this mixed train had further warned me not to travel the dead-end road to the tank. Nearby planters along the road were hostile toward Yankees. I am certainly glad that I was not trying to take pictures when the civil-rights disputes broke out—and me with an Ohio license plate on my Plymouth!

"THE DELTAN" of the Columbus & Greenville Railroad was a good-looking train in its wine-color paint scheme. The observation platform was especially enjoyed in humid Mississippi for its "air conditioning." By the time this picture was taken at Winona, on May 27, 1946, the gas-electric system of the doodlebug had worn out, and a steam locomotive was hauling it on the schedule. The engine was off getting water at a nearby water tank when this view was recorded on film.

THE FIRST PASSENGER TRAIN on the Columbus & Greenville Railway, after John L. Lewis called his coal-miners out on strike during the spring of 1946, was photographed on May 18, 1946. This 168-mile line, which crosses Mississippi from Columbus to Greenville, exactly as its name implies, had been crippled by this strike. During the strike, the C&G "Delta Route" could obtain only a single car of coal from the Birmingham area on a now-and-then basis. So, instead of a passenger train, a mixed train and generally two daily freight trains, the road was reduced to one mixed train, carrying with it a partly empty car of coal when it left Columbus. When it completed a round trip the next day, its future runs depended on whether or not some coal had arrived at Columbus in the meantime. I had been trapped at Indianola, a little town on the western end of the C&G, because my advertising materials were held up for two weeks by delays in transit due to the strike. I was definitely not enjoying my status in this community. As the company's dealer in this town reminded me, "You ah the only Yankee in Sunflower County," and I found no satisfaction in that distinction. So, I certainly was glad to find this ancient Ten-wheeler, C&G No. 178, coming along with its three-car consist—and right on time. This pastoral scene was photographed at Kilmichael, in the red-hill country east of the rich Yazoo delta.

and passenger service... from, to and through the Mississippi Valley." From Greenville a two-car gas-electric train made a daily round trip, advertised as "air conditioned" and named *The Deltan*. There was also a daily mixed train each way, requiring—if on time—four more hours than the five-hour trip of *The Deltan*. Their advertisement also gave the schedule for a daily 10-hour through freight train.

The motive power was mostly old Southern Railway engines, including a number of small 4-6-0 types, as well as 2-8-0's. For the heavy freight trains, a handful of light 2-8-2 engines were used, these Mikados having come from the abandoned Fort Smith & Western in Arkansas. The gas-electric train was wearing out by 1946, so it was simply hauled by one of the lighter Ten-wheelers. The wine-colored train was attractive, had an RPO section in the head-end unit, as well as a large "Jim Crow" compartment. The trailer car had an observation end, innovative for a

gas-electric train. The mixed train used older wooden mail-express cars and some well-maintained vestibuled wooden coaches. There were many passengers, mostly making short journeys, and there was much exchange with other lines that were crossed en route, which included several north-south lines of the Illinois Central's subsidiary Yazoo & Mississippi Valley, the Gulf, Mobile & Ohio and several roads at Columbus.

Union leader John L. Lewis called a coal-miners' strike just after I arrived at Indianola, Mississippi, to handle the advertising setup for a new dealer at the edge of this small town, about 25 miles east of Greenville. And my advertising material was delayed indefinitely "somewhere" due to the ensuing railroad curtailments and embargoes. With nothing to do but wait, I employed a lot of waiting time in taking pictures of the Columbus & Greenville, and I even went for a couple of train rides. Just east of Indianola, there was a usual water stop at the Sun-

flower tank, where in earlier times, there had been an important meeting with steamboats on the Sunflower River. The terrain across the rich cotton-growing Yazoo Delta was mostly flat, and the track was reasonably straight. East of Greenwood, it became hilly, and the land became poorer.

Eventually, the railroad began to run out of coal, its only source being from mines not struck near Birmingham, Alabama. However, the demand for coal was such that the C&G could obtain only a carload now and then. The passenger run was taken off, and the mixed dragged along, hours late—with a car half full of coal heading for Greenville. On the next day, when the train came east, it still had the car in the consist, but it was now virtually empty, and the conductor predicted that unless they found a new car of coal at Columbus, "...there'll be no train on the morrow."

Finally, the strike ended, and normal train service resumed, and before long, I got a call that my express shipment was in. Borrowing the dealer's pickup truck and a black helper, we started to leave for the C&G; however, just then, a heavy rain started, and as the helper would be soaked riding in the open bed, I told him to get in the truck cab. Upon arrival at the freight depot, the rain had stopped, and the helper quickly scuttled out of the cab. Unfortunately, the agent was holding a "white supremacist" meeting under the open-sided platform, with an audience of a dozen or more "rednecks." The agent turned on me, and in blistering language, he cataloged me as an ignorant "damn Yankee," and apparently I was the personification of all the dangers that were implied for Mississippi. There was a considerable barrage in foul adjectives about the "Lost Cause" and the evils the Yankees had left behind in the "War Between the States." When "down South," I had kept a very low profile on these matters, avoiding discus-

sions of the myths that everything was the fault of Yankees, etc.

Ordinarily, I would have ignored the comments and gone into the office to take care of my business; however, this vindictive outburst was so personal that my anger overrode my caution, and I answered the agent with a short talk to the rednecks, starting out by saying that I respected the flag under which their grandfathers fought so bravely. And I had visited, as a student of history, many of those places made famous during the War Between the States. Beyond that, I was sure that if those war veterans could return, they would stand beside me and say that they had not fought for some of the things the Confederate flag was now being dragged in the mud about. I went on to say that after listening to the agent, I was proud to be a Yankee, and I was prouder still of my ancestors who fought in the war... and so on.

None of the men made one word of re-

THE ILLINOIS CENTRAL dominated much of Mississippi with its Chicago–New Orleans route, as well as numerous branches, which operated under the name of the Yazoo & Mississippi Valley Railroad. However, the Y&MV engines were simply lettered for the IC. This is a typical Illinois Central engine of 1946, 2-8-0 No. 720, at Leland, Mississippi. As the IC hauled large quantities of coal, its engines tended to put out much smoke, as they tried to burn the mine-run coal they were given—often poor stuff, with a lot of dirt in it.

sponse, and there certainly was no applause. But the agent had nothing to say, either. He just glared at me! So, I picked up my delayed express shipment, and when I got back to the dealer's store, he had already heard of the confrontation. He told me that what I had said was right, but this was not the right place to say it. Obviously alarmed, he told me that I dare not go into the town again, that if I needed anything from the hardware store or anywhere else, he would have one of his helpers do the errand for me. Moreover, he told me that if I wished to go to dinner, I could not go to the hotel, but I would have my choice of driving to either Greenville or Greenwood. Otherwise, it seemed I was limited to the little bus station cafe at the crossroads nearby! He pointed out "...that you ah the only Yankee in Sunflower County!" It might be mentioned that the population of this county was 70 percent black.

One odd result of this was that one afternoon, I chased the eastbound mixed train toward the little place of Ittabena, where it stopped to do some switching. The conductor motioned to me, and I thought "Here comes more trouble," but instead, he warned me not to go down the dead-end dirt road to Sunflower tank, as the "...planters on both sides are those kind of people." Moreover, he told me that if I had any trouble with anyone, just to give his train a washout signal, and they would pick me up, as the engineer felt the same way he did, and that I had said the right things. All of this made me feel like a foreigner a long way from home, and I almost yielded to the urgent telephone call from my boss, telling me to drop things and come back to Ohio. However, I stayed to finish the job. That there was some very real danger was shown several years later, when Indianola became the focus of national attention from the lynching of an "uppity" young black kid from Chicago. And, of course, I was an *uppity Yankee!*

THE DE KALB & WESTERN was a little 12-mile lumber road, typical of many in the South. It connected with the Gulf, Mobile & Ohio at the junction point of Sucarnoochee, Mississippi. This was in the central eastern part of the state. The neatly maintained 2-6-0, No. 504, was typical of a time when engine crews took pride in their engines. The coach was a typical Southern combine, with one end for the "colored," while the other end was for "white folks." The little Mogul was photographed on February 4, 1942.

WOODBURNERS IN THE WOODS

BY THE TIME I was taking railroad pictures, woodburning locomotives had vanished from America's mainlines decades earlier. A few places where the railroad served a large logging operation and sawmills, some engines were supplied with the bark slash from the logs and other scrap from the mills. This would be piled high on the tender, as this type of fuel burned very fast, and even small locomotives consumed it rapidly.

While wandering around the South, I came across three woodburning lines. In Florida the 64-mile Live Oak, Perry & Gulf was owned by the lumber company that supplied all of its traffic. At Foley, Florida, where the mill was located, engines were loaded with a towering load of mill scrap; however, this was not nearly enough fuel for the 128-mile round trip to Live Oak and return. So, on the return trip the next day, one or more stops would be made along the line to "wood up." At these points, stacks of "pine knots"—irregularly shaped chunks of

pine stumps from cut-over timber lands— were piled on platforms built close to the main track. A crew of black laborers would be waiting, and as soon as the engine pulled alongside, they industriously tossed the so-called knots into the tender's bunker. Apparently, the cutting and hauling of this fuel was their sole occupation, but it was not very expensive, as wages in the backwoods were low, frequently amounting to only $14.00 for a six-day work week. During the early days of railroading, the supplying of wood for engine fuel was a source of income for many rural residents.

The freight-only Mariana & Blountstown managed to cover its 29-mile route in northwestern Florida, using just the mill scrap, which was piled as high as possible on the tenders of this line's handsome Ten-wheelers. These 4-6-0's carried straight smokestacks, and apparently the area was so humid that forest fires were evidently of no concern, despite the great amount of hot sparks the woodburners showered on both sides of the track.

The 17-mile Mississippi & Alabama line

had only two locomotives, both equipped with straight stacks. Fortunately, for my interest, the regular engine was laid-up for repairs, and the railroad was using an ancient Mogul, so ancient that she had the old-style dome castings of the 1880's. By daylight, the clouds of hot sparks were not very noticeable as the 2-6-0 switched the junction tracks at Vinegar Bend, Alabama. However, I found after watching her for perhaps an hour that my shirt was speckled with little burn holes. When I rode behind the 2-6-0 aboard the ancient, rickety caboose, I could see behind us now and then a clump of weeds aflame. The engine was burning a tender-load of pine knots at the Bend, which produced enough black smoke to please even the smokiest desires of a perspicacious Lucius Beebe. From the sawmill, the engine took on a load of bark scrap, intended to last the 17 miles back to Leakesville, Mississippi. Along the way we were met by a Heisler locomotive doing switching for a veneer mill, which also was using mill scrap for fuel.

Even though the engines of the Live Oak, Perry & Gulf were equipped with the turban-appearing Rushton smokestack, specially designed to control sparks from wood-burners, when riding that train from Live Oak at the pre-dawn departure time of 3:30 a.m., the view ahead toward the engine provided an amazing mass of red sparks showering the right-of-way. Looking back now and then, I could see a clump of weeds or bushes—missed by sparks of earlier trains—erupt in quite a column of flames, which concerned the crew not at all. The small conflagration burned itself out, and the crew apparently knew it would not spread. The only comparison to a coal-burning engine's output of sparks would be if the coal-burner had been sitting idle for a while, or if the fireman had shoveled-in a powdery residue of coal from the tender.

DRAWN BY JIM KEY
04/12/95

MISSISSIPPI & ALABAMA RAILROAD

THIS 17-MILE CARRIER featured wood-burning locomotives. At the time of my visit to Vinegar Bend, Alabama, where the M&A met the Gulf, Mobile & Ohio, this short line did not seem to be too prosperous. The rails were quite worn, and the timber trestle over the Chickasawhay River was reinforced with a variety of additional ties, which resembled slabs from the local sawmill at the Bend. And farther along the line, a veneer mill had its own switcher, a Heisler type of geared locomotive. At Leakesville, Mississippi, the end of the line, was the shop and terminal, as well as the location of another lumbering firm.

The big event of the morning at Vinegar Bend was the stopping of the southbound *Rebel* streamliner of the Gulf, Mobile & Ohio. The train stopped here to exchange a couple of passengers and some sacks of mail, which had been carried aboard the M&A's little green homemade railbus. I tarried to take more photographs of the ancient molded domes of Mogul No. 62, which was at work switching, and the crew agreed that if I wished to pay fare to ride in their equally ancient and decrepit-looking waycar, instead of the railbus, it was okay.

185

THIS ANCIENT hand-me-down Mogul from the Mobile & Ohio, was the sole working motive power of the 17-mile Mississippi & Alabama Railroad in February, 1942. The road's decrepit caboose had served as a convict car in the past. The 2-6-0 continuously poured out thick black smoke and hot sparks from its fuel of "pine knots." By the end of my round trip, my shirt was speckled with burn holes! In the background are the combined depot and warehouse of the lumber company at Vinegar Bend, Alabama.

Engine 62 lacked builder's plates, but she allegedly was formerly a Mobile & Ohio engine. The old side-door waycar had traces of paint remaining, and the crew informed me that during an earlier life, the car was used to haul convicts to work projects. The wood-burner put out plenty of sparks, and behind the train would rise blazing clumps of weeds or brush, one after another. However, this merited no attention from the crew, as the fires did not spread, and they would quickly die out.

THE "GULF COAST REBEL" of the Gulf, Mobile & Ohio exchanged mail sacks and a few passengers at Vinegar Bend, Alabama. This daily "passenger train" of the Mississippi & Alabama, homemade Railbus 301, was painted bright green! The M&A was not to be outdone too much by the GM&O streamliner!

186

THE LUSH WEEDS and brush along the Mississippi & Alabama Railroad were kept more-or-less under control by the passing of the line's wood-burning locomotives! Engine 62 was wyeing at Vinegar Bend, Alabama, in February, 1942.

The timber trestle over the river was long and not too sturdy in appearance, and within about an hour we arrived at Leakesville. There, the other engine, No. 4, a 2-8-0, seemed to be somewhat dismantled and obviously receiving a major overhaul. My return to Vinegar Bend was by the little railbus, whose operator was very sociable and expounded about the countryside, which lacked much in the way of inhabitants and seemed to be cut-over timberlands.

Upon disembarking, I noticed as a sort of souvenir of my day on the M&A that my shirt was dotted with small holes. These holes were burned by the generous amount of wood sparks that the old No. 62 lavished upon not only the countryside, but Yankee visitors as well.

THE SOUTH'S FAVORITE ENGINE THE TEN-WHEELER

WHILE DRIVING along anywhere in the South, except along the "racetrack" main-lines along the Atlantic seaboard—where there was stiff competition for the Florida traffic—it would be a safe bet that if you saw smoke in the distance from an approaching engine, it would be a 4-6-0. With both big roads and small ones, this wheel arrangement seemed to be the most popular one for handling both freight and passenger trains, and of course, for the numerous mixed-train schedules.

Ten-wheelers of the smaller classes were ideal for the often-rolling terrain, on track

THE MARIANNA & BLOUNTSTOWN Railroad was a 29-mile lumber road running from a connection near Chattahoochee, in extreme northwestern Florida. The Marianna & Blountstown's three 4-6-0 woodburning locomotives had a strange spread in numbering, as the other two Ten-wheelers were No. 101 and No. 444, all Baldwins. Another strange feature about the line was its two-inch listing in the *Official Guide*, which listed every one of a dozen places, and then, a notation next to the scheduled time that it was a "freight-only" operation. This listing was published in 1942, and the railroad made news headlines when its owners used it years later in a manipulation that raised many eyebrows in the financial world.

DESPITE A METICULOUS point-by-point listing in the *Official Guide*, this scheduled freight train of the Marianna & Blountstown was hours late. With a pile of scrap wood in the tender, No. 101, a Baldwin 4-6-0, the engines operated with straight stacks, and they showered hot sparks over the countryside. The small fires springing up along the route did not seem to be noticed by any one except me. This Florida scene was photographed on February 7, 1942.

with light rail and not much ballast. Some 4-6-0's originally intended for passenger service had fairly large drivers, while others had drive wheels down in smaller freight sizes, such as 44 inches, for example. One narrow-gauge line, the East Tennessee & Western North Carolina, employed only 4-6-0's. More than once, I would be fooled by some rather small engine, which I would guess from a distance might be a Mogul (2-6-0) or American (4-4-0) type, only to find out it was a low-drivered light Ten-wheeler. And into the diesel age, this type of engine worked until the last of steam power went to the scrap yard.

The Southern roads did not require large tenders with their Ten-wheelers. As roadmasters pointed out, the tender was the least stable item in a train, because of the fluctuations in its load of water and fuel, which sometimes resulted in dangerous rocking of the tender on "secondary" track, or should

we say third-rate track. Railfans learned early not to stand too close to branch-line trackage, as rocking tenders now and then could drop off a sizeable hunk of coal.

LIVE OAK, PERRY & GULF RAILROAD "THE FLORIDA WOODBURNER"

UPON LOOKING UP the Live Oak, Perry & Gulf Railroad in northern Florida, I found it interesting to see it was a woodburning outfit. So, I got up early one day, at 3:30 a.m., to ride their early mixed train from little Live Oak, Florida. It was dark so early in the morning, and from the combination coach, one could see a lively shower of wood sparks raining down on the right-of-way from a hustling balloon-stacked 4-6-0 up ahead. Looking back from the rear platform, one

THE 3:45 A.M. MIXED TRAIN of the Live Oak, Perry & Gulf, out of Live Oak, Florida, was waiting to be "wooded up" in the midst of the cut-over timberlands in northern Florida. The stumps were chopped up to be used for engine fuel—making thick, black smoke—and despite the screen in the big "cabbage" stack, many hot sparks were thrown out. These sparks set numerous small fires in the weeds along the right-of-way, but they soon died out.

LOWER RIGHT: "Wooding up" on the Live Oak, Perry & Gulf looked like this! Even this small steam locomotive consumed wood at a surprisingly rapid rate, and twice during a three-hour trip, the train had to stop to wood up.

A SMALL FLEET of these Ten-wheelers was operated by the Live Oak, Perry & Gulf Railroad. They were all wood-burners, which handled trains on the LOP&G's 44-mile mainline from Live Oak to Foley, Florida. At Foley, the road's owner, the Brooks-Scanlon Corporation, had a huge lumber-mill complex. Before heading back up the line, the engine's tender would be piled high with scrap wood and bark waste from the mill. Coming back, the train might stop a couple of times to "wood up" from piles of "pine knots"—old tree stumps that had been cut up for fuel. Sometimes, the train would take a branch to Mayo, Florida, following the Suwanee River (made famous by song writer, Stephen Foster). In this instance, No. 101 was at Mayo on February 20, 1942, and the engineer was oiling around while freight was being loaded.

was able to view one blaze after another, as they flared up among the trackside weeds and bushes. However, no one seemed concerned; apparently, all the flare-ups burned out without spreading in the lush but damp countryside.

Near Dowling Park, some 17 miles out and the first station stop, we stopped at a "wooding-up" platform, where a crew of black section men pitched up what looked as if they were chopped tree stumps into the tender. That indeed was what the fuel was, and they were all full of resin, and the engine ate them at a hungry pace, emitting plenty of black smoke in the process.

Not long after leaving Dowling Park, we crossed the Suwannee River on a long-and-curving trestle. The river was not at all the kind of stream expected from the song. Its water was dark from mangrove discoloring, and tangled tree roots obscured its banks. Just beyond the river crossing was Mayo Junction, and on the return trip we made a 12-mile side trip down the branch to the

namesake of the junction, a tiny settlement. The run ended at the mill town of Foley, where the Brooks-Scanlon Corporation, owners of the railroad, had a huge lumber mill.

Upon our arrival, engine No. 5, their switcher, was about to go to work. No. 5 was a neat little 2-6-2, whose dusky fireman was completing the job of wiping down and polishing the engine, including the tender. Even the Rushton smokestack gleamed. Brass candlesticks flanked the headlight, and some color and white striping enhanced its appearance. The engine's tender was heaped with waste slabs from the mill. Our road engine's tender was also stacked high with that source of fire wood.

Only a year or two after my visit, the company embarked on an ill-advised venture of converting the engines to coal. Shortly afterward, costs went up, and various other problems plagued the line. So, in the end, the Live Oak, Perry & Gulf was converted to diesel power, and the steam-engine fleet was cut up.

THE BEAVER, MEADE & ENGLEWOOD line was a 105-mile subsidiary of the M-K-T "Katy" system. The B-M-E extended way out into the panhandle of Oklahoma, a rather flat, isolated region. This was the B-M-E's sole car, and since they listed Trains 1 and 2 as mixed "irregular service," this must have been the mixed-train car you rode in, whenever it "went." While walking back out of the weeds after shooting this picture, I found that I was accompanied by a large tarantula spider. So, this day, September 21, 1946, ended my walking through weeds in either Oklahoma or Texas to take pictures. I did have a golf club to "swish" them with, but I declined to wear the "pointy-toed" boots the natives loved. Evidently, you have to be raised to wear them because they hurt my feet! It seems as though my Yankee feet were not designed for "cowboy boots."

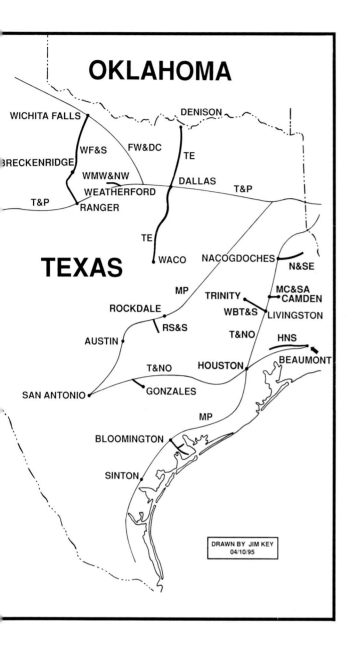

OKLAHOMA

WICHITA FALLS

DENISON

WF&S   FW&DC

BRECKENRIDGE

TE

WMW&NW

DALLAS

WEATHERFORD

T&P

TE

RANGER

T&P

TEXAS

TE

WACO   NACOGDOCHES

N&SE

MP   TRINITY

MC&SA
CAMDEN

ROCKDALE

WBT&S   LIVINGSTON

RS&S

T&NO

HNS

AUSTIN

T&NO   HOUSTON

BEAUMONT

SAN ANTONIO

GONZALES

MP

BLOOMINGTON

SINTON

DRAWN BY JIM KEY
04/10/95

THE HAMLIN & NORTHWESTERN

SOME OF THE SHORT LINES had an aura of mystery about them, with nothing much in information to be gleaned from standard sources. One such line was the Hamlin & Northwestern Railroad in western Texas. During a brief stop at Hamlin to check out our tire dealer, I hunted up the H&N. However, all I could find was a switch on the Santa Fe system, just north of Hamlin itself.

The track curved through some sandhills, and after walking a quarter-mile or more, and nothing changed, I gave up. Evidently any terminal was not near this junction.

Inquiry of the Santa Fe station agent was a disappointment, as he was a temporary agent, and he professed that he had never heard of the Hamlin & Northwestern. I tried the conductor of a local freight train, and he also professed ignorance, since he was an extra man, replacing the regular man. I did not bother to mention my wonderings to the tire dealer, as he never seemed to know anything about railroad matters. In this instance, I was really wrong... he *owned* the railroad! But I did not learn that until months later, and I was never in Hamlin again.

Long after this incident, with some time to spare in Austin, Texas, I inquired of the elderly clerk at the State Railroad Commission, and he fetched the file. It only added to the mystery. The annual report showed the road had handled 300 carloads of freight, but it owned no rolling stock, and the spaces for type and quantity of motive power were blank. Nothing was owned, leased, rented or borrowed. The clerk "tsk-tsked" at this lack of information on the form, and he declared that he would have to request them to properly make their return, but I suspect that after my departure, the file went back into the cabinet, and that was that.

The road showed 10.2 miles of line from Hamlin to Flat Top for freight service only, with the manager residing at Chillicothe, many miles to the north. Built in 1929, it was abandoned in 1956. Early listings in the *Official Guide* show that it connected with both the Katy and the Abilene & Southern at Flat Top, evidently an error for Hamlin. There was no mention of the Orient line, which became the Santa Fe—another mystery.

193

THE LOCOMOTIVE BACKSHOP of the Rock Island line at El Reno, Oklahoma, had quite an accumulation of dead motive power in September of 1946. Since most Southwestern lines were still busy moving postwar freight, I was surprised to see these three recently overhauled locomotives set aside, all heavy 4-8-4 types. These modern Chicago, Rock Island & Pacific engines were Nos. 5020, 5025 and 5017, equipped to burn oil, which was plentiful in the Southwest.

Perhaps someday someone will be encountered in information about the Hamlin & Northwestern, perhaps even with a photograph or two of whatever mysterious power moved those 300 carloads of freight!

THIS ROCK ISLAND TRAIN was typical for a gas-electric run during the 1920's–1940's period. This "doodlebug" was on the 231-mile route of the CRI&P from Little Rock, Arkansas, to Winnfield, Louisiana. All over the U.S., branch-line locals had been replaced rapidly with trains like this one. However, the trains to watch for, if the doodlebug was laid-up in the backshop, were the usual replacements, older steam power, with heavyweight passenger cars. This train was leaving El Dorado, Arkansas, on June 2, 1946, and the gas-electric unit was CRI&P No. 9071, followed by an older, heavyweight steel coach, with six-wheel trucks.

ON ALL FRISCO MAPS and folders, Floydada, Texas, was marked importantly. It was a "let down" in July of 1946, when I found only some yard trackage, a few cars and not much else at this station. The only locomotive in sight was this Decapod, which the setting sun highlighted very nicely. From the ground, the builder's plate was incomprehensible, which I thought was because it was dirty. However, when I climbed on the engine to get a closer look, the lettering on the Baldwin plate was in Cyrillic. This was one of a large number of broad-gauge 2-10-0's built for Russia, but never delivered there because of the revolution of 1918. Actually, the line into Floydada was trackage of the subsidiary "Quanah Route," the Quanah, Acme & Pacific Railway, which had been projected to go to El Paso, but never made it.

FORT WORTH, TEXAS, had received a storm on New Year's Eve which left the city with way-below freezing temperatures, and there was a sheet of ice everywhere. I had planned to spend the day driving around, but the fender-benders caused by Texans not used to driving on ice, discouraged that idea. So, I walked over to snap pictures of this switching of a Frisco 2-8-0, No. 1263. This was at their freight house, while at the left was a Texas & Pacific crew, struggling with the slippery weather. The date was January 2, 1947.

TEN-WHEELER No. 605 of the Kansas City Southern Railway was backing her train into the station of Shreveport, Louisiana, and she will shortly take off for Hope, Arkansas. It was June of 1946, and within a few years, most of the KCS system's trains will be gone. Shreveport was a very important junction point on the Kansas City Southern mainline.

MISSOURI PACIFIC EXPERIENCES

LAKE CHARLES, LOUISIANA, was interesting for several reasons, and it was worth remembering. A daily passenger train came in with a through sleeping car from St. Louis, headed by an Atlantic (4-4-2). The Missouri Pacific roster of engines showed the road's years of financial problems, for the freights struggled with 2-8-0 types, and even typically Southern with a 4-6-0. At Lake Charles, the engine crews would tie-up at the depot in town. Then, the hostlers would come into town, couple-up the three or four engines and drag them the couple of miles out to the engine terminal, out in the marshes beyond the town.

Odd combinations worth recording by camera included an 0-6-0, 4-6-0, 2-8-0, 4-4-2 and even one of the very first diesel-electric switchers of the Missouri Pacific. For the two-mile trip, the lead engine would sport white flags.

P. J. Neff, chief executive officer of the Missouri Pacific, gave a talk at the Lake Charles Chamber of Commerce while I was there, and I read his remarks in the next day's newspaper. He deplored the road's financial stringency, which forbade adding streamliners, etc., and he told his audience that changes must come slowly. Now, I had been impressed with the MP's mechanical-department people. The engines were kept clean, carried neat white striping along the running boards and sounded as though the men were doing their best. As I worked with advertising, I sat down that night in the hotel and wrote some suggestions to Mr. Neff. One was to employ the buzz-saw logo by having it made in enamel on metal, as sign companies did, which was then rather inexpensive, and to apply the logo in place of huge numbers on the tenders. I also suggested to apply the logo elsewhere, such as on passenger cars, next to the doors.

It may be that I tactlessly referred to the no-longer necessity of using huge numbers on engine tenders. However, the reply was hardly what I expected. It literally "blasted me" and my ideas, declaring that the huge numbers were needed for visibility and safety. And Mr. Neff absolutely rejected my ideas for using the buzz saw emblem as suggested. His reply was certainly no "thank you for your kind interest"! Long afterward, when I showed my boss the two letters, he laughed and reminded me of his opinion of railroad-management people. He believed they were old-fashioned and behind the times, and Mr. Neff exemplified just that.

Lake Charles' other claim to my memories was a popular restaurant outside town, whose specialty was shrimp Creole, and during my brief stay, I certainly enjoyed the best of that Louisiana dish I have ever encountered!

It is not often that a locomotive numbered "one" is encountered, even on short lines. Nevertheless, the mighty Missouri Pacific was different even in this regard. One day, while keeping my eyes fixed on approaching smoke in Arkansas, here came No. 1 at the head of the McGehee-Warren mixed train. There was no coach or combination car on the rear end of the train, just a caboose.

Later, I was to come across other low-number engines on the MP, all in the same 2-8-0 series, such as No. 25. The MoPac numbering system was wide-ranging, with lowly 0-6-0 switchers bearing numbers up to the 9500 series. Much of this had to do with the numerous large and small corporate entities included in the system, some quite small, such as the Sugar Land Railway. The railroad initials could be seen on sand domes, usually on engines far away from their initialed owner.

MISSOURI PACIFIC LINES
HOUSTON NORTH SHORE RAILWAY

THE MISSOURI PACIFIC was a huge railroad system, better known in financial circles than anywhere else. And after World War II, the MoPac was struggling to survive all the paper it was burdened under. It had scads of little branch lines, often with seasonal service, many with regular passenger or mixed trains, and it seemed to have lines extending everywhere in the lower half of Texas and adjoining states. The trend to highway trans-

ONE OF THE FEW ATLANTICS remaining on the sprawling Missouri Pacific system was No. 5535, shown here as she departed from Lake Charles, Louisiana, during July of 1946. The 4-4-2 was hauling the connection for a through train to St. Louis, Missouri. At least, the Pullman car went all the way to St. Louis.

"QUADRUPLE-HEADERS" were not needed in the flat country around Lake Charles, Louisiana—not far north of the Intracoastal Waterway, Calcasieu Lake and the Gulf of Mexico. As engines accumulated at this station, where the crews signed off, a hostler took them to the MP engine terminal, located in a marsh a couple of miles away. Engine 9450 was the 0-6-0 switcher hauling No. 2313, a 4-6-0, No. 5535, a 4-4-2 and No. 41, a 2-8-0, on August 1, 1946.

199

portation was taking away both short-haul and passenger business, and this changed the MP a great deal.

Listed as the "Electric Division of the Beaumont, Sour Lake & Western" was a 33.3-mile branch termed the "Houston, Baytown & Goose Creek." Half a dozen daily trips were scheduled from the Houston Union Station to Goose Creek, but it turned out that a bus, instead of a train or electric car—as might be expected—operated to the outskirts of Houston, to McCarty Avenue. There, the passengers transferred to a lightweight olive-green trolley car, nicely lettered in gold for the Missouri Pacific and flashing the buzz-saw emblem. At a good clip of 40-45 mph, the electric car bounced along the flat terrain, making a number of stops for refinery workers along the way, principally at Baytown. As freight service was conducted by standard MP 2-8-0 locomotives, these would often be met en route.

The town of Goose Creek had the car barn, a reversing loop and a few extra tracks,

one of which held the electric line's steeple-cab freight engine, obviously now retired. Here, too, one could get a look at the really oddball items among the rolling stock. This railroad handled a large amount of mail, express and L-C-L shipments, so the Goose Creek line had some combination road-rail contraptions that, upon reaching McCarty Avenue, a hydraulic system would move the flanged wheels up to allow the vehicle to rest on rubber tires. It would then drive off the concrete pad at the end-of-track, enabling it to use the city streets to reach the station in Houston. These road-rail buses had a small passenger compartment up front and a mail-express-L-C-L section in the rear. The railroad touch was made by a standard locomotive headlight; mounted on the roof. I was assured that it was used only while the bus was on the rail line.

There was an element of risking your life while riding on this line. Local tank-truck drivers would step on the pedal when leaving Baytown, and the one flat angular grade

SANDOW, TEXAS, in October of 1946, was the site of a lignite-coal mine and the small railroad terminal of the Rockdale, Sandow & Southern. This town did not even have a post office, and the one in nearby Rockdale sufficed. Although it showed Trains 1 and 2 operated to and from Marjorie, six miles away, at the connection with the Missouri Pacific, I learned this was just fiction. The only RS&S steam engine, No. 3, was out of service, a former M-K-T 2-6-0, built by ALCO in 1901.

THE SOLE WORKING ENGINE of the Rockdale, Sandow & Southern Railroad was this Mercury-powered No. 5, of whose manufacture it was not clear. This small unit handled the daily output of the lignite mine the six miles to a siding on the Missouri Pacific, named Marjorie. A steam shovel, that looked like a relic of Panama Canal construction days, worked in the pit. This was shot during October of 1946, and I understand that the little line prospered when a steel mill opened at nearby Daingerfield, Texas.

had seen the schedule in the *Official Guide*, and I had thought I might go for the round trip, as I was interested in railroads.

There never was a direct reply to my stated intent to buy a round-trip fare. The RS&S superintendent politely invited me to see his rolling stock (and, as it turned out, mostly un-rolling stock). A half hour later, as I drove away, I realized that this was his deft manner of informing me that there was not any Train 1 or 2, as the schedule designated them, and that they just did not do any passenger business.

There was an odd eight-wheeled internal-combustion locomotive sitting nearby, powered by two Mercury engines, and it must have been the current motive power. There was also a waycar (caboose) and some odds and ends of parts, as well as some freight cars. Not very far away could be heard the workings of a genuine steam shovel, loading lignite coal into hopper cars. This shovel used chains instead of cables and seemed to be rather elderly.

Anyway, as it became clear, passage (if any) to Marjorie would be on board the Mercury-powered 0-4-4-0 or a coal hopper. So, I had my answer, and I had learned again that what is listed in the *Official Guide* often is quite different from the actuality. As a result, I thanked the superintendent for the tour, and I drove away smiling somewhat regarding what I had learned about the RS&S.

Interestingly, the Rockdale, Sandow & Southern survived to become a much more important carrier, which served a new steel mill at Daingerfield, Texas. And for all I know, Marjorie is a shiny junction point.

LOCOMOTIVE No. 5 of the Roscoe, Snyder & Pacific, a 2-6-2 Prairie type, was departing from the depot and offices at Roscoe, Texas—way out in the west Texas cattle country. The RS&P was a strange railroad, moving freight from the Texas & Pacific 30 miles to the northwest, where it turned it over to the paralleling Santa Fe system. A number of U.S. railroads used the intricacies of tariffs and routings to build up their traffic. The date for this winter scene was January 6, 1947.

THE ROSCOE, SNYDER & PACIFIC

THIS SHORTLINE, called the Roscoe, Snyder & Pacific Railway, was a small west-Texas railroad. It was referred to by its connecting Texas & Pacific and Santa Fe agents as a "traffic thief," as it diverted routings of

A RATHER SHORT mixed train was photographed on the Roscoe, Snyder & Pacific. However, I did not try to find time to ride on this one. As I was shooting this picture from an adjacent city street in Roscoe, Texas, a man came shouting from the depot, out of sight to the right. And when he got closer, he announced if I took any pictures, he would call the sheriff! My response was, "What, not a Texas Ranger!?" Maybe the Roscoe, Snyder & Pacific had some guarded secret, but I certainly did not notice any on that day back in 1947.

through cars away from those two roads, which could have interchanged freight shipments quicker than diverting the cars for a 30-mile trip on the RS&P. The "& Pacific" no doubt referred to a 19-mile extension beyond Snyder to the little crossroads point of Fluvanna, which was abandoned and torn up long before the rest of the RS&P quit.

The freight yard of the RS&P, consisting of a few tracks, was an open space, faced by a residential street in Roscoe. The morning freight train was switching when I parked my car on the street and unlimbered my camera one day in 1947. Promptly from the combination depot and office building at the end of the yard came an office type who firmly warned me not to take any "pitchas," as they did not allow it. When I protested that I was standing on a public street, he threatened to call the sheriff—to which I must admit I sarcastically inquired, "What!? Not the Texas Rangers for something big like this?" To end the nonsense, I gave him my business card and assured him that when the office manager in Dallas was informed of his attitude, he would make sure that none of Seiberling's freight shipments would travel over the RS&P.

Only occasionally in wandering with a camera to shoot train pictures over much of the U.S. would some ignoramus as this one be encountered. If they were asked what possible harm a photograph would bring, they could not come up with a sensible answer. And I must admit, they annoyed me with the implication in their attitude that I was some kind of spy, engaged in some mysterious industrial espionage! It always seemed to me that if any lurking spies wanted to fritter away time, energy and film on things like the RS&P, they should be encouraged to do so. Perhaps the Roscoe line did have some big secret, but it surely escaped my notice!

THE TEXAS & NEW ORLEANS RAILROAD'S 4-4-0 TYPES

AT THE END of World War II, the Texas & New Orleans (SP) had the largest fleet of 4-4-0 types in America, and it was truly large. There were some rather old ones, but there also were over 20 remaining of a fleet purchased at one time from Baldwin during the early 1920's for branch-line service. The T&NO was unimpressed with the capabili-

209

IN THE EARLY 1920's, the Southern Pacific bought a large fleet of 4-4-0 locomotives for its branch lines. Many of the branches, like the Gonzales-to-Harwood line in Texas, had quite a bit of freight traffic, so they combined passenger and freight into a double-daily mixed train on the 12 miles to the mainline at Harwood. However, the diesel-electrics were coming, and when a 4-4-0 would need $500.00 or more in repairs, it would be set aside for the busy scrap lines at Houston.

WHILE RIDING on the Gonzales–Harwood train of the Southern Pacific on this April day in 1946, I partook of a rather fragrant spring trip. The long string of stock cars offset a roadbed carpeted primarily with spring flowers.

SET ASIDE at the San Antonio roundhouse, Engine 206 was one of a line of five 4-4-0's soon destined to move to the scrap line at the Houston shops. Built in 1924 by Baldwin Locomotive Works, this engine was one of about 25 such American-standard 4-4-0's delivered for use on Texas and Louisiana branch lines of the Southern Pacific. Diesel-electric locomotives were on order in 1946, so repairs on steam engines were limited to less than $500.00 per engine.

ties of gas-electric cars to haul three-car passenger trains, and as a result, the railroad went with small steam power for this task. Now, as traffic went back to normal in the spring of 1946 (following the war years), the 4-4-0 American-type engines were beginning to line up dead (permanently) on storage tracks, at places like San Antonio. Instructions went out that new diesel-electric units were on order, so any of the 4-4-0's needing $500 or more in repairs should be set aside.

The evening train from Austin, Texas, bound for Houston, with a Pullman car bringing up the rear, provided the heaviest load and toughest run for a 4-4-0. The countryside consisted of rolling terrain, and it was fun to drive out along the route, shut off the car's motor and listen to the engine make a strong run for one of the steep grades, barely crest the top, then race down through the bottoms to build-up speed for the next hill, where the engine would slow down to a crawl near the top of the next ridge. A similar train traveled from Fort Worth, Texas, on a much shorter trip to Ennis in the evening, to meet the T&NO's *Owl*, en route from Dallas to Houston.

For the 12-mile run on the Gonzales to Harwood branch—off the T&NO's main east-west line—another 4-4-0 and a combine provided mixed-train service twice a day.

During the spring, the weedy overgrown track was solid with wildflowers, which, however impressive they were from the rear of the train, gave a slippery time of it for the engine crew up ahead. Gonzales provided a lot of freight shipments, and the train often handled a long string of boxcars.

As it was on the Katy line, the 4-4-0 types would fill-in for ailing gas-electric cars. My train-chasing practice was to keep an *Official Guide* or timetables handy, so I could watch for trains. When the appearance of smoke showed up in the distance, my camera was readied and a suitable spot was selected, as it was very likely that through the wild-turkey country along the Katy would come "a-hustling" an old 4-4-0 American type hauling two passenger cars.

However, the diesel-electrics were starting to arrive, and the big T&NO shops at Houston were now busier cutting-up locomotives it seemed, rather than rebuilding them. The scrap crews had variety. Among the Atlantics, Consolidations, Moguls, etc., would be one or more 4-4-0 Americans, and sometimes, even a much larger engine. Locomotives that had remained idle at roundhouses and yards were coming in on freight trains faster than the torches could keep up with the work.

DURING THE ERA of streamliners, one of the more obscure trains was the "Sunbeam" of the Southern Pacific's Texas & New Orleans subsidiary. It was advertised as "265 miles in 265 minutes," and it ran on an early evening schedule from both Houston and Dallas. The T&NO 4-6-2 locomotive, No. 651, was being switched at Dallas Union Station for the 5:00 p.m. departure. A Cotton Belt 4-8-2 was also being handled by the hostlers, while at the left, the terminal's sole locomotive, 0-6-0 switcher No. 7, was busy. This unusual scene was shot in January of 1946.

CROSSING THE WIDE Trinity River bottoms at Irving, Texas, just outside Dallas, the Frisco's "Black Gold" was beginning its nine-hour run to Tulsa, Oklahoma. Pacific No. 1056 was the motive power for the brightly painted consist of heavyweight passenger cars. The date for this view was February 24, 1946.

RACING SOUTHWARD, the Southern Pacific's "Sunbeam" was crossing the Trinity River, headed by shrouded Pacific No. 650. This was one of two T&NO (SP) 4-6-2 locomotives specially rebuilt in this fashion for the Dallas–Houston traffic. During the train's mile-a-minute run, only two stops would be made—both conditional—at Ennis for passengers going to either terminal, or at College Station, for passengers only if they were going to either terminal. The mighty Southern Pacific did not dare to decline stopping for the all-powerful Texas "Aggies" station, i.e., the depot for Texas A&M College. The date was March 2, 1946, when this distant broadside view was photographed.

SOUTHERN PACIFIC Train 51 made a long trip daily from Waco, Texas, to Yoakum, Texas, 171 miles to the south, and return. Traffic was mostly mail and express shipments, as this empty depot platform at little Rosebud indicates. At this time, during March of 1946, the SP was giving up on its gas-electric cars, and as they needed repairs (becoming rather frequent), they substituted steam power from a sizable fleet of 4-4-0's, which hauled two-car trains. The Waco & Yoakum R.P.O. was very important for serving this part of Texas.

THE "SUNSET LIMITED," poky Train No. 1 of the Southern Pacific, had arrived—late as usual—on November 2, 1946, headed by 4-8-2 No. 4373, at the left. Dieselization had commenced, and ALCO diesel-electric No. 1390 had been put to work as passenger-train switcher at El Paso, Texas. On a few hours notice, I had driven to San Antonio, stored my car, and with a ticket to Fresno, California, I had boarded on Thursday, to find myself in Los Angeles by Saturday evening. This was a leisurely trip, with many long stops because of head-end business. And the "Sunset Limited" met and passed many other trains, with a great variety of motive power.

SOUTHERN PACIFIC'S Los Angeles-to-New Orleans Train 6, the "Argonaut," had a 4-6-0 helper on this run, which was about to depart from Tucson, Arizona. Despite streamlined SP 4-8-2 No. 4353, the train itself was not a stream-liner, because the "Argonaut" was really a local train on a long route—with much head-end work en route. (This train had come from New Orleans via the Texas & New Orleans line.) I shot this picture in Tucson on November 29, 1946.

ON MY FIRST TIME in Dallas, Texas, it was a delight to find the Texas Electric Railway. In 1945, this interurban line was a busy replica of what had been a common type of operation in Ohio (and other states)—until a very recent past. Operating big red-and-cream cars that were much rebuilt, the Texas Electric had frequent service 97 miles south to Waco, and 77 miles north to Denison. In addition, the Texas Electric had a city-car line in Waco. In Dallas, the Texas Electric operated on the tracks of the city streetcar lines, Dallas Railways. So, whenever I was in Dallas and found time on my hands, I could spend an hour or so snapping pictures of the Texas Electric. Here, No. 326—en route to Waco—was at Oak Cliff Junction on January 3, 1946.

TEXAS ELECTRIC RAILWAY

BY THE YEAR 1945, the "interurban era" was nearly over in the U.S. Of the 2,500 miles of such lines in Ohio in 1925, only one small line remained. So, it was a pleasant surprise to encounter the Texas Electric Railway when I arrived in Dallas during 1945. The Texas Electric line was a 174-mile operation, which seemed to me as though one or more of the vanished electric-traction lines had been reincarnated in Texas. Big red cars, rebuilds of what was common at the height of such railways, round-end freight trailers (boxcars), like the hundreds that once roamed traction lines in the Midwest, and steeple-cab freight motors (electric locomotives) that hauled interchange freight cars from the steam railroads. Operations on the Texas Electric were similar, too, with single track, no block signals and functioning only with timetables and train orders.

Almost every hour, the big red cars departed from the Interurban Building yard in Dallas for Denison, 77 miles to the north, just short of the Oklahoma border. Similar schedules were in force for the 97-mile line south to Waco. The routes of the Texas Electric were not hilly, mostly running through gently rolling country, with stretches of mesquite lands—and the southern line passed through cotton-growing country.

Several of the interurban cars assigned to the northern route had a Railway Post Office compartment in the rear end. So, of course, I made sure to mail as much of my personal matter as possible on these cars, in order to get the "Denison & Dallas RPO" postmarks.

After traveling for several blocks, the 11:20 a.m. run going to Waco would back into the large Texas Electric freight house to couple-on a green round-end freight trailer, which would be hauled through to the end of the line. So, I would go to lunch early when at our branch office, to shoot pictures of this interesting movement. The long building was paralleled by several tracks, always

ON SATURDAYS, many suburban residents went shopping in "Big D," Dallas, Texas. To carry them home, the Texas Electric often operated a schedule with two or three "sections" (extra cars running on the same schedule). Here, on Bryant Street, interurban No. 350 was carrying green flags, indicating a following section. No. 360 was the second section, which had a Railway Post Office compartment. Residents could mail a letter by just watching for the big car and step out to either hand it up or drop it in the mail slot. *Shades of logical good times in the past!* In this case, I was standing under shade trees in Dallas while shooting this view on April 20, 1946.

holding various freight motors and trailers. It seemed to be a duplicate of what had been in existence not too many years before in Akron, Cleveland and Toledo, Ohio, as well as at various Indiana cities. However, the General Freight Agent of the Texas Electric was not amused with my delight, but apparently disapproved of me (for some unknown reason). So, he had a TE crewman learn who I was and the name of my employer. One day, he phoned the Seiberling branch office, and after getting "Mac," the manager, on the phone, he proceeded to ask if he knew their employee, Bob Richardson, was down at the TE freight house taking pictures instead of working at his job. The freight agent was taken aback when "Mac" quickly acknowledged that he knew of my interest in railroads, and he went on to state that he hoped the TE people were being accommodating and helped my interest in any way possible. I had learned that Mac had no interest in railroads, but he did have a lively interest in my travels and experiences, and he thought that if such harmless doings would keep me happy on the job—which all my predeces-

sors had only complained about and did far less than I was doing—he was satisfied that I had an interest in railroads.

One day, we had a mid-morning call at Dallas for some badly needed tires in Waco. The dealer had to have them that day. Calls to truck lines indicated nothing further could be shipped out that day. So, I suggested using the 11:20 a.m. Texas Electric interurban to Waco. It turned out that no one from the electric-traction line had ever solicited Seiberling business. So, with barely a half hour to spare, the tires were en route to the freight house, and I had the pleasure—as I conspicuously wore my camera over my shoulder—to go upstairs so I could watch the grouchy freight agent sign the freight bills for the tire shipment. I took pains to explain in front of him how TE got the freight, as a result of my interest in watching and photographing their operations.

While spending a couple of weeks at Waco, Texas was having a heat wave in July, with highs of 109 degrees (F.). To cool off at the end of a sweltering day, several times I boarded a northbound interurban late in the

THE TEXAS ELECTRIC LINE left downtown Dallas via the trestle of the local streetcar company, spanning the Trinity River bottoms. Interurban No. 309 was heading for Waco, while behind it was a PCC trolley of the Dallas Railway & Terminal Company. Normally, the Trinity River contained only a trifling amount of water. However, occasionally, the Trinity would "do things up" Texas style, and high water would flood this wide area.

afternoon, near sunset, and rode to Hillsboro — about 30 miles north — so I could enjoy the breeze from the open windows, have dinner, and then take another breezy ride back to Waco. On the last such trip, the motorman had a train order to meet a southbound freight train at a stub siding, whose switch was on the south end. So, I sat in the front seat, camera ready, planning to take pictures of the meet, as apparently, we would take the siding, which meant that the single crewman would have to throw his own switch twice. As we approached the siding at a good 50 mph, I became alarmed and got very uneasy, as there was not any slackening of speed. And we bounced past the switch on a long tangent section of track, which ended over half a mile farther north, to wind through a mesquite-filled "bottom."

I was certain that I had read the TE train order correctly, but was also reluctant to say something to the operator, as I kept thinking I could be mistaken. Suddenly, up out of the mesquite, not more than a quarter-mile ahead, came the round green front end of a freight motor! We traveled a considerable part of that distance before we got stopped, and then we backed to the siding where we

were supposed to make the meet. Somehow, I had lost all interest in taking pictures, and I just kept my seat! My ride back from Hillsboro later that evening was my last jaunt on the Texas Electric, as I had seen some careless things happen on the north end.

Not many miles north of Dallas, the TE closely paralleled a Texas & New Orleans branch, which — for about a mile — was on a fill where at one point the TE went under the T&NO, then turned north again. At that point was a stub-end siding, with its switch on the north end. It was a Saturday afternoon, and the next northbound interurban train would be in three sections, running about a quarter- to a half-mile apart, depending on how many stops were being made, as Saturday shoppers provided the TE with substantial patronage each weekend. A few miles north of the underpass, there was a siding where I had expected the southbound freight train to pull out and stop, but it had not done so. When I saw this take place, I was on a small hill overlooking the general underpass scene, siding, etc., and I could see the three cars coming in the distance. As the first interurban approached the sharp curve at the underpass, the freight train came into view, and to my dismay, I could see the two crewmen in the cab looking at a pocket watch, and then the train slowly passed the switch and approached the underpass curve! I could see the cab of the passenger car; it was crowded with shoppers, so I hastily laid my movie camera on the ground and grabbed my hat and handkerchief to wildly wave a desperate washout signal! As a result, the two trains met a few feet apart under the T&NO, and the freight motor then backed its train to take the siding and waited for the other two sections to arrive, the first of which was also carrying green flags.

Eventually, the same freight crew that caused the above incident was killed in a headon collision with a passenger-interurban car, under similar circumstances. Their freight train was supposed to clear the passenger car by three minutes; however, the crew counted that the extra Saturday patronage, with additional stops, would make the interurban late, and their train could make it to another siding closer to Dallas. This tragic accident proved to be the final headon colli-

sion on the Texas Electric's Denison line. While driving from Louisiana toward Texas one day I heard the news about this fatal mishap on the radio, so I drove for the TE line. With my movie camera I captured one of the silver-colored electric locomotives hauling a shattered red interurban. It was Saturday afternoon, and downtown Dallas was busy with its normal heavy street traffic, while the tracks in the streets were occupied with city trolley cars, as well. The crowded downtown streets slowed everything down, and through this crowded scene the bloody wreckage of the TE was slowly trundled—to the dreadful awe and revulsion of bystanders. This was hardly a good advertising stunt for the Texas Electric. Why the management failed to wait until late at night to order the wreckage moved, I could not understand.

The Texas Electric Railway failed to last for long after this accident, and the final runs came during 1948. The postal clerk on the TE R.P.O. obligingly stamped some covers for me bearing the four train-number variations of the postmark used on that final day.

THIS FORMER "Katy" locomotive was the last operable steam engine of the Waco, Beaumont, Trinity & Sabine Railway. Track on this shortline to an oil field was so poor that when I first saw this train, I thought it had stopped. However, as I prepared to take a picture, I noticed that the drivers were turning very slowly on the dubious track of this curve.

THIS STATION of the Missouri Pacific at Trinity, Texas, saw trains several times a week. However, it also was host to this unusual "motor train" of the Waco, Beaumont, Trinity & Sabine Railway, which no doubt explains the road's local nickname of "the Wobbly-Bobbly." After bridges became unsafe for its steam engines to cross, the 33-mile run to Livingston—through cut-over pine lands in east Texas—was made by this "train." "Jim Crow" times were still around in 1946, so "colored" passengers had to ride in the trailer, along with the mail bags. Amazingly, they were expected to push, and this was done, if the thing broke down!

WACO, BEAUMONT, TRINITY & SABINE RAILWAY

BY THIS LINE'S NAME, it was all too typical of many shortlines, whose ambitions outran the financial means of its builders. It did get near the Trinity River, and its terminal was that same named town. Actually, the Waco, Beaumont, Trinity & Sabine built nothing; it had bought its trackage from the M-K-T, when that road was about to abandon it after the pine forests along the route had all been cut-over. Although in 1946, the WBT&S still proclaimed it had a daily round trip over the 33 miles to Livingston; however, in actual fact, it had been a while since that performance had ended. During the Great Depression years, maintenance of the track and bridges had dwindled to where a steam locomotive dared no longer to venture out on the line. With a mail contract, the line kept that revenue by converting a Model "A" Ford to flanged wheels, and by building a four-wheel trailer from a section man's push car (to meet "Jim Crow" laws).

The Ford soon showed evidence that it was wearing out, and now instead of making daily trips, it made only three round trips a week. The trailer had lengthwise seats, and had a top with side curtains, which could be closed in case of rain. The mail sacks rode back there with most of the passengers, who were black. Even though the route was through the flat east Texas cut-over pine lands, the struggling Ford boiled continuously, and more stops were made to replenish the radiator than for any other purpose. Traction was more difficult as weeds went uncut, and as the old vehicle rolled along, dead leaves and assorted insects disturbed by the car swirled into the Ford, requiring that I had to keep my collar buttoned despite the warm day.

The "railbus" passed through poor countryside, where unpainted general stores with post offices were located at occasional crossroad places. One water stop was at Onalaska, which was nearly a ghost town, where the crumbling-and-vandalized depot still carried

A LITTLE BUSINESS from an oil-loading rack west of Trinity, Texas, was the only freight moved on the Waco, Beaumont, Trinity & Sabine Railway. Until an ICC inspector red-tagged the last operable locomotive, the 4-6-0 took along this decrepit waycar-coach. The railroad had been in receivership for many years, and the track barely permitted the passage of the locomotive. In fact, there were frequent derailments. Shortly after this view was made in December of 1946, operations ended.

a board that proclaimed (in chalk) the schedule of trains. Near this station, five or six black passengers were picked up at a cotton-farmer's place.

The WBT&S train did not quite make it into Livingston, as half a mile out of town, at a place named West Livingston, the crossing of the Texas & New Orleans was encountered. As the "Wobbly Bobbly" (its nickname thereabouts) had not paid its share of maintenance, the big road had removed the worn-out frogs of the WBT&S. Passengers had to walk into Livingston, and volunteers heaved the mail sacks! Several men showed up to assist the motorman in turning the "No. 1," which was achieved in a manner encountered on no other railroad. A jack was placed under the crankcase, and after the car was raised as much as the jack could manage, the men firmly grabbed onto the Ford, and since it did not clear the rails, they jockeyed the thing around the best they could. The small group of men were unsmiling for my movies of this event. In fact, the motorman was rather taciturn during the entire trip, obviously not appreciating a "d--- Yankee" passenger, who was asking too many questions—which were really not the business of Yankees!

We then pushed "No. 2" (the trailer) until we came to a passing siding, where the car was switched around by hand to be in back of No. 1. The coupling was a very elementary bar-and-pin arrangement. Handing over another 70 cents to the motorman, we proceeded toward Trinity at about 20-to-25 mph. However, a mile short of that place, near the location where we used the Missouri Pacific track for the last half mile, the Ford's motor quit, and despite all efforts, it remained in that condition. The black passengers, obviously used to this, took turns pushing the train up to the Missouri Pacific depot. There was no refund (of two cents) for the mile I walked. But nonetheless, I was thankful that the vehicle did not breakdown farther out, as I had not seen much of anything in other transportation, just occasional empty dirt roads.

This was one railroad where I did not venture to its engine terminal, some distance through high weeds, a quarter-mile from the MP. I could see derelict equipment scattered around, but the intervening track was deep in weeds, which from the passage of the Ford, were smeared with oil and grease. There was a turntable, which could not be seen, but whose presence was known when the Model "A" suddenly was being turned.

220

The railroad's most important revenue was from an oil-loading rack, a few miles to the west. A former Katy engine handled a waycar (caboose) on this line, but the track was so poor that the engine simply crawled at five or six mph. For miles beyond the oil rack, nothing at all was operated. Some years earlier, the railroad had torn up another 66 miles of line that reached northeast of Trinity. This also was formerly Katy trackage, but even by the mid-1930's, it was embar-goed for both freight and passenger service, as the *Official Guide* listing explained "...account physical condition of the line." I was told the receiver of the "Wobbly Bobbly" had held the post for many years. Also, not long after I rode the line, operation on that portion was suspended permanently. An ICC inspector came by and examined the last operating steam locomotive and put a red tag on it, ending operations. No attempt was made to repair the engine.

THE PARENT ROAD, the Texas & Pacific Railway, gave up on the last locomotive of its subsidiary line, the Weatherford, Mineral Wells & Northwestern Railway. The T&P left the 2-8-0 partly dismantled at the Fort Worth shops. Engine 5 was built by ALCO in 1919. Up to the end of operations, the T&P supplied light locomotives for the 22-mile line from its ample supply.

WEATHERFORD, MINERAL WELLS & NORTHWESTERN RAILWAY

THIS LITTLE SUBSIDIARY of the Texas & Pacific was a 21-mile shortline that actually lived up to its name, for it had gone another 20 miles beyond the road's terminal in Mineral Wells prior to 1947, when I visited the line. During previous generations, Mineral Wells had become famous as the source of "Crazy Crystals," which provided much freight revenue. However, the Great Depression had ended scheduled passenger trains, and trackage beyond the terminal was abandoned. Now, the sole trains, No. 3 and No. 4, were labeled "mixed," and under this statement was: "Operated daily except Sunday, on irregular schedules. Subject to freight connections."

On the Friday when I inquired at the T&P's Weatherford depot, I was informed that the train indeed would run on the morrow, with a mid-morning departure. But when I showed up on the following morning to buy a round-trip ticket to Mineral Wells, there was another man on duty, a substitute, as the regular agent had taken the weekend off. The substitute neither knew what the fare was, nor could he find it anywhere. And it turned out that the conductor was a new man who had never sold a fare and did not seem to have a T&P tariff book with him, as he was a freight man. The train was waiting to depart, so it was decided I would ride to Mineral Wells, where the regular agent at that point would know what the fare was and could settle the matter.

The mixed train's engine was a T&P 2-8-2 Mikado, as the last engine of the WMW& NW was in condemned condition at the T&P's Fort Worth shop. The caboose also was lettered for the Texas & Pacific, as passengers obviously were so rare that no combine was needed. For 21 miles, the train wound through seemingly endless curves and mesquite groves. The several intermediate sidings indicated that there was no traffic expected from them.

Upon arrival at Mineral Wells, the agent joined the crew as they unloaded the L-C-L freight. Meanwhile, I waited at the counter inside the depot, where a large and rather tough-looking tomcat was sitting, with a bored air about him! Almost without thinking, I simply reached over and scratched him behind the ears; I had many years of practice doing that, something all cats seem to appreciate. This one, like many others, gave no recognition to my scratching thusly. Just then, the four men came in, their labors ended, and they stopped abruptly, as the agent said to me "Do that again!" And again I automatically scratched the cat. They came closer, and the agent explained in some sort of awe "Nobody touches that cat!" And he went on to say that anyone trying to touch the cat would ordinarily expect a batch of claws. I thanked him for so recklessly urging me to risk my fingers, but I could not resist commenting that perhaps the problem was the cat was a Yankee, and he just did not like Texans! That remark drew no smiles at all!

All railroad lines have some unusual feature. This one's was its wye at Weatherford, where the tail of the wye terminated at the end of a short trestle over a small stream. The trestle ended at the far bank, and the crew liked to boast that although their engines had started across the stream hundreds of times, none ever got all the way across!

Meanwhile, the tire dealer in Weatherford had tried to reach me, and on Monday he asked where I had gone. When I told him and described the train trip, caboose ride and all, he allowed that this was a "…right smart idea for something to take the family on some Saturday." Months later, upon meeting the Seiberling salesman who covered that area, I was startled to learn that the tire dealer had gone on this trip, and I immediately thought of his overactive children "on the loose" in that caboose. Furthermore, the salesman told me that the word about this railroad ride had gotten around at the dealer's church and clubs, which led a goodly number of Weatherfordites to do likewise. Imagining what this meant for the train crews, I made a mental note never to go near that T&P branch again—lest some crew member might take after me with a brake club for bringing such misfortunes on them!

WICHITA FALLS & SOUTHERN

SCATTERED OVER TEXAS were a number of decaying railroads, relics of great plans and dreams of times in the past. Wichita Falls was the headquarters for one of these lines, the Wichita Falls & Southern Railroad, 190 miles of neglected track in the dry ranch country of west Texas. There was very little in the way of wayside revenue, because the WF&S served only a handful of small towns, and most of the stations listed in the half-page coverage in the *Official Guide* were merely weedy, rusty sidings, only flag stops for WF&S mixed trains.

Since I was in and out of Wichita Falls for several weeks, I determined to ride the north-end mixed train. According to the schedule, this run took 8½ hours to make the 103 miles from Wichita Falls to the county seat of Breckenridge. This mixed train operated on a tri-weekly schedule, down the line one day and back up on the next. Departure was supposed to be at 10:00 a.m., but it was well after 12:00 noon before a sizeable-tonnage train pulled out of Wichita Falls behind a hard-working Mogul. This 2-6-0 had begun life as one of the locomotives hauling construction trains on the huge Panama Canal project.

For a railroad with so little on-line traffic, the size of the long train of boxcars was sur-

222

BRECKENRIDGE, TEXAS, was a divisional operating point on the decrepit Wichita Falls & Southern Railroad. The road's owners neglected maintenance because they expected the Rock Island and "Katy" railroads to outbid each other to buy it. However, they waited too long—and the two big railroads had so many problems of their own, they did not want to add the WF&S to them. So, the line went to abandonment. This Wichita Falls & Southern locomotive, 2-8-0 No. 31, was photographed on the turntable at Breckenridge on September 3, 1946.

prising. It turned out that the little road was good at obtaining bridge traffic, or as some unkind traffic agents working for other roads would declare, the WF&S was a "traffic thief."

We arrived in Breckenridge exactly at midnight. Adding to delays along the way was the fact that the road had too much tonnage for a tri-weekly single-engine train. As a result, our train would stop at sidings along the way and exchange some of our cars for cars that had been set out by the previous train. There was a "slow order" in effect, which called for the crew to look for "sun-kinked rails" at one point. We crawled over this section of track, where the rails obviously were warped, and were not held too securely with extra spikes applied to ties that had outlived normal life. Fortunately, not a wheel derailed in our long train!

At another point, there was a spring of very good water, something extremely valuable and appreciated in west Texas. Here, in a steel combine that once had been a component of some railroad's gas-electric train, bottled spring water was placed in an amazing collection of jugs and water containers of many sizes. As I had already learned, Wichita Falls had the worst drinking water as yet encountered, full of alum. It also made the worst coffee in the entire state of Texas, so the hotel "imported" spring water via the WF&S, so they had decent water for coffee-making.

The Wichita Falls & Southern had numerous interchange points with other railroads, including the Fort Worth & Denver (part of the Burlington Route) and the Katy (the Missouri, Kansas & Texas) at Wichita Falls. Another interchange was with the Rock Island

THE TERMINAL of the Wichita Falls & Southern Railroad was at Breckenridge, Texas. That is the mainline in the foreground, somewhat neglected. The old steam shovel had served as a wrecking crane. In 1946, the poor little WF&S was nearing its end.

at Graham, about half way down the run, while on the other portion of the WF&S, connections were made with the Texas & Pacific, the Santa Fe and the Katy. Junctions with two other shortlines, the Cisco & Northeastern and the Eastland, Wichita & Gulf, had been abandoned not long before I visited the Wichita Falls & Southern.

In the Breckenridge yard sat the spare combine for the mixed runs, an ancient open-platform relic from the Nashville, Chattanooga & St. Louis. Its paint and lettering were peeling; however, its NC&StL parentage could still be recognized. The other mixed train, which covered the 60 miles between Breckenridge and Dublin, did not trust this relic and employed a caboose, instead.

On the return run to Wichita Falls, our northbound train made better time, and although we departed about an hour late, we did not lose much time, as it was obvious that most of the revenue traffic moved southbound. The train's arrival at Wichita Falls presented an unusual scene, a small crowd of people, patiently waiting for their various water jugs.

The story was given to me that both the Rock Island and the Katy wanted to purchase the WF&S, so the owners played the two big lines off against each other for years. A sale to one or the other was believed to be certain eventually, so they spent nothing but the barest amount necessary for maintenance of the shortline. This accounted for the miserable track and a very junky shop area, full of equipment needing repairs.

However, the WF&S owners waited too long. The boom times for Texas railroads that preceded and carried through World War II were over. Both the Rock Island and the Katy found themselves in financial binds, and suddenly, the two would-be buyers found they really did not need the WF&S, which would cost enormous amounts of money to rebuild it for their type of operations. The great moments were in the past for the WF&S, and within a few years, the shortline became just another abandoned, weedy grade in west Texas.

THE REPAIR SHOPS of the Wichita Falls & Southern Railroad at Wichita Falls, Texas, looked like this in December of 1946. The old combination car's paint was peeling, revealing previous ownership by the Nashville, Chattanooga & St. Louis. Wichita Falls was a railroad center for the "Katy" lines and the Burlington Route as well.

MAKING A STATION STOP at Amecameca, some 58 kilometers from Mexico City, the morning narrow-gauge passenger train of the National of Mexico (NdeM) was heading for Cuautla and Puebla, 310 kilometers away. Gradually, the outside-frame 4-6-0 types were going to the scrap heap, and in 1962, No. 188 was one of the last of these, being replaced by outside-frame 2-8-0 types. When No. 188 was new, the train had first-class coaches, with red-plush seats, even Pullman sleeping cars, as the line then extended all the way to Vera Cruz, on the Gulf of Mexico. When this picture was taken, the cars were the distictive home-built ones of the NdeM, all but the last being second class, as few first-class passengers rode the line any more.

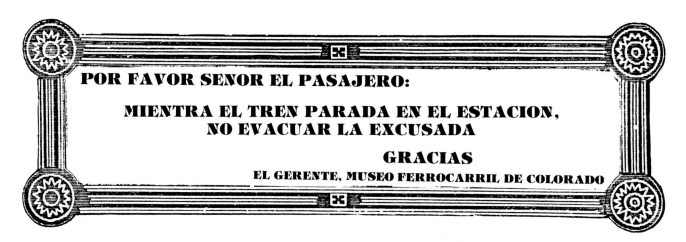

POR FAVOR SEÑOR EL PASAJERO:

MIENTRA EL TREN PARADA EN EL ESTACION, NO EVACUAR LA EXCUSADA

GRACIAS

EL GERENTE, MUSEO FERROCARRIL DE COLORADO

NOTICES SUCH AS THESE were posted in Mexican passenger cars for many years. POR FAVOR SEÑOR EL PASAJERO: "For a favor Mr. Passenger:" MIENTRA EL TREN PARADA EN EL ESTACION, NO EVACUAR LA EXCUSADA, GRACIAS. "While the train stops in the station, no... [flushing] the toilet—thanks." Another common sign read: "Do not put your feet upon the seats."

226

EXPLORATIONS IN MEXICO

IT COST ONLY A FEW PESOS, and it looked as if it had spent the past nearly half century tucked away safely in some file in Mexico City—while the outside world was a swirl of revolutionary armies and a violence that seemed to cover Mexico with blood. Its title, *Guía Oficial de Ferrocarriles Y Vapores de la República Mexicana*, the date, September 1918, pocket size, 75 pages, and the timetables therein contained everything operating in México. However, after seven years of civil war, the railroads of this land were missing hundreds of locomotives and thousands of cars. This *Official Guide* nonetheless listed schedules showing what was intended to operate, with not too many runs "suspended." The operating company was the Ferrocarriles Constitucionalista de México (Constitutional Railways of Mexico) for most of the lines listed in detail. The guide was proclaimed to be issued monthly, but another issue never turned up. It is truly a treasure of Mexican railroad information.

This pocket booklet was one of the essentials on trips to explore Mexican railroads between 1959 and the mid-1960's, while this was a world of steam, with passenger trains everywhere. At the very least, a "mixto" train went to places that really were nowhere. Pages of current *Official Guides* also were essential. And if you could find one, a copy of the thick timetable of the Ferrocarriles Nacionales de México (National Railways of Mexico) was most helpful.

One such trip was made in the winter of 1962, with Ken Crist as a very knowledgeable companion, ever hopeful of catching some new rare diesel engine with his cameras. I scorned the diesels and concentrated on the wonderful assortment of steam motive power, old and new, some dating to 1881, ranging from 2-6-0's to 4-8-4's and Mallets. With a business card declaring I was General Manager of a museum and introducing Ken as my "ayudante" (assistant), we applied for permits to visit repair shops, yards and roundhouses, making certain that no matter what the weather, we were properly accoutered in neckties and suit coats when we entered their offices. We found officialdom friendly and cooperative, and they would issue a typed permit, with an indeci-

pherable signature, which waved us past all gates and guards. Since no one could read those signatures, a Latin-American style, we often wondered if such permits really meant anything at all?

We would ride a variety of trains, sometimes a new articulated "Auto-via," with its snack bar serving the hottest-seasoned "sandweeches" one could imagine. At other times, we would ride on a local passenger train, being almost the sole occupants of the primera (first-class) coach on the rear. These trains were fine for a leisurely tour of rural Mexico, with frequent and unhurried stops. At each stop, there was great activity up ahead as the crowded second-class cars became even more crowded, and vendors handed all sorts of good-looking and good-smelling stews and tortilla-wrapped goodies through the windows. However, all of this we had to disdain trying—no matter how strong the pangs of hunger. On rare occasions, we would weaken, like eating ears of boiled corn, or some powdered-sugar-loaded baked items. Nevertheless, we were determined not to get sick, so we took care, and on none of the various expeditions did the dread afflictions "get us."

Up ahead, next to the postal car, in front of the second-class coaches, would be the train guard. This consisted of a corporal's guard of very youthful-and-bored soldiers, whose duty of riding trains was a form of military training. The postal clerk in the "Ambulante" section (Railway Post Office) was buried under an impossible amount of mail bags, a mail service so short of cars and personnel that a postcard reached home months after the trip. For some reason in Mexico and points south, postmarks are generally illegible, as if it was by design! So, my souvenir cards, despite requests for a clear postmark, "por favor, gracias," were mostly a smear. Later, I learned that I should have accompanied the request with perhaps one of the new silver pesos.

At the very small places, perhaps a small village of baked mud bricks at a siding, the train would linger while the women of the village filled all kinds of containers with hot water from the engine. Dieselization ended what was a very valued service for people afflicted with dubious water supplies. Potable water was something Mexico City politicians were always promising, and like the funds for schools, school books, medical facilities, roads and other things we Norte Americanos take for granted, somehow these funds seemed never to reach those little places. And the politicians would retire from office at the end of each six-year presidential term, very well off indeed—rich in many instances—indicating a remarkable ability to save more than the salaries they received!

It made a grim joke of all the high-sounding promises of the 1917 constitution and the politician's promises. Allegedly to prevent a return of the dictators who had spent a lifetime in office, letters from government offices would have the slogan, "Sufragio efectivo! No re-eleccion!" (Effective suffrage! No re-election!) However, all it meant in practice was that every six years a new set of officials came in and worked their best so that they could retire as wealthy men at the end of their term, with big land holdings mocking the revolutionary promises of "land and liberty" for the peasants.

Trains could be very lonely in much of Mexico. There were no nearby roads, no county sheriffs, just endless vistas of distant mountains, nearly dry river beds and hints of ranching. And you realized that the small train guard up ahead was all the police authority in a vast area. In the not-too-distant past, those train guards had fought many a little battle against bandits and revolutionary forces, and the railroad lines had countless sites of such last-ditch defenses.

To Mexicans, a train trip was an endless picnic. The people were always eating, an activity that encouraged numerous vendors to be at trainside during station stops. If nothing else was available, they would sit happily chewing foot-long portions of sugar cane, with the juices dribbling over their clothes. Men favored wearing suits with vests, but we joked among ourselves that we had never seen so many stained vests, the result of passengers trying to eat the sloppy,

dripping goodies wrapped in tortillas en route. We rather stood out in the midst of all this endless snacking, as we were not eating anything, except perhaps a banana, boiled corn or bakery goods, when those items were available. No wonder they thought Norte Americanos were odd!

While I was a little kid learning to read in grade school, our newspapers frequently had headlines of events in Mexico. And often, there were pictures of railroad disasters that fascinated kids. Perhaps trying to grasp the tongue-twisting names of the places got me started toward "A's" in spelling. A Pennsy railroader in the neighborhood would get out maps and show us where these places were. And he would add to the news stories tales he had heard from railroaders who had fled the upheavals of 1910–1920.

Now, many years later, and after studying Latin American history, the names of the stations and sidings often were familiar: Chihuahua, Torreón, Zacatecas, Saltillo, San Luis Potosí, Aguascalientes, Puebla, San Lázaro, Amecameca, Cuautla, etc. If perhaps I would ask a conductor with graying hair about some point, which seemed to recall some stirring event, a spirited lecture in rapid Spanish often would ensue. I would have to keep suggesting "despacio," slow down. Typically, other crew members and passengers would join in, as they would point out the sites of events that once made headlines throughout the world. The railroaders could not forget that many a railroader had lost his life in wrecks caused by bandits and revolutionaries. Once, a trainman pointed to a parallel stretch of the always-present telegraph line and recounted how the Federals had hung captured rebels on miles of those poles.

Trains in Mexico started on time, but as the schedules were estimated for a day with minimum stops, switching and delays for meets, the train invariably would get later and later—sometimes many hours later. So, if you got off at a station stop to take a picture, you had better not stray too far, as all of a sudden, the train was underway, and you had to run for it. They never waited for late passengers running to catch the train, and sometimes, almost making it, with the shouts of more fortunate passengers, "Adelante, muchachos, adelante!"

Mexico City had three stations. The main one was Buena Vista, where the handsome new building was under construction—with

AN "AUTO-VÍA" MOTOR TRAIN was photographed in 1964, on the popular Mexican tourist route of the Chihuahua al Pacífico ("Chihuahua to the Pacific") Railroad. This train was fast and comfortable, with a well-stocked buffet counter. Comparatively, it was a swift trip, over a 405-mile run through the rugged mountain area of Copper Cañon—the newest railroad in Mexico. Started before the 1910 revolution, this was to be the Pacific Coast portion of the Kansas City, Mexico & Oriente Railroad. However, the civil commotion ended construction, with unfinished sections in both directions from Chihuahua and an isolated section from the port of Topolobampo. Decades later, under government control, the line was completed, including the little-noted northern end to

Ojinaga, just over the border from Presidio, Texas. The Orient line folded many years ago in the U.S., large portions becoming the Santa Fe line from Wichita, Kansas, through Oklahoma and west Texas (San Angelo). And now, much of that is gone, either abandoned or parts of new shortlines. In 1972, "Auto-Vía" railbuses were running on the line north from Chihuahua, and on one day, I made the round trip. Most of it runs through barren desert country. A foreman told me how a Federal army retreating from Chihuahua in 1914 had used the unfinished railroad as far as it could. Then, the men staggered the rest of the way to Ojinaga, after blowing up their trains at the end-of-track. His first job was to work at cleaning up the wreckage, using only hand tools.

what seemed like endless expansions. The second station was for the original British-built Ferrocarril Mexicano, the first railroad in Mexico. This line was built from Vera Cruz on the Gulf of Mexico, to the capital. And the third one was the old San Lázaro, where the narrow-gauge trains departed. Within a few years, only Buena Vista remained. Yards and engine facilities were close by, as they had been located when the city was small, not the

multi-million megalopolis of today. During the steam-locomotive days, they guaranteed a perpetual smog situation for the capital.

An employee told us where we might go to get copies of employee timetables covering those lines we planned to explore. On the second floor of a small building within a few blocks of the Buena Vista terminal, we found a frosted glass door, lettered to indicate this was the right place: "Itinerarios." But the door was locked! And there was no indication when anyone might be expected to open it. Just then, a small man carrying a big bundle came down the hallway, spoke to us, and smiled as he unlocked the door and waved us in. The big room was startling to us railfans. All around the walls were shelves stacked with timetables of every railroad division in the republic. Neither of us—then or since—had ever seen or even imagined so many timetables!

The NdeM was in the beginning stage of changing-over from the large 10 x 15-inch size timetables to the more modern booklet type, as used in the U.S.A. When we expressed our interest, he happily went here and there, selecting tables, until we had a set ample for the needs of our "expedition." He offered any more tables we would like, even suggesting some, but what to do with them was the problem. So, we thanked him and left, still in somewhat of a daze because of that enormous stock of timetables.

That evening we went to a motion-picture house showing films from the Archivos Casasolas, a firm that had started taking movies back in 1899. This company had been the source of a great deal of newsreel items seen in the U.S. The films shown contained scenes of many different things, including the city's first electric trolley cars, Independence Day parades and inaugurals, as well as films of noted figures. However, in among all this history were numerous railroad scenes. Here came a double-ended Fairlie engine on the Mexicano line, with flatcars loaded with artillery guns and bandoleered troops riding on the tops of boxcars. There were wrecks of all kinds. And there were views of presidents disembarking from the famed red presidential train—and on and on.

We rode the Mexicano to Vera Cruz, skirting the great volcano, Orizaba, en route to the Gulf Coast. Our train used a three-cylinder Pacific for the first part of the trip. Then, electric engines were used to descend the steep grades through the mountains to the coastal lowlands, where steam motive power resumed. As we returned to Mexico City, we rode aboard the elegant parlor car "Huamantla," and a passenger asked me why I called Ken "the little one"? On an earlier trip, I started calling him "Kennethcito," so I replied, "Because he is not." The gentleman's puzzled look only relaxed when I smiled, and all the passengers on the car joined in the joke, as Ken was not little. Rather, he was long-legged, and his belt was almost at the chest level of most Mexican men. A name that started with a "K" was also strange to Mexicans, as only the Mayans of Yucatan used names with that letter. And by Ken's height, he certainly was not Yucataneco.

Some 210 kilometers from Mexico City, as the three-cylinder Pacific hustled us eastward across a wide barren plain in the state of Puebla, we sped by a flag stop called "Aljibes." This triggered the memory of an event that made headlines in the U.S., "Carranza Assassinated," and the date for this tragic incident was my tenth birthday. When I asked the gray-haired conductor, comfortably sharing two seats with friends, he confirmed my hazy memory. He excitedly filled out a picture of a government fleeing the capital in 15 trains, which became stranded at Aljibes because the engines were out of fuel and water. And the rebels had cut the track ahead, as they closed-in for a battle involving over 10,000 troops.

The Constitutionalist President Venustiano Carranza abandoned his special car to join a small party of officials on horseback, heading for the distant mountains, where he was murdered that night. The conductor and his friends regaled me with descriptions of running trains up the 4.1-percent grade from the Gulf Coast, with doubleheaded Fairlie 0-6-6-0's. So many engines were lost during the troubles that electrification was hurried to completion in 1923, covering the most rugged portion of the line. Now, those electric locomotives were worn out and unable to keep up with the growing traffic. So, diesel-electric engines were hauling the trains, with electrics as helpers. Ken's camera was busy along this route! Meanwhile, all the rest of the way to Vera Cruz, I was enjoying listening to the guided tour in rapid-fire Spanish of this place or that en route.

THE MUST TRIP, of course, was to take the 8:13 a.m. narrow-gauge passenger train from the old San Lázaro station. Mexico had been gradually getting rid of its slim-gauge lines, and this line, which once went under the name, "Interoceanic," had gone all the way to Vera Cruz. However, it had been cut back to Puebla, with some branches remaining. If one stuck it out—in its very circuitous route—one might make it to Puebla by late evening, hours late. We elected to go to the city of Cuautla, 144 kilometers away, and we enjoyed the trip so much that several times I went for trips to some of the places along this route.

This was a busy rail line, with many short freight trains hauling building materials of limestone and such to the capital. Most of the motive power consisted of several classes of outside-frame 2-8-0's, built during the early 1920's, with several 4-6-0's still handling passenger trains. Typically Mexican, the engines had standard short stacks and large headlights centered on the front of the smokebox. Enginemen were proud of their charges, and they kept them wiped down, even polished, and often added little extras, such as brass flag holders. As for their steam whistles, these were obviously highly prized and vied in melodious tones.

The enginehouse, a block from the old San Lázaro depot, was old-fashioned, and over the various doorways were arched signs proclaiming: "Mayordomo de la Casa Redonda," "Ayudante," etc. We thought that would be a nice touch if we ever got a shop built at Golden. The yard was a maze of dual-gauge trackage, and busy switching was accomplished with much whistling.

Our 8:13 a.m. train had an attractive old wooden mail car, titled "Correo," a couple of boxcars serving as express cars, several rather home-made-looking second-class passenger cars (with flat roofs and odd square-looking windows), trailed by an oversize first-class open-platform coach. (Incidentally, one of these first-class cars is now on the Cumbres & Toltec line in Colorado.) For many years, Pullman sleeping cars from the Denver & Rio Grande had rolled out of this station. The D&RG had sold them to the Interoceanic way back in 1902; however, none of them remained. We did not have to ask for smoke ("mas fumo, por favor") for our pictures, as the fireman was laying down a smoke screen over San Lázaro that any navy-destroyer man could envy!

There are stories claiming that this line was so crooked because the early contractors and concessionaires were paid by the kilometer, but the grades would have to have been impossibly steep if they had made the twisting route any shorter. Cuautla was reached in just under four hours, averaging about 35 kilometers per hour—a busy terminal. En route, the background was dominated by two volcanoes, Popocatépetl and Ixtaccíhuatl, and from the midpoint of Ozumba we wound down a 4.0-percent grade through many small villages, ruined haciendas (large estates) and small farms. This was Zapata country, and in my treasured 1918 guide book, operations were suspended as the Constitutionalists tried in vain to contain the popular rebels. The rebels even ventured to the outskirts of Mexico City, often attacking trains and tearing up tracks. By the end of the revolutionary times, in 1920, not much of the original railroad was left intact.

By now, the reader has no doubt gathered that we did not waste our time visiting the country's "touristy" places. We found the people at our destinations and way points to be friendly and tolerant of the not entirely sane North Americans. We joked among ourselves that we were likely helped by the Spanish belief that God has taken the "locos" (crazy ones) under His wing, and one must not harm such individuals. My rusty Spanish was politely tolerated for at least we were trying to speak their language! Ken had learned "Español" (Spanish) well, but he refused to try to speak it for fear of embarrassment. So, I had to be the "interpreter," although he would sometimes provide a word in a low aside or whisper. We learned railroad terms by studying the employee timetables. So, we did not make the North American errors of mistaking "Desviador" and "Empalme" as station names (derail and junction). However, I am sure that I made some awful bloopers. When we were in places the tourists frequented, we found an entirely different attitude from many residents—and no wonder—as we witnessed some rather rude examples from American visitors.

The railroad's dining cars were fine, although one had to watch what one ordered. "Huevos rancheros" (eggs, ranch style) came with a colorless sauce, which was innocent appearing, but it was as hot as anything from Tabasco. They used the "dollar sign" to indicate prices, which were in pesos. Once, a couple of obnoxious tourists at a nearby table loudly complained of the outrageous prices, such as "...$15.00 for eggs and $5.00 for toast!" So, when they tendered some $20.00 U.S. bills to pay the tab, the waiter glanced nervously at us, perhaps expecting us to tell them the "$" sign did not mean U.S. dollars. However, the couple had been so obnoxious throughout breakfast that I just shrugged my shoulders. So, the waiter made change, again in U.S. dollars, as he and I smiled.

Pie was something new to Mexican dining cars, but now they had it, "piña empanada" (pineapple pie), and this was a standard dessert item everywhere the cars rolled. Café (coffee) tended to be strong and black. The tab (as figured in pesos) was modest for even a large meal.

A very large coach yard at Mexico City had hundreds of passenger cars on its tracks, and it was headquarters for everything. There were dozens of parlor and office cars. Coaches represented most of the major U.S. roads, who, as they discontinued trains, sold their best equipment "south of the border."

On a later trip, 10 of us chartered the office car "Venustiano Carranza," which originally was the private car used by a copper-company's management, who credited it to Arizona's Magma Arizona Railroad. It had a large dining room, served by a factotum, who was a combination porter-chef-waiter, plus a maintenance man. Was it expensive? In the end, it cost us far less than if we had ridden aboard regular Pullmans and eaten at restaurants. We journeyed from Juarez (opposite El Paso, Texas) to Vera Cruz and return, with stopovers at Chihuahua, Aguascalientes, Mexico City, etc. We even had an opportunity to have a steam-powered branch trip with it for a little over $100.00 additional, and we got to pick the engine! However, a diesel minority vetoed that!

The history of Mexico is fascinating, and the episode of the French intervention and the "Phantom Empire" of the 1860's are particularly interesting. So, during waiting periods at Chihuahua, when loading-out a couple of narrow-gauge engines, I read many of the letters of the indomitable Indian President Benito Juárez. They are displayed at the museum that originally was the small building he used as a refuge while escaping Napoleon III's lancers.

I used to enjoy reading the inscriptions on many of the impressive monuments that are a feature of station plazas. At the time, I did not realize that one especially would come in handy. While riding along one day in the first-class coach on the narrow-gauge line, we were seated just a couple of seats away from a businessman and his family. He was having a dispute over fares with the conductor. In typical Mexican fashion, the latter included us, appealing for our opinion. Ken, in a low voice, urged, "...don't say anything. Let's keep out of this." However, that would not do; we were obliged to say something. And then, I thought of one of those monuments and "threw it into the pot" (sort of). In my creaky Spanish, I said, "El Benemérito de la Patria, Don Benito Juárez..." at one time said, "En el respeto por la ley es la defensa de la puebla." (The best protection of the people is to respect the law.) The businessman inclined his head and then produced the fares in dispute, and the conductor tipped his cap to us and nodded, "Gracias, señores." Ken muttered, "Now, you've done it." However, as we all got off the coach at Ozumba, the conductor again tipped his hat to me, and the businessman politely nodded in a friendly manner. *That is Mexico!* A North American had quoted the great benemérito Juárez himself. It was enough!

We rode the local train from Cuernavaca, something none of the tourists to-and-from Acapulco would ever do. It was a wonderful entry into the capital. We rode the Sureste route from Vera Cruz to Mérida, a 1,300-mile trip from Sunday evening through Tuesday morning—past Palenque of ancient ruins and forests of cacao trees. Again, coming from Guatemala, I boarded the mixed train at the border and entered a former New York Central coach that seemed unnecessarily huge after days of riding on the three-foot-gauge lines in El Salvador and Guatemala. That 24-hour trip, which covered nearly 600 miles to Vera Cruz, had us arrive in nearly a starved condition. We had passed several dubious-looking station restaurants, expecting to find something better farther on. Oh well, there were bananas! Nevertheless, it was all fun, and our only regret is the "bright ones" in Mexico City have imitated the North Americans and have done away with all the mixtos and almost everything else!

I wonder... if in all their changes they have taken away the telegraph keys at railroad offices. It indicated authority for an official to have a key on his desk, a status symbol. I wondered if they ever really used the telegraph keys. Once, however, in response to a question, the ayudante cut in and rapidly called someone, and in a few minutes, we had the answer!

THIS WAS THE SMELTER TROLLEY at Concepción del Oro, Zacatecas, Mexico, the western terminal of the narrow-gauge Coahuila y Zacatecas Railway. Not many years later, the C&Z was standard-gauged and partly abandoned, and it became a branch of the National of Mexico (the NdeM).

THE COAHUILA & ZACATECAS

COPPER MINING in northern Mexico, in the desert-mountain country, was the reason for the construction of the oddly named Coahuila & Zacatecas Railway—a 78-mile narrow-gauge line built from Saltillo, the capital of the Mexican state of Coahuila. There was not much between the two terminal points, only a few very small communities, barely surviving at the fringe of the western Coahuila Desert. Concepción de Oro was a typical mine-and-smelter town, and enough business was going on to require a switch engine, provided at the time I visited the place by engine No. 1, an 1897 Baldwin 2-8-0. The daily mixed train took about five hours each way. Due to the long, steep grade out of Saltillo, the mixed and freight trains had to be rather short. The mixed train consisted of only a few freight cars, tailed by a bright blue Railway Post Office and Express car, and two coaches. The rearmost car was partly "segunda" (second class) and partly "primera" (first class).

On the day I rode this C&Z (or "CyZ") mixed train with Ken Crist, the morning was damp from fog and a light rain during the night. The two freight trains that had gone out at dawn (or earlier) were having a hard time on the hill. Oil had leaked from tank cars, and the curves were so slippery that the engines would stall. Then, the second freight train came up behind the caboose, and nudged the first train to help get its engine around the curve.

Our mixed train caught up with this struggle, and with a closed coupler knuckle, our train added its push to the strange mixture ahead. As soon as the two freight engines got onto the straight-away, they could momentarily get ahead of our train, but

233

CONCEPCIÓN DEL ORO was in the mountains of Zacatecas state in Mexico. Engine 11, an outside-frame Baldwin 2-8-0, was being serviced for the return trip with the mixed train to Saltillo. Built in 1909, this engine was one of the few items among the road's rolling stock that survived the destruction of the civil wars, which gradually ended in 1920. To serve as a pattern for building new freight cars, the Colorado & Southern Railway shipped one of their boxcars from Denver.

The illiterate carmen at Saltillo faithfully copied everything, even to the style of lettering. An all-day trip on the Coahuila y Zacatecas was a treat for narrow-gauge fans. In placing little items about the CyZ in the *Narrow Gauge News* now and then, I did not realize that many readers thought the road and its names were a fictional invention! So, I had to drag out an *Official Guide* a couple of times to prove there really was a Coahuila y Zacatecas south of the border!

upon struggling into another sharp curve, the engines would stall again. The second-class passengers enjoyed the show, leaning out the windows to shout encouragement. They also became very vocal as we paralleled the mainline of the National of Mexico, near the top of the pass. A NdeM freight train, powered by some very noisy and obviously not well-functioning diesel units, was just barely overtaken and passed by our mixed train. The second-class "cheering section" was very loud in insulting shouts to the NdeM crew, who obviously could not hear the shouting. However, the crew certainly could understand the derisive gestures.

About 67 miles out of Saltillo, there was a junction called Avalos, where the mining

branch diverged from the mainline. However, more interesting for railfans was a two-foot-gauge track, upon which sat a wooden double-truck hopper car. Just as our train was about to leave, a cloud of steam at the enginehouse some distance away cleared barely enough for a glimpse of an 0-4-4-0T Mallet! It turned out that this little mining road had two of these machines and an 0-4-0T Porter switcher. Not long afterward, thanks to publicity in the Colorado Railroad Museum's *Iron Horse News*, the Porter and one of the Mallets ended up on a tourist railroad at Cripple Creek, Colorado. This was shortly after the little narrow-gauge mining line in Mexico was dieselized.

On the return trip from Concepción, the

OUR MIXED TRAIN was caught as it climbed up the steep grade out of Saltillo, on a drizzly, foggy morning, with two freight trains struggling to overcome not only the slippery weather, but an additional problem of rails coated with oil—especially difficult to manage on curves. Evidently the oil came from a leaking car in an earlier train. The first freight train, with only one engine, would stall on curves. Then, with closed knuckles, the sec-ond freight train—doubleheaded—would push against the caboose. Our mixed train did the same thing, and at times, all three trains were working hard in this fashion, the freights pulling ahead after they made it around a curve. Things like this occurred long ago in the United States, when Colorado's narrow-gauge lines employed smaller engines in places like Cumbres Pass, Marshall Pass, etc.

train limped to a stop out in the nearly barren desert. One of the siderod connections to the first driver had broken. The engine crew had to disconnect the first driver from the side rod, changing the 2-8-0 to a 4-6-0! Unable to start on the grade, the train had to be backed down to the far side of a sag, so it could make a run for it. Slipping badly, the engine managed to haul the train to a siding, where a freight car was cut out of the consist. However, the train still slipped badly, and we just barely made it around a curve, where another car had to be set out on a siding. This was a graphic demonstration of the difference in power between a 2-8-0 and a 4-6-0.

A government agency overhauled the C&Z during the 1960's, and the most outward evidence of this work was in some col-orful painting—as seen in some red and green on engines, and blue passenger cars, which had been given names. The postal-express car displayed the name "Noche Buena," while the coaches had been named for famous citizens. Nevertheless, time caught up with this little road, and it was replaced with a shorter branch from the NdeM mainline, and the Coahuila & Zacatecas is no more.

One odd feature about the freight cars was that they were lettered in a style close to that of the Colorado & Southern Railway narrow-gauge cars of about World War I times (with large block lettering). Years later, while going through C&S files, I found that a C&S boxcar had been sent to the C&Z. During the rebuilding of its equipment from the

AT THE TRANSFER TRACK in Saltillo, Mexico, a wooden Coahuila y Zacatecas gondola, loaded with ore was at the left, while a standard-gauge National of Mexico steel gondola was at the right. Where is the transfer machinery? *Señores,* that consists of *hombres* with shovels or buckets, like the bucket lying by the track! The wooden CyZ gondola looks like a Colorado & Southern or Denver & Rio Grande Western narrow-gauge gondola, does it not?

THE FIRST-CLASS COACH *(primera* class) of the Coahuila & Zacatecas was painted a bright blue, had the railroad's logo (herald) in full color, and was named for Coahuila's most famous son, President Venustiano Carranza, of revolutionary-times fame. The old coach was unique on the CyZ, as its contemporaries had been destroyed in those violent times. devastation of the 1910–1914 revolutions, the new cars were copies of the Colorado & Southern's "sample" boxcar! No doubt, among the freight cars we looked over, was that same C&S boxcar, hauling ore concentrates a long way from its original travels to Como, Leadville and Gunnison.

WHEN THIS PICTURE was snapped at the enginehouse of the Chihuahua Mineral Railway in 1964, the line was shut down, and eventually, it was scrapped. Engines 2, 7, 6 and 4 sat awaiting their certain fate of scrapping—or so it seemed. Finally, by 1972, all that was left were Engines 7 and 4, and all cars and nearly all the track were gone. The turntable was left behind at Santa Eulalia, the mining town on the mountain. On it still sits Engine 2, a low-drivered Porter 2-8-0. Engine 6, another 2-8-0, has for years been a tour-

ist attraction, sitting on a plinth at Los Mochis, the western passenger-train terminal of the popular Copper Cañon tourist trips. Engine No. 7 had come from the logging railroad at Rhinelander, Wisconsin, in 1941. And I had what you might call the "general foreman's task" of returning little locomotive No. 7 there in 1973, to exchange for an old South Park engine, also then numbered "7." Engine 4, as mentioned elsewhere, was "thrown in the pot," and this little locomotive was moved to Golden.

CHIHUAHUA ENGINES TO THE U.S.

DURING THE WINTER of 1972–1973, there came about a very involved locomotive transfer involving bringing two narrow-gauge engines from Chihuahua, Mexico—one of them being traded for an engine in a logging museum in Rhinelander, Wisconsin, which had originally worked on the Denver, South Park & Pacific in Colorado, 2-8-0 No. 191. The three-locomotive movement was worked out by a lawyer-author, the entire cost being borne by the Colorado Railroad Museum in Golden, Colorado.

At Chihuahua, the two dead engines had to be loaded into standard-gauge gondolas; however, the nearest standard-gauge track

was three-rail on an adjacent freight line with a gauge of two feet, six inches. To reach the gondolas, we laid three-foot track from the enginehouse over to the electric line, and then on top of it, to the two gondolas, where a ramp was built to those cars. The narrow-gauge electric line ran twice a week, and we had to lay the track, load the engines and get the standard-gauge cars and our track off its mainline in-between those runs.

As a result, I drove my car to the scene in Mexico. As I traveled en route to my destination, I practiced my rusty Spanish on signs and newspapers. Unfortunately, except for the mine superintendent, none of the people I was to work with had any command of English. At first, it was thought that one engine could be steamed up and used to push the other engine and itself into the gondolas, but

DURING FEBRUARY OF 1973, the end of a long 32-year round trip was made by Engine 7 of the Thunder Lake Lumber Company, returned back to Rhinelander, Wisconsin, for the logging museum. Sold to the Chihuahua Mineral Railroad in 1941, No. 7 was returned by the Colorado Railroad Museum when that Mexican line was abandoned in 1971. No. 7 was exchanged for a former Denver, South Park & Pacific 2-8-0, displayed in the park at Rhinelander.

when an attempt was made, the little engine burst some flues. So, we managed to persuade the driver of one of the local mine trucks to use his truck as a switcher, using a cable to pull the engines. His big truck moved the narrow-gauge engines with ease. Then, the smelter's standard-gauge diesel-electric engine—with a cable attached—hauled the little locomotives up the ramp aboard the gondolas.

On the final day, we worked on the job until midnight, as the electric line had a train due during midmorning of the following day. And we managed to have this line's track clear of the makeshift overlay track by the time its shrill air whistle announced its approach. This train consisted of two diminutive boxcab electric motors (electric-tramway engines), equipped with panto-

graphs, trundling a string of little ore cars.

One of the steam engines, still lettered for an earlier railroad, the Potosí & Río Verde, went to Golden, Colorado, and was routinely unloaded, with the use of a crane and a lowboy truck. However, the No. 7 2-8-0, which was being returned to its original locale at Rhinelander, was quite a different affair. Although the old South Park locomotive sitting in the park was only a few hundred feet from the gondola containing her successor, the work that was needed to switch locations of the two engines was rather difficult.

At a cost of $8,000, as well as days of hard labor in near-zero temperatures and spitting snow, the transfer was eventually accomplished. The engine in the gondola was moved out onto a track connecting it to a lowboy-truck trailer. Then, the old DSP&P

USING A MINE TRUCK as a "switch engine," Potosí y Río Verde's No. 4, a 2-8-0, was being towed out of the enginehouse of the Chihuahua Mineral Railroad at Avalos, Mexico. Without a connecting track to where the little engine could be loaded into a mill gondola for shipment to Golden, Colorado, a temporary track was built over to and on top of the neighboring 2.5-foot-gauge electric railroad. The narrow-gauge electric line had some dual-gauge track with standard-gauge just beyond the water tank. Working until midnight, this engine and another one, No. 7, were loaded aboard two gondolas, using a steel cable and a diesel-electric engine from the smelter to pull them up into the gondolas. Then, by 10:00 a.m. the next morning, all of this had to be out of the way, as the little electric mine train arrived on its bi-weekly run.

engine in the park had to be loaded onto another lowboy trailer and maneuvered among the trees in the park, power poles and a curving road to get to the gondola. The rails had to be greased on the ramps, as the engine's drive wheels were frozen and would not turn. At one point, a construction worker threw a lighted match into the firebox. After this act, a lazy wisp of smoke came from the DSP&P engine's stack for several days. It turned out that the park-cleanup people had disposed of trash in her firebox for years!

The F.C.M. ("Ferrocarril Mineral de Chihuahua") had ceased operations, as its equipment wore out, and motor trucks took over the hauling of ore from the nearby mountains. Two others of its engines were put on display, one on the turntable at the mines, and the other at distant Los Mochis, on the Pacific Coast. The 30-inch electric line, which had a stable of interesting freight cars, along with the ore cars, also had a short future, and a few years later, it went to the scrap heap. It had the impressive name of the "Minerales Nacionales de México," as well as the "Ferrocarril Industrial El Potosí & Chihuahua." Originally, it was a steam-powered line, but it had been electrified in 1924. The two little parallel lines served the same mining area and the same Asarco smelter.

On the day we finished our work at the smelter, I stopped at the local bakery near my motel and picked up their specialty: coconut cake. We sat down at noon for lunch around a fire composed of kindling from scrapped narrow-gauge boxcars—featuring sweet portions of that coconut cake for dessert, a delightful Chihuahua delicacy. And the foreman regaled us with a reminiscence of his first railroad job, working at clearing dynamited and burned engines and cars on the Orient line to the north, where the railroad was a victim of the long revolutionary period of 1910–1920.

We were very glad to obtain the old South Park engine for the museum. Dating from 1880, when she was No. 51 of that line, this engine had worked as a freight engine under the successor companies: the Denver, Leadville & Gunnison Railway and the Colorado & Southern Railway. The C&S people decided to rebuild the newest narrow-gauge power, and they offered No. 191 for sale. By early 1902, this 2-8-0 was gone, to see use on a Wisconsin lumber line, the Washburn & Northwestern Railroad as their No. 7. Then, after that road ceased operations, the engine went to the Thunder Lake Lumber Company for use on their Robbins Railroad. In 1932, the ex-DSP&P engine was given to the city park at Rhinelander, Wisconsin, and old No. 191 was still able to steam to that site.

The old engine had seen much hard usage, and despite everything, she still had her old-style dome castings of 1880. Jim Dunlop (of two-foot restoration fame in Massachusetts) built a South Park style wooden "cowcatcher." John Buvinger scaled off photographs and made a cardboard mockup of a standard Union Pacific headlight of the 1880's, which an Ohio craftsman then duplicated in metal. Plans for a Congdon smokestack were given to a sheet-metal firm, which turned out a credible replica of that distinctive South Park fixture. The tender tank was something made by the lumber-company people, and it was about to collapse. So, Bob Shank, Jr., traded us a Denver & Rio Grande Class C-16 tender tank left at the Perins Peak coal mine and ghost town. This place is northwest of Durango on what was the Calumet Branch of the Rio Grande Southern. Tom Stevanak and Brad Lester worked many hot summer days to rebuild the tender frame, a massive job requiring over 100 large bolts and other appurtenances, which required drilling holes in smoking oak wood.

Volunteers planned to replace the missing boiler jacket and restore the wooden cab, much battered from years sitting in the park at Rhinelander.

Because old records mostly were destroyed, little was learned about exact places and usages of the 2-8-0. However, what little was found indicated the engine had spent years stationed at Gunnison, used on the Baldwin Branch and as a helper on the line to Alpine Tunnel. No. 191 was one of two DSP&P engines kept at Gunnison in 1882, when Union Pacific forces were grading a route up beside Ohio Creek and over Ohio Pass to reach coal-mine properties just a few miles to the west. They had laid track for about a mile beyond what in later years was called Baldwin, when workers were diverted to build a mile-long spur to a newly opened coal-and-coking project. Tracklayers had reached within several hundred feet of the mine when the project closed down in bankruptcy, never to reopen.

The track had been laid in very poor weather, deep snow, was unballasted and right along the creek. Disgusted management in faraway Omaha ordered the spur trackage to be taken up. So, the assistant division engineer working at this spot (without authority) used one of the available engines to take flatcars out on the dubious track to load its rails and ties. It could have been No. 191, and if so, it was the farthest point on the South Park line that any engine or train had ever been. The Ohio Pass Extension shut down shortly thereafter, due to financial problems on the Union Pacific, and although the project was "revived" in 1892, under the Denver, Leadville & Gunnison name, there was neither any track laid, nor were any trains operated.

Another probable use of No. 191 was in 1895, when a work train stalled in Alpine Tunnel, while men were digging out a cave-in at the eastern portal. There was nothing under steam at the shutdown Gunnison roundhouse. Eventually, however, an engine was able to be sent with a makeshift crew to try to drag out the stalled engine, whose crew had perished in carbon-monoxide gas when the fireman had stoked the fire in the engine. Was it the 191 that went to the rescue? Unfortunately, the train registers of Alpine Tunnel vanished in some bonfire of long ago, and things like train orders also vanished in fires and due to neglect.

YUCATAN RAILWAYS—IN A VERY DIFFERENT MEXICO

THE UNITED RAILWAYS of Yucatán (Ferrocariles Unidos de Yucatán) was a very unusual segment of Mexico's railroads. Isolated until the 1950's on this peninsula that juts way out in the Gulf of Mexico, there had grown up in this state a system of hundreds of miles of narrow-gauge lines. And they were equipped with a stable of motive power that was unique in all the Republic of Mexico. However, by the 1960's, the little Yucatan railways were facing changes that would sweep them away.

In 1960, the state capital of Mérida had a large "Central Station," with a stub-end train shed consisting of half-a-dozen tracks. Connecting with the engine-and-car terminal was a yard that had a considerable amount of dual-gauge trackage. A feature of this yard was the highest switchstand targets I had ever seen. The engines used to be woodburners, and the yard had been piled high with wood for the engines until very recent times. This was the reason for the targets being so high that a ladder was necessary for the switchstand-lamp tenders.

As with most Mexican cities, the rural vendors that sold the day's vegetables, etc., came into Mérida early in the morning. Any interruption of this could quickly bring the city to a point of starvation. In Yucatán, the vendors came into town by train. From way out in the peninsula, mixed trains would start from various terminals at about 5:00 a.m. They averaged about 20 mph, considering their numerous stops along the way, before arriving for the morning outdoor farmers' market. Then, late in the afternoon, the trains would go back to their respective terminals. Several trains reversed this routine, departing from Mérida during the early morning for some distant point. So, twice a day, there was a great coming and going of trains, with fascinating consists, not to be found anywhere else in the Americas.

Yucatán is flat, and the railroad lines had minimal grades and curves. There were no bridges; all the streams were underground. As a result, there was no need for a Bridge-and-Building Department work train on the UdeY. The engines were a mixture of low-slung light Moguls (2-6-0's), Americans (4-4-0's) and Ten-wheelers (4-6-0's). For size, they would have matched the little engines the Denver & Rio Grande first bought during the 1870's and 1880's. Most of them had crosshead pumps, just like those engines of long ago. Their pilots had a long link-and-pin coupling bar, although each tender had an automatic coupler, with a slot for link-and-pin coupling. Yet, among this roster were the last 4-4-0 types built by Baldwin Locomotive Works in 1946. For branch use, way out in the remote portions of the railroad, there were still a couple of woodburners with huge balloon smokestacks. However, all other engines had been converted to burn oil as fuel.

The Mérida roundhouse could be seen only from the inside, as all the trackage was on the inside of the structure. This was a square building, with a turntable in the center. This odd construction meant that the stalls varied in length. All around the place were discarded items, including two of Mérida's last streetcars (rotting away), a der-

elict three-foot-gauge 4-4-2 and many other surprises. The shop force was rebuilding a couple of wooden-pump handcars for section crews. They also rebuilt the wooden flat-roofed coaches, and a string of a dozen wood-beam coach trucks was ready for use.

The United Railways of Yucatán (UdeY or URofY in English) also had a standard-gauge line, 29 miles in length (with third rail) to the port of Progreso. And frequently operated trains ran on this line, powered by 4-4-0 types. Among the coaches were what seemed to be former streetcars. One of the 4-4-0's came from the famed Yosemite Valley Railway of California. A group of Californians tried in vain to buy it for return; however, they failed. That was typical of most attempts to purchase engines from Mexico, as many U.S. groups learned. When dieselization finally came in the 1960's, Walt Disney's representatives arrived on the scene. They made a deal for several of the last steam engines, including a woodburner on display in front of the depot in Mérida.

Not only was the Mérida station area a center of much activity each morning, with the arrivals and departures, the trains had to be very close before one could be certain if the approaching engine was a 4-4-0 or a 2-6-0. They usually had a steel-underframed boxcar for a baggage car and faded red second- and third-class coaches. If there was a special event, such as a religious festival, fourth-class passengers would be handled in freight cars. As it rained without warning—heavily—in this tropical environment, open cars were not favored. Fortunately, these showers were brief, or else the railroad yard would have become a lake.

At some time, the railroad had obtained an outside-frame 2-8-0, but it was limited to the yard—much too heavy for the light 40- and 45-pound rail on the mainlines. The Federal Department of Public Works (SCOP initials) bought a 4-6-0 standard-gauge engine of 1888 for switching, and a couple of NdeM outside-frame narrow-gauge 4-6-0's from the lines that were working out of Mexico City. However, when the 112-mile line from Mérida to Campeche, located in the adjacent state to the west, was standard-gauged, these heavier narrow-gauge engines had little use.

The station names in Mexico proper are heavy with the names of saints and heroes, "San" and "Santa" being common prefixes. However, Yucatán had station names that

241

were really tongue-twisters, such as: "Tix-kokob," "Dzitas," "Xcanchakan," "Xucu," "Oxkutzcab," etc. The people of Yucatán were mostly Mayan, so different from the rest of the population of Mexico that they petitioned the U.S. Congress some 150 years ago to admit them as a state of the Union. Our stunned politicians never made a reply to this serious request.

For many years, the UdeY was listed in a condensed inch and a half in the *Official Guide*. However, as it neared the end of most of its activity, the company splurged with a full page in the *Official Guide*, listing in detail the schedules and all the little places on each remaining line. For general manager there was genial Ing. Gelasio Luna y Luna, whom we had met earlier, when he was rebuilding the Coahuila Y Zacatecas line. Wanting to practice his English, he insisted we speak to him in Spanish, while he would reply in English. And in that fashion, we negotiated to have our special train, amid much smiling.

In a burst of enthusiasm during one trip to Yucatán, several of us railfans asked about having a special train. For $150 we obtained Mogul No. 260, a caboose and second-class coach "Claudio Sacremento M" for a 106-mile round trip to Sotuta. At that point, the crew showed us a "cenote," a deep pool in the limestone. This supposedly was where prehistoric Mayan priests had indulged in throwing people into the pool as sacrifices. A ruined church was a relic of civil wars of this century. Lunch was at the home of some friends of the crew. It was composed of an interesting variety of food, unlike what is termed "Mexican" at restaurants. And not only was it very bland, but there were no hot condiments at all, and no salt and pepper, either. The Yucatecos (as the people of Yucatán are called) are very different from the population in the rest of Mexico. They are rather short, with different features, speak a language full of "X's" and "K's," and their places and towns are neat and exhibit a much higher standard of cleanliness.

The engineer of our special train, happy at not having to make so many frequent stops, showed us a burst of speed. However, our coach bounced so much that one marker lamp bounced out of its socket and arced over the right-of-way. At one point, we had a meet with a "train" of a sisal plantation. At one time, Yucatán had 2,500 miles of the so-

LOCOMOTIVE NO. 76, a 2-6-0, and a five-car passenger train, was photographed in the Mérida yard of the Unidos de Yucatán (UdeY), the railroad operating in the State of Yucatán. This Mexican state is located at the northeastern end of the Yucatan Peninsula, and Mérida is the capital and principal city of this state. Notice that the typical switchstand target towered above the train, a reminder that the UdeY engines were woodburners in the past, and the yard was full of high stacks of wood for fuel. A cattle car was frequently seen at the head end of UdeY mixed trains, handling all kinds of livestock.

called "Decauville" railways, small narrow-gauge affairs marketed by Europeans. No longer were there any locomotives operating on these lines, only a mule-hauled flatcar here and there, which met the regular trains. They had been very important when the peninsula produced enormous crops of henequen and sisal. At one time, these crops were the principal products of Yucatán.

For many years, Yucatán was the richest state in Mexico, primarily because it supplied most of the world's needs for henequen. This was a fiber that was made into ropes, and it was used by weavers of rugs, etc. Progreso was a busy port, with ships from many nations tying-up here to load this material. However, after World War II, the market rapidly declined, as nylon and other materials superseded henequen. And with that decline went the bulk of traffic of the UdeY, resulting in the abandonments of most of its lines, as well as the little Decauville lines that carried the henequen to the UdeY.

Highways have replaced most of the UdeY trains, and the farmers' market people now come to town by trucks and buses. And little No. 260 is somewhere in the Disney empire, hauling the much bigger loads of passengers than during the day it made our fast run to Sotuta and back to Mérida.

AYUTLA, IN GUATEMALA, renamed Tecun Uman, was at the extreme western end of the mainline of the International Railways of Central America. Generally, the line, equipment, etc., was referred to by its Spanish name, the "Ferrocarriles Internacionales de Centro America," and the lettering was simply "F.I. DE C.A." Well maintained, operated in North American style, twice-daily passenger service was offered on the mainlines across Guatemala, with mostly home-built steel cars that had replaced the original wooden cars. By 1965, on our last visit, troubles with the military governments were growing, and finally the line was nationalized in 1968. And the Ferrocarriles Internacionales de Centro America has been going downhill ever since.

INTERNATIONAL RAILWAYS OF CENTRAL AMERICA

GUATEMALA AND EL SALVADOR, the two countries just south of Mexico in Central America, had large American-style narrow-gauge railroads, which still barely exist (in 1995). These lines had hundreds of miles of mainline trackage, excellent roadbed, and their trains powered with Mikados very similar to the largest classes of 2-8-2's on the Denver & Rio Grande Western. The mainline had double-daily passenger service, with 8- and 10-car trains.

Several times between 1959 and 1965, it was a pleasure to explore these lines. A property controlled by the United Fruit Company became a victim of political changes, and in 1968 the lines in Guatemala were nationalized, with those in El Salvador following suit in 1974. However, these Central American lines remained U.S. style in equipment and operations.

The first trip Ken Crist, Ed Gerlits and I took was the 6:00 p.m. passenger train from the capital of Guatemala, en route to Puerto Barrios, the country's Atlantic port. At midnight, we stopped at Zacapa and got off the train to spend the night in the railroad-operated "Hotel Ferrocarril," (*ferrocarril* meaning *railroad* in Spanish—literally "iron-rail").

After dawn on the following morning, I

244

F. I. DE C. A. 2-6-0 No. 79, a Baldwin Mogul, was waiting for its connection at Mulua, Guatemala. Then, the engine will haul a three-car train of old wooden passenger cars up the 3.0-percent—and even steeper—grades to San Felipe, high in the coffee-growing region.

was awakened by a great commotion outside the hotel, and I wandered out onto the second-floor veranda to see what was going on. Below my vantage point the eight-car passenger train for El Salvador was being prepared, and passengers were noisily embarking. Across the railroad's yard tracks were a roundhouse and turntable, and a half dozen engines could be seen. Busily switching the yard was a husky outside-frame 2-8-0. All sorts of equipment could be seen, ranging from freight cars to extra coaches—and even a ditcher train was waiting for wet weather. For me, this was a good introduction to Guatemala's railroads.

During the early afternoon, we went on to Puerto Barrios via the daytime 10-car passenger train, consisting of an RPO-express car on the head end, followed by eight coaches for second-class passengers, and tailing on the rear was a new steel first-class coach, in which our party of three comprised most of the payload. After five hours of traveling through the jungle-like countryside along a big river, we reached the port city. That evening, we had a tour of the roundhouse and then adjourned for refreshments in the Club La Luna (*la luna* meaning *the moon* in Spanish), a dirt-floor version of a Guatemalan nightclub. As it was the evening of Christmas day, some customers were lighting firecrackers to toss out on the dance floor. However, by his presence, a *policía* (policeman) ensured that things stayed under control. On the next day, we returned to the capital, enjoying the doubleheader mixed-train consist as it wound through endless curves, crossed trestles and even passed

245

ENGINE 79 WAS ONE of the last three Moguls of the International Railways of Central America (the FIDECA), shown here on the San Felipe Branch in 1965. The light track and bridges kept larger engines away. The small engines could handle 20 tons on the up-to 3.5-percent grade on this 10-mile branch in western Guatemala's mountains. With discontinuance of the line in the late 1960's, the little engine was given to the Colorado Railroad Museum. However, no practical way to move FIDECA locomotive No. 79 out of the country ever developed. At the time, the military government was getting cash by scrapping all the railroad it could for $30.00 a ton, offered by the Japanese for steel scrap at Pacific Coast ports. And—sadly—No. 79 went to Japan for scrap.

through occasional tunnels, as we climbed out of the lowlands into the coffee-growing highlands. Guatemala City had the principal roundhouse and machine shops, where almost anything needed by the railroad could be fabricated. Shopmen were working on new steel passenger cars, steel boxcars and other cars, while locomotives were being given major overhauls. In one corner of the shop, men were fabricating hardwood pilots for the locomotives, since it seems that in wet weather a wooden "cowcatcher" was safer than a conventional steel one when encountering a rockslide, as a steel one might bend and derail the engine, while a wooden one would just disintegrate. And amazingly, the shop also was turning-out newly built 1890-style hand-pump section cars!

The 177-mile trip to the Mexican frontier at Tecun Uman was a two-day event, as there was not much in hotel accommodations at the border. So, we preferred to arrive there in the morning. En route, the train dropped through huge cuts in the volcanic region, skirting the shores of lakes, backed by distant volcanoes, and the train stopped along the line at places where roundhouses and branches were located. The last part of the journey was through jungle country, which included steel trestles over deep ravines.

Tecun Uman had an engine shed, a small yard and a low international trestle, over which the National of Mexico (NdeM) traversed to use the small dual-gauge portion of

LOCOMOTIVE 79, one of the last FIDeCA Moguls, was waiting for its train at the mainline junction of Mulua, in western Guatemala. Soon, a slightly larger 2-8-0 would arrive here, with a three-car wooden train, looking like something from the railroad's early years. This train had started at the little Pacific Coast port of Champerico, on that branch. Then, it used a few miles of the mainline to get to Mulua. Many years earlier, this route had been a separate railroad from the coast to San Felipe; however, later construction had made both ends just branches, of very little traffic importance any more.

the yard. A short branch led to the Pacific Ocean, and for that light-rail line the last 4-4-0 was employed, along with the last inside-frame 2-8-0. The 4-4-0 eventually ended-up in the Smithsonian Institution in Washington, D.C., as she had originated from a California railroad. The 2-8-0 was retained to power occasional excursions from Guatemala City. Deep in the jungle were two rusting Rogers engines and who knows what else, relics that were abandoned many years ago from some failed project.

Up early in the morning for another trip, we boarded the El Salvador-bound eight-car passenger train from Zacapa. For much of the way in Guatemala, the train followed the river, but then a series of loops were encountered to reach the frontier—via tunnels and deep cuts through a terrain that obviously had the habit of sliding and heaving the tracks. Below us, the river valley became tiny and distant. Finally, 70 miles out of Zacapa we reached Anguiatu, the small border point, where the bridge arched over a small stream.

Salvadoran customs agents eyed us curiously, as foreigners rarely traveled this way anymore. Local children acted as money-changers, using the train from Guatemala to get back and forth, and by this means, we obtained enough *colones* to pay our fares to San Salvador. The El Salvador Division train was about the same makeup, except that no Railway Post Offices functioned in that coun-

try. For 95 miles that afternoon, the train wound through brushy scenery, very rugged at times, past numerous villages, like scenes from *The National Geographic* magazine—even past an occasional lake. As in Guatemala, the distant mountains looked as though they contained the high peaks of volcanoes. This was the newest portion of the IRCA, having been opened only in 1929, to give El Salvador's coffee and cotton products an outlet to the Atlantic Ocean.

The city of San Salvador had a large roundhouse, as well as a large machine shop, which like the one at Guatemala City, could repair and manufacture almost anything the rolling stock needed. Cars on this division had an "S" prefix to their numbers. We did not have the extra days needed to go on to the end of the line at Cutuco, on the Bay of Fonseca, and we returned in the evening to the amenities of San Salvador.

Guatemala had several branches to ports, and one 10-mile branch worked its way upgrade to San Felipe. Because of light bridges and rail, the last Moguls (2-6-0's) of the railroad were kept for use on this line. From the port of Champerico, a train would work up to the mainline, 18 miles away, then use that trackage for a few miles to reach the San Felipe Branch. Meanwhile, a Mogul had backed down for about nine miles from the Mazatenango roundhouse and hauled the train on up the branch. One of the last wooden coaches was used on this branch,

247

TWICE A DAY the junction point of El Sitio del Niño ("The Site of the Child"), El Salvador—in Central America—was busy, as mainline trains from both directions met the Santa Ana Branch train. Cars, passengers, mail, express and L-C-L freight were quickly exchanged, as all three locomotives took on water in the midst of all this confusing commotion.

obviously due for repairs. Standing on the end platform, one could see the forward end of the car tilt in the direction of a curve it was entering, while the rest of the car was still vertical!

San Felipe perhaps was once an important shipping point for coffee. A nondescript wooden depot, freight house and turntable were fixtures of the small yard at this point. Nearby, a vague trail in the forest showed us where, during the 1920's, a standard-gauge electric line ran to the regional capital of Quezaltenango. Destroyed by a tropical storm a few years later, it was scrapped.

The IRCA management decided to give me one of the Moguls for the Colorado Railroad Museum. However, problems arose that made its "escape" to the U.S. impossible. The railroad was about to be confiscated by the military government, and shipment was blocked indefinitely. So, a few years later, when the Japanese were offering $30 a ton for scrap, little No. 79 joined those ship-

ments, and the branch to San Felipe was abandoned.

FERROCARRIL DE EL SALVADOR

THE "OLD RAILROAD," as the Ferrocarril de El Salvador was known, was quite different from the modern IRCA. At a large wooden trainshed a long mixed train waited in the morning, made up of a string of open-platform wooden coaches, with the road name lettered in full. There were no first-class coaches, so we squeezed in with the crowd of second-class passengers—with their kids, vegetables, chickens and other small livestock. At one point, the train skirted an active volcano, passing through deep cuts in an old lava flow, which for a few years, had cut the line in two. The 108-mile railroad, although financed by English capitalists, was American-equipped. The line had

248

ENGINE NO. 13, an outside-frame Baldwin 2-8-0, was typical of the motive power of the El Salvador Railway. The engine was equipped with a link-and-pin coupler on the pilot, while the ten-der had an automatic coupler, which was slotted, so that link-and-pin couplers could be used. This 2-8-0 was typical of narrow-gauge power Baldwin sold all over the world, begining in the late 1890's.

been constructed in the shape of a giant wye, with terminals at Acajutla, on the Pacific, and at Santa Ana, a western provincial capital. Twice a day, the junction point of Sitio del Niño ("site of the child") would see trains from all three points meet, do some switching, take water, exchange passengers, and in about half an hour, the place would be quiet again.

Link-and-pin couplers were still used, along with automatic ones equipped with slots to accept the old links. And the pilots of most engines had only the old link-and-pin type. The automatic couplers were so worn that on our return trip the next day—as we approached the town of Armenia—our rear-end first-class coach, fresh from the Sonsonate shop, uncoupled, and passengers frantically worked to tie-down the hand brakes. As the knuckles had slots, the crew

just used link-and-pins to re-couple the car to the train and did not even try to use the automatic coupler again.

Engines on this line were all outside-frame 2-8-0's, several of them secondhand from the Oahu Railway in Hawaii, as were some of the steel boxcars. At Sonsonate, the machine-shop belts were powered by what was left of ancient engine No. 1, a 4-4-0, mounted on concrete blocks. Outside the shop building, the yard had various old relics, some idle so long that small trees were growing up from engine steam chests, etc. It was obvious why the owners had simply turned the money-losing company over to the government, which kept it running on virtually no budget.

The train to Acajutla dropped steadily downgrade in a swirl of dust from the unballasted track. At one time, the old port had been important during the days when coastal steamers regularly plied the numerous small ports of call along the Pacific Coast of Central America. Now there was a new port a couple of miles away, with modern docks and heavy-duty cranes, where ships were loaded with cotton and coffee shipments—most of it transported to the port by trucks instead of by rail. The fireman on our engine indicated that they were taking the engine over there, and if we liked, we could go along. And in a short time, he came from the office, bringing a large sheet of wrapping paper, which he placed on the air tank atop the tender, providing us with a clean seat from which to watch the proceedings. Thereupon, we rode on top of the tender as the locomotive switched cars at the new docks.

It was on Sunday when we went on our way back to the capital of this small Central American country. Ahead of the mixed train went two or three gasoline-powered railbuses, reminiscent of the old Rio Grande Southern's *Galloping Goose* cars. Someone in our group dubbed these railbuses "Gal-

loping Bananas"! Overloaded with weekenders returning to their homes, the roofs of these railbuses were piled high with luggage and parcels of assorted shapes and sizes. At one station, we caught up with one of these cars that was having motor trouble. However, the crew did not seem to be overly concerned about the problem. Obviously, it was not a rare occurrence. A long bar, equipped with coupling-pin holes at each end, was brought out, and the motorized vehicle trailed our train in this fashion for the rest of the day. Our engine did not seem to notice the extra load, despite the steep grades.

When the Salvadoran government took over the IRCA in 1971, it merged the two railroad operations. The Sonsonate shop was closed, and much of the old railroad's rolling stock was either set aside or scrapped. Then came the brewing civil war, and before long, both railroads were shut down. The latest heard from El Salvador was that except for switching at the port and a suburban train in the capital, all of the railroad lines sat rusting and rotting away.

CHASING TRAINS
BOB RIDES TRAINS ACROSS THE MIDDLE EAST

IRAN STATE RAILWAYS British-built "Beyer-Garratt" (patent type) articulated locomotive No. 418 had two 4-8-2 sets of wheels (4-8-2–2-8-4). This monster was used on the line north of Tehe- ran, over the mountains to the Caspian Sea port city of Bandar Shah. No. 418 was photographed just after being rebuilt by the U.S. Army Railway Battalion in 1944.

250

THE IRAN STATE RAILWAY

THE MAINLINE of this unusual state railroad traverses some of the most rugged mountain areas in the world, 861 miles from the Persian Gulf to the Caspian Sea. In one section of 165 miles of line, there are 135 tunnels, numerous gallery-type cuts and many large bridges. Beyond Teheran, on the portion of 286 miles reaching to the Caspian Sea, there is a 65-mile section that includes 69 tunnels, totalling over 11 miles in length. Eleven of these tunnels are of spiral design, of the same type made famous on the Canadian Pacific in the Rocky Mountains. At several locations there are three levels of track on the mountainsides, and many bridges of considerable size. Grades, however, are at most just under 3.0 percent on this northern section, while on the southern portion, the maximum is 1.5 percent.

Without incurring any foreign debt, the line was constructed between 1927 and 1938.

Few foreigners had any occasion to use the line, but beginning in August of 1941, it assumed great importance in supplying Russia with wartime needs. Then, in 1942, the first of some 30,000 U.S. troops became involved in the operation of the railroad, which lasted until 1945. The railroad had not been intended or expected to handle large amounts of freight when built, and passenger business was all local. However, the railroad's capacity was greatly expanded during World War II to move millions of tons of freight.

THE LARGEST LOCOMOTIVE of the Iran State Railways was this mammoth articulated creation. Four of these articulateds were built by the respected British firm of Beyer-Garratt, and the shipment of these locomotives to Iran and subsequent unloading at Bandar Shahpur on the Caspian Sea represented the largest items the port ever received. By the time the British and Russian armies invaded Iran in 1941 (to head off an expected takeover by Nazi forces, who were advancing into the Caucusus in Russia, just north of Iran), the engines were out of service. The meager Teheran shop force was unable to keep them going. The U.S. Army Railway Battalions that arrived in 1943, went to work on this one, and finally, in 1944, they brought the monster out for trial. They proudly posed on the 4-8-2–2-8-4, and they cleared the area for my pictures. However, when the throttle was opened, the great machine just sat in place—vibrating—as each set of drivers attempted to move in opposite directions! However, the problem was corrected, and the engine was assigned to the extremely difficult line operated by the Russians, from Teheran through the Elburz Mountains to the Caspian Sea. The lettering and Imperial emblems on the sides were heavy brass plates. A huge plate, with the "Lion-and-Sun" emblem, was offered to me by one officer, from another scrapped engine. My problem was: how would I get it back to the U.S.A.?

IN TRAVERSING the Zagros Mountains that lay between the Iranian capital of Teheran and the Persian Gulf, the Iran State Railways had something like 135 tunnels in 130 miles. There were many huge stone and concrete bridges, and long stretches of galleries cut into the mountainsides. At one point, there was a spiral loop, which employed several tunnels and a bridge over a narrow gorge. Completed in 1938, the line also reached beyond Teheran to the Caspian Sea, going through another mountain area, featuring three levels of tracks, many tunnels, spirals and 3.0-percent grades. This line is where the four articulated Beyer-Garratt 4-8-2–2-8-4 engines were employed. Little known even today, this Iranian line undoubtedly is one of the greatest railroad-engineering feats of all time. Fortunately, being in the U.S. Signal Corps and supplied with a camera permit, I could take all the railroad photographs I wanted. In the times of the railroad's builder, Shah Reza Pahlevi, photography was strictly limited.

As a member of the U.S. Army Signal Corps, I traveled several times on the Teheran-to-Ahwaz *Trans-Iranian Express*, a 10-car steam-powered 505-mile trip, requiring nearly 24 hours to traverse terrain involving cold nights and searing daytime desert temperatures. Unlike in the prewar times of the Shah, there was no restriction on photography, so I saved my film for these trips. The way the train meandered through the great gorges and tunneled through enormous cliffs—passing from tunnels to cross high concrete-arch viaducts—this trip was an endless mile-after-mile delight to a railfan. I have neither seen anything since to match it, nor have I heard of any other railroad that comes close to operating on such a rugged route.

Of the 73 road locomotives available when we arrived, almost all of them were out of service, and the British and Americans brought in over 100 steam engines. The British locomotives were mostly their standard "W.D." 2-8-0's, while the U.S. imported standard 2-8-2's, produced by the three major locomotive builders. In addition, thousands of freight cars were brought-in to carry the freight.

Derelict at Ahwaz, I found the first four engines, Baldwin 2-6-0 types, with the Baldwin plates and front-end number plates in both English and Persian languages. Since everything on the railroad was in the Persian (Farsi) language, it was necessary to teach the Americans to read the numerals, and all the stations were equipped with name boards in English. For timetables, the Americans issued mimeographed sheets at Ahwaz, which had the Persian language on one side and English on the other side. Adding to the

ANOTHER TYPICAL SECTION of the mountain line on the Iran State Railways, this view shows a passenger train with a tunnel beyond. It was a great treat for me to ride the "Trans-Iranian Express" between Ahwaz, in the southern desert, about 90 miles inland from the Persian Gulf, to the capital, Teheran. We traversed about 500 miles in 24 hours, using an American Lend-Lease 2-8-2 for power, with an eight-to 10-car train. When built, this line was never expected to haul the amount of traffic World War II brought. Britain and Russia invaded Iran in August of 1941 to prevent this country from falling under tyrannical German control. During the next four years, millions of tons of all kinds of supplies were moved over this railroad to the point where construction had halted on the northern branch. Thence, the war materiel was trucked to what was then the Soviet Union, to its "back door," the Caucusus.

complications were two different calendars, the Persian years and months based on a March new year, itself being in the 1300's.

To my delight, I could wander around with my camera anywhere, and I employed many a day's pass from army duty to stroll through the Teheran machine shops and "boneyard," the latter including rolling stock and motive power from all over Europe, including several Beyer-Garratt locomotives.

While at Ahwaz, several times I would ride in the engine of the passenger train down to the wye—a few minutes of escape from the humdrum of the office in the depot. It did not do to forget the extreme heat in Iran. One time I hurried out with a message for an engine crew, and I started climbing into the cab without my gloves, burning my hands on the grabirons. The grabirons were as hot as if they had been in a raging fire!

Once, while I was riding to the wye, the engineer suddenly became alarmed at being unable to get any water reading in the water glass, and in a panic, he shouted to the fireman and me, **"Jump!"** At 20 mph, those big, jagged black rocks of the desert certainly looked like a poor alternative to going sky high, and then water surged into the glass, and the engineer yelled "Hold it!" It turned out that the G.I. fireman was lazy, and he had not blown-down the engine as he was supposed to do, and the water had foamed, giving the incorrect reading.

After working the midnight shift, I could go back to the barracks in the morning by skipping the hot bus and riding in the diesel switcher, getting a little 90-degree (F.) breeze during the three-mile trip. Even a 90-degree breeze could feel cool in Ahwaz, where the sun temperature might rise to 160 degrees!

The rail lines beyond Teheran were in Russian-controlled territory, so I never got to see the spectacular northern line to the Caspian Sea. However, I did see the unfinished

THIS WAS A STATION STOP on the Iranian State Railways in the Zagros Mountains. There were not any towns or villages in these rugged-and-barren mountains. Water was so scarce the railroad had to use many tankcars for transport-ing fresh water for the engines. The extremely high temperatures of summer would make these places almost unbearable, and they would not cool off at night, as the rocks seemed to retain the heat.

line to Tabriz in northwestern Iran, but it was uninteresting for the most part, just follow-ing barren, dusty valleys. Briefly, we were stationed at the end-of-track, in Mianeh, 272 miles from Teheran. Once, while traveling through the area in a jeep, several of us drove along many miles of the unfinished 188 miles remaining to Tabriz. It traversed a rocky gorge, where there were gallery cuts in the mountains and a huge concrete arched bridge, which had partially collapsed from a recent earthquake. This line was under con-struction during 1941, when the Russians and British invaded Iran and took over.

For a few days, we were in Tabriz itself, as a result of bringing out U.S. airmen from Russia. These Air Corps boys had been in-volved in the Ploesti oil-field raids and had landed in Russia, where they were interned until the U.S. could arrange for their transit through Iran to the Persian Gulf. The Rus-sian five-foot-gauge line from Tabriz to Julfa, at the Russian border, was 91 miles in length. It was called the Azerbaijan Railroad, taken from the name of the local province.

You can read about my brief adventure with the Russians in Tabriz, in the section about the Azerbaijan Railroad.

Strangely, I never met any other railfans among the American troops in Iran, although I heard about one through one of the men I served with, who had met him. At Teheran, I had an unusual experience when the officer in charge of the Railway Battalion at the shops issued an order that no one was to in-terfere with my wanderings or picture-tak-ing. As I had never met this officer, I was puzzled at this order. And I did not know of it until one time crew members insisted on moving an engine out of the shop, so I could photograph it. When I protested that they were wasting time, they said that it was "…by order." All I could learn was that the commander had been having a bad time

THE TRANS-IRANIAN RAILROAD was completed in 1938, after 11 years of construction pierced this very rugged and desolate mountain range. The line required over 130 tunnels in about 122 miles, in two places making loops with curving tunnels in the mountains. Seized by Britain and Russia in August of 1941, to prevent Nazi agents from either seizing it or partly destroying it, the line was used for the next four years to haul supplies to the southern part of the Soviet Union (Russia) from the Persian Gulf. At this point, to gain altitude when a river gorge diverted away from the surveyed route, the railroad connected the two levels with a spiral loop. This included three tunnels and two viaducts—one of the tunnels being almost a half circle.

with his bunch of former U.S. railroad men. So, when a lieutenant reported me for taking pictures and wondered if that should be permitted, the officer reportedly declared that he was glad to find at least one G.I. who on his time off could behave without harming anything or anyone. Hence, he gave the order. So, at times it was sort of like enjoying a photo stop on a fan trip, except that I was the only one in the photo line! However, to my amazement, even the Colonel of the Military Police agreed that my activities were okay!

At Teheran, the Americans took over the machine shop to get engines restored to operating condition. In 1942, the yard had more dead locomotives than live ones. The four Beyer-Garratt 4-8-2+2-8-4 types were completely dead, even missing necessary parts. Eventually, the American shop men rebuilt one of these large articulated engines, and I happened to be at the shop on the day they proudly shoved No. 418 out to test their workmanship. Embarrassingly, when the throttle was opened, each set of drivers tried to go in the opposite direction, and the huge machine just stood there, shaking! *It seems as though they had hooked it up like an American Mallet!*

After the shop men corrected their error, No. 418 was turned over to the Russians to operate on their section over the Elburz Mountains to the Caspian Sea. However, No. 418 was back in the shop after only one round trip. The problem was the Russian crews were slovenly, using any kind of water—in this case, muddy ditch "gunk" (runoff from the mountains) and the engine simply was plugged.

THE AZERBAIJAN RAILROAD

A SMALL U.S. ARMY detachment was in Tabriz, Iran, for a few days during World War II to supply communications for the return from internment in Russia of a group of American airmen, who had bombed the Ploesti oil fields during a one-way trip across Romania. The northwestern portion of Iran (originally called the Persian Empire) was firmly under Russian occupation, and this was the sole time American G.I.'s were permitted to enter this region.

We were amazed to see a small narrow-gauge train of the Azerbaijan Railroad in Tabriz. The tickets to ride it were large paper coupons, and the train was said to have once been a horse car. However, when we were there, it had a sputtering Model "A" Ford engine, and it hauled a trailer as well, from the heart of Tabriz to the railroad station at the north edge of this Iranian city. The gauge was about two-thirds of a meter (26-inch gauge?) I stepped it off, using my shoes to guess what the gauge was, for lack of anything else to measure it. The Azerbaijan Railroad station and rail line led to the Russian frontier, 91 miles to the north, and the Russian army was firmly in control.

After explaining to a Russian political officer my interest in railroads, and stressing that I had never seen a broad-gauge railroad, he gave me a tour of the five-foot-gauge line at the depot. However, one had to contend with a not-too-dormant suspicion of their Amerikanski allies. So, the tour was made with two booted privates, "clomping" along, carrying their rifles with bayonets fixed. Proudly, I was shown an immaculate four-wheeled open-platform coach, with spotless ancient plush seats. A neat enginehouse, with rather sparse machinery, was also shown to us. And before I left the yard, a doubleheaded freight train, with two 0-10-0 types, came around a sharp curve into the yard on very worn-out rails. My guide declined, however, to let me examine closer a cluster of rusted engines over at one side of the Tabriz yard.

At the gate, I expressed my thanks to my Russian guide and escorts, and belatedly remembered I should have brought some cigarettes for them, showing my appreciation. Although I do not smoke, I did have some

THE AZERBAIJAN RAILROAD of Iran was a 91-mile broad-gauge line from the Russian border to Tabriz, capital of Azerbaijan province. It also had this narrow-gauge (about two-thirds of a meter) streetcar line, from the railroad station to the downtown area of Tabriz, about two miles in length. The fare was two *rials*, about six cents, and passengers received a large paper receipt (or ticket) with the Lion-and-Sun emblem of Iran. The lead car was powered with what looked like a Model "A" Ford motor. As usual, it struggled to haul the two cars, overloaded with passengers on a track that—fortunately for the motor—was mostly tangent and flat. World War II had stopped construction of the Tabriz Branch of the Iran State Railways, and in 1945, there was a huge gap in a very mountainous area of Iran. Many years later, this line was completed, and the Azerbaijan Railroad was merged into the ISR system and standard-gauged. The fate of the little streetcar railroad is not known.

chewing gum with me—an American custom all three evidently had never encountered. So, I had to explain how it was used. Gingerly, they tried it, smiled broadly and perhaps three converts were made that day to the custom!

THE RAY RAILROAD OF IRAN

ONE OF THE MOST UNUSUAL, and one might use the word "antique," narrow-gauge railroads I explored was the Ray Railroad. I was able to visit this unusual line while stationed in Iran during World War II, as a member of the Persian Gulf Command. This line was the country's first railroad, designed to handle the large traffic from Tehran to the

TAKING SIDING in Iran looked like this on the meter-gauge Ray Railroad. There had been a breakdown, and one trip was missed. So, little engine No. 5, an 0-6-0T, had quite a time of it getting a double-size train underway. The fireman went ahead and shoveled dirt on the rails to help the little engine get traction. Older pictures showed overloaded trains, with passengers crowded on the car roofs. This photograph was taken on June 28, 1945, and the view shows Iran's first railroad. Getting the material to Teheran in 1887 took much of the year. Then, the engines and cars had to be re-assembled, after they were hauled over what passed for roads through Iran's northern mountains, from what was later to become the Soviet Union—now Russia.

Islamic holy city of Ray (sometimes spelled "Rhages"), seven miles away. Iran had been rather isolated for centuries; however, following some visits of the Shah to Europe in the 1870's, various European-style items were introduced into the Persian lifestyle, like the telegraph and a postal service, which joined the then-new Universal Postal Union.

The Ray Railroad opened in 1887, with a rather ornate station building located at the eastern edge of the city. The railroad's equipment, which remained unchanged to the end, was rather simple. At first, the line had only three 0-6-0T side-tank engines, built by Tubize of Belgium. The line's coaches looked like something from children's story books,

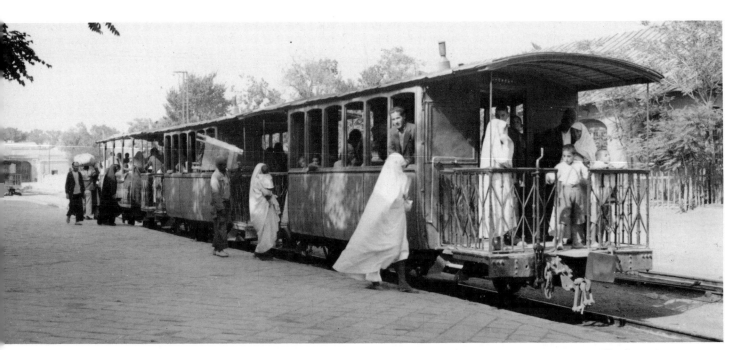

IT WAS TRAIN TIME in 1945 at the Ray Railroad station in Teheran, Iran. The country's first railroad, built to meter gauge, opened in 1887. And for over 70 years, the road has hauled hundreds of thousands of religious pilgrims to a shrine at Ray. This little city was a suburb of the capital of Teheran. So, the trains hauled large numbers of the Iranian version of commuters.

THE RAY RAILROAD'S engine No. 3 was built in 1887 by the firm of Tubize in Belgium. The engine's journey to then-remote Iran took many months, as well as extraordinary methods to get the 0-6-0T and her sisters through the Elburz Mountains from the Caspian Sea. Shah Nasr-ed-Din, who had visited Europe in the 1870's—the first Iranian ruler to do so—brought back many ideas for his backward country. These included the telegraph and a postal service. It is said that the Shah rode on the first train in 1887.

OLD ENGINE 2 of the seven-mile Ray Railroad was at Ray (ancient Rhages), Iran, a suburban community, with a shrine, attracting many passengers from Teheran, the capital. Despite the torrid summer weather, the U.S. Army insisted that we should be as uncomfortable as possible, wearing collars buttoned, neckties and long sleeves and trousers. It cost me six rials for a round trip on this line—about 20 cents—and the ticket agent was shocked when I bought $2.00 worth of tickets to send to friends as souvenirs!

ENGINE NO. 4, an 0-6-0T of the Ray Railroad, was entering the depot area in Teheran, Iran, during the summer of 1945. This meter-gauge engine, built by Tubize of Belgium, was the 1887-era railroad's newest engine. No. 4 dated from 1904, and was an exact duplicate of No. 1. The grade was steep from Ray, perhaps 2.0 percent or more, and the little engines worked hard to handle a string of five or six of the small four-wheel cars. The fare was three rials for a one-way ride—about 10 cents—so, I splurged and rode a round trip. This was my last railfanning in the Empire of Iran (Persia), for in a couple of days, my U.S. Army unit started to prepare to go home.

MANY AMERICAN CITIES have a "Railroad Street." This is the one that used to be in Iran's capital city of Teheran. The country's first railroad was installed in 1887, a meter-gauge line of seven miles to the holy pilgrimage city of Rhages (Ray). The street otherwise looked like streets all over the vanished empire. The little railroad was abandoned during the 1960's, in a dispute over taxes.

being four-wheeled, with open platforms and five windows on each side, as well as having benches end-to-end. The engines had tapered versions of the balloon stack, as the locomotives originally were intended to burn coal, but were converted to oil later. The cars had only hand brakes, but the engines had steam jam brakes. During 1904, two more engines arrived.

The line had an ascending grade to Tehran, but one engine could handle about five of the cars, typically packed with passengers. The fare was low, a mere three rials (about 10 cents U.S. in 1943). Operations were quite simple; there were no turntables, and the engine just ran around the cars at the end of the run. Midway along the route of about 35-pound rail was a passing track. To get traction for departing from Ray, the fireman would use a shovel to place sand on the rails for about 25 feet, which did the trick,

enabling the engine to get a start on the grade, with little slipping.

There was no indication of any freight traffic, although originally, before there were automobiles and trucks, there may have been many L-C-L freight shipments. There were several four-wheeled flatcars and boxcars to be seen at Tehran.

Unfortunately for my interest, the railroad was in a very old part of Tehran, off-limits to U.S. soldiers. However, one day I just climbed aboard a horse-drawn *droshky* (a four-wheeled carriage), and in that fashion, I traveled to the station. Upon departing from Tehran, the track wound down the center of a typical Iranian dirt street, narrow and flanked by seemingly endless mud-brick one-story buildings. Pedestrians seemed to favor using the track as a road. Once beyond the city, the line had a few easy curves, sometimes on sizable fills, through a treeless, barren countryside, typical of Iran. Besides the shrine at Ray, to which pilgrims constantly flowed, the other attraction was a pool fed by a spring. The water of this pool was supposed to be excellent for curing newly woven Persian rugs by washing them in the pool. After washing the rugs, they were then spread over nearby rocks to dry. Also at this point was a throne cut into the rock, dating from some forgotten ruler, who had set up his court at this spot.

Likely, I was the only G.I. to see and ride this little line. And as I had been off-limits at the time, I just kept the experience to myself. Many years later, I learned that during the great boom in Iran from oil revenues during the 1960's, the railroad got in a tax dispute and was shut down and scrapped. Evidently, the Iranian version of the IRS was a tough outfit to fight!

A BRITISH SOLDIER told me of this horse-car line in Baghdad, Iraq, in 1944, while I was passing through on a furlough to Palestine (Israel). Notice the Arabesque (Moorish) design of the car-barn doorway, at the left. This single-track line carried pilgrims to a nearby shrine of the Shiite Moslem sect. I did not dare go for a ride, because the area was "off limits" for non-Moslems, as the Britisher had warned.

THIS IRAQI STATE RAILWAYS meter-gauge passenger train was on the line from Baghdad to Basra, at the head of the Persian Gulf, a distance of 358 miles. This locomotive was a U.S. Lend-Lease 2-8-2, and most of the cars were from Britain or British India. Although the desert in December of 1944 became quite warm by day, at night it was freezing, and the coaches lacked glass windows, equipped only with shutters. In the consist, however, was a new dining car, built at Baghdad. This dining car had cuisine and service that would match many other railroads in supposedly more advanced parts of the world. The trip to Basra took about 18 hours. During the 1980's, a new standard-gauge railroad was completed, and the meter-gauge line was torn up. It is not known what happened to this line during the recent "Desert Storm" conflict in the Middle East.

IRAQ DURING 1944 had hundreds of miles of meter-gauge lines, in fact, more of them than standard gauge. This British-built engine had been their heaviest power until World War II brought some Lend-Lease American Mikados. The yard area in Baghdad had a wonderful variety of engines and cars. Some were very small, a single step being all that was required to get up into the cab. With the European disdain for handholds, footboards and other American conveniences, the crew coupled-on a small open car the switchmen could ride to switch cars.

AN AMERICAN LEND-LEASE ALCO locomotive used during World War II was on the meter-gauge mainline of the Iraqi State Railways, between Baghdad and the Persian Gulf port of Basra. The 2-8-2 was of general design, could be devised to operate on various gauges, and was sent around the world to do so. The engine's weight taxed the meter-gauge track, which fortu-nately had few grades and curves through southern Iraq. When these locomotives and hundreds of other engines and cars were shipped from India early in the war, it was feared that Turkey might go in with the Axis powers (Germany, Italy and Japan), and Iraq might become an important war zone. Fortunately, the Turks declined the Axis pressures.

IT WAS JUST AFTER 8:00 a.m., and the "San Juan," Train 115, was just departing from Antonito, Colorado, for Durango on July 2, 1941. At the left, the conductor and passengers wait for the Santa Fe train to pull up to the platform. The station agent's helper had an old-time two-wheeled baggage cart loaded with mail for the train's Railway Post Office. The combined trains had come from Alamosa, and late in the afternoon, the same operation would be reversed at Antonito. However, this was not to last much longer, for at the end of the following month, the final runs would be made on the 125-mile "Chili Line," as the Santa Fe Branch was affectionately known. I found that riding on this train to Santa Fe, New Mexico, was like taking a trip to a foreign country. (Notice the black Conoco tankcar on the siding next to the mainline.)

THE SOUTHBOUND "Chili Line" train was waiting for the northbound train at Embudo, New Mexico. Behind the water tank is a turntable for helper engines on the seven miles of 4.0-percent grade leading from the canyon of the Rio Grande (the river). The stone-covered depot remains a monument to the consumptive Station Agent H. W. Wallace, who served many years at this site. In his spare time, he covered the wooden depot, as well as all the outbuildings, with stone. Agent Wallace had first come to Colorado in 1892, probably thinking he would die, and he worked at the Rio Grande Southern's station at Lizard Head Pass, where the dry air helped him a great deal. This scene was photographed on July 2, 1941, and the abandonment hearings were over, the ICC decision had been given, and the Chili Line was going to be abandoned by the end of August.

262

THE D&RGW'S CHILI LINE

STRANGEST of the Denver & Rio Grande Western's narrow-gauge lines was the 125-mile Santa Fe Branch, from Antonito, Colorado, to the capital of New Mexico. It was like a train ride in a foreign country, earning it the nickname of the "Chili Line." This appellation was derived from the seasonal strings of drying hot peppers on the adobe houses of the few small communities along the branch. For many years, the branch was kept busy transporting agricultural traffic, but by the Great Depression, that had almost entirely vanished. Only a six-times-a-week mixed train plied the route by 1941, to be abandoned by the end of August that year.

Between Alamosa and Antonito, the two-car Santa Fe consist was combined with the *San Juan*, and the engines were double-headed. After switching out its mail-express car and coach at Antonito, the *San Juan* quickly departed for Durango. At 8:30 a.m., the eight-hour southbound trip began. On the day that I rode on the train, there were no freight cars in the consist. A peculiarity where passengers boarded at Antonito was the largest step box I had ever seen. As the third rail of the dual-gauge track was nearest the depot platform, a regular small step box would have been inadequate. So, the Alamosa shop had made an extra-large box that fitted between the near standard-gauge rail

and the inside third rail of the narrow gauge. (This box is now an exhibit at the Colorado Railroad Museum in Golden.) The open-platform coach had a bay window on each side, so the crew could keep an eye on the train ahead, somewhat like watching a train from a caboose cupola. Since this branch line seemed to be mostly curves, it was easy to watch the train from these bay windows.

Passengers were few, including some railroaders, but mostly Hispanics. On this trip, mostly Spanish was to be heard, almost as if the train was in Mexico itself. Even the two restroom facilities were bilingually lettered "Hombres/Men" and "Mujeres/Women." And a sort of "Jim Crow" order was imposed, as the crew indicated, where the Hispanics sat in the front and the Anglos sat in the rear of the partly filled coach. It was not clear to me who was being segregated, as "down South" generally the whites sat in the front and the blacks sat in the rear. No matter, though, as everyone on the Chili Line train seemed to be in good humor, enjoying joking with each other.

It seemed as though the smoke of the San Juan passenger train's engine could be seen far to the west for nearly half an hour after leaving Antonito—even after passing the stone Colorado–New Mexico border marker. Sometimes it appeared as a small black moving line, as the train worked its way upgrade toward Cumbres Pass. The crew of the "Chili Line" train offered information about points of interest along the way. They mentioned that just beyond the state border, carloads of striking miners from Cripple Creek were dumped off the train by the Colorado Militia in 1903. Later, the men were rescued by townspeople from Antonito, saving the strikers from the volcanic wasteland near the border. It was 35 miles to the first town, Tres Piedras ("Three Rocks" in Spanish), with a station agent and a water tank as railroad amenities.

This area was very dry, barren country, now and then relieved by a grove of stunted piñon trees (known for their tasty piñon nuts). One "station," which consisted of a siding and section house, was named "No Agua," as instead of a necessary water tank for the smaller engines of earlier times, there was a cistern. Crews of passing trains routinely filled the cistern from tankcars of water. For many years, the adjacent "highway" was a rather rough road, sometimes gravel-surfaced, sometimes just a dirt or sand affair—obviously having little traffic. It was to be many years before this road was paved all the way to Santa Fe. Winter storms from Cumbres Pass would blow across the route, as it skirted Mount San Antonio, and snow would occasionally block the line. Once, dur-

A NARROW-GAUGE MEET of the Chili Line trains was taking place on July 3, 1941, at Embudo, New Mexico. The southbound train was waiting at the switch, and it had just come down the seven miles of 4.0-percent grade into the Rio Grande (river) Valley.

IT WAS JULY 2, 1941, and D&RGW Train 425 had just unloaded mail, express and passengers at the depot in Santa Fe, New Mexico. The train now was backing to the engine terminal, yard and wye at the edge of town. Train 425 had just completed the eight-hour 125-mile trip from Antonito, Colorado. Passenger David Davis was waiting for me to finish picture-taking before heading our grimy selves for a hotel. The neat brick depot of the "Chili Line" still stands, although it serves as a restaurant, and it is decorated as if it was an AT&SF relic.

264

NO AGUA, NEW MEXICO, was just that, waterless. A cistern was filled with water from a tank-car carried part of the time by the Chili Line trains. No Agua was not a town, just a siding with a capacity for 22 cars, as well as a section house. Local people had just received packages from the mail-express car and a mail sack or two for a small fourth-class post office, some distance from the railroad. Notice the bay window, a feature of the three coaches assigned to the Antonito–Santa Fe train. It served the train crews in lieu of a cupola, so they could keep an eye on the cars ahead. The backup air whistle on the rear of the coach was for use in Santa Fe. After the train arrived at the Santa Fe depot and all the station business was taken care of, the train would back through city streets to its engine terminal. The date for this view was July 2, 1941.

RIO GRANDE TRAIN No. 426, the northbound counterpart bound for Antonito, Colorado, was waiting to depart on its day-long trip on July 3, 1941. A Santa Fe locomotive, No. 3200, which had come in on the AT&SF branch from Lamy, New Mexico, was doing some switching in the small yard. At the left, please notice the end view of the AT&SF's idler car (with its double couplers) for use here for switching narrow-gauge cars. However, it was seldom used anymore, as freight for transfer had diminished to virtually nothing. And by the end of next month, the Chili Line would be abandoned.

ing the 1930's, a rotary snowplow was used to open this stretch and rescue a large number of livestock trapped by the storm.

It seemed that the track wound endlessly through dry, rough country made up of scattered volcanic rock. There were few trees, and at one point the line circled the rim of an ancient volcano, where there was a siding appropriately named "Volcano."

At one point, we halted to exchange a slim mail sack with a boy who had ridden up on a horse, and then departed for some settlement, out of sight. At Servilleta, over 44 miles from Antonito, the train halted for several minutes to catch up with the timetable, its depot being a locked boxcar body, presumably for L-C-L freight. The crew told me that many years before this station had been the site of a little crossroads. At Taos Junction, Milepost 336.52 (from Denver), there was a two-story depot, with upstairs living quarters for the agent, and again we exchanged mail. This time, the mail route was served by a rather battered automobile, which negotiated a dirt road to Taos, many miles to the east. Despite its name, the place had been a junction for a lumber branch that extended into the hilly region to the southwest. There, a lumber railroad fed a considerable amount of traffic to the D&RGW for nearly 20 years. Taos Junction also was at the top of a seven-mile 4.0-percent grade, which dropped the line down to the valley of the Río Grande (Spanish for "River Grand"). The postal clerk, Mike Delgado, pointed to a timber trestle, which had collapsed several years earlier under the train. At the time, his car was wrecked, and he was hospitalized with injuries. He thought that the engineer had been traveling too fast.

Embudo, with a water tank and depot, was where we found the northbound train waiting for us. It had a few cars of freight in its consist, hauled by 2-8-2 No. 476. Our train

had Engine 473 for its motive power, another of the three K-28 outside-frame Mikados that remained in service on the railroad at the end of narrow-gauge operations—still running today on the Durango & Silverton line. At the time of my trip to Santa Fe, the other seven 2-8-2's of this class had not yet gone to Alaska.

There was time to look over the wooden depot, whose exterior was completely covered by stones (rocks, I should say). Inside was a big stone fireplace, and even the outbuildings were stone-covered. "Consumptive" telegrapher Wallace had come to Colorado in the 1890's to die from tuberculosis in the more comfortable, dryer air. He had been the operator at Lizard Head Pass on the new Rio Grande Southern Railroad, and the Denver & Rio Grande eventually sent him to sunny, dry northern New Mexico. He employed years of spare time collecting rocks from the nearby mountain slopes, and he gradually encased the Embudo depot. It still stands, used after the railroad was gone as a home and as a restaurant.

The river was high and washing at its banks, but still a couple of feet below flood stage. A few days of warm, cloudless weather in the Colorado mountains had melted snow and brought down almost

enough water for a flood condition at this point. At Embudo, we coupled on two gondolas of riprap stone on the rear of the train. These loaded cars were left on the mainline a few miles south of Embudo. At this spot, we found a couple of empties, left by the other train, which we pushed to the next siding to be loaded again.

After crossing the tributary Río Chama, also nearing flood stage, we arrived at the lunch stop of the trip, in the little town of Española. Up the north bank of the Río Chama one could see the never-used grade of what was going to be a railroad to Durango, a dream of D&RG President David Moffat, I was to learn later. When the D&RG's directors in the 1890's learned of this venture and other similar things concealed from them, they fired their president. It was hard to believe that Española had been a key point on an earlier D&RG dream to build on to Mexico City.

Beyond Española, we passed through an Indian reservation, but there was no business there, just a couple of flag stops, sidings rusting away. And with 26 miles yet to go, we crossed the river and started a long climb to what amounted to a low pass to the east. The railroad used long reverse loops through sandy areas, crossing dry washes, and at

long last—suddenly—way below us was Santa Fe. The train dropped rapidly, skirted the front steps of an Indian school, making a large half circle in the descent, finally passing a wye, small yard and engine terminal on the outskirts of town. Incidentally, the engine terminal featured a hand-cranked crane, which lifted buckets of coal for tenders.

Then, for several blocks down the middle of a street, past one of the oldest churches in America, we finally entered a small yard consisting of dual-gauge track and a neat brick depot. Across the yard was the Atchison, Topeka & Santa Fe depot, which also had a mixed train come in from its mainline six times a week. It did not take long to unload the scanty mail and express. Then, our train backed to its overnight yard and service area.

On the next morning, a husky Santa Fe Mikado was doing some switching in its yard, and for a few minutes, the contrast between the two gauges of trains intrigued this camera fan. Then, our D&RGW train was off at 10:30 a.m., to be at Antonito by 6:30 p.m., in plenty of time to be included in the San Juan passenger train from there.

The return trip was over the same dusty unballasted roadbed, soon to get the passengers coated with grit. The only real excitement was along the river, south of Embudo. The train was moving at a good 25–30 mph when, suddenly, there was a crash ahead, and we stopped as abruptly as if we had headed into a mountain. A huge cottonwood tree on the banks of the river had been weakened-and-washed out by the high water, and it had fallen across our track. It fell so closely in front of the engine that the engineer did not have time to apply the brakes, and we had crashed into it. We were lucky, though, because if the tree had toppled over a few seconds later, it could have crushed one of the passenger cars.

After about 30 minutes or more of work with axes, the engine could push the rest of the tree aside, and we were underway again. The next stop was to couple on to the now empty gondolas and push them ahead to Embudo. Again, at that point, we met the other train, this time heading south for Santa Fe. We had picked up a few freight cars, and No. 473 made sharp "stack talk" as she hurried the nine-car train up the 4.0-percent grade. Antonito was reached on time, and a small distant cloud of smoke far to the west indicated that the San Juan was traveling along just about on schedule. The clerk of the "Antonito & Santa Fe R.P.O." prepared his bags to put aboard the mail car, and the freight cars were set out. And the two-day trip into the "Land of Enchantment" was over.

Today (as of 1995), the depot in Santa Fe is a restaurant, decorated as if it were an AT&SF station! The coaches we saw that day, Nos. 306 and 320, eventually traveled far away from the Chili Line and now carry tourists on the Huckleberry Railroad during the summer at Flint, Michigan.

CHASING TRAINS...

BOB RICHARDSON COMES TO COLORADO

By Ed Haley

WHILE SERVING my first stint as president of the Rocky Mountain Railroad Club in 1948, I organized the club's second excursion through the Black Cañon of the Gunnison River. During that year, the club had only 90 members, and 22 of them lived outside Colorado. The office of trip chairman did not exist, and the president was expected to arrange all trips, chair the monthly meetings and provide programs, besides handling all correspondence. The Denver & Rio Grande Western Railroad agreed to operate a train of 11 cars, consisting of two baggage cars, seven coaches, the parlor car "Chama," stocked with food and drinks, and the glass-topped observation car, "Silver Vista." The trip was advertised in *Trains Magazine*, and announcements were mailed to all club members and to local organizations, such as the Colorado Mountain Club and the Westerners, in early August.

On Saturday, September 18, 1948, 183 passengers were gathered at the Salida depot. I had received requests for tickets from 14 states, and among them was one from two gentlemen from Akron, Ohio, Bob Richardson and Carl Helfin.

Our special train left Salida right on time at 9:00 a.m. and began the 20-mile climb up the 4.0-percent grade to the 10,856-foot summit of Marshall Pass. Providing the motive power for our train was a husky Class K-37 490-series 2-8-2. The K-37's were the largest narrow-gauge engines on the D&RGW, constructed in the railroad's Burnham shops from standard-gauge Class C-41 2-8-0's in 1929 and 1930.

Down the western slope was another 12 miles of 4.0-percent grade, which flattened out before we reached Sargent. From here we followed the broad valley of Tomichi Creek for 31 miles to Gunnison, 73 miles west of Salida. After a short stop at Gunnison, the train headed north for 28 miles to Crested Butte. Here, another short stop was made, and the train was turned on the wye and headed back to Gunnison, where the group spent the night.

Next morning, on Sunday, September 19, our special train headed west out of Gunnison, pulled by 2-8-0 No. 361, a much lighter locomotive than the K-37. The mixed 60- and 65-pound rail between Gunnison and Montrose restricted the use of any locomotive heavier than the Class C-21 Baldwins, which weighed 95,650 pounds. We would follow the Gunnison River for about 30 miles, climbing out of the Black Cañon via Cimarron Cañon to Cimarron, where the train would be turned for the run back to Gunnison. Just inside the entrance to the Black Cañon, one of the deepest gorges in Colorado, our special train paused opposite the confluence of the Lake Fork of the Gunnison and the Gunnison rivers. This stop was made so that our passengers could photograph the gracefully arched highway bridge that spanned the Little Black Cañon.

As the passengers were re-boarding, two fellows came up to me and introduced them-

E. J. HALEY PHOTO

IT WAS MY IDEA to construct a typical narrow-gauge railroad depot at the Narrow Gauge Motel at Alamosa, Colorado. This was to be for an office, with living quarters upstairs, as well as for space to exhibit the growing collection of historical artifacts, papers and photographs of Colorado's railroads. Using original Rio Grande Southern Railroad's blueprints for the two-story depot at Mancos, Colorado, we erected a duplicate building just north of the motel, and it was assigned the name "South Alamosa." After spending a never-to-be-forgotten week chasing and riding narrow-gauge trains during late February of 1954, Dick Kindig, Phil Ronfor and Ed Haley returned to the Narrow Gauge Motel to spend their last night in "narrow-gauge country" before returning to their mundane tasks of earning a living. Ed Haley captured this nostalgic scene of Denver & Rio Grande No. 346—with headlight and marker lamps aglow—standing in softly falling snow. The 2-8-0 was alongside the agent's bay window at the "South Alamosa" depot replica. This little old narrow-gauge Baldwin 2-8-0 was received by the Denver & Rio Grande in 1881, as the "Cumbres," No. 406. This locomotive can easily be envisioned as making a brief station stop alongside one of the many D&RG depots the engine served so faithfully.

269

IT WAS ON JULY 26, 1953, when the "World's Largest Narrow-Gauge Museum" opened in Alamosa, Colorado. (Actually, the station name was "South Alamosa," as one can see on the end of the depot replica). We took a locomotive bell over to the local radio station in a pickup truck. Then, we rang it, so the microphone held out a window at the station could record it for a broadcast invitation to attend. The invitation did not mention that we planned to serve free refreshments for all; however, we had that as a surprise, or else I am sure the crowd would have been unmanageable. Robertson Pitcher, the grandson of Otto Mears and last manager of the Silverton Northern Railroad officiated at the opening.

ROBERTSON PITCHER came over from his home down east of Pueblo to open the doors of the Narrow Gauge Museum on July 26, 1953. He liked our ideas of preserving things from the railroad past. His father had married Otto Mears' daughter, Cora, and he succeeded his father as the general manager of the Silverton Northern Railroad. When it closed down during the Great Depression of the 1930's, he kept it intact, as his father always felt the mining business would come back. However, the bad local-tax situation in San Juan County forced him to get an emergency furlough from the U.S. Navy in 1942. Sadly, he had to arrange for the sale and dismantling of the Silverton Northern by a Chicago firm because of the narrow-minded property-tax attitude of individuals in Silverton.

selves as Bob Richardson and Carl Helfin from Akron, Ohio. They offered their congratulations on a smoothly run excursion (just a bit prematurely, as it turned out). They were very enthusiastic about the Colorado scenery in its full fall glory and the beautiful weather. Bob informed me that he was returning to Akron, quitting his job with the Seiberling Rubber Company and was moving out to Colorado to live. And Carl said he also was quitting his job running a sheet-metal shop to join Bob "out West." I am sure I must have thought to myself, "Oh yeah, I'll bet you two actually move out here!"

Our train had been scheduled to arrive back in Salida that evening, around 6:00 o'clock. However, as it turned out (as it frequently does on excursions), fate stepped in to take a hand in the proceedings. On the return run, shortly after exiting the Black Cañon, the train slowed to a halt. Upon arriving at the front end, I learned that the 361 had broken the rod that activated the slide valve on top of the right-hand cylinder. As it turned out, we would be going nowhere for the next three hours. After a walk of about a mile east into the next station, Sapinero, a

THE INITIAL PAINT SCHEME of No. 346 was rather garish, and it was toned down over the years. "Mount Blanca & Western" was our road name at the Narrow Gauge Museum in Alamosa. This view was taken after the engine had her domes restored to the original appearance, with parts obtained from Engine 345. This was possible after the sister 2-8-0 was wrecked in a head-on collision on the Silverton Branch for the movie "Denver & Rio Grande." That is 14,390-foot Mount Blanca (also called Sierra Blanca) in the background. The mountain's alleged elevation varied with the years, depending on whose guide book was used. When I moved to Golden, Caboose 0500 was left behind. And after many years, including a journey to Cripple Creek, where the car impersonated a Florence & Cripple Creek caboose for the chamber of commerce, it ended up in Durango. There, No. 0500 was beautifully rebuilt for the Durango & Silverton line, to be used as a special car on trains.

271

YOURS TRULY was very mellow, as well as "resplendent" (as Ed Haley said) in my original Denver, South Park & Pacific band uniform, while I quaffed a libation at Delaney's Saloon Party, held on March 16, 1968. These annual St. Patrick's Day celebrations were given by the M. C. Poors and the E. J. Haleys for the "Loyal Sons & Daughters of the Rusty Spike." The interior of James Delaney's Turf Exchange, a famous "watering hole" near the South Park roundhouse in Como, Colorado, was replicated in Mac Poor's basement, and all guests were required to come in 1880's garb. A grand time was had by all. Ed said my authentic band uniform was one of the best at the party! As I recall, we were supposed to impersonate someone and have a story or explanation to back-up the choice. We had been given the South Park line's band uniforms, so I wore one and claimed to be Frank Trumbull in 1898, the new president of the Colorado & Southern Railway.

272

E. J. HALEY PHOTO

ED HALEY, DICK KINDIG AND I enjoyed lunch aboard an impromptu open-air "dining car," a Denver & Rio Grande Western flatcar—part of an empty eastbound pipe train en route to Alamosa, Colorado. May 1, 1956, was a beautiful spring day, as Engines 499 and 498 climbed steadily along the Río San Juan, a few miles west of Juanita, Colorado. The three riders had hopped off the freight train during a water stop at Gato (formerly Pagosa Junction), and we bought a six-pack of soda pop, bread and meat for sandwiches, as well as some very stale cookies at Gato's general store. Dick Kindig used Ed's camera to capture this scenic narrow-gauge line through southwestern Colorado and northwestern New Mexico.

phone call was made to the station agent at Gunnison, alerting him of our predicament. The only available engineer was out fishing, and he had to be located and brought back to Gunnison. After this was accomplished, No. 360 made a fast run down the valley to our rescue. No. 361 had limped into the siding at Sapinero, and when the 360 arrived, this outside-frame Consolidation turned on the wye and backed down onto the stalled train.

We reached Gunnison about dusk, and after some delay, a 490-series 2-8-2 locomotive replaced the 360, and we headed east for Salida. At Sargent, another 490-series Mikado was standing on the main and was quickly coupled on for what one railroad official later told me was the fastest passenger run ever made between Sargent and the summit of Marshall Pass. This fast run was probably one of the most glorious episodes

in the long history of Rocky Mountain Railroad Club excursions. It was a trip never to be forgotten. The aspen trees were at the peak of their fall glory, the sky was cloudless, and the passing scenery was bathed in the light from a full moon.

The "Silver Vista" observation car was packed with excursionists, all wishing they could capture this magnificent event on film. The firemen on the two 490's were earning their pay that night. The firebox doors opened frequently, bathing the cab interiors in a brilliant glow and illuminating the un-

derside of the smoke cloud boiling from the stacks as we roared up the steep 4.0-percent grade. The capacity crowd in the "Silver Vista" sent up cheer after cheer as the long train of lamp-lit coaches squealed around each sharp curve en route to the top of the pass. As our train pulled up beside the Salida depot a bit after midnight, a small blaze erupted around one of the oil-lamp vents on a coach roof. This was due to overheated vent stacks and was sort of an anticlimax to our long journey. It was a tired but thrilled throng that climbed down from the narrow-

gauge cars. Bob Richardson and Carl Helfin had certainly made a fine choice in selecting the club's Black Cañon excursion for their first venture into Colorado.

Imagine my surprise during the spring of 1949, when Bob and Carl's names appeared in the club's membership roster, listing an Alamosa, Colorado, address. A bit later, we learned that they had become partners in a motel venture. Their Narrow Gauge Motel was under construction a short distance south of Alamosa, alongside the three-rail track of the Denver & Rio Grande Western's

TO SAVE TIME in coupling-up sections cut apart by the streets in Alamosa, Colorado, most outbound narrow-gauge freight engines picked up their trains—as this one was doing—at a long siding at the southern edge of town. The head-end brakeman, who was riding in the "doghouse" on the second engine's tender, was looking over from the front end of what could be up to a 100-car train (the limit), with not more than 70 narrow-gauge cars in the consist. The standard-gauge cars would be set out at San Luis Valley points on this dual-gauge section. I could hardly resist taking numerous photographs here. After all, I lived just across the road at the Narrow Gauge Motel and Museum at this time, February 22, 1954.

E. J. HALEY PHOTO

BOB RICHARDSON and Dick Kindig were posing alongside the derail switch at the western end of the siding of Grady on February 17, 1953, when Ed Haley took this photograph. The Rio Grande Southern Railroad had been abandoned for over a year, and the trio had hiked-in from Colorado Highway 160 to photograph RGS Engine 42, which the dismantlers had stored for the winter months before completing their job during the spring. This harp-type switchstand controlled the derail at the western end of the siding. When cars were stored on the siding, the derail was opened to prevent them from entering the mainline and running away down the 20-mile hill to Mancos. Dick was holding his well-known postcard-size Graflex, which had a 35-mm Retina camera for color shots, securely mounted and aligned above the lens of the large Graflex camera. With this equipment and his "unipod" (seen in his right hand), he was able to take action photographs simultaneously in both black-and-white and color. Ed's Graflex and unipod were between Bob and Dick.

mainline to the south and U.S. Highway 285. Bob really settled-in and began a lifelong study of the history of the narrow-gauge lines in this large area, and he started to record the day-to-day events in his noteworthy *Narrow Gauge News*.

This motel became the Mecca for railfans visiting Colorado, and it was always booked solid during each of the three-day annual excursions the club operated to Silverton for a 15-year period. Dick Kindig and I made many trips to Alamosa and travelled all through the "narrow-gauge country" with Bob in his old GMC van he jokingly called the "Gut Buster."

Bob was a great guide to any narrow-gauge line in southwestern Colorado, northwestern New Mexico and the Gunnison area, northwest of Alamosa. He knew the best way into seldom-photographed scenic points and was on a first-name basis with most train crews. Bob's "Gut Buster" was a great vehicle in which to cover Colorado's "narrow-gauge country" during midwinter, and we never had to walk out from any of our adventures. In addition, Bob always knew the best places to stay for the night and little restaurants or hotels where good meals were available. The three of us explored many miles of abandoned narrow-gauge grades, and we had some great winter rides with Rio Grande freight crews.

276

E. J. HALEY PHOTO

THINGS COULD LOOK CROWDED at South Alamosa, with four engines, a couple of cabooses, some freight cars and a Galloping Goose. Early in 1958, it was quite a moving job when the engines had to be loaded onto lowboy truck trailers, winched, and trucked to the D&RGW railroad yard to be rolled onto flatcars. At the time, road limitations made railroad haulage the only way to move the engines out of Alamosa. The freight cars and lighter items were trucked directly to Golden on flatbed truck trailers. Gibson Truck Lines performed the task in faultless manner. Probably, what influenced the pampered care was the fact that Fred Gibson was a railfan (and did not know it), as he lamented about the gradual vanishing of the trains.

NARROW GAUGE MOTEL
ALAMOSA, COLORADO

AN "ANTONITO TURN" was rolling past the Narrow Gauge Motel sign, heading south ("west" according to D&RGW operating rules). Often, narrow-gauge engines and cabooses would be employed on mixed-gauge trains that were operated only as far as Antonito, Colorado. A pair of standard-gauge idler cars enabled the engine and caboose to couple to the standard-gauge cars.

277

THERE WERE NO TREES at the "South Alamosa" site, except for some newly planted ones, so our cat climbed to the top of Engine 346 instead! A railroader loaned us his family's set of antlers, and "Bear," the cat, enjoyed climbing on them. When we removed this headlight and put on an oider type, which was missing its glass on the lee side (until we replaced it), all the local cats squirmed and squeezed to get inside the lamp and bask in the delicious heat the afternoon sun would generate. Many of the motel guests found this something to snap pictures of, and I am sure there are many snapshots of the cats enjoying No. 346's headlight!

TWENTY-THREE of these unusual signs were placed throughout the San Luis Valley. They had to be stoutly braced to withstand the often strong winds, as well as cattle that liked to scratch their backs by rubbing the signposts. The old pickup truck was a veteran of many jaunts to remote places in the Colorado Rockies. Sometimes, on Wolf Creek and Monarch passes, when the roads were slick early in the morning, there would be several-hundred pounds of rocks in the back end, along with the usual shovel, tire chains and a carton of sand.

WHY MOVE TO COLORADO?

OFTEN, I HAVE BEEN ASKED, "Why did you move to Colorado?" To answer that, things had changed at the tire company where I had been employed for several years. A new generation, not experienced in the business, had taken over, and they were making some expensive mistakes. For one thing, they had started a branch factory in Texas, and it was losing $1 million, back when one-million dollars was truly a lot of money. The younger people did not like to travel, and gradually, the placing of outdoor advertising was turned over to local sign companies. So, I found myself working at the Barberton (Ohio) plant and office most of the time. Gradually, I got into keeping secret figures of tire costs, and I was alarmed when I found a loss of at least one dollar on every tire supplied for new cars at the Michigan automobile factories. And nobody seemed interested in changing things.

It did not look good for the future, and when I had a chance to go to Colorado and open a new motel, it sounded like a good idea. I might add that within a few years, the tire firm was in serious trouble financially, and "down the road," the plant closed. My fears turned out to be true, and I was quite saddened by the end of a very good firm.

In 1948, Colorado was in poor shape to handle the increasing post-World War II tourism. The "motel" was a new thing in the lodging industry. The small mountain communities in the Colorado Rockies mostly had old hotels, many dating back to the 1890's or before. Many a railfan tourist ended their train-chasing days sleeping in their cars—as happened to a growing number of railfans who visited the rather remote Durango narrow-gauge country, as well as other parts of western Colorado. To make matters worse, local money was not available for building new accommodations for the three-month seasonal traffic. The same problem was true for eating establishments. We railfans who were not Coloradans often existed on a lot of Hershey candy bars and bottled soft drinks. *[Local Colorado railfans usually "camped-out" while they visited narrow-gauge lines, and they cooked their own meals. However, "out-of-staters" were not aware of the rather rustic conditions in western Colorado. Ed.]*

Take the region served by the Rio Grande Southern, for example. All the roads were either rough gravel-surfaced routes, or just plain dirt and rocks. Dolores had "Benny's Hogan," a sort of converted house. At Rico, one could stay overnight in a spare room at "Charlie" Engels' place. Telluride had the old "New" Sheridan Hotel, mostly full of "hard-rock miners," with little in rooms available for tourists. Restaurants? At Ridgway, one could drive to Ouray to eat a hamburger (of sorts) at a local tavern (saloon), or one could head north to Montrose to find one or two small cafes open for business on that town's main street. During the "off season" at Silverton, one was reduced to eating a sort of "embalmed" sandwich of dubious age at the Trailways bus station on Greene Street.

So, during September of 1948, I rode the Rocky Mountain Railroad Club's narrow-gauge excursion in the company of a friend from Ohio. We were visiting Colorado in the course of looking-over the once-famous "narrow-gauge circle" area. At that time, we decided that the best locations with prospects for at least some worthwhile year-around business were Alamosa and Montrose. Thanks to its over $1-million railroad payroll and its year-around economy as the main business center for the sprawling San Luis Valley, Alamosa looked good to us.

We bought a site just south of the town, situated on U.S. Highway 285, the main road to southern valley settlements and historical Santa Fe, New Mexico. This route through Alamosa was not yet a busy through highway, as most of it south of Antonito, Colorado, was gravel-surfaced, and some of that was rather skimpy. However, each year, New Mexico managed to pave a few miles of the "highway." Still, the town of Alamosa was at the central crossroads of the San Luis Valley, with roads going in all four directions. It had the promise of increasing tourist traffic… and hopefully, there were good prospects for the motel business. As a result, we opened the first 10 motel units during the following July (in 1949).

At the time, our motel units were among the finest accommodations to be found in the western Colorado mountain region. They featured large rooms, finished in knotty pine, with central hot-air heating, as well as individual heating as a supplement. And each unit undoubtedly had the largest bathrooms to be found in the region. We had noticed that the other "tourist courts" (as motels were called at that time) en route to Colorado were equipped with rather dinky bathrooms, with shower stalls where one was always bumping an elbow. So, we figured that tourist families would really appreciate a large bathroom and ample shower space.

The name chosen for our place, the Narrow Gauge Motel, raised eyebrows locally. We learned that Alamosa had a reputation as a "cold town." True, it made the national news reports with the lowest temperature reading in the nation every now and then. However, the town—like many of Colorado's smaller communities—was rather ingrown and insular, and many of the residents did not welcome newcomers. Underlying this was the fact that it had a large population of railroaders, most of them union members, of course, while the "main street establishments" were rather solidly anti-union—outspokenly so. Sales clerks in the main-street stores were paid 40 to 45 cents per hour then, and the railroaders buying shoes, clothing, groceries, etc., and tendering their sizable paychecks aggravated the anti-union feeling. Railroad people were by far the best-paid workers in the San Luis Valley.

Anyway, living in Alamosa and getting involved in railroad-abandonment hearings turned out to be very educational. It was a "civics lesson" about Colorado on a grand scale. As one retired member of the Colorado legislature said, "We are still back in 1910, and hopefully, you new people coming into the state [and many were] will gradually bring us up-to-date."

A third sector of the community at that time was Adams State College, small and with an enrollment of barely 300 students… and only if you counted the number of part-time students who attended night classes.

When we opened the Narrow Gauge Museum in July of 1953, in our motel-office replica of the old Mancos depot, the college promptly announced in a press release that the college also had a museum. Sometime later, it became known that the "museum" consisted of various artifacts tucked away here and there on shelves or in closets, with nothing much in the way of regular displays.

By 1954, I had my fill of 16-hour work days during the summers, with not much to show for it. We had built up a fair business, booming in the summer with tourists, with some business travelers as patrons in the winter, enabling us to about break even. So, I nearly became the office manager of a New Mexico company then. The more regular work hours sounded attractive to me. Accelerating such thinking was the intrusion of several local people into our affairs, some of their suggestions being downright dishonest. Anyone who has lived in a small town will nod their head in agreement.

So, in 1958, we sold Engine 42 to a new amusement park being built west of Denver (just south of Golden), and I went into business with Cornelius W. Hauck of Cincinnati, Ohio, to set up a railroad museum with all of my railroad "accumulation." This collection of railroad artifacts was about all I had to show after 10 years in the motel business, a rather dubious profit. Colorado was in the midst of a "boom," and to buy land in various seemingly good sites was impossible, as speculators were holding out for the future.

We wanted a 35- to 50-acre site near a main highway and adjacent to the mountains. We finally settled on a 15-acre tag end of an old farm, just east of Golden, on 44th Avenue. It became both a source of annoyance and amusement during the years to follow that various individuals or business firms were going to move us (usually without discussing it with us) to some other site of theirs. Some of these people acted as if we were a temporary storage place for them and their Johnny-come-lately schemes, generally not very honest schemes, either. Along with this postwar boom, Colorado was giving space for many crooks. It almost seemed as though the worst elements of the early-day mining excitements were now being replicated in the Denver area.

IT POURED RAIN everywhere I went on vacation in the Colorado mountains during September of 1946. Most of the still-scarce Kodak 616 film I had saved for months (while I was still working in Texas for the rubber company) was still in sealed boxes, not used. So, it was great for me on a dry, sunny day to find Midland Terminal Railway Engines 55, 60, 59 and 57 making up a four-engine freight train for the Cripple Creek District. The engines were spaced six to eight cars apart,

to alleviate somewhat the smoke problems in the numerous tunnels up Ute Pass from the Colorado City yard. However, the engines took so long to make up the train and pump up the air, that it was dark before the train had travelled more than a few miles. So, I did not follow the train up the grade to the historic Cripple Creek mining district, as I had learned that the MT would return with loads late in the night. (I was not a devotee of night pictures.)

MIDLAND TERMINAL RAILWAY

JUST WEST of Colorado Springs, the Midland Terminal Railway had situated its eastern terminal and freight yard in a suburb called Colorado City. For as long as the MT operated (until 1949), the afternoon action was worth watching in Colorado City. Three, four or even five locomotives would assemble a late afternoon freight train of empty ore cars for the run to Cripple Creek. Behind each locomotive, on parallel tracks, there was

assembled roughly each engine's tonnage in empties. Then, the engines would pull up to the west end of the yard, couple up, and eventually, the train would whistle off for the long climb to Divide. One reason for spacing the engines so far apart was to ease the unpleasantness for crews in the numerous tunnels—fortunately short ones—up scenic red-rock Ute Pass, north of famous Pikes Peak.

The train would arrive at Bull Hill yard (next to Cripple Creek) after dark as a rule. Then, all but one or two of the engines would run light back to Colorado City, as

THE LOWELL THOMAS SPECIAL on the Midland Terminal Railway, on January 27, 1949, was about to take water at the Cascade tank. Cascade was only 11 miles up Ute Pass from Colorado Springs; however, Engine 59 was already thirsty after the hard climb. On board the train was a select group of mining people and so-called "civic leaders," and they were quenching their thirst with "stuff" that would not freeze! Some of the passengers showed the effects when the train arrived at Cripple Creek. Hopefully, they remembered most of their trip on the Midland Terminal.

THE MIDLAND TERMINAL Railway inherited Colorado Midland trackage at Colorado Springs, part of which involved this trestle, as well as track down the middle of a city street, used to reach the Santa Fe's station, which it used. On January 27, 1949, this two-car special was heading for Cripple Creek with celebrity Lowell Thomas as the Midland Terminal's special guest, riding to his old home town in style. Engine 59, an ex-Colorado Midland Consolidation was at the head end, trailed by Coach 20 and Chair-Observation 29. The occasion was to celebrate the opening of a new Golden Cycle Corporation ore-processing mill near Cripple Creek. This new mill rendered unnecessary the hauling of hard-rock gold ore to Colorado Springs, and therefore the MT Railway was only days away from abandonment.

A RATHER RELUCTANT Midland Terminal Railway management somehow was persuaded to operate a special excursion on the about-to-be abandoned line. For the February 6, 1949, round-trip from Colorado Springs to Cripple Creek, Engine 59, a former Colorado Midland 2-8-0, ably handled her odd consist. Full-size steel passenger cars could not be used, so the D&RGW loaned two idle wooden combination cars from its re- cently discontinued Aspen Branch mixed train. The Midland Terminal had a coach—somewhat stripped of seats—and the still intact observation chair car, No. 29. The latter had been a Colorado Midland excursion car of "Wildflower Excursion" fame. Car No. 29 now is at the Colorado Railroad Museum at Golden, after spending years at Albuquerque, New Mexico, preserved by a retiree who admired the MT shortline.

one engine could handle the loads on the return trip, perhaps with a helper engine part of the way to Divide.

The Midland Terminal's yard and shop area in Colorado City would have made a good railroad museum. Everything seemed to date from the times of the Colorado Midland. In fact, much of the equipment, engines, cars and non-revenue items belonged to the CM originally. The large stone roundhouse (now a pottery factory) dated back to 1888.

When the Midland Terminal was abandoned early in 1949, the MT storekeeper ran sort of a "yard sale." With the MT going out of business, one would expect that he would sell anything. Right? Not so. He had bins full of all kinds of printed forms, some so obsolete that they went back to the days when

electric trolley cars operated in the Cripple Creek Mining District. Many of the forms had originally been produced for the Colorado Midland or one of the other local roads, and they had been overprinted for use on the MT. One unusual item in some of the bins was a collection of dozens of lantern globes, and many of these globes bore the initials of the CM, F&CC, CC&CS, CS&CCD, but oddly, none had MT initials. The shopkeeper's price? Twenty cents each! Eventually, most of the paper forms were burned, a lot of it in an arson fire while dismantlers cut up the engines and cars. Only a few builder's plates and brass whistles were saved. The large CM three-tube shop whistle became mine for only $12.00. However, that included the rather difficult task of taking the whistle off the roof of the roundhouse!

TRAINS WERE RUNNING LATE on April 1, 1951, and during daylight hours, when D&RGW No. 1706, one of the railroad's 4-8-4 passenger engines, headed out of La Veta for the pass—with a helper working behind the caboose. During the winter months, the San Luis Valley provided much traffic for the D&RGW, in the form of hundreds of carloads of potatoes. These well-known McClure "spuds" had been put in storage in September. By March, the potato cellars were being cleared of any remaining red McClures.

AT ALAMOSA there was little opportunity to snap pictures of the eastbound trains, as their movements usually were not in the daytime. During vegetable season, the branch-line trains would get back to Alamosa late in the evening—sometimes at midnight or later. Then, the eastbound freight train for Pueblo, Colorado, would depart before dawn. On this day, during January of 1949, the eastbound train was very late. It was headed by a booster-equipped Class M-78 4-8-2, No. 1514, and a D&SL Class 76 2-6-6-0 Mallet (originally Denver & Salt Lake No. 216, the last of the famous Moffat Road Mallets), renumbered as No. 3375 on the D&RGW. Shipments at this time of the year were heavy, as the renowned red McClure potatoes of the San Luis Valley were cleared out of storage cellars. In all likelihood, another Mallet would be waiting at the foot of La Veta Pass. The station of La Veta often would be a busy engine terminal, tending to a number of Mallets and straight (i.e., "simple") articulated locomotives used over the 9,242-foot pass.

THE RIO GRANDE'S "SAN LUIS" A SHORT-LIVED NAMED TRAIN

IN SEEKING DISCONTINUANCE of the narrow-gauge *San Juan Express* between Alamosa and Durango, Colorado, the Denver & Rio Grande Western management promised they would not discontinue the connecting standard-gauge passenger train from Denver to Alamosa, via Colorado Springs and Pueblo. Showing how good their promises were, they replaced the night trains with a daytime round-trip coach train from Alamosa to Pueblo. This, of course, did not enable business people to do a day's business in either Pueblo or Denver and return that night by Pullman. It also lengthened the journey into consuming three or four days for the trip, as all the travel was by day.

Moreover, the schedule was not sped up. The former night trains had a slow schedule, in part because the U.S. Post Office did not want the mail to arrive in Alamosa before 4:30 a.m. The *San Luis* carried no mail, as the Railway Post Office had been discontinued with the end of the night trains. But the westbound train plodded along at a 25 mph

gait, just as if it was the night train with a string of head-end cars, plus coaches and a Pullman car. Passengers on the *San Luis* sat bored as all the traffic on the nearby highways passed the train. So, this named train lasted only a year, and then, it was gone. Those who would have traveled by train found other ways to get to Denver and points in-between.

The D&RGW line over La Veta Pass was a scenic route, not seen by passengers, how-

ever, until this daytime train was put on. So, one Sunday I made the round trip to the little town of La Veta. Motive power for the train was one of the handsome 800-805 series Pacifics, about to be scrapped, although sometimes a diesel-electric unit would be on the head-end. Although there was not any snow in Alamosa, there was two feet of the white stuff on top of the pass and only a few less inches in La Veta.

To my surprise, we were followed on the

THE "SAN LUIS" passenger train was departing from La Veta, Colorado, for Pueblo on April 1, 1951. This was one of the shortest-lived name trains in the history of American railroading. The D&RGW promised protestants at the abandonment hearings for the narrow-gauge "San Juan" train and the connecting standard-gauge train to Denver, that ample service to Pueblo and Denver would be continued. So, the night train that departed from Alamosa at 9:40 p.m., with arrival in Denver scheduled early in the morning, was "replaced" by a daytime round trip from Alamosa to Pueblo. The former train schedule enabled business people to spend the day in Denver and then head home in the Pullman from Denver at 7:30 p.m. The "replacement" meant they had to spend an extra night at either Pueblo or Denver. And to rub things in and make the few passengers who used the daytime train unhappy, the same "poky" schedule was used between Pueblo and Alamosa, instead of speeding it up—as the D&RGW could have done. Since there was no longer a Railway Post Office on the train and no need to avoid arriving in Alamosa too early, the schedule could have been improved. Within a year, it was easy for the D&RGW to get permission to discontinue the "San Luis" from the always-agreeable "in-its-pocket" Public Utilities Commission of Colorado, since so few people were riding the train. With no further need for its only Pacifics, No. 800 and her sister 4-6-2's went to the scrap pile.

eastbound run by a very late freight train from Alamosa, and on the return trip we took siding on the pass to let the helper engines and the freight pass us on the mainline. This gave me a good chance to snap a picture of the *San Luis* train. Expecting the train to head out the upper end of the passing track, I was surprised that they backed out instead, and the engineer told me to climb aboard the engine instead of floundering back through the snow to the switchstand and beyond. As

a result, I ended up with a cab ride aboard the comely 800-series 4-6-2 for the remainder of the run to Alamosa! The slow schedule on the 25-mile tangent track from Fort Garland was so slow that the engineer kept nodding in boredom, and the fireman just smiled and kept a watch out both sides of the cab. He had little firing to do with the light train on level track. And there were rare grade crossings—none of any importance—so the whistle was seldom needed.

THE CABOOSE TRACKS in the Alamosa yard presented much contrast. The local car force would make interior changes if requested, and the regular conductor for Caboose 0503 did not like the sunlight on his work desk. So, the car force obligingly blocked off the window. Caboose 01167 was a product of Haskell & Barker Car Company in 1913—in the 01140–01189 series. Later, during 1927, the D&RGW's Burnham shops in Denver turned out 10 similar cabooses, numbered 01190–01199, wooden cars with steel underframes. Then, during the following year, in 1928, the Burnham

shops produced 20 more cabooses of the same design, numbered 01120–01139. These 20 cars completed the 01120–01199 series of 80 wooden cabooses. As built, all of these cabooses were equipped with archbar trucks; however, all the trucks on these cars were changed-over to cast-steel sideframes about 1940. They were all painted D&RGW freight-car red, an oxide-red color, while the lettering was white. Another standard-gauge caboose of the 01140–01189 series, No. 01166, was partially behind narrow-gauge caboose No. 0503.

THIS FREIGHT TRAIN was on the San Luis Valley Southern Railway, crossing the Rattlesnake Canyon trestle, just south of Blanca, Colorado. Towering 14,390-foot Mount Blanca—also called Sierra Blanca—is in the background. The SLVS only had one new engine during its entire lifetime. The one in this view, No. 105, was bought from the D&RGW in 1945, having been built for that road in 1890. Projected to go to Taos, New Mexico, the San Luis Valley Southern ended at the Colorado border in 1910, many miles short of that goal. By the mid-1950's, the track of the SLVS was getting so poor, and derailments were so frequent, that operation of all but a half mile at Blanca was abandoned. Becoming worn out during about 1955, the railroad's manager hired some D&RGW shopmen from Alamosa to come over on weekends to do repair work on Engine 105. When he found out they had virtually dismantled the engine instead—intending to make a big-and-lucrative job out of the contract—he became outraged and fired the men. And No. 105 was never re-assembled. However, Engine 106, a sister 2-8-0, was rescued by the Colorado Railroad Museum, and this engine was restored as Denver & Rio Grande No. 583, in her original livery, complete with an oil headlight and wooden pilot.

UNDER THE UNION CONTRACT a narrow-gauge engine could be used at Alamosa as a switch engine for only one eight-hour "trick" during any one 24-hour period. Alamosa's high wooden coal dock was getting elderly by 1952, so the yard crew would use a narrow-gauge engine with an idler car to push a standard-gauge car of coal up to the top. The engine crew put on quite a show, as they took a run for the steep climb. Actually, narrow-gauge K-36 2-8-2 No. 482 did not weigh all that much less than the standard-gauge C-48 2-8-0, No. 1146, the regular switch engine.

THIS UNUSUAL "CHANGEOVER" (or as officially termed, "draw"), where the relative position of the third rail changed on a wye, probably was the most closely examined piece of trackwork at Alamosa. As this picture shows, a train of either gauge could run through the wye with no problems. However, a cut of cars, with the two gauges of equipment coupled together, certainly could not use the wye in that manner—or a coupler could be torn out. In one instance of forgetfulness, the entire end of a narrow-gauge boxcar was ripped out! At Montrose, where the switch engine usually was narrow gauge, in turning the standard-gauge passenger train, the switcher would use an idler car to push the cars onto this section of the wye. Then, the switcher had to go around the other two legs and couple onto the cars, costing 40 minutes extra. An official in Denver ordered the yard crew to cut out the extra time and just go around the wye without the extra switching move. He declined to listen to the reason for the move on the telephone. So, the yard crew went out, took Mudhen 454, and the men were in the act of following the "fool order" when someone ran up and stopped the engine. The "Mountaineer" would have been "somewhat late" departing from Montrose that evening if the boys had angrily followed a ridiculous "fool order" from Denver.

A "HEAVY" LIVESTOCK TRAIN at Creede, Colorado, is the subject of this view! The mining town of Creede never recovered from the "Silver Panic" of 1893, yet a couple of mines continued operating—shakily—on an output of lead and zinc, providing erratic traffic for the D&RGW. Otherwise, as this short train indicates, there was some traffic from the ranches along the upper reaches of the Rio Grande (river). Briefly... In 1892–1893, this yard was a chaotic scene, with thousands of people arriving, along with their goods. The tracks were jammed with cars of incoming building materials, and two daily passenger trains—tailed by through narrow-gauge Pullman cars from Denver—were needed for all the travellers. At this point stood Creede's first freight "house," a huge tent. And the agent complained that while his watchman was on one side, thieves were crawling under the tent on the other side to loot it! The only water was from the little stream coming out of the narrow canyon. And things got so bad that winter that by spring the switch engine took a layover coach on Sundays and ran 50-cent excursions to the hot springs at Wagon Wheel Gap. This was to enable the citizenry to take a bath and wash their clothing! Thanks to Conductor George Andriko, who had a sense of history, the agent's letter book and the first train register were saved.

DURING THE FINAL YEAR for the D&RGW's standard-gauge steam power—1956—a Class C-48 2-8-0, No. 1136, headed out of the Alamosa yard with a Creede Branch train. This was a five- or six-times-a-week operation. However, the train seldom went as far as Creede, as the mining traffic had greatly declined. Most of the traffic was made up of vegetable loadings (particularly red McClure potatoes), involving many setouts and pickups at Monte Vista, Del Norte and various sidings as far west as South Fork, 50 miles from Alamosa. There was an element of violation shown here, as tankcars were coupled directly behind the locomotive. It might have been that they contained nothing flammable. However, on one trip, when I was taking pictures at Monte Vista, I realized they had hauled a tankcar of very-dangerous stuff right behind the engine! Of course, this definitely was a railroad-industry "no-no"! And this practice could have resulted in a catastrophe!

D&RGW CONSOLIDATION No. 1151 was coming to wye at Wasson, Colorado, the "turn-around" for the end of the Creede Branch in December of 1956. This standard-gauge engine was making the last steam run on this branch. The D&RGW was determined to end all standard-gauge steam in 1956, and it did so, leaving the system so short of diesel power, that a number of trains had to be cancelled. Various officials and underlings of the railroad had started obtaining bells, whistles, number plates, etc., from the steam engines at Alamosa before the final runs. So, for this C-48 2-8-0 to operate this day, some items had to be replaced! And the "top brass" used to blame the railfans for such things—actually as a cover-up for their own misdeeds!

THE END OF A SNOWPLOW

MOST PROBLEMS on railroads are the result of human error, and the destruction of the plow-flanger car kept at Alamosa for occasional need on La Veta Pass is an example. This "home-made" car was about the length of a short flatcar, and it was decked over, having under the deck a load of perhaps 20 tons of slag to hold the plow down during bucking snowdrifts and avalanches. A large steel wedge plow, with a housing for a one-man crew, it was pushed by at least one locomotive.

Learning that this plow-flanger was to be used on an infrequent trip over the Creede Branch, I watched the smoke of the train as it left Alamosa. Then, I took my time to pursue it, knowing that it would be about two hours before it reached the part of the line where the snow would be piled up, beginning at South Fork, nearly 50 miles west of Alamosa. Sometimes a train would not be needed on the last 20 miles of the branch for weeks, as the mining traffic was marginal, subject to the fluctuations in the lead and zinc markets. So, trains might operate nearly daily for the lumber-and-vegetable traffic, but go no further than South Fork, and the engine would run to Derrick, another mile up the branch, where the locomotive was turned around on the wye at that point.

On this day, the snowfighting train prepared to plow out the near leg of the wye, intending to plow out the other end on the return run from Creede. So, I floundered through a couple of feet of old packed snow to get near the tail of the wye, so I could

THIS WAS THE LAST RUN for the D&RGW's Wedge Plow 066. During February of 1952, an infrequent trip was made to Creede with this plow. Derrick wye was just a mile west of South Fork, and it needed to be plowed so the turns from Alamosa could use it. So, they attempted to plow the east leg of the wye; however, No. 066 derailed. As it was getting late and the sun was getting low in the west, I left for home at Alamosa. After re-railing the plow, the crew went on the 19 miles up the Rio Grande Cañon to Wasson, location of the wye used for Creede. There, the snow was very deep, old and hard-packed. And the engine worked hard to push the plow on the sharp curve, when—suddenly—the plow jumped the track again, and before the engine could stop, it was wrecked—the car broken up. Then, it was learned why the car kept derailing. It was a heavy piece of equipment, with many tons of slag from the steel plant at Pueblo under the deck. However, in a summer-time overhaul at Pueblo, the car-repair people had forgotten to replace the slag!

shoot the action. The action was brief, for the plow-flanger had traveled only a few feet on the sharp curve when it derailed. It just seemed to lift off the track. It was now late in the afternoon, heavy clouds and a cold wind were making it evident that whenever they did get the car re-railed, there would be little light on the next 20 miles to enable use of a camera. So, I went home, while the cursing crew members labored in the snow with shovels, blocks and rerailers.

Eventually, the car was re-railed, and I later learned about the rest of the trip. The plow-flanger rode the rails poorly as far as the wye at Wasson, where the crew intended to wye the train, as the ore cars were loaded there, instead of in Creede, two miles beyond. On the Wasson wye the plow derailed, but this time the engine was working hard, and the plow just sort of crumpled into a total loss. It was then that the reason for the derailing became evident—in repairing the car in Pueblo, the repair force had neglected to replace the necessary 20 tons of slag under the deck! The roadmaster took the section crew to Wasson and burned the wreckage!

K-28 MIKADO No. 476 had been worked through the Alamosa backshop, and she was being operated westbound to Durango, working her way over the San Juan Extension. The 2-8-2 was about to serve as a mid-train helper on this freight train, which was doing switching at Antonito, Colorado. Here, the two engines were setting out the head-end idler car. It was a typically cold November day during 1948, in the southern end of the vast San Luis Valley. So, smoke and steam appeared at their best for pictures—although people on the wrong side of the locomotives no doubt failed to appreciate the sooty coal smoke pouring out of the K-28 and K-36 Mikados!

ALAMOSA'S SUNDAY FREIGHT

ON TUESDAY, Thursday and Sunday, a narrow-gauge freight train would depart from the Alamosa yard during midmorning. Routinely, the two locomotives came from the roundhouse, coupled together and then stopped briefly opposite the depot. Then, they would continue to the west end of the yard and couple up to their train. The yard crew had the train ready, uncoupled at the street crossings (of which there were several). While the air was being pumped-up, automobile traffic gradually would stack up, particularly if it was Sunday morning, from the comings and goings to and from Sunday school and church services. There would also be a few Saturday-night revelers, now urgently headed for something at a drug store, or a "pick-me-up" at the VFW, American Legion or Elks halls.

TRAINS WOULD RUN doubleheaded as far as Antonito, Colorado. Then, one engine would be cut back in the train toward the middle. Here, on February 20, 1956, one engine is going to be cut back into the snow-fighting train, behind the drag flanger and Jordan spreader. The dual-gauge track—particularly the switches—was incomprehensible to one student brakeman, who never could understand it. After derailing a train, he finally was fired. From this coal dock I watched him study this switch, then throw it against the oncoming locomotive. After my excited protest, he studied the switch some more, and then, he finally threw it correctly. To the left is my infamous "Gutbuster," a 1950 Chevrolet "carryall," which all who rode in it pronounced it to be the hardest-riding vehicle ever. Hence, its nickname. Although its springs and shocks were repeatedly checked by mechanics at garages, they never improved the rough-riding qualities, especially pronounced on Colorado's rough gravel-surfaced and dirt back roads! Cornelius Hauck at one time pronounced that it made him feel dizzy!

ON SUNDAY, TUESDAY AND THURSDAY, a narrow-gauge freight train would head west (south) from Alamosa. This train was unusual in that while switching here at La Jara ("The Reeds") they had picked up some standard-gauge cars and cut them in ahead of the road engine, No. 486, using No. 483 as the helper. At Antonito, the crew will leave the boxcar and idler cars flanking it. The date was January 9, 1949, and the train had a long group of tankcars, to be loaded at Chama, New Mexico. At this time, some 56 of these cars were engaged in this traffic, many of them simply being small standard-gauge tankcars that had been placed on special narrow-gauge Andrews trucks.

The railroad company, with plans to abandon all narrow-gauge lines by the mid-1950's, was doing all it could to get rid of this crude-oil traffic, and the Union Tank Car Line (UTLX) had a man kept busy by impediments caused by the D&RGW. Eventually, the oil field north of Chama closed down, ending the constant acrimonious disputes. The former standard-gauge tankcars were put back on their rightful trucks, and some of the narrow-gauge cars were sold to the White Pass & Yukon Route at Skagway, Alaska, while the remainder was scrapped, and many were used by some of the San Luis Valley ranchers for oil and gasoline storage.

During the winter, the light was best, and I would often try my luck with cameras, and sometimes I would be joined by a college student taking movies for an uncle. The impatiently waiting motorists eyed us in an unfriendly way, obviously irked that we were somehow enjoying their delays. I was to learn that some of these church-going folk engaged in some rather un-Christian comments about our activities. What the "hangover crowd" had to say about us can only be imagined!

Slowly, the train would move out of the yard, sometimes a limit length of 100 cars, the first 30 being standard-gauge reefers en route to various potato-loading sidings in the San Luis Valley. The run down to Antonito provided little in worthy photo opportunities, with only two easy curves and one truss bridge. The lead engineer engaged in lengthy whistle blasts for grade crossings, particularly if motorists were in sight. Many valley motorists were ranchers and farmers, used to being all by themselves out on their vast spreads, and they had the habit of not paying much attention to stop signs or traffic. And it required plenty of whistling to awaken them to the danger of an oncoming train. Even so, there were many close misses.

At Antonito, the engines would take on water and perhaps coal, also. Then, the helper engine was cut back into the train, leaving the lead locomotive—the one with the big plow reaching to the middle of the smokebox. After that was done, all the crew would adjourn to Reno Lucero's Cumbres Cafe for a second breakfast.

They also made sure to set out the two idler cars each train carried on this dual-gauge line. Once, however, they somehow forgot the one behind the lead engine, only to be discovered by the fireman as it was bumping along a quarter mile beyond the end of the third rail. Very cautiously, the train was backed, and the idler car climbed back on the third rail with no problem! Many years afterward—perhaps even yet—the flange marks on the ties were evident. On that particular day I had turned back to Alamosa as the train left town, missing out on the unusual happening. I might mention that the center of the valley received little or no snow, even when a storm was obvious out toward Cumbres Pass. However, if a storm had piled-up drifts, the routine was to send out a flanger train several hours ahead of the

freight train, to plow the way.

Returning freight trains from Chama were timed to reach the valley not earlier than 6:00 p.m., cutoff time for loading cars at the sidings. The result was that usually the eastbound freight would reach Alamosa long after dark, sometimes as late as midnight. The train would be set out on the long track at the south edge of town, and the engines and caboose would go on into town, dropping off the caboose near the depot. Once, as the 16-hour limit came within minutes, the fireman just uncoupled the engine from the train, leaving it standing on the mainline, as the crew hustled to reach the roundhouse before the deadline. The conductor came walking in to borrow the phone to call the dispatcher to get a yard crew to come to the rescue of the stranded train.

As only one engine was needed to bring a train from Cumbres Pass, the helper engine would run light, ahead of the train. During the winter, this served to plow open any drifts along the way, which helped the following train immensely. One time, though, the road crew decided not to leave Cumbres because a storm was increasing in intensity. This was a fortunate decision, as the helper engine hit a cut near Osier piled deep with snow, way over the top of the engine, and she was stuck fast. It was to be nearly a week before the engine was retrieved, as in the meantime, a flanger train sent to the rescue derailed at Osier, tying up everything.

ALTHOUGH THE SIGN SAYS: "END OF STANDARD GAUGE," it was ignored one day when a westbound freight train put marks still seen in some of the ties by forgetting to set out the idler car (behind the engine) at Antonito. The train in this view was short and unusual. It was taking a bulldozer operator to Cumbres Pass to clear out the trackage there, so normal operations could be maintained during the winter of 1951–1952. Between the two engines was a drag flanger, and following that was flatcar with the bulldozer, a boxcar of supplies, an extra tender for water, a "living" car (once a pay car, in other times), and the water-service man's outfit boxcar (containing tools and pipe fittings, and even some dynamite). Typical of the countryside in winter, there was little snow at Antonito, but there was a great amount of it beginning a dozen miles farther on. The train encountered drifts higher than the engines before it arrived at the summit of Cumbres Pass.

CHASING NARROW-GAUGE TRAINS

AFTER MOVING TO ALAMOSA in the fall of 1948, I gradually learned the routine of the Denver & Rio Grande Western narrow-gauge operations. One crew worked three times a week on the three-day round trip from Alamosa to Chama, the second day being employed to make two "hill turns" from Chama to Cumbres Pass. From Durango, another crew worked eastward to Chama to exchange cars with the crew from Alamosa. The engines of this crew sometimes were employed in helping haul cars on the hill turns to the 10,015-foot summit of the pass.

Also from Durango, there was a once or twice a week round trip to Farmington, New Mexico. Besides this, two or three trips were made weekly to Silverton, a "work-and-turn" one-day round trip. Durango also had the only yard crew on the narrow gauge, which worked from five to seven days a week.

From Salida, a crew worked a two- or even three-day round trip to Gunnison. The second day sometimes was employed to make a round trip on the Crested Butte Branch, north of Gunnison.

Busiest of all narrow-gauge lines was the Monarch Branch, which saw a round trip on this short line five or six days of each week. However, this Monarch operation was run only eight or nine months of the year, usually being closed from December into March. Also from Salida was a two-day round trip to Alamosa via the "Valley Line" about once a month, or even less frequently.

Between Gunnison and Montrose, there was a monthly round trip, except during livestock season in the spring and fall of each year. During these two periods of time, the line might see two or even three trips a week. Also operated irregularly— sometimes not for a month at a time—was the Baldwin Branch, the ex-C&S line northwest of Gunnison. Operations on this branch depended on coal loadings; however, during each autumn season, a few extra runs would occur for livestock loading.

Montrose operated trains to Ridgway, depending on traffic to and from the Rio Grande Southern Railroad at that point. The busiest times of the year were during the spring and fall livestock seasons, which might see three trains a week. The remaining portion of the Ouray Branch, between Ridgway and Ouray, had light rail and might see one train once a month, depending on ore loadings at the end of the line.

However, as you can see, there were over a dozen narrow-gauge operations on the D&RGW, but they never occurred on the same day—or even during the same week. There would be days at a time when nothing at all was operated anywhere.

Yard switching at Alamosa was done by standard-gauge motive power. At Gunnison and Montrose, switching was performed by road crews. This meant that at Montrose, some switching was done by

TO THE DELIGHT of Colorado railfans, the trains on the Alamosa-to-Antonito dual-gauge trackage presented a great variety of consists. U.S. Highway 285 closely paralleled the track, and the trains could not be missed. During much of the year, and during the summer vegetable harvests in particular, the Antonito "turns" from Alamosa often consisted of just a standard-gauge engine and caboose, with a string of refrigerator cars in between. However, many trips on this line might consist of a narrow-gauge engine on the point, with a narrow-gauge caboose on the rear—with an otherwise standard-gauge train in between. Then, there were all kinds of combinations, such as the one here, which had a lone narrow-gauge boxcar in a standard-gauge train. Crews had to be careful with such mixed-gauge consists. The wooden narrow-gauge cars were much older than their standard-gauge counterparts, and sometimes, the older cars could not take the punishing strains. Outbound narrow-gauge freight trains bound for Chama, New Mexico, generally would have up to 30 standard-gauge cars in their trains, destined for San Luis Valley points.

narrow-gauge engines using a standard-gauge idler car in that dual-gauge yard.

During the height of the vegetable-shipping season, during late spring and early summer, the dual-gauge Alamosa–Antonito stretch of trackage needed almost daily service. Chama-bound freight trains took care of this work in both directions; however, on other days, an Antonito turn would be made. This turn usually employed a standard-gauge engine and caboose; however, not infrequently, a narrow-gauge engine would be used. All trains on this line carried a pair of idler cars, rare exceptions being livestock trains for the most part.

Helper engines ran up many "light" miles (i.e., without helping trains upgrade), especially so on the Alamosa end of the line. Westbound freights had a second engine, cut back in the train beyond Antonito, en route to Chama. After helping trains on the next day's hill turns, this second engine would help on the third day's runs up to the summit, then run light to Alamosa. The eastbound train from Durango usually had a doubleheader; how-ever, when it was just a one-engine train, it would find a helper waiting at Gato on its westbound trip.

Farmington runs generally were made with one engine, but the Silverton Branch trains often used a second engine, cut into the consist back in the middle of the train. This helper engine returned from Silverton to Durango running light.

Out of Salida, a second engine was cut into the train on the Monarch turns, generally back in front of the caboose. This arrangement simplified the movements up the Garfield switchback. The extra engine would return light to Salida from Monarch. The Gunnison train would require two or three engines, one cut back in the train, the third (if used) back by the caboose. Usually, the helpers would return to Salida from Marshall Pass, running light. Helpers would be sent from Salida to meet the eastbound train at Sargent, usually two for a coal train, but in the event of a heavy livestock train, four engines would be needed between Sargent and the summit of Marshall Pass. Then, all but one engine would run light ahead to Salida.

298

NOW THE TOWN'S CITY HALL, a San Luis Valley turn was about to set off some refrigerator cars at this very important loading place. Engine 494 happened to be the available engine in Alamosa, when the train was called, since none of the 1100-series standard-gauge 2-8-0's were ready. This depot represents a period in the Denver & Rio Grande's history when specially designed depot buildings were planned for the smaller towns, replacing the old cheaply constructed wooden structures. Notice the train-order signal in front of this two-story stuccoed depot. This was the only type of signal used on the narrow gauge. The date was March 31, 1950.

The train for Alamosa required one or two helpers up the grade to Poncha Pass. Then, the helpers would return to Salida, allowing one engine to take the train on down into the San Luis Valley to Alamosa. If the returning train from Alamosa was too heavy for the 3.0-percent grade from Round Hill to Poncha Pass, a helper would be dispatched from Salida to wait at Round Hill.

Helpers were needed for the ascent to Cerro Summit, between Gunnison and Montrose—both from Cimarron for westbound trains and from Montrose or Cedar Creek for eastbound trains. "Mudhens" (K-27 2-8-2's) and the C-18 and C-19 Consolidations were concentrated at Montrose for the operations out of that point.

As you can see, most operations used the two largest classes of 2-8-2's, the K-36's and K-37's. They handled everything out of Alamosa and Salida. However, they could not be used on the Silverton Branch, or west of Gunnison. Likewise, only the last two C-16 2-8-0's could be used on the

Baldwin Branch. The Silverton Branch used Mudhens (the Class K-27 Mikados) or the three remaining "Sport Models" (the Class K-28 Mikados), plus the sole engine in Class C-25, the outside frame 2-8-0, No. 375, an ex-Crystal River engine.

The two other former Crystal River engines (also outside-frame 2-8-0's), Class C-21's Nos. 360 and 361, worked from Gunnison to Montrose. They were assisted over Cerro Summit (west of Cimarron) by Mudhens, which could not be used in the Black Cañon. Mudhens also handled the trains to Ridgway; however, the track south of that station to Ouray was limited to Class C-18 2-8-0's, Nos. 315–319.

When I moved to Colorado in 1948, finding any of the 2-8-0 engines out on a run was something requiring examining the daily "dope sheet" of the Alamosa dispatcher... and luck!

Mudhens could be found on most trains of the Rio Grande Southern, which preferred to lease them, rather than use their own motive power. Engine 20, the last

299

A MISTAKE WAS MADE when "Romeo" was named. It was intended to be "Romero." After the passenger train was discontinued in 1951, the agent was laid off, and the depot at this site was done away with. No. 494, with her Valley turn, was going to set out the refrigerator cars here, while the gondolas were for volcanic-ash loading at Antonito—something that became a very large traffic item, as the material became popular for construction. An angry farmer came by one day after the depot was closed. He had bought it, to move it to his farm. When he showed up to start moving the structure, he found a section gang busily stripping everything inside the building, piling it outside to burn. The D&RGW superintendent (who does not deserve mention by name)

was a strange and hostile individual to many people, and he was personally directing the men in their act of vandalism. To the farmer's protests, he replied, "You only get the walls, the roof and floor, nothing else." The depot furniture, which included settees, cabinets, desks, partitions and other useful things, was thereupon burned. Furthermore, at the superintendent's direction, the men used sledge hammers to smash the train-order signal lamp, the lanterns and the lamps used inside the depot. Strangely, the superintendent thought he was an efficient man. Yet, here he was spending the section men's time to waste useful things just out of spite. And the section men were needed for other work, for which they were behind in performing.

4-6-0, and No. 42, a Class C-17 2-8-0, were kept at the Durango roundhouse for use on light-tonnage trains, or they were used as helpers. Engines 40 and 41, also 2-8-0's— both Class C-19's—were usually found at Ridgway, occasionally used as helpers over Dallas Divide. The RGS ran two-day round trips to Dolores, possibly with a side trip to Rico. As traffic was light after World War II, these runs might be once a week, or not even that often. During its final years, the word "often" could not be applied to the RGS. In fact, during its final year, 1951, there were not any trains for months between Durango and Dolores, as the Colorado state highway people leisurely replaced the Franklin Junction trestle with a steel bridge. (This span was intended for some highway project as soon as the railroad was abandoned.)

PILE DRIVER OB spent most of its life just sitting in the Alamosa yard. Rarely, it would be called out to repair a trestle. This one near the ghost-town site of Amargo at MP 366.9 needed a new bent over a deep arroyo. No. 481 supplied the steam to operate the pile driver. After the Antonito–Durango line was abandoned by the D&RGW in 1971, this unique item of equipment went to the new Cumbres & Toltec Scenic Railroad. This rare scene was photographed on November 18, 1949.

UNFORTUNATELY for the popular glass-roofed "Silver Vista," the car had been placed in the D&RGW's car shop at Alamosa at the end of the 1953 "Silverton" train's season. It and some standard-gauge refrigerator cars were destroyed in a fire that consumed the car shop as well in October. Even though a switch engine was present, it was impossible to pull the cars from the building to save them, because other cars in various stages of repair blocked access. The "Silver Vista" had been placed in service in June of 1948, and it was invariably sold out before train time. Built from a former coach in non-revenue service, the designers expected the passengers would stay seated and view the scenic wonders through the glass roof. However, most passengers tried to crowd out onto the small platform ends of the car to take pictures, etc., and this space had been expected to be used only by a trainman at times. So, in use, most of the passengers crowded the "dinky" platform areas, and most of the reserved seats were empty!

301

CHASING THE DELUXE *SAN JUAN* NARROW-GAUGE PASSENGER TRAIN OVER CUMBRES

ALAMOSA HAD ONLY TWO passenger trains. The standard-gauge train from Denver was rarely to be found during daylight hours on its run, as it had such a leisurely schedule that it easily arrived at 4:30 a.m. After laying-over in Alamosa during the day, the train departed in the evening at 9:40 p.m. On the other hand, the narrow-gauge passenger train, called the *San Juan*, was a delight for camera fans. The deluxe *San Juan* departed from Alamosa at 7:00 a.m., reached Cumbres Pass just after 10:00 a.m., and arrived in Durango just after 4:00 p.m. Its eastward run began at Durango at 11:15 a.m., departed from Cumbres just after 5:00 p.m. and arrived in Alamosa at 8:30 p.m. So, especially during the summer months, the *San Juan* could be recorded on film at almost any time during its journey through southwestern Colorado.

Sometimes, on a day off from my 16-hour days at the motel during the summer season, I would take off for Cumbres Pass, even if it was a day when no freight trains were scheduled, and even if not even a "hill turn" from Chama could be expected. Despite the rough gravel road up to Cumbres, it was easy to leave after the train had passed and arrive at Los Pinos to cover the last five miles of the ascent up to the pass.

One could spend the next few hours going down to Chama, New Mexico, with the train or one could just wait at this station. Fred, the "ancient" operator at the Cumbres depot, could be counted on to deliver some of his interesting reminiscences of a lifetime at places like Cumbres. His chipmunks were friendly, and they were glad to join a visitor while getting rid of any chocolate or nut candy, and of course, I would always bring along some chocolate-chip cookies to share with the tiny fellows.

Perhaps I would walk out to Windy Point, less than half a mile from the depot, along about 3:00 p.m.—to have a view all the way to the smoke of engines at Chama, 14 miles away by rail. Or, if I felt like braving a million large-and-voracious mosquitoes, I could hike up to the crags of the Windy Point rocks for an even-more aerial type of view.

Shortly after 4:00 p.m., the coming of the *San Juan* would be heralded by distant smoke, and in the winding of the track, at times the distant train seemed to be doing more winding than coming up the 4.0-percent grade to the pass. Eventually, I would occasionally glimpse the train through the trees, still appearing to be a tiny image in the distance, and now and then, the wind would

ON A MIDSUMMER MORNING at Alamosa, the hostlers had just brought No. 476 from the roundhouse for the 7:00 a.m. "San Juan" train. They will take No. 1514 back to the roundhouse, which had arrived at 4:30 a.m. with the overnight passenger train from Denver. The arrangement was reversed when the eastbound "San Juan" arrived at 8:30 p.m., and the standard-gauge train departed from Alamosa at 9:40 p.m. During both periods, the Alamosa depot was a busy place, with off-duty railroaders loafing around, local residents with last-minute letters to post on the trains, and in midsummer, tourists aboard the narrow-gauge parlor-dinette car were looking forward to breakfast and a scenic 9½-hour trip to Durango. This peaceful scene was photographed on a warm summer day during July of 1949.

carry the sound. You could tell which class of engine was powering the day's train by the sounds. The 470-series K-28's had the sharp exhaust of a hard-working engine, busily attacking the steep 4.0-percent grade. If it was a larger 480-series K-36, the exhaust would be softer, and it would give you the impression of an engine that was not working very hard. The smoke, however, no matter which class, traveled faster than the train, partly because it did not have to follow all those curves, and of course, the engine smoke was boosted by the steady winds out of the west.

So, long before the train had even reached the road crossing far below (beyond Coxo siding), the smoke already was swirling around the summit. Unfortunately, it also put a haze into any picture of the train that was snapped from this high vantage point.

A five-minute stop was made at the Cumbres depot, during which time the conductor registered his arrival and departure, noted crew names, engine number and consist of the train. Neither he nor I thought at the time that sometime in the distant future those train passings of Cumbres Pass would become part of the library at the Colorado Railroad Museum in Golden.

After the train left the pass, I could follow the train again as far as Los Pinos, then head for home, as the green **San Juan** vanished down the valley of the little high-country Los

Pinos River. For variations on such a day, a horribly-rough trail—a relic of a pre-railroad "wagon road"—could be taken to reach points like Big Horn, Sublette, Toltec Gorge and Osier. You had to select one or another as a destination, as at this juncture, the train could travel between these points much more quickly than any vehicle could bounce along on that rough trail, despite all the winding-around the train did on the upper hillsides of the river valley. There was no trail to Toltec Gorge, but from a point where the trail came close to the canyon rim, one could see the narrow, dark cleft and the black spot of the tunnel miles away in the distance. It was a pleasure to take visitors from the Midwest or the East out to these remote places.

During the summer season, the San Juan consisted of five cars: an RPO-express car, a baggage car, two vestibuled coaches and a

IT WAS A DAILY ROUTINE at Alamosa, Colorado, for the night passenger train from Denver to arrive at 4:30 a.m. (if on time, and in this instance it was not), usually headed by a Mallet. The schedule was deliberately slow, as the U. S. Post Office people did not want the mail to arrive before that time. So, a slow-moving Mallet was just right for the final leg of the run from La Veta over Veta Pass. The mail and express cars would be spotted alongside the narrow-gauge cars for the morning's "San Juan" train. By 6:30 a.m., a roundhouse crew would have brought a narrow-gauge engine down to the slim-gauge train, and they would have taken the big Mallet back with them to the roundhouse yard. A few minutes before 7:00 a.m., the "San Juan" would be coupled to the engine—usually a Class K-28 Mikado. And right on the advertised time, the train would depart for Antonito, Cumbres Pass, Chama and Durango. The attendant in the parlor-dinette car would be busy putting rubber bands around a stack of *Denver Post* newspapers, for delivery to customers (of which I was one) along this run. The attendant would toss my paper off the car's platform as the train sped by at a good 35 mph. Sometimes, the rubber band would break, and my copy would be scattered all over the countryside, among the chico brush!

"first-class" parlor-dinette car. During the winter months, there usually was a four-car consist, with one less coach. Motive power usually was a Class K-28 470-series outside-frame 2-8-2; however, often during the last years of the train, a larger 2-8-2 of the 480-series K-36 Class handled the train. The enginemen preferred the K-28's, and a couple of the K-36's made them uneasy, as one in particular, despite much shop work on it, was rigid when it entered a curve. When snow was drifting, the engines had their winter pilot plows attached, and when it was blowing badly, the train might be double-headed on rare occasions.

The parlor car, of course, was popular with tourists, who gladly paid the small extra fare for one of the reserved first-class seats. The dinette at the end of the train served meals at prices that were in effect when the *San Juan* was modernized in 1937. Four people could be served at a time, although a tray arrangement also permitted one to be served at their seat. Seats one and two were often reserved weeks, or even months, ahead by tourists who wanted the best view of the scenic route.

West of Chama, New Mexico, the scenery of the route became somewhat less spectacular, much of it arid countryside, with few small streams. However, the track followed these streams to a high point, then dropped down, following another drainage. Most "stations" were just passing sidings or tiny communities, the only places that warranted an agent in residence were Lumberton,

ON SUNDAY, MARCH 12, 1950, the "San Juan" had hurried past our motel just after 7:00 a.m., delivering my copy of *The Sunday Denver Post* while passing. The once-a-month (or so) Valley Line train for Salida was heading out that morning, and I had gone into town to take a picture or two (if possible). However, I did not stay long enough, for as the caboose was just about to clear the road crossing at the eastern edge of Alamosa, an automobile came speeding up, with its horn honking! A D&RGW employee jumped out with an urgent message for the train to come back into town. So, the conductor quickly "pulled the air" on the caboose. From a railroad telephone at Los Pinos tank (several miles from Cumbres Pass), Conductor Stamy Edmisten had called Alamosa with the message that his train was stuck in the snow near the tank! Only one narrow-gauge engine was left in Alamosa—No. 486—and this K-36 did not have a pilot plow. Engine 499, with a permanent pilot plow, had just left, at the head end of the Salida train. So, the foreman drove his car as fast as he could to intercept that train. Meanwhile, as the foreman was chasing after the Valley Line train, section men were being assembled, and anyone wanting to earn "a few bucks" shoveling snow was welcome to come along. So... at midmorning on that day, I was surprised to see Nos. 499 and 486 hurry past the motel, with a flanger and two cabooses... a rescue train! The men on the rescue train found a strange sight when they arrived behind the "San Juan." The passenger train was working upgrade beyond the Los Pinos tank, rolling along an ordinary hillside. Suddenly—without warning—a tremendous amount of wet snow slid down on the train, piling up against the cars and packing around the wheels of the engine and cars, bringing the train to a halt. In vain, the engineer tried to free at least the locomotive. Being on the shady side of the train, with the temperature below freezing, the mass just froze the train in place. The rescue train had to free one car at a time, take it back to Los Pinos siding, and then tackle the next car. Finally, the "San Juan" was reassembled there, and the flanger train went ahead—and more of the heavy, wet snow was encountered on the big loop, a mile from the summit, and it got stuck! This time, the passenger train came to the rescue, coupling behind the cabooses. And together, the combined consist broke free—and the two trains finally made it to the summit. Here, the flanger train went ahead, but found no major problems on the way down to Chama. Meanwhile, the Salida crew earned an extra day's pay while sitting around at Alamosa, "chewing the fat"!

Dulce (the capital of the Jicarilla Apaches), Gato (formerly called "Pagosa Junction") and Ignacio. The parlor-car attendants ran errands for the people along the line, purchasing things for them at the terminal city's stores, and during the summer did a fair amount of business in ice-cream cones, especially for the children living at isolated places. Along the entire route west of Antonito, there were few good roads, even gravel-surfaced, with some paving to be seen near Durango. The train traveled through a region that had changed very little from the 1880's, when the San Juan Extension was constructed.

In its narrow-minded postwar plans to

A LONG TIME BEFORE this scene was photographed in 1950, old D&RGW No. 1146 had hauled many a passenger train, or at least the C-48 had *helped* move them through the mountains on the mainlines. Here, the chunky 2-8-0 was preparing to take the night train from Denver, Train 115, down to the wye at Alamosa to turn it around. No. 1146 had an air-operated front-end coupler that could be used for coupling to cars of either gauge. On the tender, there was a three-position casting for two couplers—used for dual-gauge switching. Early in 1950, Engine 1146 hauled her last passenger train. One day, when Cumbres Pass was snowed-in, and to fulfill the mail contract, the Consolidation hauled a three-car narrow-gauge consist to Antonito and return. As it turned out, this was the last mixed-gauge passenger train to operate in Colorado, something that was fairly common on the Rio Grande several decades earlier.

IN THIS REGION of southern Colorado, there usually is not much snow until after Christmas, as the condition of the train indicates. At Chama, New Mexico, engine crews changed; however, the train crew made the entire trip between Alamosa and Durango. The halt at the Chama depot—just below the town—enabled the parlor-car attendant to go shopping for more foodstuffs, as well as for special requests from isolated people along the line. This was for needs like thread, hardware and other household items. During the summer, the attendant sold many ice-cream cones. The poor roads of this mountainous region meant that the "San Juan" was a very necessary conveyance to connect the area with the rest of the world. This view was shot during December of 1948.

abandon all narrow-gauge lines, the Rio Grande management made its first move in applying to discontinue the *San Juan* train. In a folder, they claimed the annual loss was $80,000, a sum that was laughed at by traffic people on other railroads. During the hearings, it was brought out that the company had refused two offers of increased U.S. Mail pay, which alone would have covered the alleged loss. Nevertheless, Colorado's Public Utilities Commission definitely did not rep-

resent the people of the state, and despite the evidence presented against abandoning the train, the PUC okayed discontinuance. The final runs occurred on January 31, 1951, in the midst of a severe storm.

The end of the passenger trains, which twice daily in their movements kept the track open during most of the wintry weather, meant that freight-train operations would increase in costs and further the abandonment of the Alamosa–Durango line. If a freight engine stopped, uncoupled and bucked snow, the crew would find the train almost impossible to restart in low temperatures, and this could pull a drawbar or two. As a result, more plow-flanger work trains had to be run. The two or three days between freight trains enabled the snow to pile up—and worse yet, it would pack hard. Management hoped to be rid of all the narrow-gauge lines by the 1950's, but only the arrival of a large traffic in pipe and other supplies to a newly-discovered gas-and-oil field extended the life of the Durango line for another decade or more.

ONLY NINE MORE TIMES would the "San Juan" travel over Cumbres Pass. Then, the 70-year-old run would pass into history. No. 473 had been all "dolled up" the previous year for the Silverton train, with yellow coaches. Besides the Grande Gold yellow tender, a fake diamond stack had been placed over the straight stack, and the electric headlight had been encased in a simulated oil-period case. Postal Clerk C. C. Rollins was standing in the doorway of the mail car. He was carrying a carton with some 1,100 covers sent in from all over, to be postmarked on the last run, on January 31, 1951.

307

THE "SAN JUAN" TRAIN, on its next-to-last day, had been expanded to eight cars, and it was working up the grade between Lumberton and Amargo, in New Mexico. The classic narrow-gauge passenger train was heading for the stiff climb through Monero Cañon. The train included five vestibuled coaches ahead of the parlor car. The storm gradually worsened, and the next day's final train had to be double-headed, and it ran late due to the bad weather. The nearby dirt road was becoming nearly impassable, and my Chevy barely got me back up the hill to Monero and beyond. On the following day, the road was closed.

ON NOVEMBER 18, 1949, the westbound "San Juan" passenger train was drifting through Monero Cañon, after its station stop at the little coal-mining town of Monero, New Mexico. From the appearance of the heaped tender, it was very likely that the fireman took-on coal, as well as water. This remote location is a few miles south of the Colorado border.

IT WAS CHRISTMAS DAY, 1948, and the "San Juan" passenger train was pulling up from the water tank with its six-car consist. Conductor D. H. "Deadhead" Hines was waiting in front of the 1881 log depot. A very old non-revenue work car was on the depot spur, not to be moved except with care. It has the old-time continuous-draw-stem couplers (so-called), where both couplers were tied together by a long rod, and if it broke, both couplers pulled out. The "San Juan" had an extra baggage car in the train, to move the holiday mail and express to Durango.

WITH THE PARLOR CAR "Durango," in the foreground, the eastbound "San Juan" passenger train, has made a water stop at Gato, formerly known as "Pagosa Junction," on January 23, 1951. A week later, this D&RGW train would make its final run—in a storm and cold wave—hours late and double-headed. The old log depot dated from 1881, and it had originally been at Amargo, New Mexico, and it had been moved the 21 miles on flatcars. Trainmen liked to show passengers the numerous bullet holes in the depot, put there in earlier-and-wilder times at both places.

DURANGO, COLORADO, was the only place on the Denver & Rio Grande Western's narrow-gauge lines with a switch engine on duty daily. This relic of 1881, No. 345, was a Class C-19 2-8-0, and she was turning the combined "San Juan" and "Silverton" consists on August 7, 1950. The "Silverton" was called the "painted train" by local railroaders. No. 345 was destined to become one of the two engines used next summer for a head-on collision filmed on the Silverton Branch for the movie, "Denver & Rio Grande." Renumbered as "268," this Consolidation impersonated the real Engine 268. This is to explain to puzzled railroad-minded viewers of that much re-run TV railroad epic, why in some shots the engine racing toward destruction has rounded domes, while in other views, the engine has the ornate molded-ring domes fancied in 1881.

THE HEARING before the New Mexico Corporation Commission took place on May 22, 1951, and assent for abandonment of passenger service was given. However, the news did not reach Chama, New Mexico, until the one-car train was already en route from Dulce. I drove as fast as I could and caught the train en route, taking pictures of the last run. However, the crew did not know they were making a last run! They received the news upon their arrival at Chama. Engine 473, the combination car, No. 212, and the three coaches left from the Chili Line were given yellow paint for the 1950 Silverton season.

THIS INTERESTING SCENE will be repeated only 10 more times, for it was January 21, 1951, when this picture was taken. And both the Denver–Alamosa train and the Alamosa–Durango "San Juan" train will be discontinued on January 31. Yard engine No. 1146, a Class C-48 2-8-0, had just wyed the Denver train. Spare coaches Nos. 323 and 980 were at the right, on the "Salida track," so named for the long-vanished daytime two-car passenger train that ran on the Valley Line to Salida. (Notice the "flying" *Rio Grande* emblem on the standard-gauge coach.) A 70-year era of passenger trains at Alamosa was coming to an end. By getting rid of the "San Juan," the D&RGW management intended that the freight operations would become so erratic and costly that the line itself could be abandoned. The fortunate discovery of immense amounts of natural gas along the Colorado border foiled that plan for almost another 20 years!

THE LAST MIXED-GAUGE PASSENGER TRAIN

ON ONE OCCASION, at least the railroaders signalled that they wanted their picture taken, for they had a most unusual train. Cumbres Pass was blocked by a snowstorm, but an effort was made to fill part of the Railway Post Office mail contract. On the morning of February 16, 1949, I was busy working at the motel building in Alamosa. The regular maid had not shown up for work, and there was plenty to do to get things ready for that day's guests. My attention was caught by an inordinate amount of whistling from the direction of the D&RGW yards, and as I opened the door to look, it came even closer—a locomotive whistle in exaggerated grade-crossing blasts…

very long and very loud…

━━━━━ ━━━━●━━━━ ━━━━!

Passing by, making all this extra noise, rolled the standard-gauge yard engine, No. 1146, a Class C-48 2-8-0, hauling three narrow-gauge passenger cars from the regular *San Juan* train: an RPO-express car, a baggage car and one coach. So, I hastily locked the motel office and grabbed my camera on the run, and hurried to overtake the unusual train. And I managed to take a couple of shots before reluctantly returning to my duties at the Narrow Gauge Motel in Alamosa.

Later, I learned the reason for what at that time became the last mixed-gauge passenger train on the D&RGW—and for all of North America, as well. The only narrow-gauge locomotive at the roundhouse was under repair, and all the others were out battling the storm. Then, someone recalled that No. 1146 had the correct fittings and couplers to haul the narrow-gauge passenger cars…. So, off went this unusual train in order to honor the mail contract. It laid-over at Antonito and then returned in the evening on the *San Juan* train's regular schedule. On the following day, the narrow-gauge K-36 had been repaired and hauled the train.

Commencing in the 1880's, as third-rail (dual-gauge) trackage was added to the narrow-gauge mainline of the Denver & Rio Grande between Denver and Pueblo, all kinds of mixed-gauge trains were common, although no photographs of these runs are known. Until the late 1880's, the railroad did not have much in the way of standard-gauge passenger cars, so most trains were made up of through cars intended for the narrow-gauge lines beyond Pueblo. The mixtures ended on March 3, 1900, with the termination of the last narrow-gauge passenger service between Denver and Salida (Trains 7 and 8). And the narrow-gauge third rail along the mainline between Denver and Pueblo was removed in 1902.

THINGS WERE VERY BUSY at Cumbres Pass on February 20, 1953. The helper of a westbound freight had gone ahead to Chama, New Mexico, as No. 498 (at the left) prepared to head downhill with the train. No. 484, at the right, had just made a hill turn. The "pipe boom" had increased freight trains to daily out of Alamosa—the height being nine 70-car freight trains west in seven days. After the "San Juan" passenger train was taken off this route, the depot at the pass would soon be bull-dozed. How did I get to this scene at snowed-in Cumbres? It was accomplished by riding in that caboose from Chama. Cumbres-turn crews liked to have visitors, to break the monotony of "the same old thing" every trip up the hill. This way, they could regale their visitors with stories they could no longer tell-and-tell again among their fellow crewmen!

OUT IN COLORADO FOR SNOW

WHEN I FIRST MOVED to Colorado—in 1948—like most Easterners, I had quite a different idea from reality of what Colorado weather was like, especially regarding winter snowfall. My initial hopes of taking many pictures of deep snow and drifts, as well as severe storm conditions, soon were cancelled by actual conditions in the largely mountainous Centennial State. Despite the high Rocky Mountains in Colorado, the state does not receive a large amount of snow during an average winter. Colorado's climate is best described as "semiarid"—almost desert-like much of the time—varying only as to degree.

From reading old railroad records of various types, it was learned that on an average of every five years, the high-mountain areas would receive heavy snow of the sort that most non-Coloradans think occur every winter. Below 9,000 feet in elevation, there usually are only modest amounts of snow, and what does fall in the lower elevations, quickly melts under the impact of daily sunshine—averaging over 300 days of bright sunlight every year in Denver, for example. Besides sunshine, the wind quickly disposes of much snow, especially in the mountains.

However, above 9,000 feet in elevation, the snowfall rapidly increases in depth during average or normal winters, and it lingers longer, often lasting well into the summer. It is this high-elevation snow that provides the water for the cities and farmland irrigators. This high-country snow melts slowly as a rule, keeping Colorado's streams high, often into July. And if several hot days without clouds occur in succession, it can result in flash-flood conditions in the narrow canyons—sometimes very destructive for the railroad lines.

Contrary to common belief, the rotary snowplow was a machine seldom needed or used. A normal winter would require its use perhaps once or twice a year, or not at all. The mainline of the Denver & Rio Grande Western has never needed a rotary snowplow that anyone can recall. The standard-gauge rotary plow kept at Salida until the 1940's was for use on the branch trackage at Leadville. Flangers or spreaders were all the main standard-gauge trackage needed, and at that, not often. On the narrow-gauge lines of the D&RGW, rotaries were kept at Alamosa, Chama and Gunnison. Cumbres Pass, of course, was the reason for the Alamosa and Chama machines being kept in readiness. The Gunnison rotary plow was used occasionally on the Crested Butte Branch, but not every year. A rotary plow had not been used on the narrow-gauge mainline over Marshall Pass since 1923.

Snowstorms sometimes would sweep through Cumbres Pass from the west, and in the process of dropping an average of 156 feet of snow per winter season, they would pile up drifts much higher than a locomotive. At the same time, along hundreds—or even thousands—of feet of track, gale-force winds scoured bare long stretches, as well as the nearby hillsides. The same storms would sweep easterly and take a natural path that would drop immense amounts of snow on several miles of the Santa Fe Branch (the "Chili Line") north of Tres Piedras ("Three Rocks"), New Mexico. A rotary plow would have to open that section of the line, although for miles south of Antonito, Colorado, the amount of snow would be of no consequence.

Because of rocks and tree parts in the snowslides, which routinely afflicted the Silverton Branch and the Black Canyon route, rotaries could not be used on those lines. Gunnison had a large wedge snowplow, which was nothing more than a rock-loaded gondola fitted with an engine-pilot plow at one end (topped with a locomotive headlight up high), for use in the Black Canyon. The

Silverton Branch counted on locomotives equipped with the same kind of wedge pilot plow to buck open the line.

When I lived in Alamosa, it was soon learned—to my frustration—that the places where the snow was giving problems for the railroads, were nearly all non-accessible by automobile. The rough, old dirt road over Cumbres Pass was not plowed during the winter, and upon the first heavy snowfall, it simply remained closed until the following spring. This meant that during a mild winter, one might venture up to Cumbres as late as December, as normally, most of the snow fell during the January-to-March period—or even as late as April and May. Although Poncha Pass had a highway that was kept open all year around, the narrow-gauge railroad summit was a mile away and out of sight from the road. And the snowmobile had yet to make its appearance!

So... the only place where winter operations could be closely watched was the Monarch Branch. Unfortunately, however, this steep branch line usually closed during the snowiest part of the winter—in January—and it stayed closed until spring. The closure was not because of the winter weather, but to allow the Colorado Fuel & Iron Corporation's quarrymen to drill-and-place explosives in the mountainside, to bring down in one big blast large chunks of limestone, which could be crushed and shipped the rest of the year to the CF&I's steel mills at Minnequa (adjoining Pueblo), Colorado.

On the Rio Grande Southern's remote narrow-gauge line over Lizard Head Pass, there was a narrow road that was kept open most of the winter—a rough, winding affair that was partly gravel-surfaced and partly just dirt that turned into deep-frozen ruts. The usually constant winter winds would pile up snowdrifts quickly, and this road was not a safe place to linger. As a result, the Rio Grande Southern's train movements largely went without the attention of railfan cameras during the winter months. My determination to cover the last runs of the RGS during the winter of 1951 was locally considered to be proof that I was indeed "nuts," to say the least!

When I was living in Alamosa (adjacent to the D&RGW), I would sometimes hear the rotary-snowplow outfit slowly shuffle by before dawn, on its way to battle the results of a storm over Cumbres. Normally, there would be no snow at all in Alamosa, which gave me a laugh at the letters received venturing hope that I would be taking good rotary action shots from my upstairs windows!

Also, although a set of standard-gauge trucks was kept for possible use of the rotary over La Veta Pass, I could never determine that they were ever used. Storms would occasionally hit that location, requiring drag-flanger and Jordan-spreader trains.

At Antonito, there might be an inch or two of snow on the ground, and the rotary-plow crew would stop there to adjust the blades, have a second breakfast at the Cumbres Cafe, the favorite restaurant of hungry railroaders. They would then work another 15 miles or more before encountering the first sizeable drifts, just beyond the Lava water tank, in the cuts near the Big Horn loop. From this point, progress would be about one mile an hour, depending on how many large drifts had to be trenched to enable the big machine to be pushed into them. Two or three locomotives would be pushing, so that if one "lost its footing" by slipping, the momentum of the other engines would keep the outfit moving.

Of course, you could still ride the wintertime Silverton mixed train and hope to see some action in bucking snow; however, during my first winter in Colorado, I waited for a report of heavy snow, until I finally rode on a trip during the last day in March. More than half way up the Animas Canyon, the engine only occasionally brushed aside a few inches of snow off the rails. (There was no snow in Durango when the train departed for Silverton.) However, at the site of the vanished snowshed, at Milepost 492.5 (from Denver), about two miles past Elk Park, that snowslide had run, as well as several smaller ones beyond that location. At last, my chance had come! So, while the crew studied the

situation, I climbed up over the pile on the track and got ready beyond it. At that time, I learned that what looked like snow at a distance was actually large chunks of the frozen material, the size of sugar beets or larger. I really did not want to be too close to that stuff when it went flying through the air!

Engine 463 backed the train down a few-hundred feet and uncoupled. With a full head of steam the engine was going a good 20 mph or more when it hit the slide, and I had time for just one quick shot and then ducked myself and my camera under a heavy jacket as those icy chunks rained around. The locomotive just barely broke through, with its big plow pushing tons of the slide off the track, and then No. 463 continued for a quarter-mile or so, brushing the smaller slides aside. While it was doing that, I hastened to get back down to the track and into the warmth of the cozy combine.

As Silverton was only four more miles up the line, we were soon in the old mining town, and all of us adjourned for lunch at the *not* particularly well-named "Best Cafe" (no longer in business). However, after a winter ride up the Animas Canyon, no one was particular about food. After lunch, there ensued a long bout of switching, as the 2-8-2 had no coupler on the front end because of the big plow. As a result, No. 463 would plow up to the freight cars in the yard, and then go to the wye to turn around and back into the yard tender first in order to couple to the cars. So, it was plow and wye and back for hours. The crew did not waste any time, as they wanted to get past the snowslide area before it got dark, fearing that more avalanches might come down as the temperature dropped. Nothing of any consequence landed on the track, but the return trip was made slowly and cautiously. Despite the bright headlight, the engine crew did not have a good view of the track ahead, primarily because of the endless curves through the spectacular canyon of the Río de las Animas Perdidas (*literally* meaning the "River of the Souls Lost"), and so-named by early Spanish explorers of southwestern Colorado.

Long after we had managed to traverse the high line and had arrived in the outskirts of Durango, approaching the last bridge, the train came to a stop, as abrupt as if it had run into a stone wall. A side rod had come loose, and as it flailed around briefly, it had driven itself into the right-of-way. Fortunately, the

ROTARY SNOWPLOW OM was heading westbound in the barely snowy San Luis Valley, with three tenders being pushed by three locomotives. When the D&RGW dispatched a rotary plow, it always went equipped for the worst, as well as for a longer "outing" than planned. So, trailing the engines were two cars of coal and several bunk and cook cars for the rotary crews. When there was a possibility that the outfit might not make it through—and with the known inability of cabooses to buck through snow if the train tried backing, an extra engine would follow, but headed upgrade backwards, toward Alamosa... *just in case!* Usually, if a snowstorm was raging in the San Juan Mountains, the San Luis Valley would receive little or no snow at all.

side rod did not encounter any rock or the engine would have been pushed over. The conductor hurried to a telephone; however, the Durango roundhouse did not have any engines under steam, so we were on our own. All the crew could do was to remove the rod and place it on the empty pilot space back of the plow, and with great difficulty, No. 463—running on only one side—managed to get us across the bridge and up the slight grade beyond Main Avenue. Arrival at the big wooden depot was at midnight, and we discovered that Durango had received a foot of snow during our absence.

During February of 1953, the last big mine permanently closed at Silverton, and winter runs of the mixed train ended—as it turned out, for all time. The big pilot plow of No. 463 was cut up for other uses, and the K-27 Class Mikado was sold to a Californian

(a "Hollywood" personality). However, the engine returned to Colorado as a gift years later, and in the summer of 1994, after being nicely rebuilt by the Cumbres & Toltec Scenic Railroad, No. 463 ran over Cumbres Pass again, where long ago it had been a regular "hill-turn" engine.

CUMBRES PASS IN DEEP SNOW

DESIRING TO SEE CUMBRES PASS during the winter, one day in January of 1949, I boarded the parlor car of the Denver & Rio Grande Western's legendary narrow-gauge *San Juan* passenger train, eager to make the 79-mile trip to the pass. "Sonny," the all-purpose factotum of the car, served me a good breakfast, still using the 1938 menu, and at

PREPARING TO BATTLE a snowed-in Cumbres Pass, the D&RGW's newest rotary snowplow, the OY, was being readied at Antonito on February 19, 1952. Engine 491 and two other 2-8-2's will be pushing the big plow. This time, they faced an extra difficulty, as Rotary Snowplow OM and its train were stranded, stalled a few miles west of Cumbres Pass, at Coxo siding. At Coxo, someone made the mistake of signalling to back up temporarily, forgetting a switch at this siding. And the outfit had derailed in deep snow. Compounding the situation, the Chama rotary was not in good condition, and even the stack was burned out. The superintendent at the time at Alamosa had ruled out repairs for the plow, claiming that the thing would never be needed again. He was new to the job, and he failed to understand what could happen. It was strongly alleged that the D&RGW management was pushing for abandonment of the narrow-gauge line from Alamosa to Durango, and they wanted any excuse to shut down the line.

ABOVE RIGHT: Pushed by Engines 485 and 484, the Rotary Snowplow OY was about to start from Chama, New Mexico, on the return of a two-day round trip from Alamosa, Colorado, on March 28, 1952. Chama usually did not receive much from the winter storms that hit Cumbres Pass, but this one dropped a surprising three feet. However, the snow was melting and evaporating rapidly, as was usual under a bright sun following a snow storm.

D&RGW ENGINE 483 had been the lead engine on the flanger train, which went ahead of the scheduled passenger train to Cumbres Pass on January 21, 1949. The depth of the snow was estimated at 68 inches, but many drifts were higher than the engine. Often, an engine would arrive at Alamosa looking like this after a day out on the line.

those prices! There had been a fresh, heavy snowfall on the mountain range, and about 4:30 that morning, I had heard a flanger train shuffle by—heading out of Alamosa to open the line ahead of the passenger train. The way snow falls in the broad San Luis Valley, there was neither much snow at Alamosa, nor in fact was there much snow anywhere on the route until we reached Big Horn. This place is about 20 miles west of Antonito, as the San Juan Extension climbs out of the valley. However, drifts had been encountered in cuts miles to the east of that siding.

Beyond the Lava water tank, the passenger train frequently passed through drifts piled up to the windows. Yet, the winds scoured long stretches of track, leaving the track and the adjacent ground nearly bare of snow. Beyond Osier, the snow rapidly became deeper, and it was obvious that the flanger train had worked hard.

Pulling up to the little depot at Cumbres, we found the flanger train on the siding to let us by. It had plowed past the depot to just where the grade starts down the 14 miles to Chama, New Mexico. The snow was headlight high across the track. Although I had bought a round-trip ticket to Chama and return, I decided to get off at Cumbres and try to photograph the flanger train at work. The wind was howling and blowing great clouds of snow at times. However, with little effort, the passenger train broke through the big pile of snow on the track and vanished in seconds, out of sight in the swirling snow.

Engines 487 and 483 had the Jordan spreader, a drag flanger and two cabooses. One caboose was for the hardworking section men. They continued to open up Cumbres, and it kept me busy trying to guess the next move. Then, about frozen, I dashed into that warm-and-welcome depot and thawed out to change film. Thereupon I went back out into what they said was 68 inches of snow, but just how the depth could be measured was not explained. It seemed more like 100 inches to me, and at one point, I stepped alongside the track into a slight depression, and for a short time, there was at least a foot of snow over my head! The snowfighting train then got ready to plow the house track, so I managed to get to a boxcar standing on that track, and I climbed on the roof with some difficulty. Toward me came the two hard-working 2-8-2 locomotives with their train, snow up to the headlight — and I got

uneasy wondering if in all that blinding snow, the lead engineer might just bump into my boxcar. I think he deliberately opened the throttle to make me think just that, and I must admit I backed to the far end of the car!

However, the crew was pleased that someone was taking pictures, and the men were looking forward to obtaining copies. I learned that a handful of free handouts sure created good will among railroaders, and in the course of taking photographs, I must have given away hundreds of prints. At Alamosa, when printing enlargements in my

darkroom, I learned not to throw away the copies I did not find satisfactory; the railroaders treasured them, and anyway, after they had them for awhile in the caboose or in their grips, the prints showed they were having a rough existence.

It was a busy hour at Cumbres while the snowfighters plowed out the passing track and the wye (part of which was covered). Then, they coupled up and took off downgrade for Chama, New Mexico. Downhill they used the Jordan spreader and drag flanger to plow the sidings, a tricky business,

I HAD LEFT the attractive, warm parlor car of the westbound "San Juan," as we had caught up with the flanger train at Cumbres Pass. This snow-fighting train had gone out ahead of the "San Juan" before dawn on January 21, 1949. From a precarious perch on a snow-covered boxcar, I watched the flanger train working to open up the snowbound house track at the pass, and as it got closer, still working hard, I began to have some doubts about whether or not they would stop in time. So, I "plowed" my way (without any flanger) to the far end of the car roof! Maybe the lead engineer was just having fun with me! Anyway, the gauge said there was 68 inches of snow at the summit, and the gusts of wind would put the temperature way below zero (F.).

MIKADO LOCOMOTIVES 483 and 487, with Jordan Spreader OU coupled in between, were plowing out the side track at Cumbres Pass, on January 21, 1949. They had to come back a few days later to do it all over again!

as a miscalculation could wipe out a switch-stand or break a casting on the spreader on a rock, not an infrequent happening.

Most of the time during snow season, a flanger train was all that was needed to keep the line over Cumbres Pass open. By using a wide-wing flanger (the Jordan type), a snow-fighting train operating on the mainline could plow-out a siding. The usual makeup of this type of train — when two locomotives were used—was to place the drag flanger between the engines. The lead locomotive would have a large pilot plow, which reached up midway on the smokebox.

The large rotary snowplow was only needed when the snow became too deep for the flanger train to push aside, or after a number of trips, the drag flanger and spreader could no longer push the snow aside. Then, the rotary plow would be used, which threw the snow a considerable distance to one side or the other of the track. During some winters, rotary plows were not used; however, every few years, exceptional snowfalls would require them to be used several times to keep the line open. The greatest problem actually was not the snow, but the high winds that filled the rock cuts and created huge-and-extensive drifts.

CUMBRES TURNS ON THE D&RGW

THE MOST VISIBLE and easiest to find operations were the so-called "Cumbres turns," which operated out of Chama, New Mexico. These "turns" featured two or three locomotives as they hauled freight on their eastbound runs up the 4.0-percent grade, traversing the twisting-and-turning 14 miles to Cumbres Pass. However, after the first heavy snowfall of the winter, access to this area was usually impossible, as the rough gravel-surfaced road was not plowed over the pass until next spring's opening of the fishing season. During some years, a bulldozer operator was stationed at the summit, and the operator might do a little plowing of the road now and then, but it could not be counted upon.

Freight crews would take an entire day

to bring a train from Alamosa to Chama. Then, after eight hours of rest, they would spend the second day making what usually amounted to two Cumbres turns. Timed to meet them would be the crew working east from Durango. This crew's train not only supplied most of the cars being taken up the hill, but if an engine crew was available, they also supplied one of their engines on the turns, making them three-engine affairs. When there was much traffic, a helper engine and crew were stationed at Chama to work on the turns up the hill. Once or twice during each fall's livestock season, an eastbound stock train would employ four engines. At the pass, the three helpers would be cut out of the train, and it would go on down the hill to Alamosa with only one engine. The helpers would run light, either ahead of the train to Alamosa or back to Chama.

Division officials (or "snoopers") were not often seen at Chama. The freight crews were friendly, and they would offer a ride in their cabooses for a Cumbres-turn trip. More than once, when I had some friend along on a day's outing, a conductor would eye the visitor and ask me something like: "Is your friend all right? Would he like to go up the hill with us?" After assuring the conductor that I believed his behavior would be acceptable, a happy visitor would spend the next four hours on a round trip. Of course, he would cherish his memories of the trip as a priceless treasure for the rest of his life. If the trip was made during snow season, the visitors got a view of that remote region not otherwise accessible to anyone but railroaders. The crews welcomed visitors and enjoyed the company, often telling them their tall tales of experiences on the narrow gauge.

During early spring in the high country, while snow up in the San Juan Mountains was still deep, some of the Denver railfans would take a week's vacation to "do" the D&RGW narrow gauge. One time, author Mac Poor was along—and he suddenly realized that a helper engine was coming up to the caboose. He raced to get up in the cupola to make a recording of the locomotive sound, forgetting to duck the cross bar across the aisle. The resulting crash certainly provided some language and angry comments that made an unusual recording… much more interesting than an engine shuffling close.

K-36 MIKADO No. 483 made a snow-covered backdrop at Cumbres Pass, as I took my own picture with a delayed-action shutter on my camera, which was perched on a freight car. I had started the day intending just to ride the "San Juan," but my costume included heavy-duty galoshes, and my pants legs tied with shoe laces. Every few minutes, I made a dash into the depot at the pass, to get thawed out (and the same for my camera, too). Once outside, I stepped into a snow-covered culvert and found myself looking up at more than a foot of snow above my head and all around me!

However, no one ever heard what was recorded; Mac evidently erased the best part of the episode! Conductor Myron Henry offered the opinion that "…the cupola might have come loose from the impact…" and he would have a carman look at it! Myron could blend wry humor and sarcasm very well!

One time during the spring, the goings back and forth of the railroad's bulldozer operator encouraged us to drive as far as the Coxo grade crossing, in the valley just below famed Windy Point. While the melting snow was still a couple of feet deep, the dirt road was deep in mud in some places—a sticky gumbo—and we nearly got stuck at the Colorado–New Mexico border. The snow had a thick crust, and when you thought it was going to support you without difficulty, down through the wet white stuff you would go! Ed Haley used a unipod for his camera, instead of the more common tripod. Years later, upon seeing my movies of this experience, members of the Akron Railroad Club were curious about Ed's actions. They wrote

to ask why "…that man was jumping up and down in the snow." Meanwhile, while this was going on, the crew members aboard the caboose were having their laughs of the day, watching us flounder around in the snow as we tried to take pictures—some of which amazingly turned out all right.

The vicinity of Coxo crossing was a great place to watch and snap pictures of trains as they rounded Windy Point. The volcanic rock cliffs at this point rise high above the grade beyond the train. As locomotives worked hard on the last half mile up to the summit, many dramatic photographs were taken at this scenic place. A long three-engine turn could be strung out all around the mountainside, providing an impressive view of narrow-gauge railroading in the high country—with perhaps 30 cars in the consist. After a very windy storm, one flanger train crew told of finding the track around the cliffs built up with snowdrifts, which rose 50 or 60 feet above the track. After studying the matter, they

MUDHEN LOCOMOTIVE No. 463 was given a complete overhaul, including a new firebox, at the D&RGW's Alamosa shops during the winter of 1948–1949. Destined for use on the Silverton Branch, No. 463 was equipped with the huge snowplow, favored for engines assigned to that branch. On January 12, 1949, the engine had stopped at Henry, a siding a few miles south of Alamosa, and the crew was checking the bearings, etc. If the 2-8-2 performed okay along this part of the line, she would go the rest of the way to Antonito, to wait there to become a helper on a freight train due out of Alamosa a few hours later. Of the dozen engines in the K-27 class, No. 463 is one of only two that have survived. This Mikado went back into operation on the Cumbres & Toltec Scenic Railroad in 1994.

AN EASTBOUND FREIGHT, with 63 cars, was departing from Cumbres Pass during September of 1948. The train's conductor was standing so he could check the passing cars, and then he will swing aboard his caboose on the track below—just out of sight.

323

K-37 2-8-2 ENGINES 491, 493 and 498 were moving a tonnage train of 30 cars up the final mile of the 4.0-percent grade to Cumbres Pass. The lead engines had just passed Windy Point—where in the winter, huge columns of snow would pile up on the track. After arriving at Cumbres, No. 491 ran on light to Alamosa, while No. 493 coupled up with a cut of cars previously brought up the hill. Then, this train followed No. 491 downgrade, while No. 498 ran back down the hill to Chama. The date for this view was October 21, 1950.

decided the best way to clear the track was to take only two engines, with the flanger trailing, leaving the Jordan spreader and two cabooses at Cumbres. They then roared downgrade and hit the drifts... and they went through that huge buildup of snow... with the two engines working very hard to keep up momentum. Meanwhile, behind them many tons of snow crashed down on the grade, and while sizable piles remained on the track, most of it went on down the steep slope of the mountainside.

They then had to go on downgrade to Chama, wye (turn around), and go back

325

THREE LOCOMOTIVES were hauling about 15 loads on the 4.0-percent grade between Chama and Lobato, a typical Cumbres turn in September of 1953. This train operated at about a steady 14 miles per hour, taking approximately an hour and three-quarters to reach the summit. Before they ran out of time, they could usually make two such round trips in a day. Engines 496, 498 and 492 were hauling this train, in that order. Notice the string of tankcars behind Nos. 496 and 498.

upgrade to plow the track clear. Following this, it was back to Chama again, using the Jordan spreader to widen the cleared area, and along the way, they used the spreader to reach out over the sidings to plow them as they went along. Even the Chama yard required flanging, as it did now and then. One day I watched them go plowing up into the sawmill at Chama, to enable an engine to get out some loaded cars of lumber. Fortunately, Chama was just enough lower in elevation that the warm rays of the sun would melt most of the snow rather quickly. Once, after a three-foot snowfall, I found only half of it left two days later.

During one winter, the trainmaster hired—in desperation—a nephew of one of the conductors without much checking. Unfortunately, the young man just did not take to railroading at all, and he had some difficulty understanding the workings of a switch. One Sunday, I drove down to Antonito ahead of a flanger train and got up on the coal-tipple trestle to watch the customary re-arrangement of the train. From Alamosa it was doubleheaded, but at Antonito, the helper engine was cut back in behind the Jordan spreader and flanger cars. The train would stop short of the switch and the head-end brakeman uncoupled the

A D&RGW WORK TRAIN was heading out of Antonito for Cumbres Pass in this scene from the 1950's. The makeup is unusual, for instead of both the drag flanger and the spreader being between the engines, only the flanger was so spaced, which meant that the crew will have to uncouple at the trestle. Trailing the flanger and spreader was a flatcar (which was carrying a bulldozer), a car of coal and a living car for the bulldozer operator to use at Cumbres. After arriving at the summit, he got into a burst of activity, plowing out drifts. However, the water column at Cumbres— being buried in a huge snowdrift—was done away with, along with the drift! Of course, this water column was a very necessary item and was made useless for thirsty engines at that point. When I met the D&RGW's assistant superintendent at Alamosa, he was loud in his despair about the broken water column. The man was fearful that angry rebukes would be directed at him from parsimonious "higher-ups" in Denver after he sent another work train to Cumbres, with the water-service man's two cars of tools and supplies to repair the damage from the bulldozer.

lead engine. Then, it would back into the side track, after which the second engine would pull the two cars ahead. The engine on the siding would then pull out, couple up, and then they would reverse to couple up with the caboose.

On this day, the new man went ahead... and to my dismay, he threw the switch to the siding before the helper engine came forward and passed the switch. And he signalled to come ahead. Fortunately, the engine crews were "having a union meeting" in the cab and ignored his signal. Alarmed, I rushed down the trestle where I was opposite him, and I volunteered that if they followed his signal, the engine would derail and the switch surely would be wrecked. He never said a word; however, he eventually threw the switch back to line up with the mainline, then walked out to mid-track to study it again. And before he could change his mind again, the engine came forward. The same thing happened when it was time for the engine to come back to the main. He first threw the switch one way and then another, each time studying it in some puzzlement.

Anyway, two weeks later at Chama— still puzzled at how a switch worked—he threw a switch to another track in the middle of the yard, in front of an oncoming helper engine, which tore up the switch and derailed. Needless to say, the Cumbres turn was hours late departing from Chama on that day! Crews had noticed this fellow's apparent inability to figure out a switch. However, they had been reluctant to complain because his uncle was high in seniority, and they did not want to call this to the trainmaster's attention.

327

THE SILVERTON BRANCH needed a plow engine for the winter of 1948–1949. However, it was January before the Alamosa shop completed the overhaul of Mudhen No. 463, including a new firebox and bolting on the big pilot plow. Halted at Henry for a checkup, a few miles south of Alamosa, the 2-8-2 was making a test run to Antonito. If all went well, the Mudhen would be used as a helper on a freight train due out of Alamosa several hours later. Despite the rush to get No. 463 to Durango, the winter—which generally reaches its worst in February and March—turned out to be a mild one. And I kept waiting for a heavy snowfall in the San Juan Mountains. However, none came, and I finally went for a winter trip on the Silverton mixed train during the end of March. At that time, I shot pictures of No. 463

bucking through a slide a few miles from Silverton, where a large snowshed had once stood. Since the big plow had no coupler, switching cars was difficult. In switching at Silverton, the engine would plow snow to the cars, then have to go to the wye, turn around, and then back to couple to the cars being switched. This was a slow-and-tedious job, and the train did not get back to Durango until midnight. Years later, No. 463 was finally overhauled and placed in service on the Cumbres & Toltec Scenic Railroad during the summer of 1994. Between the Mudhen's end of service on the D&RGW and her return to service on the Cumbres & Toltec Scenic line, the engine had spent years at Gene Autry's "Melody Town" in California, before No. 463 returned as a gift to the city of Antonito.

TO SILVERTON IN THE WINTER

BY THE EARLY 1950's a few people still rode the mixed train to Silverton during the winter, relying on its rather irregular movements to enable them to make trips to Durango to visit doctors or dentists, or for other business purposes. Most residents preferred not to try to drive on the gravel highway during midwinter, which often got snow-packed and then became very slippery as the sun glazed its surface. So, the once- or twice-a-week trips usually had a handful of real passengers—not tourists—and in any case, tourists did not venture into this remote part of Colorado during winter time.

If there were some deep snowslides or drifts on the track, one of the Mudhens would be used, equipped with a big pilot plow. This huge plow reached up nearly to the headlight of the K-27 2-8-2.

If no snow-bucking was expected, just small drifts easily shoved aside, the usual

THE MIXED TRAIN that operated once a week on the Silverton Branch was passing along the High Line, hundreds of feet above the Animas River. There were no tourists yet, so the combination car was ample. Up ahead, the Mudhen, No. 463, with a big pilot snowplow, was in preparation for expected slides, which often would come roaring down the steep slopes at this time of year, in April (1950). And usually, the upper third of the 49-mile Silverton Branch was where the snow fell heavy and often each winter.

Sport Model K-28 2-8-2 (numbered in the 470's) would be used for the Silverton train. The big drawback to using these engines for any serious bucking of slides was that the cylinder cocks were on the outside, while the older K-27 Mudhens had them mounted on the inside. If a K-28 came across a small rock or hard-packed snow, the cylinder cocks were sure to be broken off, something not readily repaired out on the road.

I bought a round-trip ticket one winter morning, and although the engine encountered some rocks and small slides and drifts, when we arrived at the Snowshed Slide near Silverton—where the white stuff was piled higher than the engine, and

some tree trunks were sticking out—the engineer just opined that this was as far as we could go. And as the wye at Elk Park was somewhat blocked with snow, we just backed up all the way to the wye at Rockwood. Fortunately, no rocks or snow had come down behind us, for as Conductor Bruce declared: "Cabooses were not designed to buck snow."

However, as we started up the High Line, where the track is located hundreds of feet above the Animas River, the conductor told me that he had some paperwork to do. As I was sitting in the cupola, I should throw the airbrake valve at once if I saw a rock on the track, and I should be particularly watchful for the postmaster of

E. J. HALEY PHOTO

ROBERT W. RICHARDSON and Richard H. Kindig, a well-known railfan photographer from Denver, were riding aboard the Silverton mixed train on February 18, 1953. D&RGW Mudhen No. 463 was watched by Bob and Dick from the mixed train's combine, No. 212. At this time, the train was running on a Wednesday-only schedule. E. J. Haley, another prominent railfan photographer from Denver, shot this view from the caboose.

IN A MANAGEMENT ERROR, it was decided not to repair the snowshed on the Silverton Branch at a place where snowslides annually ran heavily. So, the shed was torn down. It was located at about Milepost 492, just three miles short of Silverton. Here, No. 463, with her big pilot snowplow, was uncoupled from the following cars, and the 2-8-2 was making a run at the slide. The Mudhen just barely broke through the slide, and in the process, threw big chunks of frozen snow and ice a considerable distance. After snapping my pictures, I ducked down and covered my head and camera, as the icy missiles rained down all around, like so many rocks. In the years when the Silverton Branch was busy with mining traffic, such plowing was commonplace. Now, when snow conditions were bad, trains might not run for weeks. This scene was photographed on March 31, 1949, at the end of what had been a mild winter in the Colorado mountains.

A DAY OF GLOOM greeted the D&RGW train when it arrived in Silverton, Colorado, on February 18, 1953. The crew of the weekly mixed train was greeted with the news that the big gold-and-silver mine, the Sunnyside, had closed its operations permanently. The empty boxcars were not needed for ore-concentrate loading anymore, and they were returned to Durango—empty. February 18, 1953, was a bad day for Silverton and the narrow-gauge railroad, as the scheduled runs were cancelled. Only the summertime-tourist trains rumbled into Silverton. The was not any use anymore for No. 463, with her big snowplow.

Tacoma on his motorcar. Conductor Bruce was worried that the postmaster might not be as alert as he normally would be, as he would be all bundled up because it was windy and cold. He surely was not alert, as around a curve he came, with his head down, and he was not looking ahead at all. I quickly turned the valve, and the train abruptly stopped, just as the postmaster crashed into the coupler. However, during the last few seconds he looked up and rolled off the section car into some rocks.

ON FEBRUARY 5, 1951, the weekly Durango–Silverton mixed train rolled along the High Line, powered with K-28 2-8-2 No. 473, in its gaudy yellow paint, "goofy" smokestack and box headlight—now a rather grimy engine. The caboose behind the Mikado carried a section crew to help clear the track of rocks and ice.

The postmaster got badly bruised, and he limped somewhat after he got to his feet, and the groceries he had loaded on the motorcar were scattered about. A huge sack of pancake flour had burst and was all over him, the section car and the general scene.

The crew set the broken-up motorcar to the side of the track, resisting their impulse to toss it down into the gorge. Then, they assisted the injured man aboard the train, and at Rockwood they looked up someone to get him to a doctor. This story illustrates why railroaders are reluctant to let motorcars out on their tracks by non-railroaders. In Colorado, they reluctantly let engineering people for highways and power companies use them, and it seemed that there was usually a collision eventually. Motorcars were considered to be the most dangerous item on a railroad. Anyway, as we never got to Silverton, Conductor Bruce handed back my ticket, inscribed to the effect that since I was not able to get there, I could use it on some later venture on the Silverton Branch.

333

D&RGW MUDHEN No. 454 was heading out of the Durango yard on September 12, 1946, with a special freight train for the refinery at Farmington, New Mexico—with orders to "run slow." Perins Peak rises behind the yard, a rather unlikely looking place for a private five-mile railroad to have operated for 25 years, built to serve the coal mine on this mountain.

THE GAS-AND-OIL BOOM of the 1950's, along the state border, but chiefly in New Mexico, brought a tremendous traffic increase to the 47-mile Farmington Branch. Long daily trains were the rule for years. Bondad water tank, 13 miles south of the mainline, became an important point. The pipe trains included many open-ended gondolas because the pipe being hauled by the D&RGW was longer than the narrow-gauge cars, and idler flats were required between the loads. Much additional siding had to be built on the branch.

POOR-QUALITY WATER was found along many of the narrow-gauge lines of the D&RGW. As a result, water cars often were carried to fill cisterns at stations and section houses, as this train on the Farmington Branch has done. It also has hauled a carload of new automobiles in one of the canvas-covered flatcars created for this traffic. It was April of 1950, and one train a week was sufficient for the Farmington Branch in northwestern New Mexico. Soon, the gas discoveries in the San Juan Basin will make long daily trains a necessity. The engine was a Class K-36 2-8-2, No. 486.

A VALLEY LINE freight train was passing the ghost town of Mineral Hot Springs on one of the infrequent trips on this little-used branch in the lonely northern San Luis Valley. Engine 497 was equipped with a pilot plow, and at Round Hill or Villa Grove—miles ahead—a helper was waiting, so the train could make it up the 3.0-percent grade to Poncha Pass. The loads were mostly untreated ties en route to the Salida creosoting plant. In the Sangre de Cristo Mountains, just above the top of the caboose, are the abandoned Orient iron-ore mine and its attendant ghost town, where the spur off this branch operated until 1942. The vandalized hotel, at the right, still had a warped piano and other furniture in the parlor. An old hot-springs pool and the ruins of a dancehall were also at this site, once popular with the iron-ore miners. The date was January 14, 1949, as the narrow-gauge train passed through this sparsely settled part of Colorado.

OVER PONCHA PASS ON THE D&RGW NARROW GAUGE

PONCHA PASS, at 9,059 feet above sea level, was not considered to be a high pass in Colorado; however, it was reached by three miles of 4.0-percent grade from Mears Junction, on the narrow-gauge mainline between Salida and Gunnison. On its southern slopes, the grades were much easier—3.0 percent or less—but the prevailing southwest winds of the San Luis Valley would pile snow deeply on the Poncha Pass trackage.

While heading southbound, a train would double the hill from Mears Junction to the summit. Two K-36 or K-37 outside-frame 2-8-2 engines could manage a drag flanger, 12 cars of Baldwin coal and a caboose to the summit. Then, they would in effect double downhill to Villa Grove, the two engines taking just the flanger and caboose to plow open that part of the line. Then, upon returning from Villa Grove to the summit, one en-

gine would take off light, heading back to Salida, while the other engine would take the train on down to Alamosa. If northbound, a train might face an unusual amount of snow, in which case a helper engine would be sent to Villa Grove, or even to the Round Hill wye to assist.

My first experience with this line in winter was during January of 1949, and heavy snow had been pushed off the gravel road. Assuming there was a wide berm, I pulled off the road to take a picture—whereupon my car went down into deep snow. There was no berm; I had driven onto a big pile of plowed snow! So, I took the pictures of the train working up the 4.0-percent grade, then, with a shovel, I started digging to rescue my car. Amazingly, I was out of the mess and back on the road in perhaps 20 minutes! A local rancher came along with a two-ton truck, but he did not have a long chain; however, a pickup truck came along shortly after that, and the driver had a chain that was added to mine. This was enough for the larger truck to pull my car out of the snow in a couple of minutes. So, there was ample time for me to chase up the road to snap the flanger "double" at the grade crossing on the south side of Poncha Pass! Later, the crew asked me how I had gotten "unstuck" so quickly!

THE SAN LUIS VALLEY LINE'S GRAND FINALE

THERE HAD BEEN NO TRAIN for over a month on the "Valley Line" of the Denver & Rio Grande Western, and I had learned from a friend in Washington, D.C., that the ICC had authorized the abandonment of most of the 75-mile line—the portion from Hooper to Mears Junction, a distance of 54 miles. With its customary reticence, the railroad had issued no information. To barely comply with regulations, the D&RGW had posted a notice of upcoming cessation of operation in the only two depots. (There was no "service" on the line, as patrons had complained.) In any case, the only two depots, at Hooper and Moffat, were closed and locked, so the notices that were posted *inside* these buildings could hardly be seen by anyone. During recent years, both places would have an agent on hand only briefly, during livestock shipping at Moffat, and for vegetable loadings at the height of the season at Hooper. Miles Wooden had closed Moffat in the fall of 1950, and had gone to Creede, where he would again be the last station agent.

Then, about February 10, 1951, the dispatcher's "dope sheet" at Alamosa showed intent to run a Valley Line train on February 14, which would return to Salida on the following day. I wondered, "Would this be the last run"? The only thing to do was to go and shoot its progress, and if there were not any more trains, then it would indeed be the final trip. I got a late start that morning, and encountered the train with Engine 482, coming along the old narrow-gauge mainline west of Poncha Springs. At Mears Junction, while taking water and switching-in some loads of Baldwin coal, the conductor (while the trainmaster was out of sight) hurriedly told me "This is it... the last!" And he suggested I had better get my pictures while I could. He briefly mentioned that the crew did not know until after the train had pulled out of

Salida, that this was the final run, as the trainmaster had told them a few minutes after they had left the end of the third rail on the edge of town.

With No. 480 acting as helper, the two K-36 engines doubled the hill to Poncha Pass, less than four miles away. On the first trip they took a long string of empty gondolas for the use of the dismantlers. The second double had nine cars of Baldwin coal, making nearly a full-tonnage trip up the 4.0-percent climb. After arriving at the pass, No. 480 wyed and returned to Salida light. No. 482 handled the long train down the 3.0-percent grade toward Villa Grove.

At that point, I drove my car ahead and stopped at Moore's General Store for a soft drink, and I tried to joke with the owner about "the lack of a band, press coverage and the populace to see the last train go by." His reply was that I was mistaken; the county was buying the line and was going to operate it, a baseless rumor I was going to learn had wide circulation in Saguache County. When I told him I was certain there would be no such operation, he became concerned about the car of Baldwin coal he had ordered quite some time ago. Then, for a few minutes, he was reassured to see those cars in the oncoming train, but his hopes were dashed, as the train—after taking water—went on down the line without setting out any coal!

At Moffat, 18 miles down the line, the scene was repeated. At Biggs Store, I had a "heavy lunch" of Hershey candy bars and another soft drink, and again the proprietor was expecting a car of coal, long overdue. However, after setting out the 33 empty gondolas, but nary a car of coal, the southbound train went on. This was quite typical of the D&RGW railroad-management's disdain for shippers on its narrow-gauge lines, wherein neither merchant was informed of the com-

THE LAST TRAIN on the D&RGW's San Luis Valley Branch, usually simply called the "Valley Line," was nearing Round Hill on February 15, 1951. The background was provided by the magnificent Sangre de Cristo Range. Mikado No. 482 had left Salida, Colorado, the morning before on the two-day round trip, and the crew did not know this was the last run until the trainmaster so informed the men after their train departed from Salida. The D&RGW was very secretive about this particular abandonment. No notices had been posted, except for ones inside locked-up, closed depots at Moffat and Hooper—rather difficult for informing anyone! There were no news releases, and the trainmaster was much annoyed when I showed up to photograph this last run, as it left Alamosa. He probably was even more irked when, in my guise as a sometimes-reporter for *The Pueblo Chieftain*, I sent the newspaper a news item and photographs! None of the little places along this route knew it was a final trip. A rumor in Saguache County was current that the county was going to buy the line and an engine and caboose to operate it. One conductor speculated that the false rumor was started by the railroad; however, no one knew for sure.

ing cessation of service, so that the coal supplier could make certain that their final shipments of coal were delivered. Baldwin coal was very popular with both businesses and householders, as it was deemed to be the best in Colorado, and this demand kept the coal mine north of Gunnison from closing.

Hooper, 20 miles north of Alamosa, was where three-rail trackage began, and it saw the train pause only long enough to pick up the pair of idler cars, which (by custom), the previous northbound train had left there. One idler car was the usual stubby steel standard-gauge flatcar, but the other one was unique on the Valley Line, as it originally was a narrow-gauge engine tender. When smaller engines were used, this tender, equipped with both narrow- and standard-gauge couplers, was employed as far as Moffat, where a water standpipe was available for a slow refill.

On the next morning, shortly before noon, the final northbound run commenced, but there was no crowd, and no newspaper reporters (except for this "Abandoned Lines reporter") were on hand to snap pictures of the last orders being handed up to the engineer. The trainmaster was annoyed at my presence at the otherwise "secret" occasion, and he barred me from obtaining copies of the "flimsies" (i.e., train orders).

Again, the train had the two idler cars, coupled at each end of four standard-gauge refrigerator cars bound for Hooper. Following these cars, there were 27 empty gondolas for the dismantler and two boxcars. Beyond Hooper, the train consisted of only the two boxcars and the caboose. It drifted down into

Mears Junction by mid-afternoon, ending the narrow-gauge connection between Salida and Alamosa. Railfans called the Valley Line part of the "Narrow-Gauge Circle," but the original narrow-gauge "Around the Circle" tour did not include the Valley Line. Rather, it used the Royal Gorge route to reach Salida and went on westward via Marshall Pass, returning eastward to the Royal Gorge line by way of Alamosa and La Veta Pass.

The Valley Line had been a busy route after its completion to Alamosa in 1890. For a few years, the Denver-to-Durango passenger trains had been routed via this line, carrying narrow-gauge Pullmans. The Valley Line must have been the most boring ride on the entire narrow-gauge system, with its 53-mile tangent from near Mineral Hot Springs south to Alamosa Junction (just east of Alamosa) consisting of little but nearly flat sagebrush land. The original portion of this line to Villa Grove was built in the 1880's up what became a branch to the iron mine at Orient, and many multiple-engine ore trains had rumbled over Poncha Pass to Salida until the 1920's. Another branch had been intended to haul the output of a large gold mine in the Sangre de Cristo Mountains, but the mine produced mostly water, which huge pump installations could not control. However, by 1951, both of these short branches were long gone, leaving the Valley Line with only seasonal shipments, and serving as a transfer route for rolling stock being moved to and from the Alamosa machine shops.

Only two days after the final run, scrap crews from the dismantling firm were on hand at Hooper to tear up the rails, which they did at a rate of two miles per day. Man-agement was taking no chances of anyone promoting a new railroad in Saguache County. The abandonment had been ignored in the Alamosa newspaper. The editors were unable to read a large wall map in their office, and they pleaded that they could not find Hooper, the second-largest town in the county! The weekly newspaper at Saguache simply ignored the subject, its publisher also assuring me the county was going to run the line. Once more, this served to emphasize how little true reporting was to be found in the mountain areas of Colorado. My snooping around and reporting these events in the *Narrow Gauge News* usually was the only coverage of railroad news and trivia. It was sad to think of lines that had been greeted with large civic celebrations were now vanishing—one after another—with not even a brief mention in the press.

IT WAS SANTA CLAUS DAY in Salida, on December 22, 1951. On this day, No. 481 was about to take the much-decorated caboose, No. 0578, to Poncha Junction, backing all the way. Then, the short train would come back to town as the "Santa Claus Train," and the old bearded gent, himself, would emerge from the caboose to hand out candy to a mob of kids. Then, all the crowd would walk up the street to the movie theater for a free kids' show. No. 1166 was the standard-gauge switcher for this day, equipped with dual-gauge couplers fore and aft. In five more years, No. 1166 will go to scrap at Pueblo, while No. 481 will end up a regularly used motive power on the popular Durango & Silverton Narrow Gauge Railroad. Caboose 0578 would be personally selected by me on behalf of the Rocky Mountain Railroad Club in 1955, after all the narrow-gauge lines out of Salida were abandoned. This caboose now is at the Colorado Railroad Museum in Golden, on permanent loan from the club.

A GENERAL VIEW of the Monarch lime-stone quarry is depicted here, much of the year the busiest destination on the D&RGW's narrow-gauge lines. Cars were loaded and dropped by gravity in coupled groups of four, to the curved storage tracks at the bottom of the picture. The usual two-engine train had spotted their empties, and the engine at left center was about to run light down to Maysville to wye and help No. 496 bring up a second cut of empty gondolas. No. 496 had gotten the loaded gondolas out of the holding tracks, and she will shortly wye at the extreme right, get on the head end and take the loads down the Garfield switchback to Maysville. It was September 23, 1948. Still to come was the exciting day when a carman forgot to turn the angle cock on the fourth car. And the train proceeded to run away—piling up cars and limestone on the steep 4.0-percent grade. The crews, operating along U.S. Highway 50, would enjoy varying the "same old thing" of every trip. So, they would invite visitors to go for a train ride, something management very much objected to, providing one conductor with a 30-day layoff without pay!

MARSHALL PASS: HIGHEST POINT ON THE NARROW GAUGE

THE MOST REMOTE PART of the Denver & Rio Grande Western's narrow-gauge lines seemed to be the old mainline over Marshall Pass. At 10,845 feet above sea level, this pass was the highest point on the D&RGW's narrow-gauge system. By the time I arrived in Colorado, this line still had a traffic of coal trains, varying from one to three per week much of the year. However, this was expected to cease during the 1950's, as the Colorado Fuel & Iron Corporation of Pueblo developed other coal sources on its captive standard-gauge railroad west of Trinidad.

Access to Marshall Pass was limited to a dubious, rough, rocky trail that followed little Poncha Creek. At Mears Junction, a fairly good gravel-surfaced county road fol-

IT WAS LATE IN 1955, and K-36 No. 483, with sister engine, No. 481, behind the caboose, had just arrived at the Monarch limestone quarry. These 2-8-2's had 14 empty gondolas for the Colorado Fuel & Iron Corporation's operation. After shoving the empties up beyond the loading tipple, the engines returned to Maysville to bring up the second half of their train. They will cut and double up the 4.5-percent double switchback at Garfield. U.S. Highway 50 is out of sight to the left, and it is several miles farther up to the summit of Monarch Pass, at 11,312 feet above sea level. Monarch itself is at an elevation of 10,030 feet. It was a gold-and-silver mining camp before limestone became the primary output of this high-altitude location.

IT WAS SATURDAY, December 22, 1950, and it was "Santa Claus Day" in Salida, Colorado. C-16 No. 268, in her Chicago Railroad Fair garb of "Grande gold," a yellow, black and silver paint scheme, was doing the honors, with a much-decorated caboose. From Poncha Junction, the short train backed into town, so that Santa Claus could hand out candy to a crowd of kids—young and old—before all would go to a free movie show. After returning from the railroad fair, No. 268 had been tucked away in one of the small bays of the Alamosa roundhouse. However, the only other C-16, No. 278, was in failing health at Gunnison. So, Engine 268, still lettered for the mythical

Cripple Creek & Tincup Railroad, and with small paintings attached to the tender, was sent up the San Luis Valley in a freight train—dead. Denver railroad officials decided there was no need to repaint the engine, since it would be seldom seen at Gunnison because trips on the Baldwin Branch were rather infrequent. So, little No. 268 kept her "bumblebee" paint scheme (as railfans called it) until the end of operations in 1955. However, the Consolidation later was relettered (in black): "DENVER & RIO GRANDE WESTERN" on the tender, with "268" on the side of the cab. Today, No. 268 sits in a spot of honor at the Gunnison museum.

lowed the railroad to Shirley Curve, a distance of 2.5 miles. A side road went up to O'Haver Lake, a popular fishing spot for local residents. This lake was situated below the railroad grade, near the siding of Keene, about six miles west of Mears Junction. Beyond this small lake, there were no roads or trails up to the summit. The railroad line worked its way high up on the forested mountain slopes below Mount Ouray, while the trail from Shirley was deep in a ravine, at times thousands of feet below the track.

At the summit of Marshall Pass, the railroad curved through a deep rock cut, roofed-over to provide a long snowshed. Inside the shed, there was a covered turntable, a depot

D&RGW ENGINE No. 489 had been rented to the dismantlers, and she was moving the scrap train at the end of the day. The narrow-gauge 2-8-2 was rolling around Shawano Curve, directly below Marshall Pass, but four track miles away from the summit. This spot had sad memories for the engineer, Henry Wolford, because in September of 1923, when he was a fireman on a freight train waiting at the summit, he was watching the train they were waiting for down below at Shawano. Suddenly, a huge cloud of steam filled the mountainside! Obtaining orders from the dispatcher, they rolled downgrade to find Mudhen No. 451's boiler had exploded, and the engine crew had been killed, their bodies blown many feet away. While searching that hillside as I was waiting to take this picture, I found the rim of a steam gauge about 200 feet up the mountain, as well as many pieces of a wooden engine cab. The date for this view was September 2, 1955.

and various other buildings for operators
and section men. All of these structures were
connected by covered passageways, which
provided protection against winter's worst.
And Marshall Pass had a reputation for getting much of the winter's worst! A long passing siding on the east side of the pass paralleled a high mountain meadow. There was a
water tank at this siding, as well as a short
spur used to load ore into cars from a mine.

There was no road or trail along the railroad grade west of the summit. Therefore,
the hopeful fan could only walk through the
dark snowshed and then sit outside the
western portal and gaze hopefully down the

miles of mountain valleys, looking for a
train. Despite all forecasts to the contrary,
this wait invariably seemed to be many
hours behind the expected time of arrival.
Any trip to Marshall Pass meant that one
had to be sure to take along a lunch. But
there was no need for a "supper lunch," as
well, as the summit was no place to linger for
night photographs, or to attempt night driving back down that extremely rocky trail on
the eastern slopes of the pass.

From the western side, one could look
down to the Shawano water tank and siding,
about a mile down the steep and slightly
overgrown slopes. Beyond Shawano, the

THE LAST TRAIN, a cleanup run from Gunnison, had entered the Marshall Pass snowshed. From my perch on the cupola of the second caboose, I had enjoyed a wonderful view during the past hour and a half—as the long train of empties snaked up the 4.0-percent grade. I also acquired an Ethiopian complexion. And my clothes received numerous burn holes they did not have when the day started, as hot sparks came my way from the helper engine. After May 2, 1955, the next trains seen were powered by the dismantler's engine, hauling cars of rails destined for Poncha Junction. Inside the snowshed, there was a turntable and a depot. During the 1920's, one telegraph operator became so affected by being kept inside by the deep snow and high winds at 10,845 feet elevation, that he sprinkled kerosene on the snowshed. Then, he sat outside and watched the place go up in flames, as reported by the crew of a helper engine! The railroad seemed uncertain as to just what the altitude was at the summit. The last roster, in 1923, reiterated the elevation as 10,856 feet; however, the station sign dating to the 1930's and in use until the end of operations, read 10,845 feet. Many early-day estimates of heights in the Colorado mountains turned out to be wrong many years later.

presence of an approaching train could be discerned only by occasional small clouds of smoke, miles away. On one of these ventures, I had for company the later well-known camera enthusiast from Long Island, John Krause, and his new wife. They were spending their honeymoon in Colorado, and Marshall Pass was his bride's introduction to one of Colorado's remote mountain places.

After assembling about 60 to 70 loaded cars of coal at Gunnison, a single engine would often take a train to Sargent, located at the western foot of the pass. At Sargent, helper locomotives would be cut into the train, and it was very likely that the hill

would be "doubled" (i.e., the train would be hauled up the grade to the pass in two sections). During wet weather, the "hard pull" on the stiffer grade the last mile into Sargent might require doubling into that picturesque helper station.

After helpers were no longer stationed at Sargent, they were dispatched to run light from Salida to meet the train at the bottom of the 4.0-percent grade. One engine would be cut-in the middle of the train, while a third engine was coupled-in just ahead of the caboose. A K-36 2-8-2 was rated at 232 tons, while a K-37 could haul only 20 tons more, which meant six cars of coal per engine. This is a good example of how costly narrow-gauge railroading and its 4.0-percent grades could be. If there was a fall livestock train, where delay by doubling had to be avoided, as many as four engines would be used. (The additional helper was added in the middle, so that if the train stalled, the first three engines could double up to the top of the pass quickly and go back for the rear portion without much delay.)

Typical of the luck railfans often had at Marshall Pass, John Krause, his bride and I waited all day without seeing a train. So, as the sun began to set, we reluctantly gave up and drove back to Alamosa. During the fall of 1945—before I moved "out West" to Colorado—I bought a ticket from Gunnison to Salida. Armed with a special permit, I boarded a caboose so I could ride over Marshall Pass on a freight train. The train had been expected to depart before 7:00 a.m., but it did not get out of the Gunnison yard before mid-afternoon. All kinds of little delays delayed the departure, resulting in an arrival in Sargent at about 5:00 p.m. The conductor and rear brakeman were "on the outs" with each other, and they almost never spoke to each other. The atmosphere in the caboose seemed to be charged with electricity! Since the train was going to have to double the pass, there were expectations that it might take until midnight before it could put the train back together at the summit. So, I had no idea when—in a starving condition—I would arrive in Salida!

Recalling that a bus came west through Sargent (on U.S. Highway 50), about 6:00 p.m., I decided to give up on a ride aboard the train under those adverse circumstances. I later learned that the engines, if not the train, had arrived in Salida at dawn, after more delays of all kinds.

As expected, the CF&I's "Big Mine" closed at Crested Butte in 1952, and the ICC okayed the abandonment of the Marshall Pass line, effective January 15, 1954. The railroad operated a couple of "cleanup trains," but finally, on May 2, 1955, the D&RGW ran the last-of-all cleanup trains. The master mechanic of the Grand Junction Division came over and spent a day setting-out old wooden gondolas for dismantling. It took several hours before a train was lined up, with far too much tonnage for two locomotives to haul over the pass. As a result, many freight cars, as well as non-revenue cars, were left behind. Jack Thode, a financial officer for the D&RGW and a longtime railfan, had prevailed on the Denver office of the railroad to add an extra caboose for a small group of Denver friends, and I was included in this historic trip.

We brought out mostly old stock cars, as these worn-out wooden cars were needed for conversion to flat cars. They were to be used for handling the immense amounts of pipe being carried over Cumbres Pass to the San Juan oil-and-gas fields. I elected to sit on top of the caboose cupola, a rather sooty and hot, cindery place, but wonderful for viewing Marshall Pass. It was also great for watching the two-engine train snake around the curves

ahead. With No. 489 just ahead of the cabooses, very few hot cinders missed me! It was a great trip, a beautiful day, and while we dropped down the east side of the pass, we could see Poncha Pass miles away, to the south.

The last Powderhorn livestock rush via the D&RGW's Marshall Pass line occurred during October of 1953. The ranchers of that area southwest of Gunnison had gathered their livestock at Iola for shipment to the Denver market during autumn for many years. However, 1953 was the last time for this narrow-gauge tradition. The D&RGW's little No. 268—still in her yellow-and-black "bumblebee" colors from the Railroad Fair doings—doubled the stock cars into Gunnison. Then, two K-36 Mikados handled the train to Sargent, where two more 2-8-2's were cut into the middle of the consist, making the last-of-all four-engine trains on Marshall Pass. Both railfan-photographer Otto Perry and I were following things on that day; however, he apparently never saw me as I stood out in the field, about a mile east of Sargent. Then, we both drove over Monarch Pass and hastened to travel to the vicinity of the big Shirley Curve to try our luck at photographing this historic train. I arrived on the scene first, and to get my car out of the way, I drove through the underpass and parked beyond. Then, I hiked up the narrow-gauge railroad grade. Way off, somewhere in the distance, could be heard the "thumpa, thumpa, thumpa" of the three helpers coming downgrade light, using their equivalent of the old water brake, instead of driver brakes. The sound would seem to be close, then vanish, as the engineers cut out the mechanism.

Meanwhile, here came Otto Perry, who parked his car on the near side of the underpass. He then started hiking up the hillside to get to the grade. He did not see me, as a large bush was below me, and just for fun—on that quiet afternoon, with no breeze blowing—I made a low call, "Hurrrry Otttoooooo. Train is coming...." He stopped, cocked his head, looked around, but he saw no one, of course, and then, to his credit, he continued climbing the hillside. "Ghosts" or strange voices were not going to intimidate Otto Perry! In fact, I repeated the low-voiced call, and although he again stopped, he continued on to what he thought would be a good spot for taking pictures. Just then, the first helper came around the hillside, and I guess we both forgot about voices. Soon, the second engine came by, and in another 10 minutes, the third helper rolled past us. They dropped by us at about 20 mph, rolled over the bridge, and almost without sounds, except for that occasional "thumpa, thumpa" noise, they vanished toward Mears Junction.

It was quite awhile before the distant sound of the train itself could be heard, a rather subdued roar. Then, as the train got nearer, but was still out of sight, the metallic clanking and creaking of the old wooden cars could be heard. The train drifted by at barely 18 mph, perhaps slower, filled the big curve, and soon it was gone.

Otto Perry immediately scrambled down, got in his old Ford and drove off, never giving me a chance to explain to him that I, too, was present and had not intended to scare him. In any case, I did not see him the rest of the day, and I never did get a chance to explain to him about the ghostly sounds!

Just before going to Gunnison to stay as the railroad liaison with the dismantlers, Gene Harden asked me if there was anything I might want off the Gunnison lines. He was not authorized to sell any cars, but he wondered if there was anything else I could use. I asked him about buying the siding signs, and we discussed what should be paid.

When I said maybe $5.00 each, he ridiculed that amount, saying that the old wooden boards were not worth anything like that. Besides, I would have to go get them myself. In the end, for only $20.00, all the signs on the Gunnison lines west of Poncha Junction were mine, cash-and-carry.

Most of the signs were some distance from any point where I could drive with my pickup truck—some of them miles from the nearest trail or road. Two of them, "Otto" and "Mears Junction," were relatively easy to get, although they were a problem to unbolt from the 12 x 12-inch wooden posts. The railroad used carriage bolts, and it was difficult to get a grip on that kind of bolt. And sometimes, I had to use a combination of a chisel and a hacksaw to get the bolt free. The "Otto" sign resisted all such efforts, so I just moved the entire thing, post and all, up the steep dirt bank. While I was sitting there, out of breath, someone drove past and noted my license number so he could give it to the railroad "hawkshaw" at Salida. On the next day, the Alamosa chief clerk was on the phone wanting an explanation. He said he had never heard of anyone paying real money for an old wooden siding sign.

With an Alamosa friend, I drove up to O'Haver Lake, and then hiked to "Keene" and "Gray's" sidings to get those signs.

SARGENT'S COAL DOCK was a very important facility during the years that the D&RGW's line over Marshall Pass was busy. This little railroad town was located at the western foot of the steep grade up to the pass, and it had a six-stall roundhouse until the larger classes of engines handled all of the trains. During the last years, engines would take-on coal at Gunnison or Salida, and they seldom needed more when they arrived at Sargent.

347

Some of the signs were very old, and peeling paint indicated they had been painted several times. In all likelihood, they were new when the line was constructed in 1881. The crew of one of the cleanup trains entered into the spirit of the thing, since the conductor thought it was a good thing to preserve the old signs. He volunteered they would bring up the "Shawano" sign. So, as the train pulled up into the snowshed at the summit and the caboose came rolling along, there it was on the rear platform... with the 10-foot, 12 x 12-inch post and all!

A couple of the signs did not survive. Fishermen used them for firewood, as I found only the burned ends of the "Tank 7" sign. The "Marshall Pass" station sign was nicely framed, with the mileage and elevation lettered on it. It had been repositioned on the section house after the depot closed. We found a rickety ladder and spent an hour reinforcing it before we could use it, but the shaky thing lasted long enough for us to retrieve the sign.

I also bought the train-order signal at Sargent, as well as the station sign. This required that I get up into the attic, which had a layer of soot up to an inch deep, as fine as carbon black! When disturbed, this old soot filled the air! You might wonder what else I obtained at Sargent, but the place was bare of paperwork and the telegrapher's items. The railroad had the habit of bringing up an empty boxcar to a station being closed so that a section crew could load everything aboard the car, to the last scraps of paper. Then, the car would be moved to Salida, where another gang of laborers would remove everything and burn it.

OVER MARSHALL PASS BY SECTION CAR

THE BRINKERHOFF BROTHERS from Rico, Colorado, got the contract to tear-up the Gunnison lines of the D&RGW, their biggest job yet. They constructed a very ingenious winch-motor and sling affair, which could "snake" rails onto several cars behind the one next to the rails being pulled up. They rented old C-16 No. 268 to use on the Sapinero and Baldwin branches, then rented K-36 No. 489 to work over the pass with the loaded cars and bring back the empties from

Poncha Junction. They wanted some pictures of their doings, and I was invited to ride on Engine 489. However, I pointed out that this was the worst place to try to take pictures, so they then offered their two motorized section cars, and amplified their offer by telling me that I could ride on them anytime. So, in the next couple of months, I made several such trips to Poncha Junction. A long round trip on a motorized section car—136 miles—allowed one's posterior to get the full effect of each rail joint. And many of those rail joints were far from smooth! After one trip from Gunnison, where I almost collided with cows grazing on the track, I cut back my starting point to Sargent. The round trip from Sargent was only 74 miles... which completely exhausted one of my Eastern friends. At a grade crossing at Doyle, automobile traffic and rain had pushed a considerable amount of gravel onto the crossing. When I hit that crossing at 25 mph, the little section car suddenly bounced up into the air... and amazingly came back down on the rails without derailing! However, everything that was loose on the car scattered all over the place—including several tools, spare parts, a gasoline can, etc.

Both section cars, the work gang's car and the roadmaster's version, needed overhauls—tuning particularly. I learned this the hard way when the carburetor assembly fell apart in a very weedy stretch of track, several miles from Sargent. I literally crawled on my hands and knees through those weeds until I found all the parts. Then, I had to reassemble them out in the middle of nowhere!

When carrying two people, the little roadmaster's car absolutely refused to start on a 4.0-percent grade. So, we would have to back down to a siding that was nearly level (built that way with locomotives in mind) to have another go at the steep grade. We started at the far end of the siding, so we could get a run at it, and the little car managed to chug steadily upgrade at a good 20 mph, or more. The big section car had much more power, but it was much work to set it off the track, as the rails often were 90-pound sections. This meant that the rail was about six inches in height (above the ties), and it was hard work for one man to lift the car over the rails and away from the track.

On the first trip with the big section car, it just did not want to run. So, we used a piece of fence wire to tie it on behind the last car of rails (on a train going up to the summit), and I rode aboard the engine to the top. From there, I coasted back down, allowing gravity help me until I finally got the thing adjusted to run at its best. When not in gear, those section cars could plummet down that 4.0-percent grade, freewheeling at speeds of at least 50 mph on straightaways. However, with frequent 24-degree curves along the line, approaching them at high speeds was reckless and definitely not to be attempted.

When the dismantling train had reached the vicinity of Shawano, John Krause again was out in Colorado, and I drove him up to the summit. We were planning to hike down the slope, and in any case, I wanted to explore some of the remnants of Otto Mears' old toll road, which zigzagged over the mountainside. Gene Harden, the engineering liaison from the railroad assigned to the dismantling crew, offered us a ride downgrade on his section car. Reluctantly, I declined his offer because I had seen the high rate of speed Gene operated his car. Nevertheless, despite my warnings, John elected to climb aboard, with his Speed Graphic camera in hand. Gene took off without the brakes applied, and the car shot out of sight. I muttered a prayer for poor John and his camera, hoping that he kept a tight grip on both the car and his large camera.

The section car traveled at least four miles to the one that I walked, and it was at Shawano long before I arrived. Along the way, I examined the rotted log cribbing at places on Otto Mears' old road. I also examined the toll gate (which still lay in place), about a quarter mile from the summit. When I hiked down to the track, there was John Krause, obviously quite shaken by his ride and very pale, and he grumbled something to the effect that his host was "crazy." They had covered that steep, crooked four miles in much less than 10 minutes! At the sharp curves, John had to hang on with all his might! Or so he agitatedly claimed!

We stayed around the place the rest of the afternoon. The engineer of No. 489 was Henry Wolford, formerly a Rio Grande Southern engineer and Galloping Goose motorman. Henry got to reminiscing that when he was a young fireman he had worked for a while out of Salida. One September day in 1923, he had been waiting aboard a helper engine at the pass for a freight train that was just leaving Shawano tank. As the train's en-

gine rounded the curve and entered the tangent track far below his helper engine, he suddenly saw a huge cloud of steam and the train abruptly stopped. Certain that something terrible had happened, the Marshall Pass telegraph operator wired the dispatcher for permission to go down to see what had occurred. There, they found Mudhen 451 had blown up, killing the crew. The engineer was known for his penchant for keeping water low and getting a full head of steam. Then, after the train got underway, he would

HENRY WOLFORD was hired by the Denver & Rio Grande Western, where he was photographed as an engineer. The narrow-gauge line over Marshall Pass was about to become history when this photograph was taken on June 14, 1955. Earlier, Henry had worked for the Rio Grande Southern.

open the injector to put more water in the boiler. Apparently, this time he had allowed the water to get too low.

After Henry Wolford told me this, I spent some of my waiting time exploring the mountainside at the site of the explosion. Along the track lay the wrecked end of a gondola that had been behind No. 451. Up the hillside were pieces of the cab, especially the roof, and at one spot was the twisted round brass rim of a steam gauge, a good 200 feet from the track.

There were many stories the crews would tell about wrecks and unusual happenings on the Marshall Pass line during the "old days." Before automatic airbrakes and automatic couplers came to the narrow gauge in 1903, there were many runaway trains and "break-in-twos." There was even a holdup site at Mill Switch (on a curve between Shawano and the next siding to the west, Chester), where the westbound passenger train was stopped by ties on the track. Thereupon, the express car and passengers were robbed. Helper engine No. 421 was drifting down behind the passenger train, when the engineer saw the holdup scene upon rounding a curve. He stopped the engine, and he was just reversing direction when a rifle shot hit the cab just above his head. The robbers evidently were aware of railroad operating practices, and they had posted a man there just to prevent the helper crew from backing up to the summit to spread an alarm. One of the funnier results of the holdup was that while for some minutes the gang was busy in the express car, the passengers hurriedly scurried around burying their watches and valuables. Later that day, they were brought back in a coach to seek out and retrieve their buried items.

Today, there is a rather good gravel-surfaced road over the abandoned railroad grade all the way to the site of Tank 7. At that point on down to Sargent, a distance of 10 miles, the route follows the rebuilt Mears toll road. The U.S. Forest Service cleared away all structures, and strangely, the last time I was up there, no sign had been posted advising visitors of the site of Marshall Pass and the narrow-gauge line. So… Marshall Pass goes unmarked for the casual visitor. This is not unusual in a state that has so many railroad points of interest to more-and-more people. Yet, most of these historic places are unmarked, unknown.

IF IT HAD BEEN FINISHED in 1882, the grade atop this rock retaining wall would have been the route of some very interesting trains hauling coal. Dreamers like to imagine the Denver, South Park & Pacific's Mason Bogies working up there on this extension. However, the railroad laborers left this wall unfinished in the spring of 1882, never to return to finish the Ohio Pass Extension of the old South Park Railroad. This stone retaining wall caused a big stir in narrow-gauge railfan circles when I accidentally stumbled on the unfinished grade in 1954.

350

WHAT "MIGHT HAVE BEEN" IN THE GUNNISON COUNTRY

EVERYONE has their favorite areas, and one of mine was "the Gunnison country" of western Colorado. Several vague reasons probably entered into this choice. I am sure it originally stemmed from reading Gilbert A. Lathrop's stories in *Railroad Magazine* about the once-mighty Third Division of the Denver & Rio Grande, with headquarters at Gunnison. The northern portion of this region includes some vast wilderness areas and impressive mountain vistas. And when I first visited Colorado back in 1948, the D&RGW roundhouse in Gunnison included some of the most elusive and nearly unique narrow-gauge locomotives in the U.S.A. It was a thrill to find them out on the rails and working.

There were some very interesting abandoned railroad grades in this region, like the South Park's lines and its Alpine Tunnel, the Crystal River & San Juan into Marble and the Denver & Rio Grande's branch from Crested Butte to Floresta, once the scene of huge anthracite-coal loadings for the D&RG.

In the summer of 1954, I stumbled onto a forgotten grade of the Denver, South Park & Pacific near Ohio Pass. Ohio Pass itself was almost forgotten at the time, as it was merely the southern exit to east-west Kebler Pass, but it lacked much of anything one could call a road. In fact, there was just a trail, with a U.S. Forest Service warning sign, as the trail descended steeply into the forest. It roughly followed little Ohio Creek into a wilderness area. With my neighbor's two boys, we were sort of exploring back-country areas. Earlier in the day, we had driven as far north of the ghost town of Baldwin as dared, to a point where a beaver pond blocked the way. Near there, we had examined a long-abandoned coal mine and an adjacent coke oven, neither of which seemed to have been used much. There was not any indication of any railroad grade nearby, and we dismissed it as just another unimportant coal-mining venture, of which Colorado had seen too many. It was to be 37 years before that mine was identified. We certainly did not have any idea that it had been the destination of the farthest rails of the old South Park line, and had we

looked south a few hundred feet, we likely would have seen faint traces of the grade.

After dropping down that steep, rough trail from Ohio Pass, it just more or less vanished into something I no longer wanted to pursue. So, we looked for a place to turn the "G-buster" carryall around, and upon spying a flat spot, we backed into that. As I looked to my left, there was a stack of old ties, very rotted, half obscured by the accumulated leaves and forest debris. After getting out of the truck, it was obvious the flat place was part of the grade, for ahead of the carryall was a trail heavily overgrown with giant ferns and brush, as well as some sizable trees. Behind, there was a fill, and there was a gap where Ohio Creek flowed. And farther on was another abutment fill, and a grade curved into the forest beyond.

As it was now late in the afternoon, and we had reservations at the Redstone Inn, down in the Crystal River Valley, no hiking explorations were made on that day. Back up the steep trail we went, and at the crest we noticed a hillside cut, much sluffed-in, but obviously a grade in both directions. At the summit of the pass just beyond, the area opened out to a wide beaver pond, into which extended an obviously man-made fill for several hundred feet—a grade. However, for whom or what was it intended?

We arrived at the Redstone Inn long after dark, following a long, dusty, winding drive from Kebler Pass, down into the valley of the North Fork of the Gunnison. Then, it was up over the dubious dirt road that topped McClure Pass, and from there, we jostled and bounced down what was then an awful road to the Crystal River Valley. We had missed the scheduled dinner at the inn, but the staff at this elegant hostelry trotted out cold cuts and leftovers, which they served to us in the grand old inn's awesome dining room.

At Denver on the following day, I made inquiries as to what railroad grade we might have seen, but no one knew of anything at that site. In fact, it was suggested that we were mistaken. Some folks who thought they knew everything about Colorado's railroads, later went on to ridicule the report we made, and it was asserted that I was seeing imaginary railroad grades. Anyway, the maps I checked around Alamosa and at the college were not of any help.

Next spring, Gunnison County constructed a road from where we had seen the little abandoned coal mine. The county road crew used the grade we had seen in part, and it made a good connection with Kebler Pass a mile or more beyond. However, we were busy at the motel at Alamosa, and I had no time to go look up the new road, and what with one thing and another, I just kept putting it off. Finally, during early August, I joined several people from Denver in a weekend of exploring the ghost town of Irwin, and we hiked to Floresta on the old D&RG grade. After lunch, the new road was mentioned, which ought to take us back to Gunnison by a shorter route, and we ought to see the remains I had noted during the year before.

The fill still extended out into the beaver pond, but no one was impressed. It was obvious they **did** think I had imagined the old grade! However, upon dropping down the steep new road, with its twists and turns, the hillside cut had vanished in the new road work. At the bottom of the hill, the grade eased, and I pointed to the left, where the obvious grade could be seen coming to and becoming part of the new road. After a short hike, and upon coming out on a fill, I looked up to see how this got up to the pass, and there was a huge unfinished rock retaining wall! It had been made of locally quarried stone, laid without mortar, and it was some 300 feet long and 75 feet high.

The afternoon was spent hiking the finished grade, which had some unusual features. A long stretch was hand-laid with slide rock, many feet deep, while where it turned to head for the rock wall, it managed to do so by crossing the little stream twice in what looked like a half circle of perhaps 24 degrees. Evidently, work had ceased when the first culvert was finished and filled, for the second culvert consisted of simply the large stones laid in place, without mortar.

From that spot along the hillside, toward the rock wall, only some grade stakes were found, still laying in the slide rock. At other places, where there was dirt, only the rotting shreds remained. Upon arriving at the rock retaining wall, we found it to be about a yard wide at the top and perhaps 20 feet wide at the base. No fill had been placed against it. From its parapet, a grand view was obtained of the Ohio Creek Valley, with the distant Castle Peaks to the southwest. There was some additional rock work farther along the mountainside, but then, there was a long gap to where the hillside cut had been.

Gradually, from bits and pieces (primarily in old newspapers), I learned this had been the Ohio Pass Extension of the Denver, South Park & Pacific. And work on this extension had ceased in the spring of 1882, never to resume. Then, when the Colorado & Southern was tearing down old buildings in its Denver yard during the 1960's, a railroad employee, Bob Munshower, found among the old papers being thrown away some engineering maps and drawings. These items evidently had been given to the new Colorado & Southern Railway by the Union Pacific system in 1898. Among these maps and drawings were profiles of the Ohio Pass line, with mileposts indicated. And they showed the line as projected going down toward the North Fork Valley, as far as a place marked "Marcellina Pass." This was the U.P. surveyor's name for a spur of Marcellina Mountain. No such place is named on any maps of this area, but the point obviously is where today's highway lays.

Then came some more information. After the C&S gave us tons of old files about to be destroyed, some letter books were included, which had come from the division engineer of the Union Pacific's Colorado Division. This included all the Colorado lines, such as the DSP&P, G&SL, Colorado Central, etc. One had copies of reports to Omaha headquarters. It turned out that in 1887, the railroad had laid track from near what is now the ghost town of Baldwin, on the Ohio Creek road of today, intending to place a one-mile spur off the unused Ohio Pass Extension to a coal-and-coke project, the one we had seen in 1954! Records in the Gunnison County courthouse showed a group of New York state's men had formed the Ohio Creek Anthracite Coal Company. However, they went bankrupt before the rail spur was completely laid during deep February snows. They had intended to supply Irwin by wagon, and the returning wagons would bring ore and concentrate for loading on the South Park rail line. The railroad company badly needed every bit of revenue, and that was why Omaha executives of the U.P. directed that the spur be built as soon as possible, despite the adverse weather. During May of 1991, the grade of this spur could be seen in places, close to Ohio Creek, despite a century of spring flooding and occasional storms. It appeared that it had not quite reached the coal mine, having missed it by several hundred feet.

One afternoon, while talking with a rancher who was raised near Baldwin, he pointed out the barely perceptible grade of the mainline of the Ohio Pass Extension. He said it passed in front of his parent's home and went a good half mile farther, to a point where it left a meadow and started up through the trees. The rancher told me how old-timers had talked about rails being laid to that point and left there for years. It was from near the end of those rails that the spur to the short-lived coal mine was laid.

Later, in reading the letter book of the Union Pacific division engineer for 1892–1893, I found more letters and telegrams concerning this line. In the fall of 1892, the U.P. sent out engineering parties to survey a line "to our workings beyond [Ohio Pass]." However, it was an early and very severe winter that year, with heavy snowfalls in that avalanche-prone area. One surveyor backed off a cliff, and he had to be taken to doctors in Gunnison by means of a dog sled to the railhead, where a train took him on into town. The U.P. owned claims to vast coal lands beyond Ohio Pass. At the same time, the D&RG was also surveying a line to reach the same area, where the Colorado Coal & Iron Company had workings. This company was later known as the Colorado Fuel & Iron Corporation (CF&I), which operated large steel mills in the Pueblo area.

At one time, the Union Pacific people got some 70 feet above the rival Denver & Rio Grande work force. This was at a point on a hillside that was made up largely of loose rock. And probably more to give the D&RG people a bad time than for anything else, the U.P. men set off black-powder blasts, raining rock debris down on the lower grade and the D&RG workers, back in those pre-hard-hat times. Once, there was a standoff at gun point, as the D&RG men climbed the hillside to the U.P. grade, with pistols drawn, to order that company's work force away. However, their threats did not work, as one telegram reported something to the effect that the U.P. men were well armed with various rifles and shotguns. (I wrote all this up at one time for possible use in a **Colorado Rail Annual**, under the title of: "Railroad Guns at Kebler Pass." However, the article laid around for years, and it was eventually discarded.)

Over the years, bits of information turned up about this project in the Gunnison country. A mining man in Oregon wrote to me to report that there was a lot of "...old original rail of the South Park..." piled up west of the pass, along what had been the wagon road to Floresta. He had seen it and thought that the Colorado Railroad Museum might like to have it. This fitted-in with the stack of ties I had seen. Another tidbit showed that two locomotives were in Gunnison at the time the farthest bit of track was torn up. Engine 191, a DSP&P 2-8-0 that now resides at the museum, was one of the locomotives in Gunnison. Was No. 191 the engine that made it the greatest distance west on the old South Park... toward that elusive "Pacific" in their corporate name?

It should be mentioned that the Union Pacific people felt that the D&RG was an interloper, taking advantage of the fact that the U.P. had constructed the first railroads into Colorado at such bankrupting costs. This feeling and rivalry that lasts to the present day, spurred the U.P. to try to extend their lines into much of the mountainous region of Colorado (west of Denver). Using the names of the narrow-gauge roads they controlled— such as the DSP&P (later known as the Denver, Leadville & Gunnison)—the surveyors drew routes for many lines on paper. And one even showed them paralleling the Denver & Rio Grande to reach the gold and silver mines of the San Juan region.

By 1893, other bits of data showed that both the D&RG and the DL&G, straining their resources to their limits, were forced to retreat to common sense. Early in 1893, they signed an agreement for a joint-track operation from Kebler Pass to the west. The U.P. would bring its DL&G narrow-gauge line down from Ohio Pass to Kebler Pass and connect there with the Rio Grande's Floresta Branch. At the time this joint-track agreement was reached, severe winter weather was raging, and it would be the summer before much could be done in the area. By that time, the terrible financial crash of 1893 was hitting hard. The D&RG was able to finish its track to Floresta, but the U.P.—with Alpine Tunnel closed, and mills and mines rapidly closing—never resumed construction in the Gunnison country. Yet, until the 1930's, the U.P. kept title to the coal lands beyond the mountain passes, and then, in the depth of the Great Depression, they sold them. Later, one U.P. official told me reluctantly that this "...was one of our greatest mistakes."

Since 1955, when the *Narrow Gauge News* reported the rediscovery of the Ohio Pass Extension, hundreds of visitors have hiked along the unfinished grade in the northwestern part of the scenic Gunnison country. They have examined the stone culverts of 1882, which still function, as well as the neat rock work, and they like to think what a little Mason Bogie engine might have looked like, working those grades with a short mixed train. It is a form of "chasing trains," in a way, and they have had a lot of enjoyment doing so.

DURING JULY OF 1952, unusual and unexplained at the time, Engine 268 was steamed-up at Gunnison to make a round trip to Crested Butte. However, these few cars of coal would not justify an eastbound freight train to Salida. As explained before, the Denver & Rio Grande Western had never repainted this C-16 from its "Grande Gold" bumblebee paint scheme of Chicago Railroad Fair times. With a friend from Alamosa, a railroad clerk and photographer by the name of John Hake, we had taken the day off to follow No. 268's progress, for it was a rare trip. At this point, we raced ahead and hastened to the sunny side of the track for our pictures. When we came back to the "G-buster," a rancher-type individual we had passed in such a hurry was waiting with a question: "You fellows shootin' gophers?" My reply was, "Oh no, we are certain it was a steam locomotive of my friend's employer, the D&RGW Railroad!" On the same day, we were asked if we were putting out fires, and, "How is the fishing?" Our cameras were ignored.

MULTIPURPOSE CAMERAS

WHILE TAKING PICTURES in Colorado, we encountered many local residents who persisted in thinking we were not taking pictures of trains, but were up to something else. John Hake, a railroad clerk at Alamosa, often accompanied me, and he used one of those old large Graflex cameras that resembled a small box headlight. One day at Gunnison the last C-16 narrow-gauge engine of the Denver & Rio Grande Western, little No. 268—still wearing her bright yellow paint scheme she had for the Chicago Railroad Fair—made a round trip to Crested Butte, and John and I tried for a few pictures.

While waiting near the bridge over the Slate River, a man in a pickup truck veered over to us, stopped and leaned out to inquire "How's the fishing?" When we replied that we did not know, but were waiting to photograph the oncoming train, he snorted "Oh, hell!" and sped off. Later in the day, as the train was returning to Gunnison, we raced ahead, then stopped and ran across the track to snap the train from the sunny side. We had passed another pickup truck, and the driver was waiting behind our car, and then, he inquired "You fellows shooting gophers?" Keeping from smiling, I replied—after turning to John and asking "Was that a gopher?"—"No, my good sir, we are sure that was not a gopher that just passed, but we are certain it was a steam locomotive of the D&RGW Railroad." He still sat there after we drove off, trying to figure it all out, I guess.

While switching cars in Gunnison during that hot afternoon in July, the little 2-8-0—despite wearing a cinder bonnet—set fire to weeds near the rodeo park. Soon, flames were shooting high, and as smoke rose, someone called the fire department. The engine crew, seeing the blaze they started, made a fast trip around the wye, so the fireman's blowoff valve would be facing toward the fire. And then, one pass was made with the blowoff open, and the fire was out. The arriving volunteer firefighters had a dry run. Anyhow, an old codger watching all of this, came over to us, eyeing John's big camera, and he inquired "You fellows putting out a fire?"

Much of the way home, we were laughing at the residents of Gunnison County who thought cameras could be used for fishing, shooting gophers and putting out fires!

GUNNISON FOR WINTER ACTION

GUNNISON, as so many narrow-gauge fans know, had been a very busy railroad center for many years. Even after the new alternative standard-gauge route was opened in 1890, it remained an importantly busy place. However, by the time I moved to Colorado in 1948, Gunnison had become a quiet place, where sometimes for as long as a week, there was nothing moving on the D&RGW. The old mainline west, through the Black Cañon to Montrose, had trains only once a month from the fall into the end of spring livestock movements. And occasionally there was a short run to serve the sawmill at Sapinero. The Baldwin Branch, on which only the last two Class C-16 2-8-0's ventured, was hardly a route of shiny rails, with weeks, or even a month, between runs. Crested Butte was busier, as the CF&I steel mills at Pueblo still maintained operations at their "Big Mine" for much of their coking coal. As a result, that branch could be counted upon for at least one train a week. And when enough loaded cars accumulated in the Gunnison yard, an eastward freight train would run over Marshall Pass to Salida. So, only by watching the dispatcher's "dope sheets" for forecasts of operations could I keep up with Gunnison's scanty steam-ups. The Gunnison country in late winter was no place to go sight-seeing. During March of 1952, I learned that there would be a Sapinero "turn" using little Engine 268, still resplendent in her "golden bumblebee" yellow-and-black paint from the Chicago Railroad Fair. (The Denver office of the D&RGW did not think repainting the engine was necessary, as who would notice this little 2-8-0 on her infrequent jaunts out of the roundhouse?)

Snow had been accumulating out Sapinero way, much deeper than in Gunnison, so a snowplow train took off one morning pushing the wedge plow (made from a gondola loaded with rock for ballast), which had a locomotive pilot plow on one end, topped with a headlight, perched up above the car on a sort of scaffold. The trainmen got the larger caboose—naturally—while the section men, along with their shovels, were squeezed into the much smaller Caboose 0524, the smallest "hack" on the narrow gauge. The train soon vanished into the canyon of the Gunnison River, out of sight

DURING MARCH OF 1952, the sawmill at Sapinero, Colorado—at the mouth of the scenic Black Cañon—had some loads of lumber ready to ship. The last Class C-16 2-8-0 on the Denver & Rio Grande Western, and the only engine small enough for that branch, sallied forth from Gunnison, pushing the railroad's rock-loaded wedge-plow car, with a drag flanger and two cabooses trailing behind. In the Gunnison Cañon, about 10 miles out, hard-packed snowdrifts—some of them higher than the engine—made the going difficult. During these times, the 2-8-0 would back out, uncouple from the train and take a run for the drifts. It took about six hours to cover the 26 miles to Sapinero. En route, a blizzard started up, so the engine had fresh drifts to plow through on the way back to Gunnison. No. 268 now sits in the museum area on the main street in Gunnison.

from U.S. Highway 50. The only side road down into the canyon served summertime fishing resorts, and it was a mess of mud and deep snow, so it was not attempted. Instead, I went on to wait at Cebolla, where the track again came within sight, along the highway, squeezing between the river and the road. But it was a long wait of several hours! Where was the train?

A couple of section men had gone ahead of the train on a motorized section car, and overconfidently, the men had been rolling along too fast. As they rounded a sharp curve, the section car came to grief on a rock. As if that did not cause enough delay, the tender was getting low, so the train backed to the Gunnison tank for a refill. And while this was going on, I was still waiting at Cebolla. The trainmen found the injured section men on their second trip. Knowing I was likely to be waiting at Cebolla, they planned to transfer the men into my car to take back to the hospital. However, they did not signal to me their intentions to stop, so I drove on toward Sapinero after I shot my pictures. So, they got the caretaker of the closed Cebolla resort to take the injured men back to Gunnison.

As the train worked its way through the canyon, there were occasional deep drifts, but the real test came as the train neared the point where the road to Lake City crossed the track. This was good for me, because the bridge enabled me to get on the railroad side of the river. Here, there was a long stretch of track covered with drifts, blown in places almost up to the top of the smokestack of the engine. Uncoupling from the flanger and cabooses, after backing up for some distance, the engine roared off down the line, pushing the plow car as hard as she could into the drifts—until she stalled. It was not very easy to take pictures, as the snow was almost as deep as I was tall, and I never knew when I might step into a trench or small channel. The plow and engine backed away from the spot where the engine stalled, and the section men went to work, clearing the rails, so it would not be so slippery for the next "running buck" with the plow. Then, all of a sudden, they were rapidly digging at one

spot along the track. And then, they reached down and came up with a man sputtering snow! It was the engine foreman, Mr. Stoecker, who had been walking outside the ties, and he suddenly stepped into a culvert location, and sank down so far that two feet of snow was over his head. With the usual heavy-handed railroad humor, the resulting kidding and remarks—such as, "...this wasn't the time to be playing around in the snow!"—had him in a bad humor long before the train got back to Gunnison.

Once the plow had been pushed through the drifts, it was coupled up with the rest of the train, and it headed off toward Sapinero.

At the Sapinero Needles curve, a place featured in old D&RG advertising, the train

LITTLE C-16 2-8-0, No. 278, handled the infrequent needs of the Baldwin Branch while its more glamourously painted and decorated fellow C-16, No. 268, was away at the Chicago Railroad Fair. One mine on the branch still loaded the popular Baldwin household coal for places as far away as the San Luis Valley. On February 28, 1950, No. 278 had brought a dozen empty gondolas from Gunnison, stopping at every road crossing to dig the track free of ice and gravel. With just the flanger car, it had cleared the wye. On the leg where it had to back the flanger the wrong direction, it was a matter of try-and-try-again. The unique squat water tank was a relic of the Colorado & Southern times, and it was still painted mineral red. The B&B crew never got to Castleton with their buckets of standard buff-yellow Rio Grande paint. This was originally the farthest few miles tracklayers got on the Denver, South Park & Pacific Railroad. Hidden by clouds is the Anthracite Range, some 25 miles beyond, where the Union Pacific managers hoped in 1882 to tap vast coal lands. However, all that remains of this ambitious plan are miles of unfinished grade, reaching to Ohio Pass.

357

approached a deep rock cut, full of snow. I could guess what was coming next, but I could not find any safe place to pull off the highway paving, as everything was a mess of mud and sloppy, wet snow a foot or more deep, on each side of the paved part of the road. If I had pulled off, I likely would have gotten stuck, and if I stayed on the main part of the highway, I would have created a dangerous situation for motorists. So, as I cruised along very slowly, I watched the little 2-8-0 "rev up" so her exhaust was a steady roar, as Engineer Clayton Braswell headed full-tilt into that cut. The pile of snow just sort of exploded, and the exhaust slowed down rapidly... to where the engine just barely got through. However, everything

was still on the rails, and everyone in the cabooses were able to relax after holding on for the likely crash! Fortunately, there were no large rocks in that snow!

The rest of the trip to Sapinero was made with just ordinary plowing, and in fact, Sapinero itself did not have any really deep snow or drifts. With a lot of slipping drivers, the train was wyed, loads of lumber were cut into the train, and after lunch, the long, slow trip upgrade back to Gunnison commenced.

While we were at Sapinero, a storm approached from the west, and soon, heavy flakes were making driving a chore—as I tried to keep the windshield clear so I could see to keep my car on the largely obscured road. The snow was so thick that, although I

could hear the train working across the river, seldom could I see it clearly. So, I headed home to Alamosa by way of the grind up to 11,312-foot Monarch Pass. Already, the highway had received a good foot of snow, and much lower Poncha Pass also had received quite a snowfall. However, long before I reached Alamosa, the road and countryside were typically bare. It had been a long day, but it was worth it to see the old 1882 veteran narrow-gauge Consolidation performing under the kind of conditions railfans used to read about in old issues of *Railroad* magazine.

The 18-mile Baldwin Branch was not badly troubled by snow, which was just as well, as in the final years—with Engine 268 away at the Chicago Railroad Fair and on display in Denver—and then, with No. 278 being given to Montrose for display, only one of these little engines was available. One such winter trip I saw was a good example. Engine 278 was hauling a flanger, a string of empty gondolas for coal loading and a caboose. The section crew went along to occasionally pick open hard-packed grade crossings, as well as to clear the switches at Castleton, at the end of the branch.

At Castleton, some three feet of snow had accumulated, so the engine, with only the flanger, plowed hard into the near leg of the wye. However, the difficult move was to clear the second leg of the wye by backing, as the flanger wings, although brought in as

TO THE DISAPPOINTMENT of narrow-gauge fans, the Gunnison terminal looked like this most of the time, with not even a simmering little No. 361, which was sitting outside the roundhouse. Out of sight, to the right, were an ancient car shop and a yard of trackage whose rails dated from the early years of the Denver & Rio Grande. Flangers OE and OK, along with homemade spreader OV, were the basic items of snow-fighting equipment. The Gunnison roundhouse stored the ex-Crystal River Railroad rotary snowplow OO, and on a stub track, there was a gondola wedge plow, designed for use in the Black Cañon. This scene was taken on May 30, 1949, and two days later, abandonment would be effective for the 15 miles through the Black Cañon and beyond, nearly to Montrose. This rendered surplus and up for scrap more of the small steam power. Here, were kept the two smaller 2-8-0's that were former Crystal River engines, Nos. 360 and 361, as well as the last two C-16's, Nos. 268 and 278. Only these smaller engines could be used west of Gunnison. As the Baldwin Branch was too light for the C-21 ex-CR engines, both would go to scrap within the next two years. In vain I tried to buy one of them, but they were cut up while I still waited for a price from the D&RGW's Purchasing Department in Denver.

close as possible, tended to bring snow onto the track, instead of away from it. The little 2-8-0 roared as she backed the flanger, stalling several times in the process, but she eventually got through. Clearing the third leg was easy.

The Baldwin Branch was embargoed during the fall of 1953 by a peculiar accident. For many years, the material for upgrading the truss bridge over the Slate River had been rusting away in the weeds. As budget money for something like the Baldwin Branch was never available, the bridge over the years became more and more doubtful, banning the use of any locomotives larger than C-16's. However, in October of 1953, after No. 278 had gone off to Montrose to become a popular target for local vandals, No. 268 took off with a caboose to pick up some livestock loadings at Teachout siding. As the engine began to cross the bridge, the huge wooden mudsill that had needed replacement for many years, collapsed. And the center support of the bridge sagged several feet. Engineer Braswell had no choice but to keep on crossing the span, because to stop would have created a worse disaster. To his surprise, the 2-8-0 made it over the bridge, with a rough trip for the trailing caboose. However, the crew was stranded on the "wrong side" of the river crossing, with no way to get back to Gunnison. So, the train tied-up at Teachout to await the Denver management's reluctant decision to call out the Alamosa Bridge & Building crew to drive their trucks to the rescue, loaded with repair materials.

The work crew made temporary repairs, replacing the shredded big wood block, jacking up the bridge. Luckily, the water was low when the repairs were made. And a few days later, No. 268 backed to Gunnison with the stock cars and the caboose, ending all operations on the branch. The C-16 was new in 1882, when the Denver, South Park & Pacific Railroad constructed this line. Their intention was to go up Ohio Creek Valley, over Ohio Pass and on down into the valley of the North Fork of the Gunnison. However, track was laid only a few miles beyond Castleton, although many miles of grading—and even some heavy rock retaining-wall work was done beyond the actual end of track. Every summer, the Baldwin road beyond Castleton sees many visitors, with many of them hiking and exploring these abandoned-and-unfinished railroad grades.

CRESTED BUTTE, Colorado, was virtually a company town of the Colorado Fuel & Iron Corporation. Almost every one who lived there was a coal miner or a family member. There were mines far to the left, out of the picture, and the "Big Mine" and others were to the right. Prior the 1930's, a switching crew was required by the D&RGW, and a daily mixed train came up the 35 miles from Gunnison. This April scene in 1951 was taken after a mild winter, which had far less than normal snowfall. On an average, at this time of the year, you could see large amounts of snow in the surrounding mountains, as well as remaining snowdrifts piled up in the town. The D&RGW depot sat at the lower end of the second street from the right. Track extended to the left for four miles to serve various coal mines, chiefly the Anthracite Mine. Behind my camera, the railroad had an 11-mile branch to Floresta, another anthracite mine site, located several miles beyond Kebler Pass.

WINTER AT CRESTED BUTTE

THE LOCATION of the little coal town of Crested Butte guaranteed that it would get a good share of any winter storms in the central mountains of Colorado. Every few years it would receive unusually heavy snowfalls, but by January of 1952, it had set a record of receiving the most snowfall in 35 years. The former Crystal River Railroad rotary snowplow was kept in the Gunnison roundhouse just for such times. During some winters it was not needed, but late every summer, the roundhouse force would move the big ma-

chine partly out of the roundhouse. There, they would steam it up to make the annual tests required. Then, the plow would be pushed back into its stall, perhaps not to appear in daylight until the next year's test.

During January of 1952, Snowplow "OO" set out to open up the Crested Butte Branch. The first few miles saw only a foot or two of snow, and several much-larger drifts. The water stop at Jacks Cabin tank was made in snow up to the cab windows, that point being 16 miles up the 28-mile branch. Soon, the machine was throwing snow from the track continuously. At Crested Butte, the slow work of plowing out the yard began, with

the section men laboriously clearing the switches. The modern split switches required much more work than the original old-time stub switches, which had been replaced when heavier rail was laid during the 1920's. The town and county had plowed out the streets, but the grade crossings of the wye tracks required some work for the crew.

Some boxcars in the yard had snowdrifts nearly covering them. Gondolas fared worse, heaped high with piles of snow as cargo. The town's main street was hard to believe. Snow was piled up so deep that the movie-theater marquee seemed to rest on snow! Home

owners and businesses had dug tunnels between their front doors and the street. Motor traffic moved cautiously, with rags tied to radio aerials helping to avoid fender benders at intersections.

However, the rotary snowplow managed to clean things out very well in the yard, for the two- or three-times-a-week coal trains, and it was back in its stall at Gunnison after dark. As it turned out, it was never to be operated again. Later that year, the CF&I steel maker closed down their "Big Mine" at Crested Butte, ending virtually all need to operate the branch. It also meant the end of

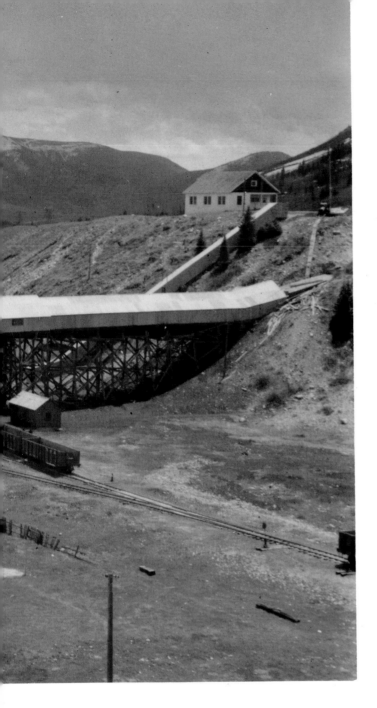

THE COAL TIPPLE of the Colorado Fuel & Iron Corporation's "Big Mine" dominated Crested Butte, Colorado—the peak of that name being just out of the picture to the left. The winter of 1950-1951 had been mild, as this April view shows. The Rio Grande track layout was typical for a coal mine. The empty gondolas were placed to the right, above the switch, and then they were dropped under the tipple by gravity as needed. And then, again by gravity, they were rolled down from the tipple after being loaded. Switching time was minimal. The long bank of coke ovens had been shut down for many years. The D&RGW's colorful depot and wye were at the far left. This mine was unusual, as some of the drifts touched anthracite coal; however, the demand for it was rather slight. Generally, the mine produced one car of anthracite coal for every 100 cars of bituminous coal. To keep the mine running through the summer months, the D&RG system urged coal customers to order their fall needs then. CF&I dominated the coal business in central and southern Colorado. By this time, coal from Crested Butte was the larger part of all traffic in the Gunnison country, and when the mine closed in 1953, the railroad line was doomed.

all the Gunnison lines and the route over Marshall Pass to Salida.

Now, Crested Butte is a big ski center, and the little wooden depot is the municipal library—with one of the largest donors leaving a sum of money to purchase railroad books for the library's shelves. The Brinkerhoff Brothers got the contract to tear up the line. The Brinkerhoffs contributed to Western State College having its best football season ever. This was because the laborers the Brinkerhoffs hired were from the football team of the college, and they easily romped over all their opponents that fall. Interest

ingly, there were reports in college circles that other school's football coaches were seeking to find some railroad lines their teams could tear up!

The dismantling was accomplished in part by using Galloping Goose No. 7, in its flatbed configuration. The Goose was mainly used for rail removal in the yards of Crested Butte, Gunnison and elsewhere. The main tracks were removed by using a homemade (but very efficient) rail-slinging device, which lifted the rails quickly into a string of gondolas, using a winch and overhead cables.

CRESTED BUTTE, Colorado, received more snow in the winter of 1951–1952 than any time during the past 35 years. In January of 1952, the rotary snowplow stationed at Gunnison opened the branch, a rare procedure. Here, on March 29, 1952, Engine 486 had brought a long train of empty gondolas for coal loading at the CF&I facility at the far left (in the background). No. 486 spent about an hour flanging the yard, and after taking on water, the 2-8-2 returned to Gunnison with her two-car train. Out in the valley, the Floresta Branch went upgrade to a large anthracite-coal mine, until business declined and the mine closed. As a result, this branch was torn up during the 1930's.

THE WINTER OF 1951–1952 was just the opposite of the previous mild winter. Crested Butte had a mind-boggling amount of snow during this season! The rotary snowplow kept at Gunnison made its final trip to open the Crested Butte Branch, not long before this picture was taken by the "Abandoned Lines Reporter" on March 29, 1952. The depot buildings are the snow-buried cluster at the left. This scene shows why the area was selected many years later to become a popular ski resort.

CIMARRON AND THE BLACK CAÑON

THE ORIGINAL MAINLINE of the Denver & Rio Grande through the Black Cañon, which exited at Cimarron Cañon and then went over Cerro Summit, was abandoned in 1949. For years, there had been little on-line traffic; the former through traffic having been diverted from Montrose via the standard-gauge line to Grand Junction. Immediately after the narrow-gauge line was declared abandoned, a Texas firm began the work of removing the rails. They employed one or the other outside-frame 2-8-0 of the two ex-Crystal River 2-8-0 Consolidations to haul the cars of scrap and ties to Sapinero, where a D&RGW crew from Gunnison would retrieve them. It was sad to watch No. 360 back across the bridge over the Cimarron River and pull flatcars of rails out of the little yard, over which towered giant cottonwood

ALTHOUGH SNOWSLIDES frequently covered the track in the Black Cañon, the rotary snowplow stationed at Gunnison could not be used because of so much rock in the slides. Too many locomotives equipped with pilot plows like this were derailed and wrecked when they attempted to buck such slides. So, the D&RGW's operating forces came up with this solution, a gondola loaded with rock (for ballast), with a locomotive headlight perched high. The idea was that it would be better to lose a gondola than an

engine. This was a very effective plow, too, as I followed along one day in a trip to Sapinero, where it was pushed by the last C-16 2-8-0, No. 268. The little engine uncoupled from its train, then took a run for drifts higher than the engine. Then, the engine backed out, waited while section men cleared the rails, then hit the drifts again with this plow. The Brinkerhoff company gave me the headlight off this plow. They joked that I ought to buy the entire car in case a big snowstorm hit Alamosa.

A FINAL EXCURSION through the Black Cañon of the Gunnison was hauled by former Crystal River engine No. 361, an outside-frame 2-8-0. This run was on May 30, 1949, the last use of what was the original mainline of the Denver & Rio Grande Railway to Utah. The rocky canyon walls are some 1,000 feet above the narrow-gauge track. The train was close to the Curecanti Needle, the odd 800-foot volcanic cone the railroad depicted in its herald for about 50 years. Sadly, two days after this excursion train passed, abandonment became effective for this track.

trees. Then, slowly retreating, the engine backed with the workmen down toward the Black Cañon.

With No. 268 away at the Chicago Railroad Fair and No. 361 laid-up, needing repairs, the chore of taking more empties to Sapinero to bring out the scrap loads fell to ancient C-16 No. 278. This engine was also somewhat in need of an overhaul. Selecting a tonnage load of scrap, the engine would work its hardest to get the train underway.

Never before had I seen an engine under these conditions actually rock from side to side, and how the rods and machinery stood that brutal work puzzled me. It was slow going through the Gunnison Canyon, with all of its curves, and as the train came within a couple of miles of its goal, the road closely paralleled the track. However, the train was moving so slowly that I could not keep my pickup truck in gear, or it would outpace it. It was quite a show, with a tall column of smoke as—at four or five mph—doing her best as she finally pulled into the Gunnison yard. Today, where No. 278 worked so hard, is the center of present U.S. Highway 50, as it swings into town.

Back up the grade, Cimarron is now a National Park Service site, with a rebuilt stockyard, original stock and bunk cars on some track, and a great attraction is little No. 278, along with a boxcar and caboose. The 2-8-0 and caboose sit on the bridge that crossed the Cimarron River a mile down the canyon. Here, in 1982, on the centennial of the arrival of the first train, a gala occasion was held, and it was my pleasure to be among the speakers. I related how my first visit to the place was to arrive all "sooty and cindered," as I rode on top of the caboose of a hardworking freight train, back in 1945. The audience agreed and laughed that I must indeed have been the only person present who had come into Cimarron in that fashion!

THROUGH THE BLACK CAÑON

THE BEST PLACE to visit a truly spectacular gorge in Colorado was the Black Cañon of the Gunnison, between Gunnison and Montrose. Even better than riding on a dome car on the Rio Grande mainline was to sit on top of the cupola of a caboose as a train snaked its way through the Black Cañon. Before the advent of the nefarious Alfred Perlman (who gained control of the D&RGW after World War II), one could usually obtain a permit to ride freight trains by applying to the Denver office of the railroad. A passenger ticket was required, of course, as conductors were not permitted to accept cash fares. So, getting a ticket to ride on a narrow-gauge line without regular passenger service often was a slow accomplishment. Most station agents had to hunt to find the tariff rates, and some could not find them at all.

Fresh out of the Army in October of 1945, I headed west from Ohio to see and experience the Colorado narrow-gauge lines once again. Learning at Denver that in a couple of days the monthly freight was going to run from Gunnison to Montrose, a combination of a ride on the Royal Gorge train to Salida and a Rio Grande Motorways bus trip from there got me to Gunnison. Luckily, I arrived in time to board the caboose of the narrow-gauge train on the following morning. A little Class C-21 2-8-0 up ahead whistled off (with two loud blasts), moving out of the Gunnison station with a fairly long train of miscellaneous loads. As the legal form I had signed waived any objections from the crew, I climbed on top of the caboose with my Kodak 616 camera. We were several miles west of Gunnison, on the stretch of track that extended much of the way to Sapinero, former junction point for the Lake City Branch. Today, there is more than 70 feet of water where we paused at that very small community before entering the famous Black Cañon immediately beyond this station.

Although it was a bright, sunshiny day, the gorge was well named, for at places the train wound along close to the cascading river in dark shadows. This made it difficult for me to take good photographs, because of the extreme contrasts in the amount of light. In some ways, it was a scary place, with huge rocks all around, obviously having fallen from the steep cliffs that rose 1,000 feet above the track. Other large rocks seemed to be separated and ready to fall, some of them being the size of multi-storied buildings. It was not much consolation to think that "ready to fall" in geological terms meant sometime during the next thousands of years!

The brakeman came up as we neared the place where the line left the canyon to point out a huge rock lying in the river, and then told its story. Back in 1882, when the railroad was new, it seems that a passenger train was approaching this spot. Suddenly, an enormous rock fell, hitting and destroying the wooden trestle, exploding bridge timbers all around. One of these timbers entered the locomotive cab, killing the engineer. Fortunately, no one else was even injured. It was about 13 miles west to this point from Sapinero, the only intermediate station being Curecanti. This is where the huge 800-foot volcanic cone stands, which the railroad used as its herald emblem for over 50 years. All that was left at Curecanti was a siding sign and a locked-up section house. When this line was busy, I was told that the children of the section foreman would be sent off to relatives in Gunnison, so they could attend public school.

Engine 360 worked hard as she pulled the tonnage up the side canyon of the Cimarron River, the mile and a half to another once-busy little railroad settlement, Cimarron. The canyon winds blew the smoke and hot cinders back my way, and I must have looked like one of the end men in an old-time minstrel show by this time. First impressions are not forgotten—and I remember the station of Cimarron as a quiet place, with scattered railroad buildings (locked up). A huge water tank served both the mainline and one leg of the wye and yard, and there was a small three-track yard, under a grove of huge, old cottonwood trees, arching over the track. At the tank sat Mudhen No. 456, waiting to couple on behind the caboose. Up ahead on the main track, at the beginning of the 4.0-percent grade to Cerro Summit, waited the other ex-Crystal River C-21, No. 361, which would become our head-end helper.

It was really something different to look back from the cupola to the Mudhen working hard behind the caboose, and then ahead to the two C-21's, occasionally curving sharply to the left or right. At a steady 15 miles per hour (or thereabouts), we only took a little over half an hour to get to the summit. The scenery had changed to barren land, with some brush-covered hillsides, and a valley stretching toward Montrose, 17 miles further on downgrade. Cerro Summit had a telephone box, the usual siding sign, a wye and a passing track. The helpers were cut off, and they went on ahead, about five minutes apart. For most of the rest of the trip, I could see them at times a mile or two ahead. At one point, they were going in the opposite direction, way below our train. Again, the brakeman pointed out places of interest, mostly wreck sites. At one place, he pointed out a rusting oil-headlight case, lying not far from the track, where a C-16 had hit a snow-slide and rolled over. Not quite half way to Montrose, we passed Cedar Creek, with its rusty wye. For many years in the past, this was a telegraph station, from which many four- and even five-engine trains had started "up the hill."

A LONG DAY'S TRIP TO OURAY

LITTLE ENGINE No. 278 held down the infrequent trips to Baldwin, while her sister, No. 268, was away in "Grande Gold" livery at the Chicago Railroad Fair. These two locomotives were the last of the Rio Grande's longtime fleet of Class C-16 2-8-0's. They had formed the major portion of narrow-gauge motive power since the early 1880's—until new K-27 outside-frame 2-8-2's began arriving in 1903—the first Mikados ordered by the Denver & Rio Grande.

The dispatcher's dope sheet showed that No. 278 would be making a round trip to Baldwin from Gunnison one day during the summer of 1951. So, taking along a teenage summer helper at the motel, we headed for Gunnison one morning at dawn, 5:00 a.m. It was a three-hour trip, much of it on gravel-surfaced roads. What's worse, there was not even a spot to get a cup of coffee in the 146 miles, including the climb over 11,312-foot Monarch Pass.

At 8:00 a.m., we pulled up to the roundhouse in Gunnison, where No. 278 sat simmering halfway outside the enginehouse. However, we got bad news. The hostler said that word had just come from the station agent that the run would be cancelled until tomorrow, when some additional cars would be fully loaded. What should we do? Nothing else was moving in the Gunnison region; however, I recalled that the dope sheet had also forecast that a Ouray turn would be made that day from Montrose. So, without even a thought of wasting time for breakfast, off we went in the pickup truck for the 56 gravelly (and sometimes rough) miles to Montrose.

SEVERAL TIMES between Montrose and Ridgway, Colorado, the Ouray Branch of the D&RGW crossed the Uncompahgre River. This bridge was the final crossing, near the Ridgway yard limit. Because of the lighter rail on this narrow-gauge branch, No. 318 was the only engine left on the branch that could be operated the next 10 miles to Ouray. By August of 1951, such trips were weeks apart, as the mining traffic at Ouray gradually declined to almost nothing.

THE CONTRAST between the two gauges was frequently emphasized at Montrose, Colorado. Engine No. 784, a standard-gauge 4-6-0, had just brought in the Denver & Rio Grande Western's "Mountaineer" from Grand Junction and Denver. Narrow-gauge "Mudhen" No. 454—with an unusually short train—was heading for Ridgway to meet the Rio Grande Southern's crew, making that road's final runs on the Northern District. No. 454 was not going to have much to do after this date, as the standard-gauging of the Montrose–Ridgway portion of the Ouray Branch would soon begin. On its return from Ridgway, Mikado No. 454 became the switch engine, and she had to wye the passenger train, using an idler car. Under the union contract, the switching crew was not supposed to use the road engine, No. 784, just one of the archaic arrangements that frustrated officials seeking more efficiency. The date for this view was November 21, 1951.

THE AUTUMN of 1951 was the last busy livestock season on the Denver & Rio Grande Western's narrow-gauge Ouray Branch. In any case, the Rio Grande Southern brought in as many cars as usual to the connection at Ridgway, Colorado. Here, on October 10, 1951, the last Class C-18 2-8-0, No. 318, had brought back empty stock cars from the Montrose transfer. These cars were for the Rio Grande Southern to work back to Durango, Colorado, before the RGS abandoned operations.

My teenage companion had set his heart on seeing No. 278 run, and he was very downcast. So, the thought of having a chance to see No. 318, a Class C-18 2-8-0, perform surely made him brighten. Neither of us wanted to waste a day after setting such high hopes for a narrow-gauge run.

We drove on past Sapinero, with only a glimpse of the abandoned grade vanishing into the Black Cañon, winding through the rugged country to the west. Finally, we reached Cimarron, where again the grade of what had been the original narrow-gauge mainline to Utah came into view. Then, we drove past the slide at Cedar Creek, which had obliterated the grade and pushed its yellow folds close to the highway. Finally, we entered Montrose, and a quick loop past the enginehouse told us that engine No. 318 was gone.

Nevertheless, we were not far behind the little train, and just a few miles south of town, we caught up with the 2-8-0 bubbling along with a short train at a 25 to 30 mph gait. There were no cars either to pick up or set out at any of the sidings or at Ridgway, where the train stopped briefly. Now, the grade stiffened, and

the engine worked with a sharp stack exhaust on the final 10 miles up to Ouray, at one point climbing along a ridge way above the Uncompahgre River. Upon arrival at the small yard in Ouray, along the river, the crew spotted the engine at a hydrant, and while it slowly filled the tender, all adjourned for lunch.

After lunch, switching consisted of picking up some ore-loaded gondolas and spotting the empties brought from Montrose. Then, the engine moved onto the old "armstrong" turntable. The worn center casting made turning the table difficult, and not only the crew, but any handy spectators joined in straining against the old wooden arms. In fact, over the years, it had become an expected diversion for younger tourists to join in turning the engine at Ouray.

The Ouray yard had never been rebuilt from its early days, when it was new in 1887. Six of the stub switches were still controlled by old harp switch stands. The enginehouse was long gone, as well as the depot. The colorful little depot had burned down a few years earlier, due to a short circuit in the telegraph wires. In its place, two outfit boxcars sufficed to house the agent for a while, and for what ever space he needed for his meager needs. Until the Great Depression struck during the 1930's, Ouray had been the terminal of the through passenger train from Salida. West of Gunnison, the little T-12 4-6-0 passenger locomotives of the D&RGW were usually used. Until the very end, the town had parlor-car service.

We followed No. 318 on its return trip to Montrose, where we watched her shuffle loads in the mixed-gauge yard, and finally, she tied-up at the two-track enginehouse. Then, it was back on the long drive to Alamosa by a pair of weary, but satisfied, railfans. We wished that we could stay over in Gunnison to follow Engine 278 on its outing over the weedy tracks to Baldwin, but this was not possible.

LAST RUN TO OURAY ON THE D&RGW

THE WINTER of 1952–1953 piled most of its snowfall rather late in the season, and in March most of it was arriving. About March 18, 1953, I learned that the final run on the narrow-gauge Ouray Branch of the Denver & Rio Grande Western would be made on the

21st of the month. And this run would be a round-trip from Montrose over the 35-mile line.

I could not get away on March 20, so very early on the 21st—about 4:00 a.m.—I took off for the Ouray Branch. There was not much choice of routes. I could go either via Poncha Pass and Monarch Pass, and then, west via Gunnison. Or I could use the so-called "shortcut" via Cochetopa Pass, which is shorter in miles. However, it would be the slower of the two because of normal winter conditions, let alone any that would not be normal.

Upon reflection, I elected to go via a longer southern route, via Wolf Creek Pass to Durango, and then travel north by way of Silverton and Ouray, expecting to reach Montrose before the usual midmorning departure, when the infrequent Ouray Branch trains ran.

At a breakfast stop in Durango, I learned that the "Million Dollar Highway" was being plagued by numerous snowslides, and there might be delays of hours if I drove over Red Mountain Pass (in particular). It now was rather late to go back and take the round-about route via Gunnison. So, knowing that the Dolores County road maintenance man

THE LAST DAY for the narrow-gauge Ouray Branch was March 21, 1953. C-18 No. 318 was steamed-up and ready at Montrose, Colorado. The standard-gauge line from Grand Junction, Colorado, had been all steam-powered until now. However, a GM Electro-Motive Division GP-7 "general-purpose" diesel-electric engine, No. 5102, had arrived on the scene for the first time. At the right, Mudhen No. 454 sat alone, dead, never to steam again. During the fall of 1953, the engine's boiler was placed in a sawmill. The "diesel age" had begun on the Grand Junction–Ouray line.

HANDING UP ORDERS at Montrose, Colorado, for the last narrow-gauge run to Ouray, Engine 318 was about to depart on March 21, 1953. C. L. "Clayt" Braswell, engineer, John Collett, conductor, Frank B. Wright, fireman, Joe Mazza and John Chiodo, trainmen, made up the crew for this final run. Notice the big brass whistle, a favorite of about-to-retire Engineer Braswell, a veteran narrow-gauge railroader of the Denver & Rio Grande Western's Gunnison lines.

did his best to keep Lizard Head Pass open, I headed for Dolores and Rico. The Lizard Head portion of this state highway—Route 145—then all gravel-surfaced (and in some places very little of that), was not used much by through traffic. In fact, there were virtually no through automobiles at all, just local folk going back and forth on weekends.

Not much snow was encountered between Mancos and Dolores. However, as I neared Rico, the snow depth rapidly increased, and I found that this little mining town had big piles of snow down the middle of the main street (also the highway). Inquiry determined that the road crew had not attempted to keep Lizard Head Pass open, because there was much wind... so, the road was not open! Back to Durango I hurriedly drove, and I turned north on Highway 550—reluctantly—hoping that any snowslide delays would be short ones. What a surprise I had when I discovered that the road was open, despite the gloomy early reports! Surprisingly, the highway was nicely plowed, and despite the evidence of numerous slides, some with trees sticking out of them, they were passed with no problem.

A few miles north of Silverton, while the light was good, I stopped to take a picture. But before I shot it, something caught my eye, and upon looking up on the mountainside immediately above me, I could see movement, as two or three aspen trees were bending, under the weight of slow-moving snow. I am sure I made a record jump into my pickup truck, and I rapidly gunned the motor, not hesitating to look back until I was a good half mile farther down the highway. However, no slide had run, and there was no plume of snow to be seen. Continuing northward on the downhill side of Red Mountain Pass, as I was entering the narrow, rocky Uncompahgre Canyon, I found the narrow road blocked by a slide that was higher than a car. However, I had just passed a road grader, which came along in a few minutes. And within 10 minutes, it had pushed the snow and rocks off into the canyon, allowing me to continue.

Ouray had about six inches of snow on the ground, and the attractive little town looked especially scenic, surrounded by high snow-covered mountains—as a brief bit of sunlight bathed the settlement with radiant illumination. Farther north, Ridgway had just a couple of inches of snow on the

THIS WAS THE LAST TIME an engine would be switching cars at Ouray, Colorado. The date was March 21, 1953, and this was the last day for narrow-gauge operations on the 35-mile branch between Montrose, Ridgway and Ouray. When constructed in 1887, Ouray was the terminal of a busy through line of 387 narrow-gauge miles, which operated Pullman cars from Denver. The Ouray yard was the last yard on the D&RGW with stub switches, still fitted with old "harp" switchstands of the 1880's.

ground. And the farther I drove toward Montrose (25 miles away), the less snow laid on the ground, until long before arriving there, the ground was bare. Typical of Colorado in the winter, this phenomenon is a constant surprise to those who drive in the Colorado Rockies during the winter season.

Down at the enginehouse in Montrose, the last operating Class C-18 2-8-0, No. 318, was under steam, ready to back down to the depot and pick up its "train," the caboose. This 1896 Consolidation was a veteran of service on other Rio Grande branches, long abandoned. No. 318 had been the motive power on the D&RGW's Pagosa Springs Branch, and long before that, the engine had worked hard on its original road, the Florence & Cripple Creek, in the Pikes Peak Region. Mudhens—Class K-27 2-8-2's—could

operate only as far as Ridgway, so only No. 318 could manage safely on the 10 miles of lighter rails to Ouray.

With no ceremony and no crowd of onlookers, Conductor Collett handed up the train order to Engineer Braswell, and during late midmorning, the little engine took off with its "heavy" train of one car. There was nothing to do at way points, as no cars remained at these sidings. Beyond Ridgway, snow began falling, and soon it was coming down in silver-dollar-size flakes—heavily. At Ouray, the crew coupled-up to the last boxcar loads of ore, picked up the "depot," which was an outfit car (made from an old boxcar), which had partially replaced the attractive station building destroyed by fire a few years earlier. Ouray's yard featured stub switches, with old-time harp switchstands of

REVERSING DIRECTION on the turntable at Ouray, Colorado, for the last time, on March 21, 1953, Engine 318 was about to head back to Montrose. This locomotive had been built in 1896 for another narrow-gauge mining road, the Florence & Cripple Creek Railroad. No. 318 was saved from scrapping by her purchase by Cornelius W. Hauck of Cincinnati, Ohio. This Class C-18 2-8-0 now is on display at the Colorado Railroad Museum in Golden, Colorado.

the 1880's. Then, the 2-8-0 was turned on the armstrong table, which had a worn-out center bearing and required plenty of manpower to turn it around. The engine was then backed to the water standpipe to fill the tender, while the crew walked uptown for lunch.

The townspeople of Ouray ignored the occasion, probably because none of them knew it was the last time the train would be seen in their little mountain town. During the early afternoon, the engine whistled off, trundling the odd train behind, which would have made a good *"Believe It or Not"* by taking the depot with it, the old outfit car. At Ridgway, a handful of old railroaders from the legendary (but vanished) Rio Grande Southern Railroad were on hand at the big wooden depot to exchange a few words of farewell and wave the last narrow-gauge train off. The snowstorm had not reached Ridgway or the good-byes would have been dampened in more ways than one.

Along the way, the clapper fell out of No. 318's bell, but it was rescued. However, the 318 was not going to need a bell much longer anyway. The engineer made up for the bell's silence by extra-long blasts of the

large, special brass whistle the 2-8-0 featured. The whistle had come from some passenger engine that was scrapped long ago.

At Montrose, the train was switched, the boxcars going to the transfer track alongside standard-gauge cars, providing the last of such work for the laborers. The Ouray "depot" was spotted beside the freight house, and one might have said this, too, was another *"Believe It or Not"* oddity, with two depots side-by-side. Foreman Lutkiewicz put the ex-F&CC engine in the two-track enginehouse, dropped its fire and drained it, and No. 318's 57-year career was over. Except during the 1960's, No. 318 was steamed-up again at the Colorado Railroad Museum in Golden for a brief period of use. Then, the fires were dropped again when it was learned that the firebox side sheets were "dead" from improper hostling sometime on the D&RGW.

To my delight, the pictures taken of the last run turned out all right, and they are a good memento of one very long day of trainchasing. The return to Alamosa was made via the longer, but less arduous route along the Gunnison River and over the Great Divide at Monarch Pass.

FAMED ENGINE 20 of the Rio Grande Southern was on its next-to-last trip from Durango to
Rico. The Ten-wheeler was taking-on water at
Bear Creek Tank, also known as Priest Gulch, 12
miles south of Rico. Engineer Lee Lynton was oiling around, while veteran fireman, George Thomas, was handling the spout. George McLean, the
conductor, was to become a big help in saving
many of the railroad's records. No. 20 was still
carrying the colorful ship painting on the tender,
used in the movie, "Ticket to Tomahawk," in 1949.
The date for this run was November 16, 1951.

FINAL RUNS OF THE RGS ON THE DURANGO END OF THE LINE

THE WINTER OF 1951–1952 turned out to
be one of early and what seemed to be con-
tinuous snowfalls throughout the San Juan
region. Early in December, the last interchange loads from the D&RGW for the Rio
Grande Southern had arrived at Durango. At
Alamosa, transfer crews had loaded some
cars with utility-company poles and two cars
of automobiles, all of them destined for Dolores. The poles were longer than the largest
flatcars of the D&RGW, requiring "idler"
flats to be coupled between the loaded cars.
The automobiles were loaded onto the two
specially fitted flatcars with canvas sides and
tops. These two cars were seeing their final
use for such service, and upon their eventual
return to Alamosa would have this extra material removed. During this period, hauling
utility poles across the mountain range via

Wolf Creek Pass was something that no one
wanted to undertake by highway.

So, on December 17, 1951, rented Mudhen No. 464, equipped with a big pilot plow,
which reached halfway up the smokebox, attempted the first trip from Durango in
weeks. Knowing that this run (or perhaps
the next one) would be the last of all operations on the RGS, I departed from Alamosa
at about 5:00 a.m. for the 152-mile trip to Durango. Chains, a bucket of sand and a couple
of long-handled shovels were "must" acces-
sories. Chuck Gilmer, a railroad machinist,
had a boy who was very interested in trains,
and Chuck asked me to take Billy along. We
arrived at Durango to find big snowflakes
adding more white stuff to an engine terminal already liberally supplied with it. No. 464
was being hostled, and her tender being
filled at the water tank when we arrived.
Then, the 2-8-2 switched out Caboose 0404
and coupled onto what was perhaps a tonnage train of poles and automobiles. How-

ever, there was 16 inches of snow on the track, heavily crusted, and the grade out of Durango averaged about 2.0 percent for miles.

Roadmaster Rhodes went behind, gunning the motor of his Goose No. 6, which was loaded with all the things he might need. And on the RGS, that meant many things in the way of track tools, besides shovels and chains. Billy and I drove ahead of the train for the first good location for pictures, the road crossing, just a half mile from the water tank. Engine 464 was working hard after crossing the Animas River and was sending up a tall column of smoke and steam, but it was evident that the engine was having a hard time plowing through the crusted snow. The Mudhen slipped on occasion, and when she got to the road crossing, the engine stalled, unable to resume progress, despite repeated attempts. (Incidentally, several years later, this site was employed for a motel swimming pool!)

Finally, the train backed down into the Durango yard, where it was decided to leave the cars of poles (after much discussion) and try to open the line with only the two cars of automobiles and the caboose. Meanwhile, Rhodes had been out at the grade crossing with a couple of section men, who cleared the hard-packed snow from the rails at this point. After all, there was no need to complicate matters with a derailment!

By this time, it was getting close to noon, when No. 464 came charging up the grade. As she still slipped a little, the engine made it across the highway and continued heading for Franklin Junction and the new bridge over the highway. There, the 2-8-2 tackled the grade up through Wildcat Canyon. This grade from Durango was 12 miles long, and it was not unusual for heavy trains to use so much water they would have to "cut and run" for water, meaning that the engine had to leave the train while it went ahead to Hesperus and tanked-up.

Wildcat Canyon posed another problem. For long stretches, the road was alongside the track, and the county crews had no choice but to plow snow over onto the railroad track. Now, No. 464 not only faced the 16 inches or so of packed snow, but all this additional snow piled on top of it. There were two road crossings, too, so Billy and I grabbed our shovels and worked at clearing the tops of the rails. Otherwise, with all the

delays, the train would get later and later, and we were supposed to be back in Alamosa by evening. It was really quite something to watch the engine working its hardest, plowing into all that snow! It undoubtedly caused much dismay to the few users of this old road, not to mention the county road crew, who found all that snow piled back on the road, with interest added one might say! It certainly became a one-lane road that morning.

Beyond the canyon, the RGS took off on an alignment far away, out of sight from the county road. So, we drove ahead and waited near Hesperus for the train to come into view again. It was a rather long wait, as the railroad had to negotiate what was called "Muleshoe Curve," in its tortuous route to the top that long grade from Durango. (It might be mentioned that this curve was the scene a couple of years earlier for several days of movie-making for "Viva Zapata." This movie employed about 200 local citizens—their complexions artificially darkened and wearing even more bandoleers than they would during hunting season!)

The snow had stopped falling an hour earlier, and when the train came along, the day had become bright and sunny, with a background for pictures of the very snowy La Plata Range. After filling the tender at Hesperus, the train soon got out of sight, as the railroad diverged from the road just beyond the tank. So, watching it vanish, still plowing snow—at places in great showers of the white stuff, as the plow hit drifts—the Mudhen was gone. It would be hours before the train would come into view again, after skirting the La Platas and working to the summit point of Cima, and then dropping down to Mancos, as the crews viewed that location as "two water tanks from Hesperus." So… reluctantly, we headed back to Alamosa, finding the road mostly bare of snow, and the crossing of Wolf Creek Pass was uneventful.

Two mornings later, we were back again at the Durango yard. Again, No. 464 was steaming up. It had come in the day before, after setting out the two cars at Dolores for unloading. Now, the Mudhen coupled-up to the cars of poles, and the engine again tackled the long grade up to Hesperus. With very little in new snow or wind-blown drifts to contend with, No. 464 managed very well in negotiating the long upgrade. The county

ROADMASTER C. A. RHODES had just brought RGS "Galloping Goose" No. 4 from Durango, and he did not mind posing with the railbus at Dallas Divide (Peake) on May 23, 1951. This was the last year for the Rio Grande Southern. In the background is part of the rugged San Juan

Mountains, with one of the high peaks being named for Otto Mears, the builder of the RGS. Mr. Rhodes will be dropping down the 13-mile grade to Ridgway, with most of it averaging 4.0 percent. Although the Rio Grande Southern had changed the name of 8,970-foot Dallas Divide in the 1920's,

road crew possibly had conceded the plowing contest, or else the men found other more important things to do. As a result, very little snow was shoved back on the track. Again, we did a little shoveling of packed snow on the rails, caused by recent motor traffic, but the day turned gloomy, and snow began to fall heavily. Hesperus was poor for pictures, so—knowing there was a "baby sitter" at the Alamosa motel, willing to stay late—we headed out of Hesperus, intending to go on to Mancos and wait for the train at that point.

However, the sunshine earlier had made that rough gravel road a very treacherous affair, with hard-packed snow, glazed with a sheet of ice in places. Just beyond Hesperus, on a straight section, my pickup truck veered sharply to the right… and in seconds we were in the borrow pit! This situation did not last long, as two other trucks came along, and we were soon out of that embarrassing predicament. However, the pictures at Man-

cos were skipped, as we decided this was a bad day to attempt a rendezvous with an RGS train at that place. So, back to Alamosa we drove, only to find a new winter storm had piled snow on the road, and while we were crossing Wolf Creek Pass, we came across a snowslide as well. Going upgrade at the pickup truck's steady 22 mph (or so), suddenly snow was flowing onto the road immediately ahead. If I had braked, we would have ended up in the middle of the slide. So, I gunned it, and after the wheels spun for a few seconds, we were through the slide!

The day after Christmas, I learned that on the 27th, a caboose hop would go out to Mancos to bring in the empties. The RGS train of December 19 had waited at Dolores while the utility-company poles were unloaded. Then, the engine brought all the empties as far as Mancos, where it had to leave some on the siding. Considering the experience of being stuck in the borrow pit

from habit, RGS dispatchers would occasionally issue train orders years afterward using instructions for meets "at Dallas Divide," a serious infraction of rules on most railroads. In any case, the geographical name for this pass remains "Dallas Divide."

and almost being caught by a snowslide on Wolf Creek Pass, plus the fact that slides were reportedly occurring frequently on that highway. I reluctantly decided not to attempt to make a third trip to Durango for what might be the "last run." And then again, it might not be the last. No one knew for sure. However, as it turned out, it was indeed the last of all RGS runs on the south end of the line (if you ignore the dismantler's operations the following year). Instead of using No. 464, the last run was fittingly made by No. 20, the road's ex-F&CC 4-6-0. She was steamed up, and with a caboose, made the round trip to Mancos, apparently without any problems, on a sunny, cloudless day. The crew later said they had looked in vain for someone—hopefully me again—to be taking pictures of their train, but they saw no cameras for the entire day!

No. 20 was put away in the Durango roundhouse, the fires were dropped, water was drained, and she was never to steam

again. Months later, when it was learned that the Rocky Mountain Railroad Club was buying the Ten-wheeler (with contributions from railfans), a couple of enginemen concerned that plans might be in the works to operate the engine, cautioned me not to steam her up. When I asked why, they declined to say just why, but hinted that they had made the run of December 27 knowing that some serious defect existed, which an ICC inspector would have cause to "red tag" the engine. What they were hinting at was never discovered, although one time, years later, a large flat spot was found on the boiler, evidently caused by some turnover accident. The firebox also did not seem to be as thick as it should be, one authority on such things opined later. However, it remains a mystery to this day.

THE RIO GRANDE SOUTHERN DURING A SAN JUAN WINTER

MOST ELUSIVE of Colorado's mountain railroads was the Rio Grande Southern narrow-gauge line, located in the extreme southwestern part of the state, in a region with few good all-year roads. By 1950, operations were irregular on the RGS; sometimes, a couple of weeks went by between trains. When, in September of 1951, I learned that this was to be the final year for the RGS, a fact not publicized, but just sort of whispered among the employees, I resolved to make an effort to capture some of the final action on the line.

September livestock runs kept the rails shiny on the north end for a short period, but nothing much operated after that until the final cleanup runs in late November. Winter, however, was a time of the year when no one wandered around the Rio Grande Southern with cameras. However, I spent five days chasing the final operations between Ridgway and Rico. The narrow road over Lizard Head Pass was snowpacked, and the country lay under a blanket of three or more feet of snow. But fortunately, it was a week of little wind and cloudless blue skies. After the first day, I scuffed marks across the road, and during the five days I was shooting pictures, no other vehicles used the road between Rico and Ophir. (Later, I learned that only on weekends was there any traffic during the

WHILE GALLOPING GOOSE No. 4 took siding on September 15, 1948, to wait for Extra 455 West at Peake, the household goods of a section crew moving to section house at the summit were being unloaded. Train 372 would then continue on its run to Ridgway, 13 miles downhill. Mudhen No. 455 had been wrecked in a runaway on the same hill on June 16, 1943. The Class K-27 2-8-2 shows how a cab from a standard-gauge D&RGW engine looked on the Mikado after the RGS rebuilt the engine. The D&RGW had traded No. 455 to the RGS for Ditcher 030 in 1939.

A FINAL LIVESTOCK EXTRA from Lizard Head Pass was being made up on September 26, 1951. A string of loaded cars was being set out on the passing track. Then, the engine will go out on the wye to pick up the other cars, the caboose will be coasted down the mainline to be coupled up, and the train will head for Ridgway. Two helpers will be picked up en route at Placerville. The stack of new untreated ties will never be used by the RGS, and they will be sold by the dismantlers later for 10 cents each—although, in the meantime, most of them will be stolen.

THE LAST ORE TRAIN from Rico came rumbling past the photographer on November 17, 1951. The engine had just taken water at Coke Ovens tank, and the train was approaching the steep grade to Lizard Head Pass. It is a tonnage train, with the four boxcars each having a heavy load of frozen concentrate, piled over the trucks in each car. There was no need to close the doors, as there was no danger of the rock-hard material either falling out or being stolen. At Montrose, the transfer crew will have to use a paving breaker to get the frozen ore out of the cars.

winter, when people in the area traveled to Telluride on visits, etc. Through traffic avoided the road, as part of it was still nothing but dirt, and the rest often was of an indifferent gravel surface.)

Temperatures at night at Rico would go below zero, and it would be 10:00 a.m. or later before the sun came over the surrounding mountains, and by 4:00 p.m., the Dolores Valley was again in shadow. However, up at Lizard Head Pass, the sun seemed very warm, so warm in fact that I changed clothes to get rid of my "long johns," which kept me none too warm in Rico.

Back in September, I had located a rocky outcropping in-between the trestles of the Ophir Loop, excellent for possible photographs. However, now (in November) the vague path down from the road to the track was lost in deep snow, and some chin-high drifts. By hanging onto low branches, I managed to more-or-less slide down to the RGS roadbed. The train had packed the snow on the track, and the ties could not be seen. To cross a trestle, each tie had to be located by gingerly testing. And even then, a couple of times what seemed to be a tie was only packed snow, which gave way under foot! It was slow going, but I finally reached the photo location. Thereupon ensued a long, very cold wait in the shadows of the mountainside. The sun did not reach the Ophir Loop trackage at this time of the year, which was located on the north face of the steep slopes of Yellow Mountain.

There was just enough breeze to ruffle the trees to make one imagine that a train was close, but eventually the unmistakable clank and soft exhaust of the helper engine drifting light downgrade could be heard. So, I clicked the camera's shutter a couple of times to "warm it up" and then snapped pictures of D&RGW No. 452, as it came through the cut and across the trestle. The startled fireman did not even wave, but his face showed disbelief that I was standing there.

Again there was a long wait—maybe an hour or more—and "my goodness," it was getting cold there amid all those rocks and snow! Then... the sound of the train could be heard again, at first just a low rumbling noise. As the train got closer, the exhaust of the airpump could be heard, and along came RGS No. 461, with an odd mixture of revenue loads and deadhead non-revenue cars. Again, the fireman was startled when he saw me, but he smiled as he passed. The resulting photographs are among the ones I treasure most of this little narrow-gauge road.

It would have been almost impossible to climb back to the pickup truck the way I had come, so I followed the train across the trestles to Ophir. Then, I hiked up the road for nearly half a mile to the truck. While hiking, I watched the train now and then, at first way below, then, stretching out as it rounded Windy Point—very tiny below the high cliffs at that location—and the train vanished as a small black line as it neared the Ames water tank. I believe I never put so much effort and incurred so much risk in taking pictures as my struggles at the once-famous Ophir Loop of the RGS on that cold long-ago November day in 1951.

THE SUMMER SCRAPPING OF THE RIO GRANDE SOUTHERN

AS THE SUMMER OF 1952 approached, in my guise as "Abandoned Lines Reporter" of the *Narrow Gauge News*, that single-sheet mimeographed publication issued occasionally at Alamosa, there was much wondering as to when and in what manner the Rio Grande Southern was to be dismantled. The once-famous narrow-gauge line was appraised at $500,000. However, the terms of sale set by the District Federal Court in Denver were such that the dismantler would be bidding only on the rails and track fittings, and such engines and rolling stock not sold separately by the receiver. The real estate, buildings and trestles were not up for bidding, but were involved in a partial settlement with the counties on claims based on years of unpaid real-estate taxes. During July of 1952, the scrap contract was awarded to the Hyman-Michaels firm of Chicago, who subcontracted the work to the Luria Brothers of California. They, in turn, hired the Brinkerhoff Brothers of Rico to do the actual rail-removal work.

The only operational locomotives remaining on the RGS roster were: No. 42, the 1887 Class C-17 2-8-0 stored in the Durango roundhouse, and No. 461, the Class K-27

2-8-2 at Ridgway. All the remaining cars were at Ridgway. Many stretches of track between Dolores and Rico had been washed out, including the grade. So, the dismantling crews began tearing-up track at two places, working back to both Durango and Ridgway, the southern and northern ends of the line. Offices of the dismantler were set up in part of the RGS offices located upstairs in the Durango depot of the D&RGW. Their man, Charlie, was thus handy to talk to RGS General Manager C. W. Graebing, who—despite having virtually nothing to do then—showed up five days a week at his office in the depot. (I once caught him reading a copy of *Trains* magazine one day!) As I had bought Caboose 0404, Charlie made a deal to borrow my caboose to use with Engine 42, and he offered to pay rental in the form of scrap "goodies" of one kind or another. This was an offer I found very rewarding, better than cash for me. To avoid much running back and forth to water tanks, he rented the tender of Mudhen 452 from the D&RGW, to use for an auxiliary water supply. Engine 452 was currently dead and ready for scrapping, so the tender was not in use by the D&RGW.

On September 11, 1952, RGS No. 42 headed out of Durango, with my caboose trailing behind, as well as the extra tender. The summer growth of weeds, plus a thick coat of rust on the rails, made it hard work for the worn-out engine, whose crew used the whistle for extra-long warnings at grade crossings. However, the 2-8-0 put on a good show as she crossed the Lightner Creek trestle at Franklin Junction and came along through Wildcat Canyon, mowing weeds with occasional stretches of bad slipping. Eventually Engine 42 reached a point a few miles north of Dolores, where the removal of rails had already begun. Beyond this point, there were huge washouts, and track was in the Dolores River.

Up at Ridgway, workmen had demolished the bodies of various cars, which were originally built for the Colorado & Southern. The RGS had purchased them when the old South Park line was abandoned. They made useful, sturdy flatcars, with their steel underframes and heavier and more modern trucks than the D&RGW used. The Brinkerhoffs, used to moving mining machinery in the Colorado mountains, found no large problems in trucking these flatcars down to where No. 42 was working. They also de-

BELOW THE OPHIR NEEDLES, one of the last northbound Rio Grande Southern freight trains was doing a little switching at Ophir. Engine 461 was coupling cars that had been left on that station's spur. The date was November 17, 1951, and snow had blanketed the Ophir area. In No. 461's train were the last revenue loads, concentrates from Rico, destined for transfer at Montrose to go to a smelter in Utah.

cided that it was a waste of time and energy to use a steam-powered work train alongside the highway, when scrap could be loaded on motor trucks. From there, it would be hauled down to a stockpile at Gallup, New Mexico, on the Santa Fe system. So, No. 42 backed down to Dolores, wyed, and with the caboose, extra tender ahead and trailing flatcars, moved to a point up in Lost Creek Canyon to start work there.

The Brinkerhoffs converted the No. 7 Galloping Goose into a flatbed "truck," and it was used along with the roadmaster's No. 6 work Goose, with a flatcar trailing, to salvage track material between the washouts. When finished at one place, they then trucked the Goose and its flatcar to the next segment of isolated track. The same method was used north of Rico, using a combination of Galloping Geese, highway trucks and a steam-powered work train, hauled by engine No. 461.

For living quarters for their workers, the dismantler employed some of the work cars from the Bridge & Building Department. These old passenger cars long ago were converted to sleeping and commissary cars. Incidentally, two cars got away at Coke Ovens and went into the ditch a couple of miles to the south, where the track was washed out. The steam-powered train began work at this point.

I took several days off in October to go over west of Durango to watch the works. A Californian railfan happened to come by the Alamosa motel the day before, and being a friend of another good friend of mine, I took him along on the trip. He had never been in Colorado before, and he had exaggerated ideas of what winter was like in the Centennial State. And it turned out he was apprehensive about blizzards, snowslides and avalanches, of which at this particular time, Colorado had none for him to see! We walked down the track about a mile from the top of the Lost Cañon grade, to see No. 42 and the crew of track scrappers. It turned out that the engine crew made my friend very uneasy by looking at the clouding-up sky and predicting, "...sure looks like snow before morning...." Late in the day, when it was time to haul the loaded cars up to a point on the highway for unloading, we climbed aboard Caboose 0404, as Engine 42 struggled to get underway. The heavy loads of rails trailing behind, while the extra tender

and caboose were ahead of her. The old 2-8-0 was gradually getting going, when suddenly, she slipped badly and at the same time the airpump quit!

I had jumped off the caboose to watch, when I realized that while the engine was in forward motion, the entire train was slowly going backward, and the fireman was beating the airpump with a big wrench without coaxing it into action. Beyond the loaded flatcars I could see the end of the rail, only a few hundred feet away, or so it seemed. I instantly had visions of the entire outfit rolling off that end of track, with my caboose ending up as kindling wood between the engine and that extra tender! I cannot remember the Californian's name, but I handed him a brake club and told him to get out on the other platform of the caboose and start twisting the brake wheel as hard as he could. At the same time, I was doing the same thing on the platform next to the engine—fully prepared to "pull the pin" if necessary. Of course, I was hoping to save the caboose and tender from joining any derailment. It was not a very good hope, with some 25 tons of tender on a 2.0-percent grade pushing against the caboose.

The California railfan showed that he was alarmed, and he told me later how he had read about the awful results of runaways in the Colorado mountains. And he did not expect to take part in one! Anyway, looking beyond the slowly backing engine, I could see the end of the rails looking mighty near, and I uttered a prayer to bless that wrench being wielded by the fireman to awaken that pump, and then—suddenly—it came alive, and within what seemed to be only a few seconds, the train stopped. While the engine kept working away, once again the engineer got the train underway, and this time, we topped the end of the grade—with a general feeling of great relief all around. It really was not much of a "runaway," but my friend did not feel that way about it at all! Later, he expressed the opinion we had been in great danger, and I learned later that was what he informed all his acquaintances out in the Golden State.

After staying overnight in the rather rudimentary "diggings" at "Benny's Hogan" in Dolores, we headed northward to see what was going on with the scrapping on that portion of the line. The dismantler had torn up rail as far as within a short distance of Lizard

THE SOUTH-END dismantling train of the Rio Grande Southern was having to work hard to get over the rusty rails, with plenty of weeds making the rails slippery as of September 11, 1952. Engine 42, the 1887 Class C-17—formerly a D&RG 2-8-0—was the only engine left on the south end of the line, although the Consolidation was nearly worn out. The sole caboose had been sold to me by the receiver, and it was loaned to the dismantler, to be paid for with assorted artifacts instead of money. To save many trips running for fuel and water, the tender off dead Mudhen 452 was rented from the D&RGW. The train was about halfway to Hesperus, location of the first water tank. Later, the crew told me that No. 42 was using water at an alarming rate, and they had 10 miles yet to go, most of it up grades as steep as 2.5 percent. I bought old No. 42 during the following year, to keep it from being scrapped, confident that someone eventually would want it. After years of wandering, the 2-8-0 returned to Durango as part of the Durango & Silverton Narrow Gauge Railroad, who is rebuilding No. 42 for operation on their line late in 1995 (at the last report).

Head Pass, where No. 461 was simmering, with flatcars being loaded with rails and fittings. The workers were having some slow going due to most of the spikes being the old doubleheaded Greer type (nicknamed "Jeffery" spikes), which resisted quick-and-efficient use of a clawbar in the usual manner. The men had hunted all over for some type of special bar for this use, but nothing could be found—because there was not any! Belatedly, they learned that the regular clawbar was used. However, instead of placing it at right angles to the rail, the base of the bar should be placed on the base of the rail, and in line with the rail. Meanwhile, they had struggled, and many of the spikes were in untreated ties and would not come out, with the heads breaking off when forced. After all of their problems, the dismantler's men found they had wasted their time salvaging these odd spikes, as people came from many miles around to load up their cars and pickup trucks in the belief that they were rare and valuable. A short boom in Jeffery spikes saw antique dealers pricing them at $5.00 each... then at $10.00... and—amazingly—at one time, I saw an advertisement offering these old spikes at $40.00 each!

Approaching Rico, we came to a place where a couple of trees spread their branches out over the gravel road. Just then, my companion cried out in great alarm, pointing down the road ahead! Not seeing anything alarming, I nevertheless jammed on the brakes to slide to a stop! Ahead on the road was about a half inch of snow that had fallen as No. 42's engineer had predicted. However, the sun had evaporated all of it from the road, except in that shady spot. My friend had never seen snow up close, and he handled it with considerable curiosity and was concerned that I was going on toward Lizard Head. When I left him the next day at Montrose to catch a bus to Grand Junction and then head west for home, he told me that he had never been so worried. He was thankful he had escaped from a region where trains ran away and one might at any moment be buried in snowslides or blizzards—all of this on a bright, sunny day, with not a flake of snow around! Months later, some of his friends asked me what I had done, and I said his version of Engine 42 losing her air was much more frightening than mine! And this is not to mention what he said about the great dangers of snow in Colorado!

On a later trip, I found No. 461 was working on removing rails from the Butterfly Trestle, which was the northernmost of those included in the Ophir Loop. And again a sunny day seemed somber, as one realized that this was indeed the last train on that once-hailed engineering marvel, the Rio Grande Southern's famous Ophir Loop. Down at Vance Junction I was prepared a few days later to photograph what would be the final operation on the Telluride Branch. The last run to Telluride, as originally intended for the previous November, had not taken place. A break in the power company's water flume near the junction had resulted in ice forming over the track up to three feet thick. Now, the dismantler had the same problem again, and no engine ever went up to Telluride to bring out the six stranded D&RGW boxcars. The cars were scrapped in place, and a Goose was trucked-in to scrap the branch.

Snow was starting to fall heavily in the high places, so the dismantler decided to tie up the steam outfits for the winter. As it turned out, the north end did not use steam power again, relying on the Goose and highway trucks. On a gloomy morning in November of 1952, I waited at Mancos as little No. 42 took on water at the old tank where so many engines had done this over the years. A small boy on his way to school, stopped to watch, and he and I were the only observers as the old engine slowly steamed away from the wooden water tank. There was no band and no crowd, as the last steam locomotive in Montezuma County moved away. I wondered what the kid's teacher said when he explained why he was late? The train worked through deepening snow as far as Grady siding "…out in nowhere, up in the hills." There, the engine was drained for the winter, and then the crew had a rough ride out over a dirt trail in a pickup truck.

Some of us hiked in on a March day during the following year, expecting to take pictures of the train buried in snow. What a surprise we had! The sun had reflected heat from the engine and cars, and the open area was bare of snow. It almost appeared that it was a summer scene. We had made a long slog through a foot of snow for nothing! After being steamed up again, the engine worked into Durango on March 30, 1953, and

the dismantler elected to use Galloping Geese for the remainder of the south-end rail removal. By the end of April, the work was finished, and the workers completed the job at Hesperus. They posed near the same oddly crooked tree that showed in the only known photograph of the first passenger train over 60 years earlier.

I had an unsuccessful chase of Engine 42 later that year, after buying it from the dismantler. The D&RGW agreed (without any quibbling this time) to move the 2-8-0 dead in a freight train to Alamosa for the same rate it hauled new diesel engines for Western roads over its mainline, $1.79 per mile. So, I oiled the engine liberally at Durango, went home to Alamosa. When I learned No. 42 had reached Chama, I got up before dawn one winter morning and drove there by way of Cumbres Pass, so I could oil the engine one more time. At that time, the pass was open in the fall until it just naturally was closed by snow, whenever that might occur. Then, the road would not be plowed again until the following year, when fishing season approached.

It was snowing lightly as I drove up the Conejos Canyon east of Cumbres Pass. The person driving ahead of me had obviously been part way up La Manga Pass, changed his mind about going on and turned around so he could head back toward Antonito. Still, the snow was only a few inches deep on the road, so I kept driving up the grade toward the pass. However, when I got near Cumbres, I was shocked to discover that my chains, shovel and bucket of sand had been removed. I remembered that this had happened when the car had been employed for some Boy Scout expedition, and I had not replaced these items. My goodness! What a time to discover this!

The snow was starting to drift across the old dirt road near Cumbres Pass; however, I made it on down into Chama, New Mexico, where I found my engine coupled into the eastbound freight train, due to head out soon. I used some warm oil from the engine supply house to lubricate old Engine 42 liberally, as the snow started falling thickly. After the doubleheader whistled off, I drove out to the first grade crossing west of Chama to watch and maybe take a snow picture. By that time, the snow was coming down so heavy that I could not see the road, and the train quickly vanished in the storm. It was obvious that I had been the last person to drive over Cumbres Pass this winter. So, it was home via a long detour to Española, New Mexico, and then up U.S. Highway 285, where I found the train just arriving at Antonito—long after dark—plastered with snow. So, once again I oiled those worn bearings on No. 42.

RGS EPILOGUE:

An historical 171-mile railroad had been abandoned. You would expect to see headlines in the press? And there would at least be a big story? Amazingly, neither was the case! So, when a good friend requested that I pick up copies of the local daily newspaper for a week before and after the final runs of the RGS the next time I was in Durango, I complied with his request. Knowing that he had a good sense of humor and appreciated the ridiculous, I did indeed pick up the couple dozen copies for him. While waiting for the copies, I told the lady clerk why I was getting the papers. I said to her my friend wanted to clip them for items about the abandonment of the Rio Grande Southern Railroad. She replied, "The Denver & Rio Grande hasn't been abandoned." To which I asserted, "Of course it hasn't; I'm talking about the other narrow-gauge railroad out of here, the Rio Grande Southern." She: "We have only one railroad, the D&RG." Me: "You do *now*, as the other railroad has been abandoned!" This was also the desk where the local news was turned in, but she made no move to pick up a pencil and make notes.

Noting the sign also read "Society Editor," I then tried another tack, and I asked if she knew Mrs. Clayton W. Graebing, whose name I had seen occasionally in the newspaper's club doings. She admitted that she knew Mrs. Graebing very well. So, then I told her that Mrs. Graebing's husband had been the general manager and auditor of the Rio Grande Southern Railroad, and for many years had his general offices upstairs in the Durango depot. Again, there was no move to pick up a pencil, and the abandonment and last runs of the RGS went ignored insofar as Durango's daily newspaper was concerned. Many railfans found this attitude incredulous, but it was the norm in much of Colorado. Where else in the United States was there a place or region where a 171-mile railroad could close down and be completely ignored by the press?

MY FAVORITE RAILROAD: THE COLORADO & SOUTHERN RY.

WHEN FIRST ASKED what my favorite railroad was, it took some thinking to come to the conclusion that it must be the Colorado & Southern Railway—now a vanished line that became part of the vast Burlington Northern system. Why the C&S? There was a very different aura about this railroad, casting it as very much unlike the Denver & Rio Grande Western. The Colorado & Southern came across as a sort of family line; everyone seemed to know everyone else, and usually they were on friendly terms. It was more like a shortline than the amount of miles it operated indicated. The C&S had always been far from prosperous, and although it had the only north-south mainline in a large area of the West, the expected traffic from that alignment never materialized.

Although the Colorado & Southern Railway started out in 1898 as an independent, early in this century the road became a stepchild of the Burlington Route. Although its offices were in Denver, its president until the final years, was some Burlington official in Chicago. It was the last railroad in Denver to dieselize, and it operated many steam locomotives well into the 1960's (including CB&Q steamers), symbolic of its red-ink bottom-line figures. In fact, it was only because of its subsidiary Fort Worth & Denver, that the C&S was able to report good statistics at its annual meetings.

When I moved to Golden, Colorado, in 1958, I was amazed to see all the 2-8-0 types operating short consists, with wooden cabooses, which worked out of Denver's Rice Yard. Most of these runs were just switching turns, undoubtedly all losers in revenue. However, for mainline work, there were a number of husky 2-8-2's and a half dozen

WITH A BACKGROUND of the highest mountains in Colorado, the Colorado & Southern Railway's rotary snowplow was heading for Climax to clear this branch, on a rare trip during February of 1960. Enthusiastic photographers followed its progress up the grade above Leadville. One fellow—somewhat mixed up in what a rotary plow would do—placed himself *downhill* from the track just outside Climax, and he was momentarily buried under huge amounts of snow, thrown out by the machine. He had seen the plow throwing snow to the right, not realizing that it could switch to throwing it to the left, as well! C&S Engine 641, a 2-8-0, provided the motive power for the big C&S rotary snowplow.

THE ISOLATED 14-MILE BRANCH of the Colorado & Southern Railway attracted railfan photographers. It ran from 10,200-foot Leadville to Climax, at 11,316-foot Fremont Pass. C&S Engine 638 was a chunky 2-8-0, working a train across a snowslide area in March of 1955. This branch had been the last few miles of the old South Park narrow-gauge line from Denver to Leadville. And after all track beyond Climax was abandoned in 1937, this remainder eventually was standard-gauged. It connected with the D&RGW at Leadville, and it turned-over to them the many loads of molybdenum ore and concentrates from the big AMAX mine at Climax. Many years later, the mine closed due to world competition and the price of molybdenum. Eventually, the owning railroad, then the Burlington Northern, sold the branch for use as a tourist railroad.

heavy 2-10-2's. The Denver roundhouse and its area still had some third-rail trackage in place (in concrete areas), relics of the narrow-gauge C&S lines, the last of which operated as late as 1941. In fact, there was still a "South Park" in their list of lines, although it was standard gauge, a remnant of the mainline. This had been part of that much-storied narrow-gauge route and was now only a yard turn serving industries in southwest Denver. Several C&S men still liked to say: "I'm a South Park man," dating their seniority back to the 1930's.

The Colorado & Southern's attitude toward freight shippers and passengers contrasted markedly with the Denver & Rio Grande Western, to the latter road's disfavor. Shippers received good service, and there was no grumbling about short hauls. Special groups found a passenger department ready to clean dusty, idle equipment and operate excursion specials.

If you ventured into the main offices, a genial chief clerk, Patrick Walsh, was ready to help find answers to questions. He might sit you down to look through old timetables or other files. The resident vice-president was easily to be seen, and his affable successor and the last president, John Terrill, was a friendly sort, not puffed-up with the title of his position.

After dealing with the D&RGW, it was a very refreshing experience to encounter Superintendent G. B. Hoover in Denver. This was when I was inquiring about handling my three flatcars of locomotives from Alamosa out to the end-of-track on the Federal Center line in Lakewood. Fortunately for me,

there had been a delay in shipping, and it was the C&S's turn to manage this jointly operated former interurban line in the western part of metro Denver. The D&RGW people had given me a firm "no" about moving the engines out to Lakewood, and they insisted that I must unload the cars in downtown Denver, at their local freight yard. Superintendent Hoover wanted to talk about the "old days," and it was a nervous wait for me at last to hear his casual, "Oh, certainly, we will move the cars for you. Just tell our people where you want them spotted, and we'll wye them for you if they need it." That was to typify all my dealings when I had to

do business with the C&S. Road Foreman of Equipment R. E. "Mickey" Hansen, another old-time railroader who had risen from the job of fireman, was another genial-and-helpful person.

When the C&S gave us their Leadville rotary snowplow, the D&RGW at first declined to handle it to Pueblo, offhandedly alleging that it was "unseaworthy." President Terrill sent off a couple of C&S mechanical people, demanding a joint inspection with D&RGW people, and suddenly, the snowplow became "seaworthy." However, the D&RGW still charged $1,400 to move the rotary plow— which paid for a work train doing some

ballasting their roadmaster had long requested. From Pueblo to Denver the plow trailing along behind a C&S caboose on the "Joint Line" (operated by the C&S, Santa Fe and Rio Grande).

The extended use of steam engines on the C&S provided camera fans with years of interesting operations, extending from Texline in the south to the windy wastelands and rocky canyons of Wyoming. Their handsome *Texas Zephyr*, which ran between Denver and Dallas until the end, was one of the West's best streamliners, despite dwindling patronage. When I ate breakfast aboard this train en route back to Denver from Mexico in

THE ROTARY SNOWPLOW kept in Leadville by the Colorado & Southern was making one of its infrequent trips—sometimes as much as five years apart. The big plow was setting out to open the line to Climax on February 11, 1960. Behind the train is the stormy mountain range that includes Colorado's highest mountains, a dramatic scenic backdrop for Leadville. After dieselization of this line during the 1970's, the C&S gave the rotary plow to the Colorado Railroad Museum. However, we would have to pay the $1,400 the D&RGW wanted to trail it behind a freight train to Pueblo, to interchange with the C&S. At first, the D&RGW refused to move the plow; however, after a joint inspection insisted by C&S President Terrill, the big plow was hauled by the D&RGW.

1965, it was truly a delight. I looked out from the dining car at the beautiful, snowy Front Range of the Rockies—as this sleek train glided along toward Colorado's mile-high capital. However, my trip was over-toned by the knowledge that not many more trips were ahead for this immaculate, silver Colorado & Southern streamliner.

THE ONLY ROTARY SNOWPLOW the Colorado & Southern Railway owned was kept at Leadville, Colorado, where it was needed sometimes only once in every five years or so. The plow was last used in 1960 and 1965. Then, with dieselization of the Climax Branch, the standard-gauge 2-8-0 was given to Leadville, and the rotary plow was given to the Colorado Railroad Museum in 1972. This snowplow was built in 1900 for use on the Alpine Tunnel portion of the South Park line; however, the big machine was too heavy for this part of the old South Park narrow-gauge line. So, the plow spent the remainder of its years alternating between narrow- and standard-gauge usage. For years, it was stationed at Como, in South Park. Then, it went to Cheyenne, for use on the Wyoming line. The plow had been so infrequently used that its running gear was virtually in new condition when we examined it in 1972, showing very little wear.

THE BURLINGTON ROUTE

THE CB&Q RAILROAD—or the "Q," as the sprawling Chicago, Burlington & Quincy often was called—was like many other Midwestern and prairie roads and had a number of mixed trains and "doodlebug" routes. During the 1920's and earlier, the company had replaced many secondary steam-powered passenger trains with gas-electric cars (called doodlebugs), but as such lines had less and less traffic, the CB&Q rebuilt a number of these cars into diesel locomotives. Other gas-electrics had their power units removed and became good steel combination cars for use on mixed trains. On some branches, the resulting trains were unusual in appearance, for at first glance, it looked as if there was a gas-electric at each end of what was often a considerable train.

One of the CB&Q's tri-weekly operations was the Sterling (Colorado)–Cheyenne (Wyoming) route, a 103-mile remnant of a line that had once been bright with hopes for expansion, where wooden Pullmans and "silk-and-spice" express cars were handled daily. Now, the little High Plains stops were nearly ghost towns or just weedy sidings.

During the early 1960's, the "Q" kept one last light 4-6-0 as a reserve engine for the line, for heavy seasonal traffic normal for that region of northeastern Colorado, but it looked as though the handsome Ten-wheeler, No. 919, would no longer be needed. After being approached by railfans, CB&Q officials agreed that for the payment of an extra hundred dollars, they would substitute No. 919 for the former gas-electric engine. And this made for an excellent one-way fan trip one beautiful summer day, with a couple of stops and even "photo run-bys" en route from Cheyenne to Sterling. School children of the

SUPPLEMENTING the "Texas Zephyr" on the Colorado & Southern and Fort Worth & Denver roads between Dallas and Denver was this very necessary "local" train. The train handled the head-end material shipped on this route, and it served all the little places and post offices along the line. Train 8–28 was on the final leg of this 801-mile run, photographed as it departed from Trinidad, Colorado. At this time—during April of 1951—heavy Pacific No. 551 had a short train, the sparse passenger traffic being handled by the single coach.

THE CHEYENNE ENGINE TERMINAL of the Colorado & Southern Railway was largely used by steam power until the early 1960's. Even the switch engine was a steam locomotive, sometimes this chunky 800-series 2-8-2. With the end of steam power, down came the roundhouse and the former terminal became sort of a "clearing house" for a large assortment of non-revenue cars, most of which sat idle for years. One day during the 1980's, the C&S trainmaster invited me to come up to Cheyenne to look at a wedge plow, now surplus. After looking at it and wondering how we could get rid of the extra 25 tons of rock ballast, I drove back to Golden to see what could be arranged. On the same day, the trainmaster had the snowplow tied onto the rear of a Denver-bound freight. And it was spotted in the Denver yard later that day—with no place to get rid of that rock. It took two big cranes to move the C&S car onto our property at the museum, most of the cost being caused by that darned rock!

FOR AN EXTRA $100, the Chicago, Burlington & Quincy agreed to substitute 4-6-0 No. 919 for this excursion trip northeast of Denver. No. 919 had been retained as standby power for this train by the Burlington Route. This scene was photographed on a two-day round trip from Sterling, Colorado, to Cheyenne, Wyoming, in 1956. Normally, this CB&Q mixed train looked as if it was a train with a gas-electric "doodlebug" at each end of the consist. The one at the head end had been converted into a diesel-electric locomotive, while the one at the rear was now just a combination baggage-coach, after the motors had

been removed. They managed the tri-weekly 103-mile trip (each way) through rolling prairie and natural grasslands.

BURLINGTON ENGINE No. 919 sits in a public park in Nebraska now. However, in 1956, she was standby power for the CB&Q's tri-weekly mixed train from Sterling, Colorado to Cheyenne, Wyoming. Heavier CB&Q locomotives did not dare to venture out on the 1880's light rail of the branch. This train normally was handled by one of the "Q's" distinctive homemade diesel-electrics, converted from gas-electric passenger cars.

nearly ghost town of Grover, Colorado, descended upon the train dressed as ghosts, and we had a brief escorted tour of the almost-vanished town, amid tumbleweeds and thistles. It was a great day for all, and the company took the opportunity to move over 30 freight cars that accumulated along the line. Today, No. 919 sits in the park of a Nebraska town, having escaped the scrapper's torch by a sympathetic management.

Incidentally, it should be mentioned that the Burlington Route also operated gas-electric units and trailers from Sterling to Holdrege, Nebraska, for a number of years—sharing station tracks with the Cheyenne–Sterling equipment. The CB&Q was an early convert to the "doodlebug," or self-propelled railbus, and the railroad used them for secondary mainline runs, as well as for branchline local trains. And by the early 1930's, the "Q" had garnered the largest fleet of gas-electrics of any American railroad up to that time. Beyond that, it can be said that the Burlington's fleet of gas-electrics led to the development of the first streamlined train in 1934, *The Pioneer Zephyr*. The power unit for this sleek silver train incorporated an engine compartment, baggage section and RPO compartment (gas-electric style). Therefore, the first *Zephyr* might be called a "streamlined doodlebug train"!

THE BURLINGTON ROUTE adopted gas-electric cars for many of its branch lines, and then —as such trains were discontinued in the 1930's and 1940's—instead of scrapping the cars, the motors were removed, and they were converted into combines, like this one at Sterling, Colorado.

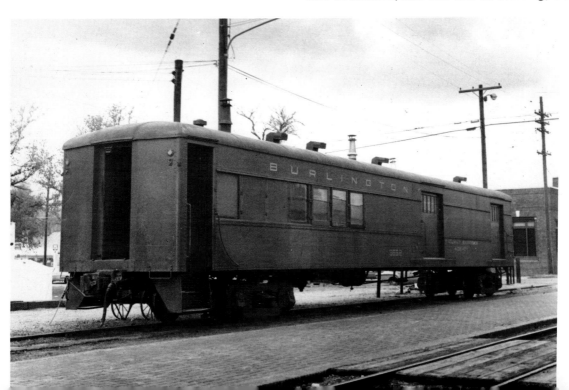

IF YOU WERE LUCKY to find a day with good weather at Tennessee Pass—and I never did—and a day when freight trains were moving eastbound, some very impressive action occurred. From Minturn, north of Tennessee Pass at 7,825 feet in elevation, it was customary for the Denver & Rio Grande Western to assign three of their L-131 or L-132 2-8-8-2 articulateds to haul a freight train to the summit tunnel at Tennessee Pass, at 10,240 feet—over 21 miles of steep grades. U.S. Highway 24 more-or-less paralleled the railroad for most of the way, and numerous possibilities for action photographs might occur. However, even on a rainy day, it was show worth watching, as a visitor from Norway and I did on a stormy day, with intimidating lightning effects. By the end of 1956, the 3600-series articulateds had gone to scrap, but trains are still impressive along this mountain mainline in the diesel age—with as many as 10 multiple units being used on coal or ore trains.

CHASING TRAINS

MAINLINE FREIGHT TRAINS OVER TENNESSEE PASS

By Robert A. LeMassena

RIO GRANDE mainline freight trains, running eastward from Grand Junction to Pueblo, were hauled by the railroad's enormous single-expansion 2-8-8-2's in the 3600 series, which had been built by ALCO in 1927 and 1930. At Minturn, at the foot of the ascent to Tennessee Pass, at 10,220 feet in elevation, the grade increased from 1.6 percent to 3.0 percent for the 21 miles up to the summit tunnel. Each train required the addition of two helpers at Minturn, usually the Class L-96 compound-expansion 2-8-8-2's in the 3400 series. One was cut into the middle of the train, while the other one was added just ahead of the caboose. Including a stop for water at Pando, in Eagle Park, the upgrade trip would require about two hours. When diesel-electric engines began to displace the big Class L-131/132 3600's elsewhere, they superseded the older articulated helpers at Minturn, as well as at Tabernash (on the Moffat Tunnel route). Eventually, all three locomotives were 3600's, as this scene—taken at Rex, a few miles south of Minturn—illustrates.

Just east (south according to the compass) of the depot at the summit, the two helpers were cut out of the train and individually reversed on the wye. Then, the articulateds were coupled together, and they drifted downgrade, back to Minturn. These locomotives were so satisfactory that they remained in daily service until the very end of steam operations in 1955–1956. The Denver & Rio Grande's original narrow-gauge line diverged from the present location at Pando and circled the eastern rim of Eagle Park. After crossing the present grade at Mitchell, the narrow-gauge track traversed a sharp half-circle curve and attained the summit of the pass at the 10,443-foot saddle, directly above today's standard-gauge tunnel.

The new standard-gauge line added two tunnels, eliminated two full circles of restrictive 20-degree curvature and reduced the climb by more than 200 feet. The new route shortened the distance by three miles and reduced the maximum gradient from 4.0 percent to 3.0 percent. Because of its steep gradient, the Tennessee Pass line has been considered for abandonment by the present management. However, it still appears to be more practical than the much longer Moffat Tunnel route through Denver, with two summits and 2.0-percent grades, to reach Pueblo.

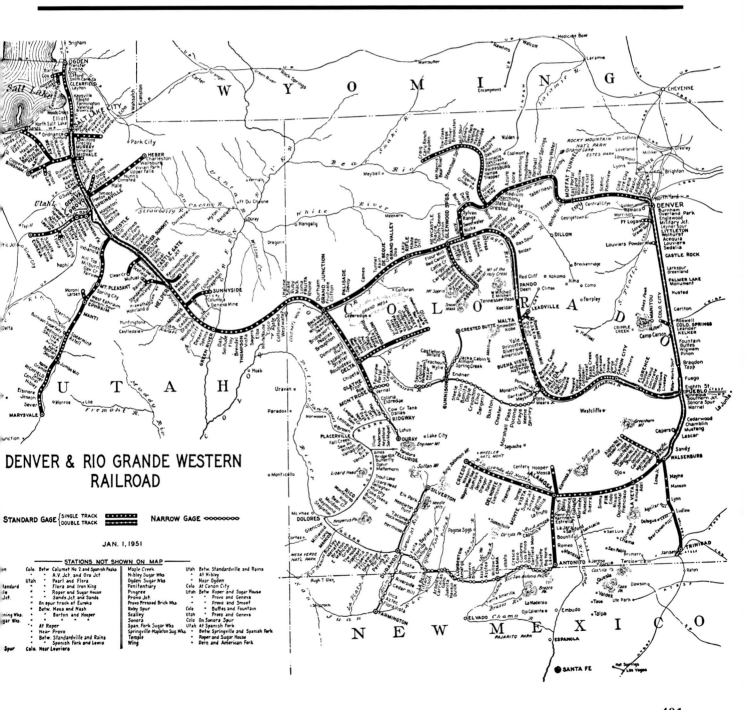

DENVER & RIO GRANDE WESTERN RAILROAD

STANDARD GAGE { SINGLE TRACK / DOUBLE TRACK }   NARROW GAGE

JAN. 1, 1951

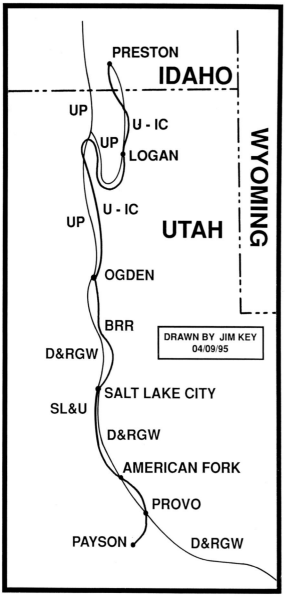

DRAWN BY JIM KEY
04/09/95

ELECTRIC INTERURBAN LINES IN MORMON COUNTRY

THREE COMPANIES combined to provide an electric interurban system that operated from Payson, Utah (67 miles south of Salt Lake City), to Preston, Idaho (130 miles north by rail from Salt Lake City). By 1945, the interurban era had passed them by, and abandonment had only been postponed by the advent of World War II.

After riding Colorado narrow-gauge lines in October of 1945, one night I boarded the westbound *Royal Gorge* passenger train at Grand Junction for the overnight trip to Provo, Utah. There, I intended to board the southernmost of the three electric lines, the Salt Lake & Utah Railroad. The *Royal Gorge* was overloaded with post wartime traffic and was running late. So, it was not long before the first southbound train of the electric line came along, an impressive bright-red steel combination baggage-coach head-end

car, trailed by a coach-observation car. The striped head-end car proclaimed this was the "Orem Route."

The observation car was locked, but the conductor let me go out on the platform, and for the next 18 miles, I had one of the roughest interurban rides ever! The car rocked and rolled as we hurried along at perhaps 50 mph. With difficulty, I managed to hang on and snap a picture of the receding landscape of the valley, backed with snowy mountains.

After arriving in Payson, I just had time for a restorative cup of coffee and a brief look at the repair shops before the return trip began. En route to Salt Lake City, two and a half hours away, we made numerous stops at small towns. And along the way, we had meets with two southbound trains of two cars each, and we overtook a freight train, headed by a steeple-cab electric locomotive. After entering Salt Lake City, we rolled past a number of city blocks in the center of the street. Then, we entered a large interurban station, with trackage shared by the Bamberger Railroad.

The Bamberger, my host for the next 36 miles, used both its older wooden cars and some lightweight steel "bullet" streamlined cars. This line had much better maintained track, and despite numerous stops, the trip took less that an hour and a half. On the left, there were views of the great Salt Lake, and closely paralleling on the right, were the Denver & Rio Grande Western and the Union Pacific, which had been glad to cede to the electric line their local passenger traffic. As the motorman told me, the Bamberger was running parallel buses until the war started. Then, the buses were discontinued in favor of the electric line. Unfortunately, within several years, the buses took over again, ending the electric line.

After a few minutes in the Ogden joint terminal, I boarded a big car of the Utah–Idaho Central Railroad. This car was of typical wooden construction, steel-plated, with truss rods to support a slightly twisted body. It took three hours to reach Preston, the trip slowed by poor track and meets with freight trains moving cars of sugar beets. At one point, there was a branch connection, where there appeared a twisted heavy car. The reason for its condition was apparent, for it was hauling a couple of heavily loaded gondolas of beets. *This was an interurban mixed train for sure!*

The line did not go directly to Preston. Rather, it made a long detour on the alignment of a mountain ridge, so that two points a few miles apart in a straight line were in fact some 25 miles apart by the long route of the interurban line. This enabled the line to reach the Cache Valley, from which the line took its slogan, the "Cache Valley Route." It

A TWO-CAR TRAIN of the Utah–Idaho Central Railroad was photographed at its northern terminal, Preston, in extreme southern Idaho. The

"Cache Valley Route" served a farming area north of Ogden, Utah. However, the line was abandoned several years after my trip in October of 1945.

served a number of small farming communities and one large town, Logan. Only the final 10 miles or less were in Idaho, Preston being another farming center. Here, the interurban line seemed to share a small yard and terminal with a branch of the Union Pacific.

The motorman of the car had to keep changing the speed of the car, notching up his controller and then notching it back down. The problem was that the now poorly maintained track had been laid with parallel rail joints. So, if he kept at a uniform speed,

the passengers soon would be rising and subsiding with the low joints, and it seemed that if he sped up, we would bounce off the rails. Sitting in the rear of the car, I must admit I could not help smiling at the ridiculous appearance of the passengers, seeming to rise and fall, as if on a merry-go-round.

It had been a long day for me, and when the return trip brought me into Ogden, Utah, at about 9:00 p.m., I hurried to a hotel. Soon, I was sound asleep after about 260 miles of interurban riding.

ASSEMBLING A RAILROAD MUSEUM IN COLORADO

WITHOUT REALIZING IT at the time, and certainly with no thought in mind of forming a railroad museum, I made a couple of trips to the yard and terminal of the just-abandoned Midland Terminal Railway at Colorado City (now part of Colorado Springs). The final runs had been made between that place and Cripple Creek during February of 1949, and scrapping of the line was immediately commenced by a Texas firm. The storekeeper at the MT shop was in charge of the sales of almost everything on hand, and there was what really was a railroad museum, engines and rolling stock (for the most part being originals from the late-and-lamented Colorado Midland Railroad, and many items of a smaller nature from the various Cripple Creek District lines).

For example, the storekeeper had bins with dozens of lantern globes—many with initials of those former companies, oddly none at all marked for the Midland Terminal. Not only were there white globes, but ones of various other colors. The only lanterns were a string of damaged ones that had been turned-in by trainmen. There were some rather ancient stampings on these lanterns. All kinds of parts filled hundreds of bins, while the stationery portion had many thousands of printed forms. It was obvious that "housecleaning" had not occurred for many years, indeed if ever, for there were forms of the Colorado Midland, the Florence & Cripple Creek, the Golden Circle Railroad, the High Line and Low Line trolley lines, etc.

AFTER CORNELIUS W. HAUCK of Cincinnati, Ohio, saved Engine 318, the C-18 arrived from Montrose in 1954. No. 318 was moved to the motel site by lowboy trucks. Forty-five years earlier, this 2-8-0 had operated into Alamosa from Salida during a period when the Denver & Rio Grande rented some Florence & Cripple Creek engines. One old-timer, upon seeing the engine on this flatcar, told us of having fired her on a special run to the Crestone Branch back in 1909, substituting for the regular fireman. And he described how the C-18 was lettered and numbered for the F&CC as No. 8. Then, in 1917, No. 8 was bought by the Rio Grande system after the F&CC was abandoned, along with sister engines, 3, 5, 9 and 11.

Many of these forms had been overprinted with the Midland Terminal name.

Tickets? There were virtually thousands, and a big sample book of hundreds of types of coupon styles designed to be issued to include travel over nearby railroads, as well as distant lines.

The equipment of various MT stations had been brought in, and 400-pound cast-iron stoves with the initials of the CM could be obtained for a mere two cents per pound.

So... I bought a couple of pickup-truck loads of items, including a three-wheel velocipede (for only $12), the huge three-tube shop whistle, the Cripple Creek ticket case, and even a Colorado Midland ticket-dater from Buena Vista (still set for the last day of use in 1918). It was a fascinating place to look through; however, the shopkeeper had his moods of reluctance to part with some things. It was as though he just did not want to see items leave, in spite of the fact that he knew that the torch and bonfire was inevitable.

He did give several of us visitors a tour of the place. On the upper floors of the office building were mostly empty shelves, marks in the deep dust and soot, showing that at some time not too far in the past, large quantities of unknown things had been removed for destruction. However, scattered around on the floor were numerous open-top cartons, with the records of various mining firms, even including their corporate seals and stock books. None of these would the storekeeper part with, and in fact, he did not even want us to look into these papers. This was an instance showing why records of the mining industry do not survive for researchers and historians. The people involved simply did not want "outsiders" to go through and read their "doings."

In charge at the end and during the final years of the Midland Terminal Railroad was

BUILT BY BALDWIN in 1890, this is the only surviving standard-gauge steam locomotive of the Rio Grande system. No. 583 was one of a large number of Class 113 2-8-0's, the first Denver & Rio Grande engine designed strictly for standard-gauge use. Later reclassified as Class C-28 Consolidations, this engine became No. 683 during one of those occasions master mechanics seemed to indulge in—when all of the 2-8-0's in this class were renumbered from 636 through 669. In 1947, No. 683 (nee 583) was sold to the San Luis Valley Southern Railway at Blanca, Colorado, and the 2-8-0 became their No. 106, the last steam engine the SLVS used. We obtained the engine in 1955 and transported the engine to Denver on a flatcar. We had a typical "Wabash"-patent oil headlight fabricated in Ohio by supplying a cardboard mockup. Jim Dunlop of California fabricated the old wooden "cowcatcher" (pilot) of the original Denver & Rio Grande style. A builder's-plate collector found that he had acquired one of the original plates, and he gave it to us, so we could have a duplicate cast and placed on the locomotive.

Vice-President and General Manager W. H. McKay, who might best be described as a typical mining man, both in demeanor and attitude. He had no sympathy for those who were history-minded, and he made that brusquely clear. With this sort of "boss" looking over his shoulder, the storekeeper's attitude could be understood. The mining people who controlled most of Cripple Creek and the owners of the railroad, had no interest in tourists or any other activity except mining and the mining district. This typified the negative attitude of people in other mining areas of Colorado, such as Silverton, Creede, Telluride and Leadville. I was to encounter Mr. McKay some 10 years later, and he reminded me forcefully of this recalcitrant attitude.

However, there was almost no one with the dollars and will to save the historic MT engines and rolling stock, so nearly all this equipment went to scrap. An exception was the MT observation chair car No. 29, which was new in 1887, as a coach for the then brand-new Colorado Midland. A retired druggist from Albuquerque, with a sentimental attachment from his boyhood days in Colorado Springs, bought this passenger car and moved it to the New Mexico city, placing it next to his home on the outskirts of the community. Unlike most people buying old railroad cars, he did not just take the body;

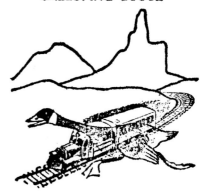

Carried Thru
"NARROW GAUGE COUNTRY"
on the
GALLOPING GOOSE

NARROW GAUGE MOTEL
ALAMOSA, COLORADO

406

THE BURLINGTON ROUTE built a number of these large 4-8-4 types during the final years of steam-locomotive construction. These Northerns were for use on both heavy freight and passenger trains. By the 1960's, they were set aside, no longer needed in the diesel age. Bob Wood persuaded his uncle, General Wood of Sears Roebuck & Company, to put in a word with his close friend, Harry Murphy, president of the Chicago, Burlington & Quincy Railroad. The upshot was the gift of this locomotive to the National Railway Historical Society, to place the 4-8-4 at the new Colorado Railroad Museum. It cost just over $10,000 to build a grade and lay temporary track into the museum grounds, including borrowing an extra girder bridge from the Colorado & Southern Railway, part of the Burlington system. Interestingly, the old Denver, South Park & Pacific locomotive, which sits alongside No. 5629, could be placed inside the tender of the Burlington engine.

he saved the complete car, and he carefully maintained it. He and his wife liked to sit on the big platform late in the day and enjoy the sunsets.

A Californian bought one of the MT cabooses, and it still exists out there somewhere in the "Golden State." A retired conductor bought the beautiful business car, but he saved only the body—stripping it of trucks, etc. Eventually, this car went to a location near Aspen, after a railfan by the name of Del Gerbaz bought it. Later, it was moved to a casino in Las Vegas, Nevada.

Still with no thought of forming a museum, I bought the former D&RGW narrow-gauge 2-8-0 No. 346 in 1951 (as described elsewhere in this publication). The defunct Montezuma Lumber Company had owned it, and the moving of this 1881 relic—a Class C-19 Consolidation—to Alamosa contrib-

uted considerably to the graying of my hair! A determined Rio Grande intent on showing declining freight revenue on its Alamosa–Durango narrow-gauge line, found all sorts of excuses to avoid moving No. 346 "dead" in a freight train. Help from old-timers who wanted to see the engine survive, enabled the movement finally to occur, no thanks to D&RGW management types.

The year 1951 saw the final runs of the remote Rio Grande Southern Railroad, located in scenic southwestern Colorado. This secluded shortline—for one reason or another (chiefly poverty)—was a narrow-gauge museum, not only of ancient rail and other track material, but also of engines and cars, all second or third hand (with the sole exceptions of its "Galloping Goose" railbuses and one caboose).

Unfortunately, 1951 was a bit early for

THE ADOLPH COORS COMPANY operated a fleet of 30 refrigerator cars like this during the 1930's. However, in that era of the steam locomotive, keeping a white car presentable was difficult, so the fleet vanished, despite their advertising value. For a replica of this Coors reefer, the Burlington system brought a similar refrigerator car from Virginia, and Coors provided a billboard sign painter to do the lettering. This car made a very attractive addition, and it is a popular photographic subject with many of the people visiting the museum.

the schemes brought forth to continue operating the RGS as a tourist railroad (at least too early for such things in the U.S.A.), and no one with the appreciation of the problems or with deep pockets showed up to save the poor old RGS! Knott's Berry Farm in Buena Park, California, had dickered with the receiver, and purchased an engine (No. 41, a sister to my No. 346), a 17-foot caboose, a business car and the best operable Galloping Goose, No. 3. People in Boulder, Colorado, had earlier bought RGS Engine 74, a handsome 2-8-0, which had been built for a local line, the Colorado & Northwestern, as well as one of the cabooses.

This left the dismantler with two operable locomotives, a K-27 2-8-2, ex-D&RGW No. 461, on the north end—which he used in

the dismantling of the line—and after seeking a buyer, cut it up for scrap. On the south end, there was No. 42, a worn-out 1887 2-8-0, originally Denver & Rio Grande No. 420, a Class C-17 Consolidation. The dismantler offered to sell me No. 461 for $3,500.00, and offered No. 455 for the same price, which sat largely dis-assembled in the Ridgway roundhouse—with new brasses and other parts rebuilt. I felt that if the two Mikados could be saved, eventually someone would want one (or both), and the investment might be profitable, in addition to keeping the engines from being scrapped. But the logistics were against me, with no cooperation from the D&RGW likely regarding loading or hauling them around to Alamosa. And with the cantankerous D&RGW in all likelihood wanting

WHEN I MOVED TO ALAMOSA in 1948, the D&RGW still had some of its much older wooden "idler" cars, and in poor condition. One day, they went off to Pueblo for scrap. The old cars looked like any old wooden flatcar, except for the coupler arrangements. The newer cars were shorter and made of steel, designed to holdup better, since all standard-gauge cars now had a steel underframe. It was difficult to snap a picture of a trainman changing a coupler's position, as he did it in just seconds. Between Alamosa and Antonito, all freights carried at least two of these cars, as

did freights on the dual-gauge line as far north as Hooper. However, most of the time, one of the idlers was an old narrow-gauge tender in the trains going north, equipped with triple-coupler positions. One of these cars was used at Montrose when switching was done by either gauge engine. The narrow-gauge switcher used an idler while wying the standard-gauge passenger trains. Narrow-gauge railroads learned that to use a narrow-gauge engine directly coupled to standard-gauge cars would result in damaging strains to the locomotive's frame and machinery.

to charge a prohibitive combination of local rates, I had to give up on that hope.

Pierpont Fuller, Jr., the receiver of the RGS, knew of my interest in railroad history, and he was dismayed that the Colorado Historical Society was unable to accept more than a small amount of the old records, and he directed the auditor and general manager, C. W. Graebing of Durango, to give me all of the old paperwork at Ridgway and at other RGS stations. Unfortunately, Mr. Fuller did not tell me about his generosity, and "C. W." just sat on the instructions in Durango. Railroad auditors were trained never to "give away" anything, and it was completely foreign to their way of thinking.

So, Graebing contacted a Ridgway man instead, Billy Talbert, and offered to pay him to clean out the office building and the Ridg-

way depot, and haul the stuff to the dump to burn it! However, Billy viewed the tons of paper and realized that it was more of a task than he cared for, so he urged me to just take it. He was also authorized to sell it to a scrap-paper company if they would buy it, but Ridgway was too distant from Denver, and no one wanted it. So, we made a deal, and he sold me the works for $40.00 that day. His father, Grover Talbert, a retired RGS engineer, who was the Ridgway watchman, urged both of us to make the deal. Grover hoped that somewhere in the massive amount of paper, I would find some of the early papers about his career—and sure enough, one day I was able to present him with the dispatcher's train sheet recording his first trip as an engineer on the RGS back in 1909, plus other assorted papers.

409

RGS GALLOPING GOOSE No. 2 could carry five passengers and 3,000 pounds of freight, mail, or whatever. It was built in a desperate attempt by a poverty-stricken railroad to survive, to keep the mail contract, yet quit operating money-losing mixed trains. The debut of this railbus in the summer of 1931 was a success, and No. 2 was immediately put in regular service between Ridgway and Dolores. Learning from this first Galloping Goose, No. 3 was built with a larger motor, two more sets of wheels—making it much more powerful, with a greater capacity, too. By late 1932, steam-powered trains were uncommon for long periods on the RGS, operating only when enough carload freight was offered. And in the grim years of the Great Depression, that was not much. At times, the road seemed plagued by all manner of troubles, washouts and wash-ins, broken axles, burned-out motors and clutches. And yet, again for weeks at a time, nothing at all would interrupt their regular passing. Bucking snow was hard on motors and clutches. If snow was rather deep, then a "snow train" would be sent ahead over the worst areas, like Lizard Head Pass. A "snow train" simply was a locomotive equipped with a pilot plow larger than the Goose had, and at times, a drag flanger would trail behind the engine with a caboose.

LAST BUILT AND LARGEST of the Galloping Geese, No. 7 retained the old Pierce-Arrow body until the end. However, somewhere along the way, she had lost the distinctive fenders. Seven passengers could crowd into the cab portion. During 1949, the freight body was rebuilt as shown, and bus seats for 30 were installed, with an end door replacing the side doors. Quite a number of excursions were run during the next two years, despite General Manager Graebing at Durango thinking it was more bother than it was worth. After abandonment, the dismantlers stripped off the box body, and the flatbed that remained was used to haul scrap. The ex-railbus would be trucked between washouts. Then, in 1955, the Brinkerhoffs got the job of tearing up the Gunnison lines of the D&RGW. Fortunately, the dismantlers had kept the box body, as well as the rest of old No. 7, and—with considerable work on the motor—the Goose is operated occasionally at the museum. Notice that headlights were missing from No. 7.

THE RGS WORK GOOSE, as it was known, saved running a steam-powered work train, greatly benefiting the cash-starved Rio Grande Southern. The roadmaster could use this car to haul a load of ties, and as the pilot plow indicates, No. 6 could do light snowplowing when needed. As motors wore out, replacements were located in nearby junk yards.

It turned out that I underestimated how much paper there was in that not-very-large building. For $250.00 each I purchased three freight cars from the dismantler, and I spent many very sooty days loading them with RGS paperwork. Then, one day, I learned from the old files that one car, No. 01789, was an 1887 D&RG boxcar originally sold to the RGS to use in construction work. When the old boxcar was about to be burned for scrap during the early 1900's, No. 01789 was twice saved for use in work trains, first as a bunk car, and eventually survived by becoming a water-service work car. Along with it, I discovered (to some dismay) that I had acquired some old crystallized dynamite, and the dismantler suggested giving it to some rancher… and that while he was loading in his truck, we should retire to a local beer joint, a block away. With our mouths open,

ATTACKED VICIOUSLY by woodpeckers (as you can see from the large holes close to the roof line), we wondered how long this relic might survive. When the Florence & Cripple Creek quit in 1915, a new intrastate mining road was equipped with F&CC engines and cars. This was the Montana Southern Railway in southwestern Montana. However, the mine was a great financial disaster, and although most of the narrow-gauge line was torn up, this boxcar and some others remained out at the end of the line, at the ghost town of Coolidge (Elkhorn Mines). Back in the 1930's, some CCC boys went for a "joyride" on this car, but the brakes failed to work, and when No. 588 went off the track, the boys were thrown all over the rough countryside. Gradually, over the next 30 years, the Montana Southern lettering wore off, and "Florence & Cripple Creek 588" began to reappear. On a grand expedition, we rented a diesel flatbed truck and brought the car out of the wilderness. However, the car truly was a sad sight, which brought comments from bystanders along the way. They made incredulous remarks like, "You went all the way to southwestern Montana to get that ruin!?" And a wreck it was, as in the last year, some careless hunters and fishermen had found it a source of firewood. Once repainted with the attractive golden herald, "The Gold Belt Line," model manufacturers chose No. 588 as a good item to produce in scale-model kit form. And thousands of narrow-gauge model railroads have included this F&CC boxcar.

we watched his pickup truck bounce out of the depot driveway, loaded with the dangerous stuff, heading out to blowup old tree stumps... *if not himself as well!*

The other cars were former Colorado & Southern rolling stock: a boxcar and a refrigerator car. The RGS had acquired them when the old South Park line was abandoned in 1937. Their long careers ended eventually as the underframes of tourist cars operating on today's Georgetown Loop Railroad (1995).

A fourth car was also purchased, from a string of stock cars left at Dallas Divide. Into No. 7302, also a former C&S car, I loaded various hardware items, handcar wheels, Telluride's baggage cart, track items and all the miscellaneous odds and ends I could find that should be saved. The dismantler found such small stuff cost more to cleanup than he could obtain for it, so he sold it to me whatever I wanted for $70.00 a ton. This ex-C&S stock car and the other three cars were trucked to Alamosa via Gunnison for only $150.00 each, by one of his drivers.

Long-derelict Galloping Goose No. 2, the first successful one, was mine for another $150.00, plus the same charge for trucking. Into No. 2's body was loaded more paper files, but the condition of the body was so uncertain that we did not dare load it too heavily. The driver decided to go to Alamosa via Ouray and Red Mountain Pass over what was then a gravel-surfaced road, not much improved from its wagon-road days. At a couple of places, the truck driver tied-up traffic, as he had to do some "switchbacking" in order to manipulate his trailer around the sharper curves.

Meanwhile, I was hauling pickup-truck loads of assorted items. The old ex-D&RG harp switchstands took my fancy, and I was able to save about 40 of them, at the cost of many pinched fingers. There were some other early and rather unique switchstands,

412

THIS WAS THE KIND of dump car the Denver & Rio Grande Western used on its narrow-gauge lines for most coal loadings. When new and in good condition, the half-dozen drop-floor sections on each side worked very well. However, with age and neglect, gaps would often occur, sometimes amounting to an inch or more, and the power company at Alamosa complained of the loss of two to five tons of coal during the 112-mile trip from the Monero mines. It was not a good idea to stand close to the track as a train consisting of these cars rolled by, or you might get assaulted by a fairly large chunk of coal. The Alamosa car-repair force did their best, but the cars had far outlived their normal lifetime. Incidentally, these gondolas were called "coal cars" by the D&RGW.

and I had to keep in mind old-man Archimedes and his principles to single-handedly load them. One can laugh now about the 400-pound dwarf stand at Dolores and my awkward efforts to load it on a frosty morning. Twice—just when the stand was nearly up to the truck bed—the thing slid back down to the ground. However, by using blocks and leverage, reinforced with several trips to the nearby cafe for cups of strong black coffee, I finally managed to haul it up into the truck.

At first, the dismantler was not going to bother with small sales, but after he realized that switchstands took up too much space in his truckloads, he agreed to sell them to me at the rate of $70.00 per ton, if I would find the ones I wanted and load them myself. Some of them presented me with quite a task to load aboard my truck. The one in the de-rail at Leopard Creek was down the bank from the highway berm, a good 20 feet. The bank was steep and consisted of loose dirt. I got the target end of the stand up the bank several feet and then lift the heavy foot up several feet. But as the bank got steeper, it was very slow going to manipulate it to the place where I could finally attach the truck's

tow chain to the stand—aided by some old fence wire—and drag it the rest of the way up the embankment.

At Ute Junction (west of Durango), there were four old switchstands that had been laying in the weeds for many years, ever since the Ute Spur had been torn-up in the early 1900's. An old section-man's push car, in rather poor condition, was used to retrieve them and haul them to the nearest grade crossing. At one point, the wooden brake broke, and we were able to just barely stop the car. After stopping, I paused to contemplated what would have happened if it had gotten away on the long downgrade into Durango, with four 220-pound switchstands for ballast!

The Dolores yard had a complete three-way stub switch, consisting of 40-pound rail. At first, the dismantler did not want to bother selling it to me, and he had his men pile it all on the depot platform. I had intended to mark all the pieces, so I could correctly re-lay all the parts. Then, after the dismantler agreed to sell the switch to me, I had a three-ton puzzle to unscramble so I could re-lay it, getting all the pieces in the right places at the museum.

The Rico yard, depot, water tank, other buildings, car bodies and everything else were sold (with the real estate) to the Rico-Argentine Mining Company. The freight section of the depot had hundreds of "pigeon-hole" filing slots along the wall, in which there were still rolls of train orders and messages written when Rico had been the dispatcher's headquarters in 1892–1893. The mining company's management refused to allow anyone to have these historic records, or to buy them, but ordered all of them to be burned. However, a wind came up when the bonfire was started, and RGS papers were blown all over the valley—including places beyond the company's property. A local man retrieved the few papers that were saved, including the first train register, showing the arrival of the first trains in Rico. Besides the RGS papers, the mine also had two kegs of never-used doubleheaded Greer (alias "Jeffery") spikes, but the manager would not let anyone have any of them.

RGS Receiver Pierpont Fuller wrote me that he had the larger Caboose 0404 for sale for $250.00, and he had to get that price because it was entered in some kind of court paper, as the Southern Pacific was going to buy it, but then changed their corporate mind. So, I went to Durango, got the key from grumpy manager Graebing so I could examine the car, and subsequently, I agreed to buy it—using his clerk's typewriter to reply to Fuller. Graebing, auditor to the last, said something like this to me "...now you just get the car body, floor, walls and roof, trucks and couplers... no marker lights, no lanterns, no tools or anything else."

My reply was that when the caboose had last been used, all those items had been used, and all of them had been in the car, "...so, where did they go?" Reluctantly, he admitted that he had taken them, so I told him that now that the caboose was mine, I did not want him to take the couplers or wheels or anything else off *my* car! The dismantler needed a caboose on the south end, so I "rented" it to him for dismantling use in exchange for a couple of pickup-truck loads of RGS artifacts. After he was through using No. 0404—to my surprise—the D&RGW hauled it to Alamosa in a freight train for about 30 cents per mile (as I recall).

During the winter of 1951–1952, the D&RGW scrapped about 500 narrow-gauge cars at Alamosa. This, it turned out, was a

mistake, as in about two years, the railroad needed most of them for the oil-and-gas pipe traffic that arose. Scrapping was done by a Texas firm, and all of the remaining short cabooses and short refrigerator cars were included, as well as eight of the remaining baggage cars. I learned that the Texans had paid $240.00 each (overall) for the cars, and their offer on a complete baggage car was $800.00. I was eyeing all the RGS stuff at the time, and I was not inclined to pay a big premium price for the D&RGW baggage car.

Under the Alfred Perlman administration of the D&RGW, the Rio Grande management scrounged the system for things to get rid of, and the company took what the U.S. Internal Revenue System later ruled were excessive write-offs. So, the company did not want to sell things for scrap prices. The Alamosa Division was limited to $50.00 per month in sales, and that was not very much, considering that could amount to only a few sections of rail sold to the county commissioners or some rancher. Friendly tips from railroaders enabled me to learn of some small things that would be for sale. So, on the first of the month, I would go "hit up" the foreman to buy the items I wanted. Once, in this fashion, I was able to buy about a dozen AT&SF marker lamps consigned for scrap for only two cents per pound. Also, some train-indicator number boards were obtained when they were finally deemed to be no longer needed on the K-28 and K-36 classes of narrow-gauge engines.

Later, I tried to buy one of the former Crystal River Railroad outside-frame 2-8-0's when it was in the Salida yard. However, when waiting for a price for months, the locomotive was whisked away to Pueblo to be scrapped. I only learned about it after this unusual Consolidation was no longer in existence, when I drove up to Salida one day to do some measuring and consider problems regarding the movement of the engine.

There were only two exceptions during this period of D&RGW management: Knott's Berry Farm purchased engine No. 340, a Class C-19 2-8-0, and the movie star Gene Autry bought No. 463, a Class K-27 2-8-2, for a reputed $5,500.00 in 1955.

The scrapping of the Rio Grande Southern was completed in the spring of 1953. All that was left was Engine 42, the 1887 2-8-0 mentioned previously. With a largely-rotten cab, thin tires and other indications of the

WHEN YOU HAVE A GROUP of freight cars, it is a good idea to move them around a little. So, during one fall "steamup," we operated a "livestock extra," as in the days of yore. Visitors and fans enjoyed these variations in operation, and any visitors present could ride aboard the old Rio Grande Southern caboose, No. 0404. On the 4.0-percent grades of Cumbres and Marshall passes, Engine 346, under the best of conditions, could handle a six-car train of these stock cars. Incidentally, Rio Grande Southern's Caboose 0404 was the only caboose built by the RGS. It was constructed in the Ridgway roundhouse by RGS men during 1902.

need of a complete overhaul, it had to come into Durango in March, with the scrap train, which was trailed by my caboose, No. 0404.

Earlier, the Rio Grande Southern's dismantler had offered Engine 42 to me for $3,500.00, but I pled poverty, having gone beyond my limits. Then, he came down to $2,500.00, explaining that he did not have a crew expert on cutting-up an engine, and he knew it was not going to be profitable or quickly done. Then, one day, I stopped by his office in what used to be the RGS clerk's room upstairs in the Durango depot, and he said, "I have an offer you can't refuse. I will sell you the No. 42 for $1,200.00, and you can pay me $100.00 a month. Now, you just can't turn that down!" He was right! So, I was preparing to pay him $100 a month and scrape-up the $800.00 or so to move the engine dead by freight train, and by lowboy truck to the motel grounds in Alamosa. Then, along came Ed and Paula Landrum of Dallas, who had learned of the deal, and to speed things

up, they loaned me the $2,000.00 to buy and transport the locomotive.

This time, with the obtuse Perlman gone to "do his thing" with the New York Central, I had no problems in moving No. 42 over the Alamosa–Durango line. Well-oiled and greased, the engine made the 200-mile trip to Alamosa without problems. Dead steam engines had a tendency to run hot o*n one* or more bearings. I oiled No. 42 well at Chama, New Mexico, and I was planning to do so again at Cumbres Pass (in Colorado), but a sudden blizzard-like storm swept in just as the train headed for the climb up the west side of the pass. And the swirling, blowing snow halted me dead in my tracks only a quarter mile out of Chama—I simply could not see the road! I had to travel home to Alamosa by driving down to Española, New Mexico, then north again—encountering the same storm again, only slightly diminished on a few miles of the road just north of No Agua, where in years past "Chili Line" trains

IT COST OVER $8,000.00, and it took a week in bitterly cold weather to trade engines at Rhinelander, Wisconsin, in February of 1973. It looked so simple, too! The engine in the Mexican gondola was in sight of the old South Park relic in the city park. A sort of trestle had to be built out of one end of the gondola to pull the Mexican engine onto. Then, No. 7—the Thunder Lake Lumber Company's number—had to be removed from the park amid trees, utility poles and winding, narrow driveways. In this scene, the DSP&P engine was being slid on greased rails into the gondola. After 40 years of sitting in the park, coupled with zero weather, No. 7's wheels would not turn! After the engine was finally loaded, a workman threw a match into the firebox after he had lit his cigar. And for the next several days, a wisp of smoke came out of the stack. It turned out that for years, park employees had thrown paper trash into the engine's firebox! Townspeople thought we had fired-up the engine and ran her onto the gondola under her own power! The wheels of the 2-8-0 were still frozen after the engine's arrival at Golden. It took a couple of weeks of application of gallons of penetrating oil, plus strong nudging by the little Peewee gasoline-powered locomotive, before the drivers finally turned.

IN THE GOLDEN YARD of the Colorado & Southern Railway, the crane was unloading Potosi y Rio Verde No. 4, a narrow-gauge 2-8-0 from Chihuahua, Mexico. This engine was thrown in, as the traffic man said, to "sweeten the pot" during an involved transfer of an engine in Chihuahua to trade for an old South Park engine at Rhinelander, Wisconsin. Engine 4 was worn out and had a huge blister on the side sheets of the firebox. We were willing to sell the engine, and a middleman came along who engineered a deal to sell the engine to a new operation at Flint, Michigan—over my protests that the 2-8-0 no doubt could not be operated until the engine received a new boiler and firebox. Meanwhile, we painted No. 4 as static display and put a bell on the little engine. A group of juvenile "volunteers" stole the bell, and we only got it back after plastering five counties with reward posters, and some very good detective work was done by two of our older volunteers.

AFTER WE BROUGHT the Denver, South Park & Pacific engine from Rhinelander, Wisconsin, in 1972, we replaced several key items on the locomotive with replicas of the originals. From original Union Pacific drawings, we had a Congdon stack made locally of sheet steel. Meanwhile, Jim Dunlop, in California, built the wooden pilot. And John Buvinger made a cardboard mockup of the early U.P.-style headlight, which was then shipped in a large crate to an Ohio specialist, who made the headlight in metal. The handsome 2-8-0 dates from January of 1880, and was then No. 51. Then, in a system renumbering, The Consolidation became No. 191. The engine came into the new Colorado & Southern Railway as their No. 31, but they put the 2-8-0 up for sale. In shipping the engine to a Wisconsin lumber firm, someone forgot to drain the tender of several tons of Colorado water, and the lumber company declined to pay the freight bill until the water was deducted from the freight bill! I should note that the long coupling bar on the pilot is an original from the old South Park, lost a long time ago in a misfortune near Alpine Tunnel.

417

THIS PASSENGER TRAIN at the museum consisted of Railway Post Office–Railway Express car No. 60, and one of the Denver & Rio Grande's standard 1887 coaches, No. 284, which was used until the 1960's on the Silverton train. Handling a passenger train was nothing new to Engine 346 in its hundred-year career. Its last such use was regularly in the 1930's, between Gunnison and Montrose, Colorado. There, the engine could handle a four-car train without a helper over the 4.0-percent grades of Cerro Summit. No. 346 had been built as a Class 70 engine in 1881.

had been stalled, and even snowbound, by such intense weather.

My motive in buying No. 42 was not primarily to acquire another narrow-gauge locomotive, even if it was the sole survivor of its class. I was positive that eventually someone would want the 2-8-0 for some project or other, and they would take it off my hands, perhaps at a modest profit. I just did not want to see the engine scrapped.

Next came the abandonment of the 35-mile Ouray Branch of the D&RGW, with the last run on March 21, 1953. A trickle of people indicated to the Rio Grande management an interest in buying equipment to run a tourist train somewhere, so the D&RGW

hit upon the novel idea of having an auction, which was done, using the theater at Montrose on April 27, 1953. The results were disappointing, and all bids were rejected. Some scrap dealers bid a high of $1,100.00 and $1,400.00 respectively for the two locomotives, Nos. 318 and 454. Farmers and ranchers were willing to pay perhaps $50.00 to $100.00 for a boxcar, but they did not want the trucks and other hardware. No cabooses or passenger cars were involved.

Cornelius W. Hauck of Cincinnati, Ohio, urged that I "save" No. 318; however, my reply to him was I had gone to the limit in "saving" narrow-gauge equipment. So, maybe he could save the engine, and perhaps

THIS LITTLE BUSINESS CAR was last used on the Uintah Railway in western Colorado. However, it originally was an 1872 coach of the new Denver & Rio Grande Railway, numbered "4." During the early 1880's, the expanding railroad needed business cars, and No. 4 was one of the coaches converted and given the designation "K." At the time the mainline beyond Leadville to Aspen was being converted to standard gauge in 1890, this car was used with the work trains as the crews changed the line to the new gauge. At that time, the car was placed on standard-gauge trucks and used by the same Leadville superintendent who worked on the conversion. Then, in 1925, when the Gunnison Division offices closed, the car was surplus and sold to the Uintah line. There, the B-8, as the car was later designated by the D&RGW, was used with the new and famous articulated 2-6-6-2T side-tank engines of that line. After abandonment, with only the car's trucks and

couplers sold for scrap, a farmer bought it and kept it well maintained at Grand Junction, Colorado. In old papers, bits of the car's history were learned—one of the more interesting facts being that upon departing from Cimarron one day, on the tail-end of a westbound passenger train, the entire train derailed and overturned. Many years later, the wife of a section foreman gave the museum a steak plate, with the railroad emblem, salvaged from that wreck. One of the dramatic moments of the B-8 was, while in transit to the museum in Golden, it was nearly hijacked off U.S. Highway 40, when the trucker was about to pass the new amusement park called "Magic Mountain." Their special deputy sheriff stopped the truck driver, and the manager tried to persuade him to deliver the business car to them instead of to our museum. Not surprisingly, the amusement park ended in bankruptcy, amid charges of all kinds.

take it to Ohio? Eventually, the D&RGW agreed to sell No. 318 for $2,500.00, and "Corny" put up the money to buy the 2-8-0. Even then, there was a hitch, as it appeared that the cost of transportation from Montrose would be a combination of the local rates— no small sum. But the local agent checked with the purchasing agent in Denver, who pointed out that the price was F.O.B. anywhere via the standard gauge, a very different matter indeed in costs. So, eventually, the little 2-8-0 arrived at Alamosa aboard a standard-gauge flatcar.

So... now we had four engines at Alamosa, some freight cars, a Galloping Goose and two cabooses. And during July of 1953,

we opened the "Narrow Gauge Museum," a free-admission affair, with a few hundred feet of track. It was to last until the partnership of the motel (and museum) was split-up in 1958, and most of the equipment was moved to a new site at Golden, Colorado, just 12 miles west of downtown Denver.

Once located at the Golden site, it seemed that one item after another came along, which seemed to be worthy of adding to the collection, and within a few years, the museum collection numbered over 50 locomotives and cars, some of which were standard gauge. On permanent loan to the museum were the several narrow-gauge items belonging to the Rocky Mountain Railroad Club (in addition to RGS Engine 20, the RGS business car "Rico" and a D&RGW caboose). Three more narrow-gauge engines, including a Porter 2-8-0 from the Chihuahua Mineral Railroad, a former South Park 2-8-0 (dating from 1880, brought from Rhinelander, Wisconsin), and after a plant was destroyed in a storm at Loveland, Colorado, an eight-ton Plymouth gasoline locomotive was obtained, which was very useful as a switcher.

At a sheriff's sale at Ouray in 1962, we bought a former Rio Grande Southern coach, which had been converted to an outfit car and then abandoned at Ridgway by a Wisconsin promoter. In building some new steel coaches for the *Silverton* train in 1967, the D&RGW sold me three coach bodies after the Burnham shop crews had removed their trucks, most of their couplers, about half of the coach seats and some other items. New Denver laws banned burning the bodies, the normal disposal method of old wooden-car bodies. So, at a bargain price of $10.00 each, these coach bodies were ours, if we could remove them immediately. At about $500.00 each, the nearby Duffy's moving crews came over, and by using the transfer table and shop lifts, this firm removed each body as soon as it was ready.

From Grand Junction, Colorado, came the well-preserved body of D&RGW Business Car B-8, which dated from a coach built in 1872. Missing only trucks and couplers, it was used on the little Uintah Railway. En route to the museum via a flatbed truck, it was almost hijacked off U.S. Highway 40, near Golden, where an amusement park was being constructed. The park's special deputy sheriff flagged down the driver, and he and the new park's manager tried to persuade the driver to deliver the car to them!

A four-wheel Colorado & Southern narrow-gauge caboose body was retrieved from Leadville and rebuilt by a C&S car man into a useful item. We had asked for several types of freight cars from the D&RGW, but we did not receive a favorable reply, so we proceeded to purchase one of each type from the dismantler. Months later, we learned that four cars held in the yard at Alamosa were ours, a gift of the management! These became very useful to store our growing volumes of old railroad files, which belonged to the RGS, D&RGW, C&S, etc., estimated to weigh over 30 tons!

One final narrow-gauge locomotive ac-

quisition was what had been the D&RGW's only narrow-gauge diesel. In an attempt to reduce switching costs at Durango, after only the *Silverton* train really needed such overtime work, No. 50 was bought in 1963 from the defunct Sumpter Valley Railway in Oregon (their No. 101). However, No. 50 was sold to a California tourist line in 1970, the Big Trees line south of San Francisco, after a balloon loop was laid in Durango for turning trains, eliminating the need for switching. One day, No. 50 ran away on a very steep grade on the Big Trees line, and when the little four-wheel diesel was stopped by ties on the track, heavy damage was done to its main gears.

After being hauled back to Durango by Bob Shank, Jr., the Colorado Railroad Museum acquired No. 50 when Bob gave up his accumulation of narrow-gauge equipment (which he had intended to utilize in a local railroad museum). Along with the little diesel engine, we obtained two RGS Galloping Geese—No. 7, the largest RGS railbus, and the roadmaster's "work Goose," No. 6. Also acquired from Bob was a Railway Post Office car and D&RGW freight cars. Eventually, all three of our Galloping Geese were put into operating condition, providing very popular rides for many visitors on operating days. Unfortunately, repair parts for the crippled No. 50 eluded us, but the search goes on to this day (1995).

From the forest near the Elkhorn Mine in Montana, we obtained an abandoned boxcar of the Montana Southern Railway, whose peeling paint revealed that its original owner was the Florence & Cripple Creek Railroad of Colorado. At Monarch, Colorado, a similar boxcar (converted into an outfit car) was found, wearing the lettering of the Western Union Telegraph Company. However, this car is the sole surviving boxcar of the Colorado & Northwestern, later known as the Denver, Boulder & Western. Other items added were an old "drag flanger," the "OC," which was used in winter snow-plowing trains from Alamosa to Cumbres Pass, and one of the standard-gauge "idler cars," used to couple narrow- and standard-gauge cars and engines together on the dual-gauge line between Alamosa and Antonito.

Car bodies are not cars, of course, the difference being that large amounts of material usually are missing—slow, costly and laborious to reproduce and install—so, museums

A SMALL GROUP of dedicated volunteers maintained-and-operated trains at the museum in Golden. The Hartford Insurance firm's steam-boiler inspection man once declared something to the effect that the way "...they baby that engine, it will last a hundred years." When a syn- thetic engineer we allowed to run No. 346 one Sunday got malicious and jerked the throttle wide open, I almost had to restrain physically two of the outraged volunteers from seeking him out and committing heinous mayhem! Here, a volunteer was showing a visitor the engine's gangway.

learn to be cautious about adding this type of item to their collections. Sometimes, it takes years of work and heavy costs to translate this type of equipment into a functioning car. However, we did save some old car bodies. One was a D&RGW narrow-gauge baggage-car body, and what had been a narrow-gauge Pullman car. This piece of equipment had been converted into a coach (and used as such for many years) and then became an outfit car. A D&RGW coach body of the original early "duckbill" roof style (built in 1876) was saved, as was another coach body, dating from 1881.

Attempts to construct passenger-style trucks for these car bodies have been frustrated by the lack of numerous patterns and castings, not to mention special springs and many small parts, all of which would cost thousands of dollars per car. When we acquired Bob Shank's collection of equipment, we also acquired his ownership of car bodies located at Vance Junction, which were in much better condition when he first sought their acquisition. One was an early standard-gauge D&RG boxcar body. The other bodies were from a very early D&RG round-roof postal car and a coach that had been stripped down to its body frame, useful only to illustrate how such wooden cars were built—a lost art.

The first standard-gauge engine obtained was a saddle-tank 0-4-0T from the oil refinery at Casper, Wyoming. Next came the last surviving Rio Grande standard-gauge steam locomotive, which ended its service-life at Blanca, Colorado, as No. 106 on the San Luis Valley Southern Railway. In 1890, this D&RG locomotive had been part of a large fleet of 2-8-0's, which could be seen everywhere on the Rio Grande system. During the same summer, the largest of all items came to the museum, Chicago, Burlington & Quincy No. 5629, a massive 4-8-4. This was a gift from the railroad to the National Railway Historical Society for placement at the museum. Outwardly, No. 5629 was a splendid example of a modern steam locomotive; however, volunteers discovered that when the 4-8-4 was last used, the engine had not been drained. And in the below-zero winter climate of Lincoln, Nebraska, water had frozen inside the engine and great damage had been done throughout, rendering steaming very unlikely.

In 1968, the Manitou & Pikes Peak Railway donated their No. 4, the M&PP's last operable steam engine. A few years later, they decided they would like to run some steam for special occasions, so they traded us their No. 1, which had been on display, and No. 4 has since operated for excursion trips up the mountain. The last engine acquired was originally a Union Pacific 0-6-0 switcher, No. 4455, which served on the Monolith Portland Cement Company's intrastate Laramie Valley Railway at Laramie, Wyoming. The little 0-6-0's arrival in 1972 coincided with the gift by the Colorado & Southern Railway of their last rotary snowplow. This plow had been built in 1900 for use on the old South Park narrow-gauge line, but proved to be too heavy, so the snowplow spent most of its life on standard-gauge trucks at Denver and Cheyenne, rarely seeing any use.

Providing useful contrast with the narrow-gauge items were some standard-gauge cars, including a steel Railway Post Office-Railway Express Agency car of the Colorado & Southern. From the Great Western Railway came its sole passenger car, a wooden combination baggage-coach, which in addition to serving on their mixed trains since 1902, was also used by the company's officers for directors' outings. After the establishment of Amtrak, the Union Pacific donated one of their "City" fleet of passenger cars. Meanwhile, the National Railway Historical Society had obtained the original tail-end observation car of the Santa Fe's famous *Super Chief* passenger train, as well as a Burlington business car. We also added a number of standard-gauge freight cars, not only to show the diverse types, but for their valued use as storage "vaults." The most outstanding of these was a Burlington refrigerator car, which the Adolph Coors Brewery of Golden repainted like one of their former fleet of white beer cars.

The Colorado Railroad Museum's collec-

DELL A. McCOY PHOTO

STANDARD-GAUGE ENGINE 583 had only switcher footboards when the San Luis Southern Railway bought the 2-8-0 in 1947. The old C-28 also had three-way couplers for the engine's use as a switcher at Salida, Colorado. Shortly after we purchased No. 583 in 1962, we started adding the little things that made the engine look somewhat as she did when the old Class 113 2-8-0 was a road engine on the Denver & Rio Grande Railroad. From a Baldwin front-end plate, we had a new brass casting made, which replaced the D&RGW's iron number plate. The old-style oil headlight is an exact copy of the patented "Wabash" type that the D&RG used for many years, until electric headlights began to replace older types in 1914. Still to come (after this picture was taken) was the splendid wooden "cowcatcher" fabricated by that experienced craftsman, Jim Dunlop, known to many two-foot-gauge fans for his skillful work on the Edaville Railroad in Massachusetts.

tion was intended to show the kinds of locomotives and rolling stock formerly used in Colorado and the adjoining states, especially in the mountain areas. No attempt was made or intended to obtain items from distant lines. We had to depend on a small number of volunteers for most of the track construction and restoration of the equipment. It is due to them that most of the rolling stock is well maintained, with authentic paint and lettering schemes.

DURING THE EARLY DAYS at Golden, in order to avoid having most items lettered for the Denver & Rio Grande Western, we decided to choose a name for our museum line and came up with the "Golden City & San Juan Railroad." Stan Rhine designed and applied to the the tender of No. 346 a triangular herald, and thousands of decals of it were distributed to modelers. However, after several years, we decided to letter items for the railroads the engines and cars had operated on, and the triangle vanished. For printed matter, "Corny" Hauck designed a circular logo, which was lettered "Colorado Railroad Museum." But we did not apply this art work to rolling stock. Corny also came up with a line drawing of No. 346, which has been employed for many years on stationery and in headings for the *Iron Horse News,* our occasional museum news sheet, based primarily on museum news, as well as regional railroad news and bits of items about narrow-gauge lines the world over.

FAMOUS K. ITTY, our revered cat, posed beside a cast-iron spittoon relic of the South Park line. There was much joking around Colorado about a couple of photograph collectors, who placed on every picture a warning (no matter how poor the photograph was) that no one could ever copy this photograph. So, when using pictures in the *Iron Horse News,* we would credit them as "...by K. Itty. This photograph must not be copied in whole or in part without written permission of K. Itty." Then, one day, Randy Dannemann found a little cast-plastic imitation camera some kid had lost. So, he put it on a string and hung it around K. Itty's protesting neck, and the picture was then used in an issue, alleging that this was a view of K. Itty on the prowl to take a picture! During all this nonsense, we learned that not a few people had no sense of humor. One woman visitor, upon reading this issue posted on the bulletin board asked her husband, "Joe, a cat can't take a picture, can it?" K. Itty prowled the museum grounds for 14 years and had many special habits. She disliked the shushing noise of an engine when fired-up, but loved to get in the cab when all was quiet to enjoy all that heat! She could climb end ladders of cabooses to get up on the roofs to chase—but never catch—birds that liked to tease cats. And if you had a ladder against a building, before putting the ladder away, it was best to check for the cat, as she loved to climb ladders and wander over roofs.

COLORADO RAILROAD MUSEUM

P.O. Box 10
Golden, CO 80402-0010

COLORADO RAILROAD MUSEUM

17155 West 44th Ave.—Route 58   Mail to Box 10, GOLDEN, Colorado 80402

ROBERT W. RICHARDSON
ABANDONED LINES REPORTER
IRON HORSE NEWS

"NOBODY'S INTERESTED IN THAT STUFF"
—REMARK OF A TOUR "DIRECTOR"

THE DENVER PUBLIC LIBRARY'S Western History Department had a very fine display of my photographs at the 14th Narrow Gauge Convention in Denver during September of 1994. However, I really had not realized the pictures were "classics," though!

RAILROAD PRESERVATION EXPERIENCES

WE WATCHED IN DISMAY and sadness during the 1930's as one after another, the interurban lines vanished and the cars were hauled off for scrap. We hopelessly wished that at least one of our favorite cars might be saved. However, the same severe economic depression that killed the interurban lines also made such hopes financially impossible. The prize of the Lake Shore Electric Railway's older cars—No. 166—was a 65-foot wooden combination car, with the ornate woodwork and window arrangements of the early 1900's, during the days when it was the daily *Lima Limited* from Cleveland, Ohio. We had used No. 166 on one fan trip, and we talked among ourselves about the possibility of buying it and saving it, but even if it had

been given to us, we had no safe place to keep it. So, that grand-and-beautiful electric interurban car became a rotting body (minus its traction trucks) on a farm.

The next year, another line we had enjoyed trips on, the Ohio Public Service Company, ended its Sunday runs between Toledo and Marblehead on June 25, 1939, a distance of 53 miles. This company had the last two wooden interurban cars in Ohio, of the type the Niles and similar transit-car builders excelled in building. Normally, the two interurbans seldom were used, but they were kept in reserve to back up the company's small fleet of lightweight steel one-man cars, only two of which were required to maintain the schedules. Wooden car No. 6 was a straight passenger, with arch transoms on the sides and arched front-end windows, while No. 21 was a combination baggage-passenger car, favored on our fan trips. Passenger traffic had been declining for many years, and the final 12 miles from Port Clinton, via Lakeside, to Marblehead had only a couple of through runs at this time. On a couple of other runs, anyone wanting to go beyond Port Clinton could do so by paying a small fee, plus regular fare, traveling to points beyond the normal end of service on the route. This was an option we railfans enjoyed, and more than a few times, several fans would avail themselves of this, and in the process, we had all the aspects of a private car, including a chance to operate the electric car. So, we had a strong affection for the Ohio Public Service interurban line.

For the final Sunday service, we persuaded the OPS management, in the person of the very agreeable Superintendent Lester Bennet, to substitute the old wooden cars. In order to do so, we put up $100 to pay for the cost of two-man crews, electric power, etc. In return, he urged us to print a modest-priced all-day pass to sell to local fans, to recoup our $100 outlay. It was a beautiful day, and fans came from several states, and we even made a slight profit! The company also had a very good day, as many residents along the line also went for trips, so it was a financial success as well.

With the end of passenger service on the OPS line, the old interurban cars were going to be sold to a scrap dealer. And after pleas from various railfans to save one of the wooden cars—especially No. 21—early in 1941, I boarded a Big Four train at Columbus to travel to Cleveland to make a deal with the power company's lawyer. He had an offer of $300 for each of the company's seven cars, and he agreed to sell us one for that amount. Expecting to be reimbursed for a good part of that amount, my personal check sealed the deal. However, in the end, only a scant dozen of those who had urged saving the car, ever contributed anything to its cost, or to the coming cost of moving and storage, and my permanent investment must have been about $150. As a result of this experience, I should have learned that wishes do not translate into practical help, especially in the form of money.

We had several places to store the car, but each in turn became impractical for various reasons. Finally, the operator of the Canton–Massillon line of the Intercity Rapid Transit company offered to let us store No. 21 at his carbarn. We could have trips over this line by paying the costs of the crew and electric power, and in return, he could have the use of the car for his excursions or private-group outings. We were about to move the car from the Oak Harbor carbarn when disaster struck. The city council of Massillon had demanded the Intercity Rapid Transit to repave its tracks through town, and faced with this impossible financial load, the line converted to motor buses (which did not have the requirement of paving the town streets they used). Now, we had a homeless 27-ton interurban car, stored at Oak Harbor, and we learned we were to be charged $10 a month for storage. These monthly bills followed me around the world while I was serving in the U.S. Army, even in the mail I received during World War II in Iran! However, Superintendent Bennet had quietly passed the word not to worry, as the OPS was continuing its freight operations, and I should just ignore the bills, a power-company formality.

Finally, during the spring of 1946, by a mail vote of our small fan club, we gave No. 21 to the newly forming railroad museum at Columbus, later named the Ohio Railway Museum. The museum moved the car by truck trailer to a field, where just what we feared would happen at our other sites happened—severe vandalism took place. One man even stole the rear platform steps for use at his home! Since then, No. 21 has suffered other attacks at the museum at Worthington, Ohio, which have required extensive repair work; however, the car is still operable.

After all of the above, one would expect that I would never again get involved in "saving" anything as a railroad item of rolling stock. But in 1951, I yielded to the sight of the forlorn narrow-gauge locomotive sitting in the weeds at Dolores, Colorado, and plunked down $800 to the scrap dealer who had discovered he would make at most a

425

THE SUMMER OF 1951 was a busy one, and after moving No. 346 onto the motel grounds, we did not have time to do much with the old 2-8-0. So, she stayed lettered like she had been since the D&RGW sold her to the lumber company in 1947. With the destruction of sister engine, No. 345, in a movie that summer, we obtained some missing parts from the scrapping. Principally, the

dome rings were missing since the engine had been wrecked on Kenosha Pass while on loan to the Colorado & Southern. Some of the railroaders were especially pleased to see the domes complete again, and one of them that helped us to accomplish this job was a Durango foreman, "Knuckle-Joint" Spearman, and Road Foreman Tom Cummins.

mere $50 if he scrapped it, after paying the high freight rates from Dolores to the Pueblo steel mill. As was the case with interurban No. 21, "saving" the Denver & Rio Grande's No. 346 2-8-0 of 1881 vintage, was fraught with all kinds of problems, even though there was narrow-gauge trackage all the way to within sight of its Alamosa destination.

Among the problems was the slow replacement of a trestle on the Rio Grande Southern by highway contractors. Then, the D&RGW declined to quote a rate to haul No. 346 dead in a freight from Durango. And the D&RGW made a promise if they found something wrong, they would reject moving it, anyway. Beyond this, if the 2-8-0 did make it to Alamosa over their objections, they made it very difficult to move off their trackage. The overcoming of all these obstacles could fill a lengthy chapter, but in August, the engine finally arrived in Alamosa. This finale erupted in comedy when the night switching crew assumed No. 346 was an engine en route to the shop for repairs (and it *did* appear to need them, what with rust and peeling paint), so the crew spotted the engine on the arrival track, just outside the office of the general foreman. Upon arriving at

his office on Monday morning, that harried individual looked out the window and exploded in dismay and frustration at his lack of parts, as well as the people to repair such a relic! This provided snickers among his underlings for days. And then, he learned that No. 346 was not there for repair, and he was equally loud in demanding that the yard crew remove it elsewhere immediately, characterizing me as a "nut."

And so began my involvement in the preservation of things on wheels that had operated on the vanishing Colorado narrow-gauge lines. The year before, I had engaged in a minor purchase of an about-to-be-burned caboose for $125, which required that a local lowboy operator could take time off from spring contract-plowing work to spend the five hours for the move. The several months delay he caused had one local rail official threatening to charge me demurrage! That caboose—after much travel—is now an extra-fare car on the Durango & Silverton line (as of 1994). Originally, this car was D&RGW caboose No. 0500.

Well, it is true that if I had not been foolish enough to scrape up the money, time and work to save a lot of "stuff," it would not have been saved. However, we are all young and foolish at some age I guess! In Colorado, part of it was that I remembered how many times we fans back East were saddened by our inability to save favorite engines, cars and interurban trolleys from destruction. Most of us felt haunted by scenes of big wooden cars being torched, or of steam engines lined up to be cut up for scrap. Probably, that was why so many fans kept urging me to save "this" or "that," even though only a very few ever contributed anything to do so. You will find very few pictures in my collection of such sad scenes. Most of us did not linger when such things were to occur.

When Engine 346 came into Durango in a Rio Grande Southern freight train on that rainy day so long ago, one man came up and hugged me—so carried away with emotion. A railroader had just told him, "No… the engine isn't en route to be cut up. That man over there bought it to preserve it…."

A GIFT DECLINED—an obsolete crane, which used a clamshell to move coal, was offered to the Colorado Railroad Museum by a power plant near Boulder. However, it was a low time for finances at the museum. So, the extraordinary costs involved in moving the machine to Golden and the museum grounds, convinced us that it was something we really did not need.

END OF THE AGE OF STEAM

THE STEAM LOCOMOTIVE was the outstanding visible machine of the "Age of Steam," the prime mover on American railroads for over a century and a quarter. Then, rapidly in the 1940's, it began to vanish, and by the mid-1950's was all but gone. Diesel-electric locomotives had made their first appearance at Akron, Ohio, in 1925, when the Erie Railroad brought in several black "oil-electrics." In fact, this term was stated in small letters on each engine. The Akron yard crew was used to steam power, and the men had a difficult time with them. Occasionally, something would go wrong, and out would pour dense clouds of overpowering oil smoke. Intended to replace the smoky coal-burning 0-6-0 switchers on a belt track that wound behind Akron's Main Street, which actually had a small yard partly under some business buildings. One of the newfangled diesel units initiated a "fire sale" at the largest department store in Akron, forcing clerks and customers to flee dense black smoke!

The Akron, Canton & Youngstown Railroad had a number of its customers and officials gather one frigid winter day to look over their first diesel engine inside their old wooden roundhouse. Unfortunately, all the doors were closed because the day was so cold. So, the debut was turned into a rout, as everyone fled from an enormous amount of oily smoke. As the roundhouse force hastily opened the big engine doors, the visitors sought fresh air outdoors, coughing as they beat a hasty retreat.

Despite things like the above, the diesel-electric gradually took over. At first, this new type of motive power was used just for switching cars. Then, on the Baltimore & Ohio, the number one passenger train, The Capitol Limited, was dieselized. Railroaders expected the conversion would be very slow, and they went ahead overhauling steam engines. Often, the result was that expensively rebuilt locomotives went to scrap without ever being used.

Railroad fans were mostly like the railroaders. We did not like the diesels. I suppose we resented the way they pushed to extinction the steam power we loved. And the shopmen and engine crews resented having to work with an entirely different type of

TRAINS SELDOM OPERATED over the last 20 miles of the Creede Branch, as the mines operated so irregularly. However, in 1956, the price of lead and zinc advanced slightly, so No. 1151 was taking some boxcars up the line on this winter day for loading with concentrates. The cars

prime mover. Crews trained to operate only steam engines could hardly conceive of working without an oilcan or torch to check over their engines before leaving a station. However, eventually the engine crews began to like the new power, and during the changeover, they preferred it.

We did not waste much film on diesels, at least not at first, but if one was in good light and position, we just could not resist their colorful paint schemes. Later, we were to regret not snapping pictures of all those early diesel units that we encountered. Many of them had short and obscure lives. The very landscape changed after dieselization began to take hold. During the Age of Steam, we

were to be set out by the C-48 2-8-0 at the old mining town of Creede, which had seen its boom collapse in 1893—never to have good times return.

could determine what was near by the smoke. However, as diesels took over, they managed to make their comings and goings a much less obvious passing. Instead of pleasant steam whistles, their tinny bells and air horns were two other things we did not like.

Today, diesel fans chase those locomotives as avidly as we steam fans tried to capture on film their predecessors. If only there had been as many fans recording steam engines, the reference sources of information on steam power would be immense. However, for most of the Age of Steam, there were not all the magazines and other publications reporting the railroad scene as there are now during the diesel era.

Perhaps I should consider myself fortunate to have been able to see so many years of the final decades of the Age of Steam. By the 1950's, the urgency to hunt out the remaining steam engines was compelling. Mainline use of steam locomotives had become scarce in most of the United States by this time. When the Great Western Railway, the sugar-beet carrier in northeastern Colorado, had its annual harvest "campaign" (as it was called), camera enthusiasts would fly to Denver from California, or from other distant points, just to chase the steam-powered trains for a weekend. (For many years, the GW line hauled many carloads of sugar beets from "beet dumps" to the Great Western Sugar Company refineries every fall.) After seeing all the action on the GW—including a sleek 2-10-0 Decapod—the fans would fly home, just as happy and satisfied as some of us had been driving home from some earlier outing during the past decades.

Oddly, the largest group of operating steam locomotives remained on the narrow-gauge lines of Colorado—and this fact remains true to this very day. These engines were expected to be sent off for scrap, along with their trackage, by the mid-1950's. However, a combination of a sudden resurgence in freight traffic, due to new oil-and-gas discoveries along the main narrow-gauge line was coupled by a dramatic rise in tourist traffic on one remote portion of the D&RGW, the scenic Silverton Branch. This "love affair" with the narrow-gauge Silverton train was difficult for old-line railroad people to understand. So, a group of 19 engines remains operating (or at least not scrapped) in Colorado and New Mexico. Engine 473 (for example), the K-28 2-8-2 that I rode behind in 1941, on the soon-to-be abandoned "Chili Line" to Santa Fe, is still hauling thousands of tourists on day-long round trips up the beautiful Animas Canyon as of 1995.

THE LAST FOUR-ENGINE TRAIN over Marshall Pass departed from Sargent on October 6, 1954. Annually, the ranchers of the Powderhorn country, southwest of Gunnison, gathered their cattle at Iola, 11 miles west of Gunnison. Earlier in the day, the last C-16 engine, No. 268, had doubled the stock cars into Gunnison, where a K-36 2-8-2 moved them eastward to Sargent.

There, three other K-36's were waiting as helpers. By placing two engines in the middle of the consist, the first part of the train could be hustled to the top of the pass, if for any reason the engines stalled during their ascent to the summit. Cattle trains could not be delayed, as the livestock would have to be transferred at Salida to be watered and fed if unduly detained en route.

Colorado Railroad Historical Foundation, Inc.

P. O. Box 10, Golden, Colo. 80402

430

APPENDIX
OF SUB-CHAPTER HEADINGS

APPENDIX CONTINUED